Teaching in a Diverse Society

Herbert Grossman
San Jose State University

Allyn and Bacon
Boston • London • Toronto • Sydney • Tokyo • Singapore

For the many students and citizens of Tuskegee who treated me like just another conga drum–playing professor, the Black Forest, the Elks Club, and Groovy

---

Series Editor: Virginia Lanigan
Editorial Assistant: Nicole De Palma
Production Administrator: Ann Greenberger
Editorial-Production Service: Spectrum Publisher Services
Cover Administrator: Suzanne Harbison
Composition Buyer: Linda Cox
Manufacturing Buyer: Louise Richardson
Marketing Manager: Ellen Mann

Copyright © 1995 by Allyn & Bacon
A Simon & Schuster Company
Needham Heights, MA 02194

Library of Congress Cataloging-in-Publication Data

Grossman, Herbert, Ph.D.
  Teaching in a diverse society / Herbert Grossman.
    p. cm.
  Includes bibliographical references and index.
  ISBN 0-205-16247-9
  1. Multicultural education—United States. 2. Minorities—
Education—United States. 3. Discrimination in education—United
States. 4. Educational equalization—United States. I. Title.
LC1099.3.G76 1995
370.19′6′0973—dc20
                                        94-759
                                        CIP

Printed in the United States of America

10 9 8 7 6 5 4 3 2 1   99 98 97 96 95 94

Contents

Preface

The American educational system serves an extremely diverse student population. Students come to school speaking different languages and dialects and with different levels of English proficiency. They have diverse learning, behavior, relationship, and communication styles because of their ethnic, socioeconomic, and regional backgrounds and gender.

Extremely high rates of immigration in recent years have led to a situation in which many students currently in school were born in other countries or are brought up during their early formative years by parents who were born elsewhere. Very often they are brought up in neighborhoods populated by people with similar backgrounds. As a result, these students come to school with few of the mainstream experiences that most schools expect and require.

The living conditions of students are extremely diverse. Although many live in a two-parent family in the same middle-class neighborhood in which they were born, this stereotype fits fewer and fewer students. Many students live in one-parent families. Some students live in more than one home and shuttle back and forth between the apartments or houses of their divorced, separated, or never-married parents. Many students are required to move every few years because of their parents' jobs. Migrant students live in different parts of the country at different times of the year. Depressingly large numbers of homeless students live in shelters or even on the streets.

Too many employed and unemployed poor parents cannot provide the support systems that enhance students' learning in school. Many parents with adequate incomes have personal problems that prevent them from giving their children the child care, attention, and love that all children need. Statistics on child abuse are horrendous.

Neighborhoods that offer students healthy environments in which to grow are becoming an endangered species because of drugs, crime, gangs, drive-by shootings, and so on. As a result, appalling numbers of students are more concerned about surviving in their neighborhoods than doing well in school.

Although in the past some students did not conform to traditional gender roles and sexual orientations, their preferences typically remained submerged in school and created few issues for their fellow students or their teachers. More recently, males and females are exhibiting great diversity in their gender-role preferences in and out of school. Gay and lesbian students are beginning to come out to their friends and teachers in greater numbers, and increasing numbers of students have gay and lesbian parents.

It is no easy matter for schools to provide for the educational needs of such a diverse group of students. It would be impossible for schools to be all things to all students or to solve all the problems facing today's students.

Educators can do little to make neighborhoods safer for students or to prevent child abuse and abandonment. Even the best-intentioned and best-prepared educators cannot compensate sufficiently for the destructive effects of such problems to enable students who face them to achieve to their potential. However, educators can become much more relevant to the many students who enjoy the least success in American schools.

Schools and the educators who staff them should do everything possible to assure that all students have the same opportunity to succeed in school regardless of their ethnic, socioeconomic, and linguistic background; the geographic area in which they live and study; their gender and sexual orientation; and their living conditions. Unfortunately, this is not the case. Many students from non–European ethnic backgrounds, especially African American, Native American, and Hispanic American students, students from employed and unemployed poor families, rural students, migrant students, homeless students, students whose school experiences are adversely affected by gender biases, and many others are poorly served by the education system.

The goal of this text is to help educators recognize and reduce ethnic, socioeconomic, gender, contextual, and communicative disparities and inequities in school. This book is designed to help preservice educators understand the influence of diversity factors on students' educational careers, to make them more knowledgeable about how schools fail large numbers of students, and to assist them to take diversity into account when they assess, instruct, and manage their students. Chapter 1 describes the problems that need to be addressed. Chapters 2 to 4 examine the causes and solutions of ethnic and socioeconomic disparities. Chapters 5 and 6 include the knowledge educators need to provide students with contextually and communicatively appropriate education services. Chapters 7 and 8 help educators deal with the impact of students' gender and sexual orientation. Chapters 9 to 11 assist educators in selecting nonbiased/nonsexist assessment, instructional, and classroom management approaches for all students.

Acknowledgment

Thanks to Harold Chu, George Mason University, for his careful review of the manuscript.

The Problem

To be truly just, society should guarantee that all students have an equal opportunity to succeed in school regardless of their ethnic and socioeconomic background, their gender, living conditions (the contextual aspects of their lives), and English proficiency or dialect. Unfortunately, many students are poorly served by and fail to succeed in the American education system. Among these are students from non-European ethnic backgrounds, especially African American, Native American, and Hispanic American students; students from employed and unemployed poor families; rural students; immigrant and refugee students; limited English proficient students and those who speak a nonstandard English dialect; homeless students; and students whose school experiences are adversely affected by gender biases. This introductory chapter describes the many school-related problems of such students.

Ethnic and Socioeconomic Disparities

The population of the United States is rapidly becoming less European American (1–5). By the year 2000, non–European Americans are expected to comprise one third of the U. S. population. The three fastest growing groups are Hispanic Americans, African Americans, and Southeast Asian Americans. The two largest minority groups, 30 million African Americans and 20 million Hispanic Americans, will comprise almost a third of the total school enrollment. Currently, non–European American students are the majority in the 25 largest school districts in the country. The number of children and youth living in poverty is also continuing to rise. Between 1979 and 1989, the numbers of Hispanic American, European American, and African American children living in poverty increased by 29%, 25%, and 6%, respectively, leading to an overall increase of 19%.

Many non–European American students and students from employed and unemployed poor families do very well in school. However, as the following statistics indicate the lack of educational success that characterizes these students as a whole is a national disaster:

1. The average achievement of African American, Native American, Hispanic American, and poor students is consistently lower than that of middle- and upper-class European American students at every grade level (6–17). By the eleventh and twelfth grades only 25.7% of European American students have repeated at least one grade level; the corresponding figures for African American and Hispanic American students are 39.0% and 40.8%, and for Hispanic American males, 54.2% (16).

2. A smaller percentage of African American, Hispanic American, and Native American students graduate high school (7, 18–28). Although the dropout rate of African American students has improved dramatically in recent years, in large cities where the vast majority of African American students are poor more than half of them drop out (7). On a nationwide basis, Native Americans have the highest dropout rate. In Alaska and California, their dropout rate has been estimated at 90% and 70%, respectively (25, 28). The Hispanic American dropout rate is almost as high. In some areas, such as New York City, the rate has been as high as 80%. As a group, Asian and Pacific Americans have a low dropout rate; however, combining the statistics for all Asian and Pacific Americans is misleading. Those immigrant and refugee students who come from developing countries where they and their families had little access to formal education have very high dropout rates.

3. African American students, especially males, are also more likely to get into trouble in school and to be suspended (14, 29-34).

4. Although many non–European American high school students perform very well during their high school years, the average achievement level of these graduates leaves much to be desired. In comparison to European American students, African American, Hispanic American, and Native American students who graduate from high school are less likely to be computer literate or to have enrolled in high-level academic courses such as algebra, geometry, trigonometry, chemistry, physics, biology, and foreign languages. They are also more likely to have taken remedial math and science classes (9, 16).

The results for students who are poor and have either an African American or Hispanic American background are especially discouraging. In comparison to middle-class African American and Hispanic American students, they are even more likely to drop out of school, to achieve less while in school, and to earn lower grades. They are also more likely to be enrolled in general and vocational programs than academic programs and remedial rather than advanced or honors classes.

Gender Disparities

Although students' performance and participation in school cannot be predicted on the basis of their gender alone, on the average, males and females have somewhat different experiences in the American education system. These differences are discussed next.

When students are given the opportunity to select their courses and activities, males and females make somewhat different choices (35–45). Females tend to enroll in fewer advanced math courses, especially intermediate algebra and calculus, computer courses, and science courses—the courses that are important for college admission and for success in many technological and scientific fields. This generalization characterizes females from many Asian and Pacific American backgrounds, those who are Native Americans, and European American and Hispanic American females from poor backgrounds. It is not true for African American females in general or for females from European American, Filipino American, and Vietnamese American middle-class backgrounds.

There is considerable evidence that males and females choose very different vocational education courses and aspire to different careers (46–60). Females comprise more than 90% of the students in cosmetology, clerical, home economics, and health courses, and less than 10% of the students in courses that deal with agriculture, electrical technology, electronics, appliance repair, auto mechanics, carpentry, welding, and small engine repair. In general, Hispanic American, Southeast Asian American, and poor European American males are more likely than females to plan to work outside the home and to aspire to professional careers that require at least a bachelor's degree. These gender differences do not apply to the same extent to middle-class European American, Vietnamese American, Filipino American, and African American students.

Although the gender gap on standardized achievement tests and school grades has narrowed in recent years (61–66), male and female students still have different success rates in many academic subjects and skills (67–101). However, many of these differentials do not apply to all ethnic groups and socioeconomic classes. African American, Hispanic American, European American, and Native American females receive higher grades than males on tests of verbal skills in both elementary and secondary school. In elementary school, females, with the exception of Native Americans, tend to score higher than males on mathematics skills tests. Beginning in high school, females, again with the exception of Native Americans, score better than males on tests of basic computational skills. However, with the exception of African American females and some Asian groups, they score less adequately than males on mathematics tests involving complex mathematical skills, word problems, and visual-spatial tasks.

In elementary school there are few, if any, gender differences in students' science achievement. In secondary school, males tend to score higher than females on tests of physical and earth science information, but not on tests of health science information. Poor and African American males are exception to this generalization.

Females are less likely to get into trouble for behavioral problems, and they are less likely to be disciplined by their teachers or suspended from school (14, 102–105).

In comparison to males, European American and Hispanic American females are more fearful and anxious in courses such as science and math, traditionally thought to be in the male domain (108, 109). African American females are no more and perhaps even less anxious than African American males in these courses (107). Recently, females have become less anxious in these courses, perhaps because they are less likely to be perceived to be in the male domain (106).

With the exception of African American students, females tend to be less self-confident about school than males, especially in courses that are considered to be in the male domain such as mathematics and science courses, in competitive situations, and when they lack objective information about how well they have done or can do (110–118). They react less positively than males to difficult and challenging situations and are less likely to take risks in school (119, 120). Females are less persistent and perform less adequately than males following failure or the threat of failure (116, 121). Finally, female students tend to seek the assistance and approval of adults more than males do (122–125).

These characterizations do not apply to all females. They are more likely to apply to poor females and to Hispanic American and Asian and Pacific American females who are brought up in families that adhere to traditional ideas about sex roles, rather than to European American middle-class females and African American females (50, 126, 127). However, these characteristics do apply to other ethnic groups and to many females regardless of their ethnic or socioeconomic backgrounds.

Contextual Disparities

The contextual aspects, or living conditions, of many students affect their achievement in school. Migrant students' dropout rate, which has been estimated at between 45% and 57%, is the highest rate of any group in the United States (130–132). Even while they are attending school these students often fail to actualize their potential for learning. The dropout rate for rural students, between 40% and 50%, is more than twice the national average (see Chapter 5).

Between 1,000,000 and 1,500,000 children and youth run away from home each year (133). Because they attend school erratically, move from place to place, do not have the documents required by schools, and lack parents or guardians to speak and sign for them, they are unlikely to receive the education services they require. Estimates of the number of homeless children range from 272,773 to 1,600,000 (128, 129). The problems that confront homeless children interfere with their schooling to the point that many of them do not even attend school.

Communicative Disparities

The limited English proficient (LEP) population is the fastest-growing in the United States. Although estimates of how many LEP children and adolescents are now in the schools vary, it is probable that almost 8 million American youngsters have a non-English background, either because they were born elsewhere or because they grew up in a home in which another language was spoken. More than 3 million of these students scored in the lowest 20% on tests of English proficiency. More than 5 million scored in the lower 40%. Whichever of these two figures one uses, it is clear that millions of students are not proficient enough in English to function in English-only classes without considerable difficulty (134, 135). Unfortunately, many LEP students do poorly in school because they are taught by monolingual English-speaking teachers. The problems of students who speak nonstandard English or who use non–European American non–middle-class communication styles are similar but not nearly as severe (see Chapter 6).

Research-Based Approach

This text emphasizes research findings. Enough is known about the role of ethnic, socioeconomic, gender, and contextual factors in education for teachers to take these factors into account when they assess, instruct, and manage their students. The following are two examples of how knowledge of these factors can help educators.

Some educators employ competitive instructional techniques because they believe such techniques bring out the best in students. Other educators stress cooperative approaches because they think these improve relationships among students, prepare them to function in a democratic society, and lead to higher levels of achievement. However, research indicates that, with exceptions, males, in general, and European Americans and certain Asian and Pacific Americans perform better in competitive learning situations, whereas females, in general, and other ethnic groups such as African Americans, Hispanic Americans, and Hawaiian Americans perform better in cooperative learning situations.

Educators who act on their preference for competitive or cooperative learning without considering their students' preferred learning styles will only meet some students' needs. Educators who are aware of differences in students' learning styles can make reasonable choices. If they want to maximize students' academic achievement, they can use cooperative techniques with some students and competitive ones with others. However, if their goal is to help students to act competitively when competition is required and cooperatively when cooperation is required, the educators might employ techniques designed to expand students' behavioral repertoires. In either case, a knowledge of gender and ethnic differences in preferences for competitive and cooperative learning environments would certainly help.

Some primary-grade teachers tend to use material reinforcers, such as food, toys, and time to use especially desirable classroom equipment, or symbolic rewards, such as gold stars, checks, and points that can be converted into material rewards to motivate students. Others prefer to use interpersonal motivational techniques, such as praising students, telling students they are proud of them, patting them on the back, sending home a note, and so on. Research indicates that females, Hispanic Americans, African Americans, and certain other groups are more receptive to personal rewards. Males and European Americans are more responsive to impersonal rewards, especially in the lower grades. A knowledge of students' ethnic- and gender-influenced preferences can help an educator select effective reinforcers.

Some words of caution about research-based teaching are in order. Although we know a considerable amount about some topics, many important issues remain to be studied. What we do know is sometimes obsolete. What was true of group a few years ago may not be true today and even less so tomorrow. For example, generalizations that characterized the Southeast Asian students who were brought to the United States by their well-educated, middle- and upper-class, urban parents in the early 1970s do not describe the children of the uneducated, poor, rural, boat people who came here in the 1980s and 1990s. The first group of children may have had considerable difficulty adjusting to American schools; however, the second group of children, most of whom have never attended school and who have had to survive the trauma of running blockades, avoiding pirates, and confinement in detention camps for many years, typically have much more serious academic and emotional problems.

Many researchers fail to consider socioeconomic differences when they study the cognitive skills, learning styles, and so on of different ethnic groups of students. Since a smaller percentage of European American children currently live below the poverty level than Hispanic American and African American children, differences that are observed among uncontrolled samples of these groups cannot be attributed solely to ethnicity. Conclusions about educationally relevant differences between African American and European American students based on comparisons between African American poor students and European American middle-class students should have no influence on educational policy and practices. Unfortunately, this is not the case.

Avoiding Stereotypes and Overgeneralizations

Educators who wish to take their students' ethnic, socioeconomic, and gender characteristics into consideration must avoid misleading stereotypes and overgeneralizations about these groups. All students do not conform to the stereotypic behavior patterns of the gender, ethnic, and socioeconomic groups they belong to. Even when people behave in stereotypic ways, they all do not behave the same. For example, subgroups within larger ethnic groups differ. Although not all Mexican American students fit the following generalizations, they tend to be exposed to much more traditional values and role models than the Nicaraguan American students, who were exposed to values that were encouraged by the Sandinistas after their assumption of power. Filipino females tend to grow up in a society in which the roles that the genders fulfill are much more similar than in Vietnam. Chinese American, Japanese American, Samoan American, Vietnamese American, and Hmong American students have very different experiences and cultural backgrounds. Native Americans who maintain their traditional life-styles live differently than those who have assimilated to the mainstream European American culture.

There are important differences among students raised in families with similar ethnic backgrounds. Parents who want their children to maintain their ethnic identities may pressure them to follow traditional values, attitudes, and behavior patterns to a much greater degree than parents who wish to assimilate into the mainstream culture. Migrant workers and their children who plan to return to Mexico may be less apt to adopt European American values and behavior patterns than those who plan to settle in the United States permanently. Native American students who plan to continue to live on their reservations may be less motivated to adapt to European American ways than those who plan to leave the reservations. Similar differences occur between African Americans who want to integrate fully into European American society and those who want to maintain their African American identities.

Although students from poor backgrounds are more likely to fulfill traditional roles than middle-class students, this may be less true for students in upwardly mobile families and students who identify with and wish to join or emulate the middle class than for those who are content with their life-style. This may also be less important for poor students growing up in Appalachia than for poor students from New York City, who have somewhat different life experiences and much more exposure to middle-class values and behavior patterns.

Students from different socioeconomic backgrounds are also influenced by dissimilar cultural experiences. Students from the same socioeconomic class may not be equally motivated to maintain their cultural heritages. Students in upwardly mobile low-income families and those who identify with and wish to join or emulate the middle class may be less likely to accept traditional values or roles than students who are content with their economic situation.

Regional differences create diversity among ethnic and socioeconomic groups. For example, Mexican American students who live in "border towns" in Texas, New Mexico, and Arizona, and Cuban Americans who live in areas with large Hispanic American populations such as Miami are much more likely to be exposed to the traditional Latino cultural life-styles and attitudes than Mexican American and Cuban American students who live in other parts of the United States. Likewise, students from low-income families in Appalachia have somewhat different experiences and exposure to middle-class values and behavior patterns than students from cities such as New York, Detroit, or Atlanta, and they may be more likely to behave in traditional ways than urban students.

It is extremely important to avoid stereotypic overgeneralizations about all non–European American, poor, immigrant, or refugee students. Therefore, research is included on the various subgroups of these large groups.

For these and other reasons, generalizations about gender, ethnic, and socioeconomic differences among students can be very misleading. Despite these cautions, however, it is important to recognize that some descriptions of socioeconomic or ethnic groups tend to apply to the majority of their members, and some gender differences cut across socioeconomic, ethnic, and geographic boundaries.

Such generalizations can be helpful. They can sensitize educators to the *possibility* that students may have certain stereotypic attitudes, preferences, values, learning styles, and behavior patterns. However, educators should never assume that students will *necessarily* think and behave in these ways. It is as important to avoid relating to students on the basis of incorrect stereotypes as it is to avoid being insensitive to the role ethnic-, socioeconomic-, or gender-influenced attitudes and behavior may play in some students' lives. As long as educators keep these limitations in mind, they will be more effective with students, especially with those groups who traditionally have not performed well in today's diverse society.

Summary

There are great ethnic, socioeconomic, gender, contextual, and communicative disparities in the extent to which students succeed in American schools. This text examines their causes and includes much of the information teachers need in order to provide students with the nonbiased/nonsexist assessment, instructional, and classroom management approaches necessary to reduce these disparities.

Activities

1. Compare the ethnic composition of the classes and program in which you are studying to the ethnic composition of the community your college or university serves. If there are disparities, determine whether they fit the patterns described in this chapter.

2. Ask the administrators of one of the local school districts in your area about the success rates of their LEP students and their students with contextual problems.

References

These references discuss population trends.

1. Bureau of the Census. (1988a). *Hispanic Population in the United States: Current Population Reports, Series P-20, No. 438.* U.S. Department of Commerce, Washington, DC: U.S. Government Printing Office.

2. Bureau of the Census. (1988b). *Money, Income and Poverty Status in the United States: (Advance Data from the March 1989 Current Population Survey). Current Population Reports, Series P-60, No. 166.* U.S. Department of Commerce, Washington, DC: U.S. Government Printing Office.

3. Bureau of the Census. (1988c). *The Black Population in the United States. Current Population Reports, Series P-20, No. 442.* U.S. Department of Commerce, Washington, DC: U.S. Government Printing Office.

4. National Information Center for Children and Youth with Handicaps. (1988). *Minority Issues in Special Education: A Portrait of the Future.* Washington, DC: Author.

5. Puente, T. (1991). Latino child poverty ranks swell. *Hispanic Link Weekly Report, 9*(35), 1, 2, 8.

The following references deal with the low success rates of non–European American and poor students.

6. Educational Testing Service. (1989). *Who Reads Best*? Princeton, NJ: Author.
7. Individuals with Disabilities Education Act. (20 USC., Sections 1400–1485; Education of the Handicapped Act Amendments of 1990).
8. Johnson, M. L. (1984). Blacks in mathematics: A status report. *Journal for Research in Mathematics Education, 15*(2), 145–153.
9. National Assessment of Education Progress. (1988a). *Computer Competence: The First National Assessment.* Princeton, NJ: Educational Testing Service.
10. National Assessment of Education Progress. (1988b). *The Mathematics Report Card: Are We Measuring Up?* Princeton, NJ: Educational Testing Service.
11. National Assessment of Education Progress. (1988c). *The Science Report Card: Elements of Risk and Recovery.* Princeton, NJ: Educational Testing Service.
12. National Assessment of Education Progress. (1990a). *The Reading Report Card, 1971–1978: Trends from the Nation's Report Card.* Princeton, NJ: Educational Testing Service.
13. National Assessment of Education Progress. (1990b). *The Writing Report Card, 1984–1988: Findings from the Nation's Report Card.* Princeton, NJ: Educational Testing Service.
14. National Black Child Development Institute. (1990). *The Status of African American Children: Twentieth Anniversary Report.* Washington, DC: Author.
15. National Center for Educational Statistics. (1989). 1987 High school transcript study. In *National Center for Educational Statistics. Digest of Educational Statistics 1989.* Washington, DC: U.S. Department of Education.
16. National Council of La Raza. (1990). *Hispanic Education: A Statistical Report.* Washington, DC: Author.
17. Office of Educational Research and Improvement, National Center for Educational Research. (1990). *National Education Longitudinal Study. A Profile of the American Eighth Grader: NELS: 88 Student Descriptive Summary.* Washington, DC: U.S. Department of Education.

The high dropout rates of non–European American and poor students are the focus of the following references.

18. American Council on Education, Office of Minority Concerns. (1989). *Minorities in Higher Education: Eighth Annual Status Report,* 1989. Washington, DC: Author.
19. Arciniega, T. A., & Moray, A. I. (1985). *Hispanics and Higher Education: A CSU Imperative. Final Report of the Commission on Hispanic Underrepresentation.* Long Beach, CA: California State University, Office of the Chancellor.
20. Aspira. (1983). *Racial and Ethnic High School Dropout Rates in New York City.* ERIC ED 254–600.
21. Astin, A. (1982). *Minorities in American Higher Education.* San Francisco, CA: Jossey-Bass.
22. Bureau of Indian Affairs. (1988, March). *Report on B. I. A. Education: Final Review Draft.* Washington, DC: Department of the Interior.
23. Hirano-Nakanishi, M. J., & Diaz, R. L. (1982). *Differential Educational Attainment Among "At-Risk" Youth: A Case Study of Language Minority Youth of Mexican Descent and Low Socioeconomic Status.* Los Alamitos, CA: National Center for Bilingual Research.
24. Illinois State General Assembly. (1985). *A Generation Too Precious to Waste.* ERIC ED 268–198.
25. National Public Radio Broadcast. (1990, September). *On the Alaskan Native American.* Washington, DC: All Things Considered.
26. New York Alliance for Public Schools. (1985). *A Study of the Identification, Monitoring, and Tracking of Potential High School Student Dropouts for the New York City Board of Education: Executive Summary. Final Report.* ERIC ED 273–720.
27. Rumberger, R. W. (1983). Dropping out of high school: The influence of race, sex, and family background. *American Education Research Journal, 20,* 199–220.
28. Steinberg, L., Blinde, P. L., & Chan, K. S. (1984). Dropping out among language minority youth. *Review of Educational Research, 54,* 113–132.

The following references document that African Americans and poor Americans get into more trouble in school and are more likely to be suspended for misbehaving.

29. Bennett, C., & Harris, J. J. (1982). Suspension and expulsion of male and black students: A

case study of the causes of disproportionality. *Urban Education, 16*(4), 399–423.

30. Bickel, F., & Qualls, R. (1981). *The Impact of School Climate on Suspension Rates in the Jefferson County Public Schools.* Paper presented at the annual meeting of the American Educational Research Association, Boston.

31. Grossman, H., & Grossman, S. (1994). *Gender Issues in Education.* Needham, MA: Allyn and Bacon.

32. Moore, W. L., & Cooper, H. (1984). Correlations between teacher and student background and teacher perception of discipline problems and disciplinary techniques. *Psychology in the Schools, 21,* 386–392.

33. Stevens, L. B. (1983). *Suspension and Corporal Punishment of Students in the Cleveland Public Schools, 1981–1982.* Cleveland, OH: Office of School Monitoring and Community Relations.

34. Woolridge, P., & Richman, C. (1985). Teachers' choice of punishment as a function of a student's gender, age, race and I. Q. level. *Journal of School Psychology, 23,* 19–29.

The following references deal with gender differences in academic interests and activities.

35. Alspach, P. A. (1988). *Inequities in the Computer Classroom: An Analysis of Two Computer Courses.* ERIC ED 301–180.

36. Chen, M. (1986). Gender and computers: The beneficial effects of experience on attitudes. *Journal of Educational Computing Research, 2*(3), 265–282.

37. Goertz, M. (1989). *Course Taking Patterns in the 1980's.* Princeton, NJ: Educational Testing Service.

38. Klinzing, D. G. (1985). *A Study of the Behavior of Children in a Preschool Equipped with Computers.* ERIC ED 255–320.

39. Lee, V. E., & Ware, N. C. (1986). *When and Why Girls "Leak" Out of High School Mathematics: A Closer Look.* Paper presented at the annual meeting of the American Educational Research Association, San Francisco.

40. Linn, M. C. (1983). *Fostering Equitable Consequences from Computer Learning Environments.* ERIC ED 242–626.

41. Lockheed, M., & Frakt, S. (1984). Sex equity: Increasing girls use of computers. *The Computing Teacher, 11*(8), 16–18.

42. Parsons, J. E. (1984). Sex differences in mathematics participation. In M. W. Steinkamp & M. L. Meehr (Eds.), *Women in Science:*

Advances in Motivation and Achievement, Vol. 2. Greenwich, CT: JAI Press.

43. Rampy, L. (1984). *We Teach Children: Computer Literacy as a Feminist Issue.* ERIC ED 240–028.

44. Silvern, S. B., Countermine, T. M., & Williamson, P. A. C. (1982). *Young Children Interacting with a Computer.* Paper presented at the annual meeting of the American Educational Research Association, New York.

45. Stage, E. K., & Kreinberg, N. (1982). *Equal Access to Computers.* Paper presented at the semiannual meeting of the American Educational Research Association Special Interest Group, Research on Women in Education, Philadelphia.

These references are concerned with gender differences in vocational training and career aspirations.

46. American College Testing Program. (1989). *State and National Trend Data for Students Who Take the ACT Assessment.* Iowa City: Author.

47. Dao, M. (1987). *From Vietnamese to Vietnamese American.* Unpublished manuscript. San Jose, CA: San Jose State University, Department of Special Education.

48. Falkowski, C. K., & Falk, W. W. (1983). Homemaking as an occupational plan: Evidence from a national longitudinal study. *Journal of Vocational Behavior, 22*(2), 227–242.

49. Farmer, H. S., & Sidney J. S. (1985). Sex equity in career and vocational education. In S. Klein (Ed.), *Handbook for Achieving Sex Equity Through Education.* Baltimore: The Johns Hopkins University Press.

50. Grossman, H. (1984). *Educating Hispanic Students: Cultural Implications for Instruction, Classroom Management, Counseling and Assessment.* Springfield, IL: Charles C. Thomas.

51. Gupta, N. (1982). *The Influence of Sex Roles on the Life Plans of Low-SES Adolescents.* ERIC ED 235–434.

52. Hannah, J. S., & Kahn, S. E. (1989). The relationship of socioeconomic status and gender to occupational choices of grade 12 students. *Journal of Vocational Behavior, 34*(2), 161–178.

53. Holmes, B. L., & Esses, L. M. (1988). Factors influencing Canadian high school girls' career motivation. *Psychology of Women Quarterly, 12*(3), 313–328.

54. Jensen, E. L., & Hovey, S. Y. (1982). Bridging the gap from high school to college for tal-

ented females. *Peabody Journal of Education, 59*(3), 153–159.

55. Kelly, K. R., & Cobb, S. J. (1991). A profile of the career development characteristics of young gifted adolescents: Examining gender and multicultural differences. *Roeper Review, 13*(4), 202–206.

56. Odell, K. S. (1989). Gender differences in the educational and occupational expectations of rural Ohio youth. *Research in Rural Education, 5*(3), 37–41.

57. Pido, A. J. A. (1978). *A Cross-Cultural Change of Gender Roles: The Case of Pilipino Women Immigrants in Midwest City, U.S.A.* ERIC ED 159–244.

58. Smith, E. J. (1982). The black female adolescent: A review of the educational, career, and psychological literature. *Psychology of Women Quarterly, 6,* 261–288.

59. Vasquez, M.J. T. (1982). Confronting barriers to the participation of Mexican American women in higher education. *Hispanic Journal of Behavioral Sciences, 4*(2), 147–165.

60. Wells, J. (1983). *Statement of the National Coalition for Women and Girls in Education.* Washington, DC: National Coalition for Women and Girls in Education.

References that deal with the narrowing of the gender gap in academic ability and achievement are listed next.

61. Becker, C., & Forsyth, R. (1990). *Gender Differences in Grades 3 Through 12: A Longitudinal Analysis.* Paper presented at the annual meeting of the American Educational Research Association, Boston.

62. Coladarci, T., & Lancaster, L. N. (1989). *Gender and Mathematics Achievement: Data from High School and Beyond.* ERIC ED 308–207.

63. Feingold, A. (1988). Cognitive gender differences are disappearing. *American Psychologist, 43,* 95–103.

64. Halpern, D. F. (1989). The disappearance of cognitive gender differences: What you see depends on where you look. *American Psychologist, 44,* 455–464.

65. Hyde, J. S., & Linn, M. C. (1988). Gender differences in verbal abilities: A meta-analysis. *Psychological Bulletin, 104*(1), 53–69.

66. Mullin, I., & Jenkins, L. (1988). *The Science Report Card: Elements of Risk and Recovery.* Princeton, NJ: Educational Testing Service.

The following references discuss gender differences in verbal and mathematics achievement.

67. Allred, R. A. (1990). Gender differences in spelling achievement in grades 1 through 6. *Journal of Educational Research, 83*(4), 187–193.

68. Armstrong, J. M. (1981). Achievement and participation of women in mathematics. *Journal for Research in Mathematics Education, 12,* 356–372.

69. Benbow, C. P., & Stanley, J. C. (1982). Consequences in high school and college of sex differences in mathematical reasoning ability: A longitudinal perspective. *American Educational Research Journal, 19*(4), 598–622.

70. Benbow, C. P., & Stanley, J. C. (1983). Sex differences in mathematical reasoning ability: More facts. *Science, 222,* 1029–1031.

71. Brandon P. R., Newton, B. J., & Hammond, O. W. (1987). Children's mathematics achievement in Hawaii: Sex differences favor girls. *American Educational Research Journal, 24*(3), 437–461.

72. Conner, J. M., & Serbin, L. A. (1980). *Mathematics, Visual-Spatial Ability, and Sex Roles* (final report). Washington, DC: National Institute of Education.

73. Eastman, S. T., & Kendrl, K. (1987). Computer and gender: Differential effects of electronic search on students' achievement and attitudes. *Journal of Research and Development in Education, 20*(3), 41–48.

74. Fennema, E., & Carpenter, T. (1981). Sex-related differences in mathematics: Results from the national assessment. *Mathematics Teacher, 74*(7), 554–559.

75. Fox, L., Brody, L. A., & Tobin, D. (Eds.). (1980). *Women and the Mathematical Mystique.* Baltimore: The Johns Hopkins University Press.

76. Fox, L., & Cohn, S. (1980). Sex differences in the development of precocious mathematical talent. In L. Fox, L. A. Brody, & D. Tobin (Eds.), *Women and the Mathematical Mystique.* Baltimore: The Johns Hopkins University Press.

77. Harris, C. S. (1986). *A Summary of the Language Arts Achievement of Students in a Phase-Elective Mini-Course System as Compared to the Language Arts Achievement of Students in a Traditional Program.* ERIC ED 280–064.

78. Hyde, J. S. (1981). How large are cognitive gender differences? A meta-analysis using w and d. *American Psychologist, 36*, 892–901.

79. Marshall, S. P. (1984). Sex differences in students' mathematics achievement: Solving computations and story problems. *Journal of Educational Psychology, 76*(2), 194–204.

80. Midgley, C. (1983). Expectations, values, and academic behaviors. In J. T. Spence (Ed.), *Achievement and Achievement Motivation.* San Francisco: W. H. Freeman.

81. Scott-Jones, D., & Clark, M. L. (1986). The school experience of black girls: The interaction of gender, race, and socioeconomic status. *Phi Delta Kappan, 67*(7), 520–526.

82. Sharp, L. M. (1989). *The SAT-M Gap: Looking at Micro Level Data.* ERIC ED 307–292.

83. Sherman, J. (1981). Girls' and boys' enrollment in theoretical math courses: A longitudinal study. *Psychology of Women Quarterly, 5,* 681–689.

84. Simmons, W. (1990). *Black Male Achievement: Strategies for Ensuring Success in School.* Paper presented at the annual meeting of the National Black Child Development Institute, Washington, DC.

The following references relate to gender differences on visual-spatial tasks.

85. Burnett, S. A., & Lane, D. M. (1980). Effects of academic instruction on spatial visualization. *Intelligence, 4*, 233–242.

86. Fennema, F. H., & Carpenter, T. P. (1981). Sex-related differences in mathematics: Results from national assessment. *Mathematics Teacher, 74*, 554–559.

87. Harris. L. J. (1981). Sex-related variations in spatial skill. In L. S. Liben, A. H. Patterson, & N. Newcombe (Eds.), *Spatial Representation and Behavior Across the Life Span.* New York: Academic Press.

88. Linn, M. C., & Petersen, A. C. (1985). Emergence and characterization of sex differences in spatial ability: A meta-analysis. *Child Development, 56*, 1479–1498.

89. Linn, M. C., & Petersen, A. C. (1986). Gender differences in spatial ability. In J. S. Hyde & M. C. Linn (Eds.), *The Psychology of Gender: Advances Through Meta-Analysis.* Baltimore: The Johns Hopkins University Press.

90. McGee, M. G. (1979). Human spatial abilities: Psychometric studies and environmental, genetic, hormonal, and neurological influences. *Psychological Bulletin, 86*, 889–918.

91. Nash, S. C. (1979). Sex-role as a mediator of intellectual functioning. In M. A. Witting & A. C. Petersen (Eds.), *Sex-Related Differences in Cognitive Functioning: Developmental Issues.* New York: Academic Press.

92. Petersen, A. G. (1979). Hormones and cognitive functioning in normal development. In M. A. Witting & A. C. Petersen (Eds.), *Sex-Related Differences in Cognitive Functioning: Developmental Issues.* New York: Academic Press.

93. Richmond, P. G. (1980). A limited sex difference in spatial test scores with a preadolescent sample. *Child Development, 51*, 601–602.

Gender differences on science achievement are the focus of the references listed as follows.

94. Becker, B. J. (1989). Gender and science achievement: A reanalysis of studies from two meta-analyses. *Journal of Research in Science Teaching, 26*(2), 141–169.

95. Hueftle, S. J., Rakow, S. J., & Welch, W. W. (1983). *Images of Science.* Minneapolis: University of Minnesota Press.

96. Hyde, J. S., & Linn, M. C. (1986). *The Psychology of Gender: Advances Through Meta-Analysis.* Baltimore: The Johns Hopkins University Press.

97. Maehr, M. L., & Steinkamp, M. (1983). *A Synthesis of Findings on Sex Differences in Science Education Research.* ERIC ED 229–226.

98. Malone, M. R., & Fleming, M. L. (1983). The relationship of student characteristics and student performance in science as viewed by meta-analysis research. *Journal of Research in Science Teaching, 20*, 481–495.

99. Shaw, E. L., Jr., & Doan, R. L. (1990). An investigation of the differences in attitude and achievement between male and female second and fifth grade science students. *Journal of Elementary Science Education, 2*(1), 10–15.

100. Steinkamp, M. W., & Maehr, M. L. (1983). Affect, ability, and science achievement: A quantitative synthesis of correlational research. *Review of Educational Research, 53*, 369–396.

101. Steinkamp, M. W., & Maehr, M. L. (1984). Gender differences in motivational orientations toward achievement in school science: A quantitative synthesis. *American Educational Research Journal, 21*(1), 39–59.

The following references indicate that females are less likely to get into trouble for behavior problems, be disciplined by their teachers, or be suspended from school.

102. Center, D. B., & Wascom, A. M. (1987). Teacher perceptions of social behavior in behaviorally disordered and socially normal children and youth. *Behavioral Disorders, 12*(3), 200–206.

103. Duke, D. L. (1978). Why don't girls misbehave more than boys in school? *Journal of Youth and Adolescence, 7*(2), 141–157.

104. Epstein, M. H., Cullinan, D., & Bursuck, W. D. (1985). Prevalence of behavior problems among learning disabled and nonhandicapped students. *Mental Retardation and Learning Disability Bulletin, 213,* 30–39.

105. Ludwig, G., & Cullinan, D. (1984). Behavior problems of gifted and nongifted elementary school girls and boys. *Gifted Child Quarterly, 28*(1), 37–39.

The following references describe gender differences in emotional reactions in school.

106. Hadfield, O. D., & Maddux, C. D. (1988). Cognitive style and mathematics anxiety among high school students. *Psychology in the Schools, 25,* 75–83.

107. Haynes, N. M., Comer, J. P., & Hamilton-Lee, M. (1988). Gender and achievement status differences on learning factors among black high school students. *Journal of Educational Research, 81*(4), 233–237.

108. Marsh, H. W. (1987). *The Content Specificity of Math and English Anxieties: The High School and Beyond Study.* ERIC ED 300–402.

109. Wynstra, S., & Cummings, C. (1990). *Science Anxiety: Relation with Gender, Year in Chemistry Class, Achievement, and Test Anxiety.* ERIC ED 331–837.

Gender differences in self-confidence are discussed in the following references.

110. Armstrong, J. M., & Kahl, S. (1980). *A National Assessment of Performance and Participation of Women in Mathematics* (final report). Washington, DC: National Institute of Education.

111. Brush, L. (1980). *Encouraging Girls in Mathematics: The Problem and the Solution.* Boston: Abt.

112. Eccles (Parsons), J., Adler, T. F., Futterman, R., Goff, S. B., Kaczala, C. M., Meece, J., & Midgley, C. (1983). Expectations, values, and academic behaviors. In J. T. Spence (Ed.), *Perspective on Achievement and Achievement Motivation.* San Francisco: W. H. Freeman.

113. Fox, L. H., Brody, L., & Tobin, D. (Eds.). (1980). *Women and the Mathematical Mystique.* Baltimore: The Johns Hopkins University Press.

114. Hyde, J., & Fennema, E. (1990). *Gender Differences in Mathematics Performance and Affect: Results of Two Meta-Analyses.* Paper presented at the annual meeting of the American Educational Research Association, Boston.

115. Levine, B. (1990). *Arithmetic Development: Where Are the Gender Differences?* Paper presented at the annual meeting of the American Educational Research Association, Boston.

116. Reyes, L. H. (1984). Affective variables and mathematics education. *Elementary School Journal, 84*(5), 558–581.

117. Sherman, J. (1980). Mathematics, spatial visualization, and related factors: Changes in girls and boys, grades 8–11. *Journal of Educational Psychology, 72,* 476–482.

118. Stevenson, H. W., & Newman, R. S. (1986). Long-term prediction of achievement and attitudes in mathematics and reading. *Child Development, 57,* 646–659.

The focus of the references listed below is gender differences in risk taking and reaction to failure.

119. Ginsburg, H. J., & Miller, S. M. (1982). Sex differences in children's risk-taking behavior. *Child Development, 53* (2), 426–428.

120. Licht, B. G., Linden, T. A., Brown, D. A., & Sexton, M. (1984). *Sex Differences in Achievement Orientation: An "A" Student Phenomenon.* ERIC ED 252–783.

121. Miller, A. (1986). Performance impairment after failure: Mechanisms and sex differences. *Journal of Educational Psychology, 78*(6), 486–491.

Gender differences in seeking teacher feedback, support, and help is the focus of these references.

122. Brutsaert, H. (1990). Changing sources of self-esteem among girls and boys in secondary school. *Urban Education, 24*(40), 432–439.

123. Nelson-LeGall, S., & Glor-Scheib, S. (1983). *Help-Seeking in Elementary Classrooms: An Observational Study.* ERIC ED 230–286.

124. Stewart, M. J., & Corbin, C. B. (1988). Feedback dependence among low confidence preadolescent boys and girls. *Research Quarterly for Exercise and Sport, 59*(2), 160–164.

125. Sullivan, H. J. (1986). Factors that influence continuing motivation. *Journal of Educational Research, 80*(2), 86–92.

These references deal with ethnic differences in female roles.

126. Dao, M. (1987). *From Vietnamese to Vietnamese American.* Unpublished manuscript. San Jose, CA: San Jose State University.
127. Simpson, G. (1984). The daughters of Charlotte Ray: The career development process during the exploratory and establishment stages of Black women attorneys. *Sex Roles, 11*(1/2), 113–139.

Contextual disparities are the focus of the following references.

128. Burns, S. (Ed.). (1991). Homelessness demographics, causes and trends. *Homewords, 3*(4), 1–3.
129. Cavazos, L. F. (1990). *U.S. Department of Education Report to Congress on the Education for Homeless Children and Youth Program for the Period October 1, 1988 through September 30, 1989.* Washington, DC: U.S. Department of Education.
130. Henderson, A. (1987). *The Evidence Continues to Grow: Parent Involvement Improves Student Achievement.* ERIC ED 315–199.
131. Interstate Migrant Education Council. (1987). *Migrant Education: A Consolidated View.* ERIC ED 285–701.
132. Lawless, K. (1986). *Neediest of the Needy: Special Education for Migrants. Harvesting the Harvesters. Book 8.* ERIC ED 279–473.
133. Powers, J. L., Eckenrode, J., & Jaklitsch, G. (1988). *Running Away from Home: A Response to Adolescent Maltreatment.* ERIC ED 296–228.

These references document the prevalence of LEP students.

134. Individuals with Disabilities Education Act. Education of the Handicapped Act Amendments of 1990. (20 USC, Sections 1400–1485).
135. Woodrow, K. A. (1988). *Measuring Net Immigration to the United States: The Emigrant Population and Recent Emigration Flows.* Paper presented at the annual meeting of the Population Association of America, New Orleans.

Chapter 2

Intrinsic Causes of Ethnic and Socioeconomic Disparities

Educators do not agree about the causes of the ethnic and socioeconomic disparities in school. Some educators believe that many non–European American and poor students are predisposed to have problems in school because they are exposed to more biomedical problems, are less intelligent, and come from disadvantaged cultural backgrounds that do not prepare them to learn effectively. Other educators consider these explanations to be examples of blaming the victims for problems inflicted on them by others. These educators blame the schools and society at large for these ethnic and socioeconomic inequities.

Educators who locate the causes of these disparities within students themselves tend to favor solutions that change students or accommodate educational approaches to their assumed differences or inadequacies. For example, educators who believe that some students are brought up in disadvantaged cultures that do not prepare them to succeed in school usually favor modifying the students' culturally influenced attitudes and behavior. Examples of these are encouraging students to work at a faster pace and encouraging them to function more independently. Educators who believe there are genetic differences among students from different ethnic and socioeconomic backgrounds that make it difficult for them to use higher-level cognitive processes typically suggest that teachers should reduce the goals they hope to achieve with these students and should adapt their methods for achieving them to these students' assumed limitations.

Educators who hold the school system responsible for these disparities want the schools and the teachers who staff them to improve so that all students can realize their full potential. By and large they support multicultural education as a way of combatting cultural insensitivity and prejudice in schools. Many of them favor a redistribution of the educational pie—with more money spent on educating non–European American and poor students, and economic reforms that will provide poor parents with the financial means to assist their children to succeed in school.

This chapter and Chapter 3 examine these different points of view. In particular, this chapter discusses explanations that locate the cause within the students; Chapter 3 deals with causes that exist in the educational system and society at large.

Biomedical Problems

The living conditions of many poor African American, European American, Hispanic American, and Native American students place them at greater risk for biomedical problems. Poor health care and nutrition can cause neurological problems, which in turn can cause them to do poorly in school. Most poor parents do not abuse drugs while the mothers are pregnant. However, some people believe that in comparison to middle-class European American children, children of poor parents are more likely to suffer the results of exposure to harmful substances because their mothers abuse drugs and alcohol while they are pregnant. (Whether this is actually true is discussed later.) If current trends continue, poor African American, European American, Hispanic American, and Native American students may also suffer the unfortunate effects of being born HIV positive in greater relative numbers than their European American middle-class peers.

Health Care and Nutrition

As a group, poor families, especially the millions of families whose incomes fall below the poverty line, do not have adequate access to prenatal and postnatal health care (7, 10). In fact, the percentage of poor mothers who receive prenatal care has actually decreased in recent years (1). As a result, poor children are more likely to suffer the consequences of complications of pregnancy and delivery, prematurity, and low birth weight, and the learning, emotional, and behavior problems these conditions can cause (2, 3, 6, 7, 13, 14–16). Six to 8% of children who are born with a moderately low birth weight will have developmental problems. Among those born with severely low birth weight the percentage is twice as large (5, 8). As the mortality rate from these complications has declined and more infants who are born with these risky conditions survive, the number of poor children who experience the learning and behavior problems caused by these conditions has increased.

Poor parents are also less able to provide their children with the same nutrition and medical care that their more advantaged peers receive. This can also cause their children to develop learning and behavior problems (11, 12). Thus, because of inadequate medical care and nutrition, poor children may experience a higher incidence of learning and behavior problems (4, 9). Because African American and Hispanic American children are more likely than European Americans to be born poor, they are at greater risk to experience these problems.

Fortunately, the deleterious effects of low birth weight and other perinatal problems can be counteracted in many cases by providing youngsters with proper care. In addition, the harmful effects of malnutrition appear to occur primarily when severe malnutrition is present, which is typically not the case with most American students from poor or poverty backgrounds. And these effects may also be reversible.

We do not know the exact effects of limited access to medical care and poor nutrition on students' school careers. When considered as a whole, it seems reasonable to expect that the disproportionately small share of the medical and nutritional benefits received by the families who earn the least in our society contributes at least to some degree to these students' problems in school. However, whether these problems are a very significant factor is a point that can only be answered by more research.

Substance Abuse

Some individuals believe that parental substance abuse contributes to the lack of academic success of African American, Native American, and poor students. They claim that African American, Native American, and poor parents abuse substances such as alcohol, marijuana, cocaine, and so on, during pregnancy more frequently than middle-class European American parents, and that as a result their children perform less adequately in school.

Substance abuse does cause both severe and subtle birth defects and a variety of learning and behavior problems (17–19, 22, 26–28, 30, 32–35, 38, 39, 41, 43–46, 52, 53). Even supposedly less severe forms of substance abuse, such as smoking cigarettes during pregnancy, can cause children to develop learning, social adjustment, and behavior problems (24, 30).

Fortunately, only some substance-exposed children actually develop the difficulties these dangerous substances may cause (49, 53). The reasons for this are largely unknown. However, one has been identified—good prenatal care reduces the likelihood that substance-exposed children will actually suffer the potential problems for which they are at risk (32, 41).

Substance-exposed children do not suffer all of the possible problems that their exposure can cause (27, 32, 41, 49). The problems children of substance-abusing parents can experience vary. Approximately 2% to 17% suffer from severe congenital defects, developmental disabilities, cerebral palsy, seizure disorders, and so on (23, 49). Many others develop normally at first, then demonstrate learning and behavior problems as they approach school age.

Substance-exposed students often function adequately under adult guidance and in structured learning and play situations. However, they have great difficulty in adjusting to situations that require them to provide their own structure, initiative, or organization. They do much better in one-to-one situations or when they have to cope with only one individual, task, or toy. When they have to deal with group situations or multiple activities, materials, tasks, or people, they quickly become overstimulated, overwhelmed, and disorganized.

Many, but not all, substance-exposed children suffer additional insults and injuries (21, 23, 29, 31, 32, 34, 42, 43). Their parents tend to have a host of additional medical and social problems. Mothers who are unable to stop abusing drugs for their children's sake during their pregnancy are often unable to care for them after they have been born. (The fact that mothers abuse drugs during pregnancy is often an indication that their children will receive inadequate care.) Those who are poor tend to abandon their children in the hospital, which often leads to eventual foster care placement. Mothers who do decide to care for their children often provide inadequate care for them because of their drug problems.

> *Growing numbers of crack babies simply are being abandoned in hospitals by their crack-smoking mothers. As for those babies who are discharged, the vast majority go from the hospital nursery to chaotic home environments characterized by deep poverty and little physical or emotional nurturing. With one strike already against them, these babies are at high risk for the second strike—neglect and abuse by crack-using adults. (43, p. 19)*

Presently we are unable to determine when and to what extent exposed children's problems are caused by physiological factors or the environmental disadvantages often associated with substance-abusing parents. For now, the prudent position is that these students' learning and behavior problems can best be understood as resulting from the interaction of both biological and environmental factors.

The actual number of mothers who abuse drugs while they are pregnant and the number of drug-exposed infants is unknown. Surveys of the percentage of parents who expose their unborn infants to harmful substances have yielded results that range from 0.4% to 27% of the parents tested or questioned, depending on the hospital and the neighborhood surveyed (21, 25, 37, 48, 51), and their number is growing at an alarming rate (36). Estimates of the number of infants that may be affected yearly by crack alone range from 48,000 to 375,000 (20, 21, 43, 47, 51).

There appears to be evidence that poor, African American, Native American, and inner city mothers in general abuse these substances while they are pregnant more frequently than other mothers (40, 43, 49, 50). However, some researchers believe that the difference between these mothers' rates of drug abuse and those of European American middle-class mothers is overstated because European American middle-class mothers are better able to hide their substance-abusing behavior from the authorities (24, 43).

> *A minority woman who uses drugs or alcohol during pregnancy is almost ten times more likely to be reported to child-abuse authorities than is a white woman. White middle-class mothers—along with other white middle-class cocaine users—find it easier to hide their substance abuse than do poor, minority women. (43, p. 21)*

Even if the difference is overstated, there is evidence that substance-abusing poor parents in general, and non-European poor parents in particular, are less able to obtain the good prenatal care that reduces the likelihood that substance-exposed children will actually suffer the potential problems for which they are at risk. Thus, it may be that their children are at even greater risk than European American middle-class children.

Although African American, Native American, and poor students are currently more likely to suffer from such problems than European American middle-class students, it is unclear what proportion of their school problems is caused by their parents' substance abuse during pregnancy. It may well turn out to be too small to account for much of the disparity between the educational experiences of different ethnic groups and socioeconomic classes.

> *The media have painted a dire picture of infants who were exposed to alcohol and other drugs in utero. . . . Children who were prenatally exposed to substances are unique, but as a whole they are more like than different from other children. . . . There is a danger in this label in that it can engender a self-fulfilling prophecy: Children will become what their parents and teachers expect them to become. Given the current view of drug exposure this would be an unfair prophecy. (49, p. 1, 24)*

Acquired Immune Deficiency Syndrome

The dramatic increase in the number of AIDS-exposed infants who are born HIV positive is adding to the number of children who demonstrate problems similar to those who are drug exposed (54–56). As better methods of prolonging their lives are developed, more and more HIV-positive students will experience difficulty in school.

Non–European American poor children are disproportionately affected by AIDS (57–58). In one national study, African Americans and Hispanic Americans represented 53% and 23% of the reported cases (58). Although the number of students affected by AIDS is still small, their numbers continue to grow.

Genetic Differences/Inferiority

In the not-too-distant past, it was both acceptable and commonplace to justify colonialism, slavery, gross economic inequality, the inferior status of women, racial segregation, immigration restriction, sterilization of the poor, unequal educational opportunities, and a host of other inequities on the basis of imagined genetic differences (59, 61, 69, 72). Abraham Lincoln was not immune to the point of view prevalent during his time. Despite his emancipation proclamation, he maintained that

> *There is a physical difference between the white and black races which I believe will forever forbid the two races living together on terms of social and political equality. And inasmuch as they cannot so live, while they do remain together*

there must be the position of superior and inferior, and I as much as any other man am in favor of having the superior position assigned to the white race. (63, p. 35)

Most of these conditions are no longer acceptable in our society. However, some individuals still believe that certain groups of students, most notably African American, Hispanic American, and poor students, are less successful in school because they inherit different amounts or kinds of intelligence (62, 64–76). The following quotes by Shockley and Jensen are representative of this position.

Nature has color-coded groups of individuals so that statistically reliable predictions of their adaptability to intellectually rewarding and effective lives can easily be made and profitably be used by the pragmatic man-in-the-street. (70, p. 375)

The most parsimonious hypothesis—one that would comprehend virtually all the established facts about the white-black IQ difference without the need to postulate any environmental factors besides those that are known to affect IQ and on which blacks in general are less advantaged—is that something between one-half and three-fourths of the average IQ difference is attributable to genetic factors, and the remainder to environmental factors and their interaction with genetic differences. (67, p. 227)

Currently, there are two major theories of how genetic differences operate to create presumed ethnic- and socioeconomic-based intellectual differences. These theories and the evidence regarding them follow.

Meritocracy Theory

The meritocracy theory offers an explanation for why poor students, especially those that come from poverty backgrounds, tend to have lower IQ scores than middle- and upper-class students. According to the theory, our society is a meritocracy in which all people have an equal opportunity to succeed. Those who do not succeed lack either the ability or motivation to do so. Thus, it is to be expected that those who remain in the working class, especially those who are below the poverty level and those who do poorly in school, lack either the motivation or the intelligence to do better. In other words, proponents of this theory offer a simple explanation for poor students' lack of achievement in school. If their parents were smarter, they would learn more and earn more. As Herrenstein puts it:

1. If differences in mental abilities are inherited, and 2. if success requires these abilities, and 3. if earnings and prestige depend on success, 4. then social standing (which reflects earnings and prestige) will be based to some extent on inherited differences among people. (64, pp. 58–59)

Various authors (60, 65, 68) have suggested that there are many millions of people in the working class, especially among those that fall below the poverty level, with what they call cultural familial retardation. They believe that these individuals suffer from two related problems. They inherit limited intellectual potential from their parents. And they are brought up by their parents in

> *families which are unable—due to their own lack of intellectual ability—to provide their children with the support that they need to acquire and maintain a reasonable standard of living. . . . Having low mental ability, exacerbated by a lack of parental encouragement, support, and proper modeling, the cultural familial retarded settle permanently into the lowest of the lower socioeconomic strata of society, become life-long clients of welfare programs, drift from job to job, are easily exploited, and reproduce an inordinately large posterity that will perpetuate this grim circumstance. (68, pp. 3, 4, 8)*

Levels of Cognitive Ability

For many years, educators and others who believed that different ethnic groups and socioeconomic classes inherited dissimilar intellectual potentials claimed the groups inherited varying *amounts* of intelligence. Since 1969 however, many of them have accepted a theory of intelligence, first proposed by Jensen, that states that poor and African American students tend to inherit different *types* or *levels* of intelligence rather than different amounts of intellectual ability. According to Jensen, there are two types of intelligence, which he calls Level I and Level II.

> *Level I ability consists of rote learning and primary memory; it is the capacity to register and retrieve information with fidelity and is characterized essentially by a relative lack of transformation, conceptual coding, or other mental manipulation intervening between information input and output. Level II ability, in contrast, is characterized by mental manipulation of inputs, conceptualization, reasoning, and problem solving: it is essentially the general intelligence (g) factor common to most complex tests of intelligence. (66, p. 99)*

Although all individuals and groups supposedly inherit the ability to use Level I (rote learning and associative learning) to solve problems more or less to the same degree, they supposedly inherit different capacities to use Level II (conceptual ability). Jensen and others claim that African Americans and poor students do not score as high as European American and middle- and upper-class students on "intelligence tests" because they tend to be endowed with a diminished capacity for Level II intellectual functioning. "The hypothesis in its most simple and extreme form states that low and middle socioeconomic-status groups differ in Level II but not Level I ability" (66, p. 104).

Implications

Individuals who believe that genetics play a role in causing socioeconomic and ethnic differences in school outcomes do not agree about how educators should handle these differences. Educators who believe the influence of genetic differences can be mitigated typically recommend that schools provide students with experiences and training that will counteract the effects of genetic differences.

Those who think the effects of genetics are unmodifiable suggest that teachers should accommodate their goals for students, their instructional approaches, and their classroom management techniques to the intellectual differences among their students, and they have provided suggestions for adapting instructional approaches to the different kinds of operations characteristic of Level I and Level II intellectual functioning. Believing that ethnic groups and socioeconomic classes require different educational approaches, these individuals are not troubled by the fact that European American middle- and upper-class students are more likely to be assigned to courses of study (tracks) for high-potential students in which teachers stress independent study and higher-level cognitive skills, whereas Hispanic Americans, African American, and poor students are overrepresented in tracks for low-potential students, in which teachers stress instructional techniques that involve concrete repetitive drill and practice, and in special education programs for students of limited intellectual potential, and are underrepresented in programs for gifted and talented students.

Criticisms

The claim that different ethnic groups and socioeconomic classes inherit different kinds or amounts of intelligence is based on four assumptions. (1) American society is a meritocracy. (2) Individuals from different ethnic and socioeconomic backgrounds inherit different amounts of intelligence or learning potential. (3) Ethnic groups and socioeconomic classes differ in their abilities to use Level I or Level II types of intellectual operations when solving problems. (4) Level I and Level II differences are genetically determined. These assumptions and the arguments against them offered by their critics are now discussed.

1. *American society is a meritocracy.* Many people have argued that the United States is not a meritocracy (73–76). They claim that schools do not provide a level playing field that enables all students to achieve up to their potential. Instead of being designed to provide all students the knowledge and skills they need to succeed in life regardless of their ethnic and socioeconomic backgrounds, schools are biased against the very groups that do so poorly. In fact, some individuals propose that myths about the democratizing influences of schools are propaganda used to legitimize the privileged positions of middle and upper socioeconomic classes by convincing poor and non–European American students and parents that they are not capable of profiting from the education offered them. In this way, poor and non–European American students and their parents will blame their lack of success in school on themselves and will believe that they merit their eventual inferior positions in society because they did not take advantage of the opportunities afforded them in school. (See the section on structured reproduction in Chapter 3.)

The evidence presented throughout this book confirms that schools are not a level playing field. Schools that serve primarily middle- and upper-class European American students have many more resources than schools that serve primarily non-European and poor students (see Chapter 3). The United States is far from a perfect meritocracy. For example, even when certain groups of students do well in school, the amount of money they earn is not commensurate with their educational attainment. It is true that European American males who have earned a high school diploma obtain higher-paying jobs than those who have not graduated high school. However, research indicates that non–European American students, especially African Americans and Hispanics who graduate from high school, do not earn significantly more than those of their peers who do not complete high school. Given the same level of education, students' earnings depend more on how high up the socioeconomic ladder their parents are (75, 76). Moreover, despite the corrective effects that affirmative action has had, middle- and upper-class European American job seekers still receive preference over their non-European and poor competitors in certain sectors. (See the section on structured reproduction in Chapter 3.) Thus, there is no justification for believing that poor students who do not do well in school and families that remain poor or below the poverty level are responsible for the state of affairs they find themselves in.

2. *Individuals from different ethnic and socioeconomic class backgrounds inherit different amounts of intelligence or learning potential.* There are a number of reasons for questioning this assumption. Supporters of the genetic explanation base their conclusion that intelligence is inherited primarily on the results of research that studies twins. They claim these studies indicate that

- Intelligence test scores of identical twins are more similar than those of fraternal twins.
- Identical twins reared apart have very similar intelligence test scores despite being brought up in different environments.
- The IQ scores of adopted children resemble those of their natural parents to a greater degree than expected.

However, these studies have been criticized on a number of grounds (77–87). Researchers who are critical of the theory claim that the studies were flawed methodologically. They suggest that because identical twins are treated more similarly by their parents than fraternal twins, the greater similarity in their test scores could be caused by the similar treatment they receive. They point out that the twins in the adoption studies tended to be placed in homes of families with the same socioeconomic backgrounds as their natural parents, thereby introducing the possibility that environmental factors accounted for the similarity between their scores and those of their natural parents. They note that African American children adopted by European American families score much higher on intelligence tests than one would expect if they had inherited a fixed amount of intelligence from their biological parents.

Another reason for doubting that some non–European American groups such as African Americans inherit less intelligence than European Americans is the fact that environmental factors are the more likely explanation of the difference in scores between African American and European American students. For example, within each socioeconomic class African American students who grow up in racially mixed neighborhoods score higher on intelligence tests because they are exposed to the contents of tests that reflect the experiences of European Americans (83). In addition, almost without exception, studies of African American children's performance on tests that purport to measure their intellectual functioning indicate that poor students do not perform as well as their middle-class peers and that socioeconomic class is a more powerful predictor of how children will perform than ethnic background (78, 88–92).

3. *Ethnic groups and socioeconomic classes differ in their abilities to use Level I or Level II types of intellectual operations when solving problems.* Research on Jensen's two-level theory has indicated that poor, African American, and Hispanic American students do score lower than middle-class and European American students on tests that purport to measure Level II abilities (78, 87, 93, 99–103, 105, 107), but a number of researchers (94–98, 104, 106, 108, 109) have criticized the results of these studies for the following reasons.

- The differences obtained in these studies are not as strong or as consistent as those originally reported by Jensen. Some studies have found relationships between Level II scores and ethnicity but not socioeconomic status, for one ethnic group but not another, or for socioeconomic status but not for ethnicity, and contrary to Jensen's theory, most studies have found differences between ethnic groups and socioeconomic classes on tests that purport to measure Level I abilities.
- The differences observed between the scores of European American middle-class students and African American, Hispanic American, and poor students on so-called intelligence tests are more likely to be due to test bias than to real differences in intellectual ability (see Chapter 9).
- There is also evidence that the difference between the scores of European American and middle-class students and African American, Hispanic American, and poor students on tests of Level II abilities is greater than the differences between their scores on tests of Level I abilities because tests of Level II abilities are even more biased against these groups than tests of Level I abilities. Finally, because training students on the use of specific strategies for solving Level II–type problems has been shown to raise the low scores of poor, African American, and Native American students, it appears that the difference in scores on these tests are due to exposure rather than heredity (95, 106, 108).
- Tests of intelligence, including those used to study students' Level I and Level II abilities, are poor predictors of scholastic achievement and therefore are invalid measures of "intelligence." There is no reason to look for explanations for why groups of students have different Level I and Level II intellec-

tual abilities because the tests used to measure these intellectual abilities neither measure intelligence nor predict how students will perform in school (see Chapter 9).

As will be seen in Chapter 9, the results of studies that appear to support the levels theory are based on invalid assessment instruments that cannot be used to measure or evaluate students' intelligence. The content, language, and format of standardized tests that purport to measure intelligence are neither culture-free nor culture-fair; assessors employ them in a biased manner; and they are poor predictors of non-European and poor students' academic achievement or their learning potentials. Comparisons of the assumed intelligence of different groups based on the results of biased instruments and assessors are invalid, misleading, and harmful. They do not explain or justify ethnic or socioeconomic differences in students' achievement.

4. *Level I and Level II differences are genetically determined.* Some educators grant the possibility that the differences between ethnic groups and socioeconomic classes on intelligence tests reflect real differences in intellectual ability but disagree that their cause is genetic. They argue that there have been no studies to investigate why some students do poorer on problems that involve conceptual learning (Level II) than on tasks requiring associative and rote learning (Level I), and they claim that because there is no evidence that these differences are inherited, there is no reason to attribute them to genetic factors rather than to such environmental factors as different exposure at home to the kinds of mental operations measured by the tests, inadequate preparation for the tasks on the tests in biased and prejudiced school systems, and so on.

Conclusions

There is no evidence that genetically determined differences in intellectual ability contribute significantly to ethnic and socioeconomic educational disparities or that ethnic groups and socioeconomic classes inherit different intellectual potentials. Differences that have been observed occur because current methods of evaluating intelligence are biased against the groups who perform least adequately on them and because our imperfect society has not yet achieved the assumptions underlying the meritocracy theory.

Cultural Deprivation/Educational Disadvantage

In the 1960s, at the same time that the genetic explanation of the low rates of success among non–European American and poor students was rejected by increasing numbers of educators, the theory of cultural deprivation gained a great deal of acceptance (110–123). According to this theory, certain non–European American students—especially African Americans, Hispanic Americans, and the children of poor parents—are brought up in inferior cultural environments that deprive them of the skills, attitudes, and acceptable behaviors that are transmitted to students who grow up in the superior European American middle-class culture. As a result, they are ill-prepared to succeed in school either academically or behaviorally. As Bloom described them, culturally deprived students have "experiences in homes which do not transmit the cultural patterns necessary for the type of learning characteristics of the schools and the larger society" (112, p. 4).

The term used to label such students has undergone a number of modifications since the 1960s. First it was changed from "culturally deprived" to "culturally disadvantaged" to signify that these students were not cultureless—deprived of a culture—but brought up in a culture that placed them at a disadvantage. Then "culturally disadvantaged" was replaced by "educationally disadvantaged" to indicate that the whole of students' cultures were not being indicted, merely the way they prepared students to function in school. Today, although few educators would publicly proclaim that certain non–European American and poor students are brought up in inferior cultures, numerous educators are on record as believing that some students are ill-prepared to succeed in school because their culture places them at an educational disadvantage. In fact, the U.S. Department of Education spends millions of dollars on educational programs for "educationally disadvantaged students."

Characteristics

According to the theory, disadvantaged and advantaged students differ in terms of their cognitive and linguistic ability, self-concept, level of aspiration, locus of control, and social behavior.

Cognitive Skills

Educationally disadvantaged students are assumed to have "special difficulty in developing concepts of an abstract nature and generalizing" (112, p. 71). They are also considered to be deficient in the "semiautonomous essential processes demanded for adequate skill in the use of linguistic and mathematical symbols and for the analysis of causal relationships" (117, p. 236). In other words, their thinking processes are concrete and convergent/conforming, rather than abstract and creative.

According to the theory, these cognitive deficits occur because educationally disadvantaged students' parents do not interact sufficiently with them; stimulate them intellectually through conversation, field trips, books, magazines, encyclopedias; correct their misperceptions; or encourage their curiosity. As McCloskey put it,

> *Intellectual stimulation between adult and child is relatively slight. Adults seldom talk with children. Parents who work at physical tasks for long hours, often during evening hours, are too tired or inaccessible for conversation with children . . . .*

Disadvantaged children have not developed sufficient cognitive and reasoning skills essential for typical rates and dimensions of school progress. These deficiencies accumulate partly from prolonged restriction to the limited experiences of culturally and intellectually impoverished homes and neighborhoods. . . . Disadvantaged children's communication capabilities are elementary. Analytic conversations with adults at home are limited. There, children learn, think, and speak largely about concrete matters of immediate import. Generalities and long-range goals are seldom discussed or recognized. (121, pp. 6, 16)

Katz stated it this way:

In crowded lower-class homes, where mothers often are away at work during the day and both parents lack intellectual sophistication, the child's early efforts at verbal and cognitive mastery are less likely to be favorably reinforced than in middle-class homes, resulting in lower expectations of reward for intellectual effort. (138, p. 19)

Linguistic Ability

The language of educationally disadvantaged students is supposedly deficient for two reasons. First, it is perceived to be structurally deficient. It is full of grammatical errors, lacks prepositions and other forms that are necessary to perceive and express logical relationships, uses tenses incorrectly, and is repetitive, dull, and colorless.

Language in the lower class is not as flexible a means of communication as in the middle class. It is not as readily adapted to the subtleties of the particular situation, but consists more of a relatively small repertoire of stereotyped phrases and expressions which are used rather loosely without much effort to achieve a subtle correspondence between perception and verbal expression. Much of lower class language consists of a kind of incidental "emotional" accompaniment to action here and now. In contrast, middle-class language, rather than being a mere accompaniment to ongoing activity serves more to represent things and events not immediately present. Thus middle-class language is more abstract and necessarily somewhat more flexible, detailed and subtle in its descriptive aspects. (118, pp. 118–119)

Second, educationally disadvantaged students' use of language is supposedly inadequate because the environments in which they grow up "offered inadequate opportunities to use language in cognitively complex ways" (158, p. 303). These deficits are attributed to parents who provide children poor language models and spend insufficient time communicating with children (112, 114, 116, 167). "In the deprived home, language usage is more limited. Much communication is through gestures and other non-verbal means. When language is used, it is likely to be terse and not necessarily grammatically correct" (112, pp. 70–71).

Compared with other children whose families provide them with adequate or extensive spoken language stimulation, children from lower socioeconomic families may be less fortunate. . . . For example, often missing is an atmosphere of family conversation where a child's questions are answered—extending his vocabulary and giving him a right to stand up for and explain his point of view. Also missing in some homes of this type is a family environment which sets an example for acceptable speech and reading patterns. And, children from meager family situations are too often not exposed to a variety of toys and play materials of different colors, shapes, and sizes which challenge the child's ingenuity with his hands and mind, and learn only "restricted" types of language. (167, pp. 332–333)

Self-Concept and Self-Esteem

Non–European American students, especially those from African American, Native American, Hispanic American, and poor backgrounds, are thought to have poor self-concepts and low self-esteem. This is attributed to a variety of causes. They are supposed to lack successful role models in their families and communities with whom to identify; repeated failure in school and other competitive situations is assumed to lower their self-image; and they are believed to suffer a loss of self-esteem when they compare their lives and living conditions with those of their middle-class and European American peers. "Disadvantaged children have relatively impoverished self-concepts. From quite realistic appraisals of their experiences, these children have acquired the attitude that they cannot achieve as much as their middle- or upper-class counterparts" (127, p. 5).

Educational Aspirations

Disadvantaged students are assumed to have low educational and career aspirations. "Their expectations and aspirations are correspondingly low. Many have learned to *'not hope for too much'*. As a result, they are less motivated by goals that fuel the efforts of pupils who have acquired larger aspirations from richer experiences" (121, p. 5).

Disadvantaged students' supposed low level of aspirations are attributed to four factors.

- Their parents do not expect them to do well in school.
- They perceive that their culture and environment does not prepare them to compete successfully with their more advantaged peers.
- Their life experiences, and those of their parents, quickly teach them that it is unrealistic to expect that they will accomplish very much.
- Many of them, especially African American males, lack role models because of the absence of fathers in the house. Because the male parent represents the external world and serves as a role model for dealing with life outside the family while the female parent represents the internal/family world, students without fathers are not motivated to succeed because they do not see that model at home (115, 120, 123).

Locus of Control

Theoretically, disadvantaged students have little faith that they are in control of their own lives. Their fatalistic, pessimistic, and dependent attitude amounts to an external locus of control. Their poor performance in school is assumed to be caused in part by the fact that they attribute their poor performance to fate, chance, and various circumstances beyond their control, and do not believe they can determine whether they will succeed.

Disadvantaged students' presumed external locus of control is attributed to three factors. They are as follows:

- Parents of disadvantaged students do not train their children to function independently or praise them for doing so.
- These parents are too harsh and authoritarian and as a result fail to encourage autonomy or positive self-expectations.
- The very conditions of being poor and powerless convinces students that they and their parents cannot exercise control over their lives. "Deprivation impels a child to adopt fatalistic attitudes about the probability that he can meet even his most basic physical needs, let alone his emotional and social needs" (121, p. 24).

Behavior

Disadvantaged students are described as misbehaving more often and presenting more discipline problems in school than other students. The theory of cultural deprivation also offers a number of explanations for why this is so (110, 113, 115, 120–122).

- The environment in which disadvantaged students grow up does not encourage acceptable behavior because much of the behavior they observe in their neighborhoods would be unacceptable in school.
- Because their parents stop supervising them at an early age, they are socialized by peer groups that model socially unacceptable values and behavior.
- The lack of fathers at home leaves many of them, especially African American students, without models of appropriate behavior for them to emulate.
- Raising males in a matriarchal setting causes them to overcompensate in exaggeratedly aggressive, masculine ways and leads to

  "desperate efforts of males in lower class culture to rebel against their early over-protective, feminizing environments and to find a masculine identity" (113, p. 9).

Implications

Some educators who subscribe to the theory of cultural/educational disadvantage are pessimistic about the possibilities that schools can overcome its presumed effects. This was especially true in the 1960s and 1970s.

Class-cultural factors largely account for the conspicuous differences between the slum and the suburban school. Each school has a class character imposed upon it by the social setting in which it exists; this, and not staff inefficiency, racial discrimination, or inequitable provisions of resources, is the main reason for the virtues of one and the defects of the other. The implication is one that reformers find hard to accept—to wit, that no matter how able, dedicated, and hard-working the teachers, no matter how ample the facilities of the school or how well designed its curriculum, no matter how free the atmosphere of the school from racial or other prejudice, the performance of pupils at the lower end of the class-cultural scale will always fall short not only of pupils at the upper end of the scale, but also of what is necessary to make them educated workers. (124, p. 142)

Educators who do not believe that the effects of cultural disadvantage can be reversed tend to favor lowering expectations for educationally disadvantaged students, modifying their curriculum, using alternative instructional strategies that involve concrete teaching techniques, and segregating them from the mainstream by placing them in separate tracks. Many other supporters of the theory believe that it is possible to combat the characteristics they attribute to the educationally disadvantaged. They tend to support additional funding to schools that serve educationally disadvantaged students; programs such as Head Start and Upward Bound to compensate for students' educational disadvantage; school integration to expose non–European American students to the influence of the more positive, advantaged culture of majority students; affirmative action to provide students with the added resources they are thought to require in order to compete successfully with their more advantaged peers; and parent education programs to help parents prepare children to succeed in school.

The litany of past and present innovation, strategies, and acronyms is endless—Parent Child Centers, Upward Bound, Chapter 1, Head Start, Job Corps, Follow Through, Home Start. These programs, including their predecessors and progenitors, are primarily the Great Society's compensatory efforts based on beliefs and assumptions that if only the appropriate method, environment, parenting style, money, program, materials, and personnel were implemented, underachieving minority students would catch up with white children. This deficit view assumes that black children, because of cultural, biological, environmental, and social differences lack the adaptations and knowledge necessary for school achievement. (136, pp. 1–2)

Criticisms

These beliefs concerning the supposed impact of cultural disadvantages have been criticized on a number of grounds since the 1960s (125–152). In general, critics claim the descriptions of so-called disadvantaged students and the cultural/familial factors these characteristics are attributed to are incorrect, unscientific, and prejudiced. "These terms carry the weight of authority and scholarship instead of the label of ignorant prejudice" (133, p. 63).

Some of their specific criticisms include:

- Many of the characteristics that are attributed to cultural disadvantage are actually the result of poor people's inability to afford and obtain the resources available to the middle and upper classes and the disadvantages many poor immigrants experience because of their limited English proficiency (126, 145–150). Since many more non–European American students than European American students come from lower-class backgrounds, many of the apparent cultural differences between them are actually the result of financial factors. Although poor parents want their children to do well in school, many of them are unemployed, underemployed, underpaid, and undereducated. Thus, they are unable to provide their children with the childhood experiences needed to prepare them for school or the educational and financial support they require to assist their youngsters during their educational careers. The following comments by educators about the poor parents of the Hispanic students with whom they worked illustrate this point of view.

> *Spanish-speaking parents believe in the educational system but do not know how to help their youngsters. . . . How can a man with a second grade level of education help his son figure out an algebra equation? (134, p. 169)*
>
> *Among poor families, the necessities of the day-to-day existence such as trips to the grocery store or laundromat, emergency health needs, car trouble, etc. are of primary importance. . . . It is not uncommon for a 7- or 8-year-old girl to stay home from school to baby sit for younger siblings so that Mother can go to work, for a bilingual child to be taken along as "translator" when monolingual parents have medical or legal appointments, or for ten-year-olds to take major responsibility for preparing meals at home for working family members. (134, p. 72)*

Critics complain that society spends less on the economically disadvantaged. They believe that local and state governments should spend more, not less, on schools that serve predominantly poor students. They favor programs, such as day care and preschool programs, designed to assist and supplement poor parents' efforts, programs that train parents to participate in their children's education, and equal opportunity, open admissions, and affirmative action programs that provide students with access to educational programs and the added resources they require to compete successfully with their more economically advantaged peers. They believe such programs are necessary for poor European American and non–European American students to achieve their potential in school; they maintain that educators should have a realistic picture of both the kinds of educational support and assistance parents can provide their children, and how their financial situation impacts on their children's functioning in school; and they advise educators to adapt their educational approaches to these realities. They believe that until this happens, many children of poor parents will continue to fail in school.

- Because students with similar socioeconomic and ethnic backgrounds (for example African American poor students) are actually exposed to very different living conditions, the theory offers misleading overgeneralizations. Within the same socioeconomic class or ethnic group, there are great differences in terms of such factors as parents' educational aspirations for their children; family size; housing conditions; frequency of parent-child cultural activities such as trips to the zoo, library, museums, and movies; frequency and type of adult-child conversation; preschool and kindergarten attendance; and so on. Students with similar socioeconomic and ethnic backgrounds often grow up to be very dissimilar, and many of them do not conform to cultural stereotypes (146, 151, 152).

There are substantial variations in children's outcomes across families that are identical in parents' education and work history, family income, family size, and other standard measures of social and economic well-being . . . differences in family behavior and attitudes have large and important long-term effects on children's academic performance. (131, pp. 528, 543)

A broad rubric such as "educationally deprived" does little if anything toward defining characteristics and educational needs of children. . . . Defining children by social economic level and then designing educational programs for this group will not suffice. . . . The terms "educationally deprived" or "disadvantaged" therefore are of little or no use for educators seriously concerned with providing meaningful educational experiences for Afro-American children, in particular, and for all children in general. (143, pp. 127, 133)

- The theory has a harmful effect on students because the curriculum offered educationally disadvantaged students is based on lowering standards, modifying content, utilizing less effective instructional strategies, and placing the students in separate tracks (125, 128, 132, 139, 140). (See the section on structured reproduction in Chapter 3.)

The development of compensatory education programs has traditionally been informed by the belief that disadvantaged students can benefit most from a less challenging curriculum and limited achievement goals. Thus, Chapter 1 services, provided through the Federal Education Consolidation and Improvement Act, comprise curricula stressing basic skills in reading and mathematics, vocational rather than academic programs, and a slower instructional pace. . . . Students receive more instruction in factual and lower-level skills—drill and practice— and less in higher-order skills. [This] hampers the ability of low achieving students to develop thinking skills, lowers their learning expectations and stigmatizes them as inferior. (140, p. 1)

The cultural deprivation explanation has provided the substance for the educational self-fulling prophecy which shackles the lives of these low-status children. Because they are "culturally deprived," low-status children are not expected to perform academically up to the norms of other children—the curriculum is watered down and they are placed, for the most part, in slow-learning classes or slow tracks. And because they are treated that way and, at times, told that they are intellectually slow and culturally deprived, they are not motivated to learn and they do not learn. (129, p. 7)

- The theory blames the victim and diverts people's attention away from the school's contribution to students' problems (127, 130).

Since both the academic opportunity structure and the occupational opportunity structure of the larger society are assumed to be open and accessible, failure becomes the fault of the individual, his family, his environment, or his culture. Since the cream rises to the top, *it is implied that the people who remain at the bottom are either low in ability or psycho-motivationally defective. Further, if whole groups remain at the bottom, it follows that something must be wrong with their particular form of social organization or culture. . . . The cultural deprivation theory, because its focus is on the family and individual personality traits, subtly calls attention away from the schools themselves as precipitators of school success and failure. (130, pp. 340, 341)*

Research

Cognitive Ability

Poor parents' and some non–European American parents' communication, teaching, and parenting styles impede their children's cognitive development and academic achievement.

The evidence does not support this claim. First, as discussed previously, there is no evidence that students from different socioeconomic and ethnic backgrounds differ in cognitive (intellectual) ability (discussed earlier and in Chapter 9). Second, there is little reason to accept the claim that poor parents impede their children's cognitive development by providing them with an impoverished language environment (154, 155). Early researchers believed that poor parents restrict the development of thought in their children because they "use a restricted language code, in which messages are short, are not made explicit, and are bound to the context in which the message occurs. Middle-class speakers, in contrast, use an elaborated code in which messages are made explicit and context-free." Middle-class mothers also differ from working class parents on the "quality of speech, sentence length, syntactic complexity, use of abstract nouns and verbs, and adjective-verb-ratio" (174, p. 280).

However, the studies this claim was based on were typically not conducted in natural settings such as children's homes, but in laboratory settings, which have been shown to make poor parents anxious and less fluent (144, 168, 178). Research in naturalistic settings indicates that poor parents do not use a restricted language code with their children (162, 163). In addition, there is no evidence that complex linguistic forms are superior to simplistic forms or that complex linguistic forms are necessary for adequate development of children's cognitive skills, reading ability or academic achievement (161, 174, 175). In the absence of such evidence, there is little reason to assume the type of language employed by students' parents affects their cognitive development.

Third, as was noted in the previous section, parenting/teaching styles do not affect students' cognitive development.

Fourth, although parenting and teaching styles do contribute to students' school success (165, 169, 177, 181) there is no evidence that the styles used by different ethnic groups and socioeconomic classes affect children's academic achievement. The early studies that appeared to demonstrate that African American and poor people's parenting styles impeded their children's success in school were poorly controlled. Like the studies on communication styles referred to earlier, the studies did not take into account the fact that poor parents behave differently in experimental settings such as laboratories and in more natural settings such as their own homes and apartments, and they did not control for the fact that parents use different teaching techniques for the real-life tasks and those involved in laboratory experiments.

Later studies that better controlled for these factors found fewer and often no class differences in parenting/teaching styles (153, 156, 159, 164, 172). As a result, researchers concluded that earlier researchers who claimed that ethnic and socioeconomic differences in parental teaching styles cause differences in cognitive development and academic achievement and asserted that the teaching style of poor parents is less efficient than the style employed by middle-class parents were merely expressing their biases and preferences for middle-class norms (174).

Linguistic Proficiency
Non-European and poor students do not have the linguistic skills necessary to succeed in school.

Many studies of students' linguistic proficiency have affirmed the existence of socioeconomic-class and ethnic group differences in oral language (167), vocabulary (166, 180), and syntactic usage (170). To some educators these differences indicate that middle-class and European American students have acquired a higher level of linguistic skills than poor and African American students. Other educators, however, interpret these results in terms of linguistic differences rather than linguistic deficiencies. They feel that certain groups of linguistically able students *appear* to have poorly developed linguistic skills because of a mismatch between the way they and their teachers use language. For example, Slaughter and Epps state that

> *Lower income Black children are quite "verbal," but . . . the norms governing when and how they should speak are different from middle-class norms. To be effective educators, teachers need to know some of these norms, to adapt them to their own classroom behaviors, and, conversely, to point out the differences between in-school and out-of-school speech to the students. (176, p. 9)*

A number of studies have documented the poor match between how teachers engage African American students in conversations and how these students use language in their homes and communities. For example, African American adults seldom ask questions that require children to state something that the children realize adults already know. Rather, they are asked to talk about things about which adults are unaware. Teachers, however, often ask questions about things that they obviously know more about than their students. Thus, in the early grades African American students are often puzzled why teachers are asking them for information that they already know. African American adults ask about things related to children's experiences, whereas teachers often ask questions about things outside their students' life experiences. As a result, students are unprepared to discuss things about which they have no direct experience or understanding. African American parents issue direct orders to students such as "do such and such" whereas European American teachers are often more indirect and say things such as "Why don't you do such and such?" or "You might want to do such and such." Therefore, African American students are not always aware that their teachers have required them to do something and not merely made a suggestion that they can choose to accept or reject (157, 163).

The use of nonstandard speech by African American and Hispanic American students does have an effect on students' academic achievement. But this effect is the result of the way teachers react to their speech patterns, not the speech patterns themselves. Teachers of nonstandard English speakers, especially those who believe standard English to be a more preferable/correct version of English, tend to spend too much time correcting students' "grammatical and dialectic pronunciation errors" instead of teaching them the skills they need to acquire (158, 171). In addition, teachers think that students who do not speak standard English are less intelligent, they have lower academic expectations for them, and they evaluate both their oral and written work to be lower than comparable work of standard-English–speaking students (160, 179), and they are also more likely to disapprove of them (169). (Also see the section on teacher prejudice in Chapter 3.)

Auditory Discrimination
Disadvantaged students have poor auditory discrimination skills.

Although there is a modest relationship between auditory discrimination and reading achievement, there is little evidence that African American, Hispanic American, or poor students have poor auditory discrimination skills. During the 1960s a number of researchers reported that these students scored lower on tests of auditory discrimination (182, 185, 190, 191). However, these differences were actually the result of biased assessment procedures.

Many African American, Hispanic American, and poor students speak nonstandard forms of English that utilize somewhat different sounds. As a result, when they are required to discriminate between unfamiliar sounds that are included in standard English but not in their dialects and languages, they are unable to do so. On the other hand, when they are given auditory discrimination tests in their own languages or dialects, African American, Hispanic American, and poor students do not demonstrate any auditory discrimination problems (183, 184, 186–189, 192).

Self-Concept
Educationally disadvantaged students' poor self-concepts interfere with their achievement in school.

Research reveals that students' self-concepts, the characteristics they attribute to themselves, have a significant effect on the way they behave both in and out of school. Positive self-concepts have been shown to enhance learning and encourage acceptable behavior; poor self-concepts impede achievement and lead to emotional and behavioral problems. However, there is little evidence that poor, African American, and Hispanic American students have poorer self-concepts than their European American middle-class peers.

Some studies, primarily those done in the 1960s, found weak, but statistically significant relationships between students' self-concepts and their ethnic and socioeconomic backgrounds. In general, poor, African American, Native American, and Hispanic American students had lower self-concepts than European American middle-class students (196, 198, 199, 201, 203, 204, 208, 213, 216).

More recent studies of Native American students completed since the 1960s confirmed these earlier findings. Many Native American students, especially those with the greatest exposure to the European American culture and school system, have lower self-esteem than European Americans (207). Most studies of Hispanic American students' self-concepts done since the 1960s indicate that they do not have lower self-concepts (202, 206, 209, 217), and the vast majority of studies, especially those done after the 1960s, have revealed that poor and African American students' self-concepts are at least as high as, if not higher than, those of middle-class European Americans (193–195, 200, 202, 205, 208, 210–212, 214, 215, 218).

Following are four of the common explanations for why African American and Hispanic American students, including those from poor backgrounds, do not have low self-concepts despite their poor neighborhoods, the discrimination they experience, and their low academic success rates.

1. The prevailing view that African Americans and other non–European American groups suffer from poor self-concepts is a product of a European American centric perspective. European American researchers and commentators do not realize that most non–European American children and their parents do not accept the dominant society's view that they are inferior and incapable. They are not aware that African American, Native American, Hispanic American, and other non–European American families have always attempted to counteract the messages students receive about their "inferiority" and have done so with increasing success since the black, brown, and red power movement of the late 1960s and 1970s (197, 210, 212).

> *To act as if the only influence upon the formation of self-concepts is that of the dominant culture negates the idea of the child having any other culture or a socialization process that might counteract such a negative view. Such conclusions assume that all a Black or Indian child will get from his family socialization is a carbon copy of the negative stereotyping and evaluation of the white racist culture. . . . Either from ethnocentric distortion or from the negation of the culture of the minority group, researchers leave only psychopathological explana-*

tions for observed behavior (i.e., academic failure due to "poor self-concept.") (210, p. 17)

Blacks have not really believed that white equals goodness and purity. Their self-concept has never entirely been controlled by whites. . . . Blacks have struggled to show their children that the white view of blacks as inferior is incorrect as well as immoral. (212, p. 139)

The supposed negative self-image of the Mexican-American is, in reality, our own stereotype projected onto him. "Anglos" tend to think of Mexican-Americans in negative ways, and conclude they see themselves in the same light. (197, p. 218)

2. Many non–European American poor students grow up and attend schools in their neighborhood primarily with students like themselves and are not actually exposed to the more advantaged groups or to the prejudice many have against them.

3. Many poor non–European American students do not have poor self-concepts because they experience less stress and tension than middle-class European American students. Unlike middle-class students, they are not trying to live up to high expectations because family's, teachers', and self-expectations for them are not as high.

4. Non–European American and poor students who believe that discrimination, not lack of effort or ability, is the cause of many of their problems, do not accept blame for not doing well and do not lose self-respect. Middle-class students tend to blame themselves for their lack of success and thus experience a loss of self-esteem.

Academic and Vocational Aspirations and Expectations
Disadvantaged students, especially males, do not aspire or expect to do well in school because their parents do not have high aspirations for them, do not expect them to do well, and do not provide them with acceptable male role models.

Research offers little support for this supposition. The most telling argument against it comes from studies of students' academic and vocational aspirations done in the 1960s, 1970s, and 1980s, which have consistently indicated that African Americans' aspirations are as high as, if not higher than, those of their European American peers (219–222). The difference between the groups is not their aspirations, but the extent to which they believe they will achieve their aspirations.

African American students start off placing even greater value on education than European American students. However, after attending school for a few years they often expect that they will not achieve the level of education to which they aspire.

Parents' aspirations and expectations for their children in school and their evaluations of their children's academic ability do affect students' confidence about their academic abilities, their academic and occupational aspirations, and the courses they choose to enroll in school. However, research about ethnic and socioeconomic differences in these parental characteristics is inconsistent. Some studies have found that poor, African American, and Hispanic American parents expect their children to do less well in school and do not encourage them as much as European American middle-class parents (126, 223–225). Other studies indicate that African American and poor parents have as high if not higher *aspirations* for children than European American middle-class parents. Again, the difference lies in the fact that African American and poor parents do not expect their children's academic or vocational achievement to fulfill their aspirations for them, so they are willing to accept lower levels of achievement than European American middle-class parents (135, 141, 142, 226–228).

Research that appears to indicate that African American students do not have high educational aspirations and are not encouraged to set high goals for themselves is often culturally insensitive, biased, and invalid (135, 137, 142). European American researchers do not consider the role of the African American community. Through individuals such as teachers, trusted adults, neighbors, community groups and agencies, and so on, outside the family, the community encourages African American students to set high achievement goals for themselves. Therefore, research that only includes the influence of students' families does not present a true picture of the encouragement African American students receive within their culture. Researchers also focus too exclusively on individual achievement. Because African American students are more cooperative and interested in group goals, researchers who do not take include students' desire to contribute to the advancement of African Americans as a group underestimate their achievement orientation.

Locus of Control
Many disadvantaged students have an external locus of control, which has a negative effect on their academic and vocational achievement.

The research evidence used to support this claim is questionable for two reasons.

1. Research about the locus of control of poor, African American, and Hispanic American students has produced mixed results. Some studies have found that they have an external locus of control (177, 229); others have found they do not (126, 231, 233, 234).

2. It is unclear whether or not the research that shows that students with an internal locus of control tend to achieve more in school than those whose locus of control is external applies equally to middle-class European American students and to poor and non–European American students (181, 231). Studying locus of control from a European American point of view, researchers failed to recognize the special circumstances of many poor and non–European American students. These researchers mistakenly thought that all students with an internal locus of control attributed their successes and failures to their own ability and effort, whereas all students with an external locus of control attributed their successes and failures to fate and chance. In so doing, they did not realize that many non–European American students with an external locus of control believe, often correctly, that the environment they encounter both in and out of school is so hostile and prejudiced that despite their best efforts, skills, and abilities they will not be able to accomplish their goals (138, 230, 232).

In a society that is fair, as it tends to be for most middle-class European Americans, students with an internal locus of control should do better in school. This is because they will try harder to succeed and to improve when they do poorly. However, in the case of poor students, African Americans, Native Americans, and Hispanic Americans, who exist in a racist and prejudiced environment, an internal locus of control may be self-destructive because it may lead students to blame themselves or hold themselves responsible for failure caused by unfairness, prejudice, and economic injustice. Students with an internal locus of control who are not doing well because of discrimination may blame themselves and give up, but students who correctly understand that external factors are to blame may strive to change them, especially if they are supported by others who hold similar beliefs and have similar characteristics.

> *"Feelings of fate control" may in fact be valid perceptions of institutional barriers (for example tracking and negative teacher attitudes) which prevent black students from actually exercising any significant and meaningful control over their own lives. . . . The way to solve the learning difficulties encountered by black students is to remove the institutional barriers which prevent them from exercising any significant and meaningful control over their intellectual and personal destinies rather than* blaming *the black family for something over which it has no control. (232 p. 75)*

Father Absence
Many of the educational and behavior problems of poor students, especially African American males, are caused at least in part by the absence of a father in the family.

During the 1960s and 1970s a number of studies found that students, particularly African American males growing up in one-parent families headed by females, performed less adequately on tests purported to measure intelligence and moral development, had lower academic and vocational aspirations, achieved less, were more aggressive in school, and were less well-adjusted (115, 165, 235, 237, 239, 240, 242, 243, 246, 249). However, these early studies have been justly criticized.

Most of them failed to control for socioeconomic differences. This is a very important omission because families that are deprived of the income of fathers were and are more likely to fall into the poor or poverty groups. Currently, 46% of European American, 66% of Hispanic American and 67% of African American children living in single-parent female-headed families live in poverty (256). In the 1960s and early 1970s fewer women were in the work force, the discrepancy between what working women and men earned was even greater than today, and there were fewer resources such as day care centers and other supports available to single-parent families. Thus, the differences observed in these studies could well have been due to socioeconomic factors.

Most subsequent studies that were better controlled, and a number of studies done in the 1960s and 1970s reported results that contradict the findings of the early studies (173, 181, 219, 236, 241, 242, 247, 250, 253). They typically found either no relationship between the presence of students' fathers at home and their adjustment in or out of school, or a relationship that was so small that it accounted for very little of the differences observed between successful and unsuccessful students. In addition, the relationship tended to be confined to poor students. These facts suggest that the small relationship between children's adjustment and the presence or absence of their fathers is primarily the result of the loss of income poor families experience rather than the absence of a male role model.

The early studies misunderstand and misrepresent the nature of poor and African American families (238, 244, 245, 251, 252, 254). Culturally insensitive European American researchers underestimated the strength of black families. They designed studies and interpreted the results of these studies while unaware of the role the African American extended family, teachers, trusted adults, neighbors, community groups and agencies, and churches play in encouraging, guiding, and supporting African American students. It is also incorrect to assume that fathers who are legally not a part of the family are actually absent. Many males who are separated or divorced from the children's mothers, or pretend to be absent and uninvolved so their families can qualify for welfare and other forms of assistance, often play significant roles in the children's lives.

Researchers may have also projected their sexist points of view on the African American family (137, 238, 248, 255). African American families are much more egalitarian and nonsexist than many European American families. Gender roles are much less stereotyped; mothers can be role models for activities and functions that are usually reserved for males in the European American culture. So even when males are absent, females can often provide the necessary role models.

Conclusions

The validity of the cultural deprivation/educational disadvantage theory can be evaluated in terms of three questions.

1. *Do the characteristics attributed to educationally disadvantaged students negatively affect educational outcomes?* Research indicates that students' auditory discrimination skills, locus of control, level of aspiration and self-concept do affect their achievement in school. The assumed negative influence of students' use of nonstandard English, parental teaching styles, and father absence are not supported by research.

2. *Do African American, Hispanic American, and poor students have these characteristics to a greater degree than European American and middle-class students?* There is no evidence that poor, African American, and Hispanic American students have poor auditory skills. Research on their locus of control is mixed. However, it is likely that even when these students appear to have an external locus of control, they may be accurately perceiving the obstacles they face in a society rife with prejudice rather than attributing their successes and failure to fate, luck, or chance. Contrary to what the theory predicts, these students have aspirations and self-concepts as high as, if not higher than, middle-class European American students.

3. *If African American, Hispanic American, and poor students have these characteristics to a greater degree than European American and middle-class students, are the differences caused by cultural/familial factors rather than racism, economic disadvantage, and so on?* The few differences observed between African American, Hispanic American, and poor and European American and middle-class students and their families that have been confirmed by research are more likely to be caused by the prejudiced and hostile environment they face and the limited opportunities their lack of financial resources impose of them than by cultural differences.

Summary

Some educators believe that many poor, African American, Native American, and Hispanic American students are more likely to suffer biomedical problems, to inherit less intellectual potential than their peers, and to come from culturally deprived or disadvantaged backgrounds. They attribute the high percentage of failure among these students to the educational problems these conditions can create.

Although poor, African American, Native American, and Hispanic American students are more likely to suffer biomedical problems, it is unlikely that these problems are a major cause of their lack of achievement. Research does not support the contention that they inherit less intellectual potential than others. The early research on cultural deprivation/disadvantage was done from a European American point of view. Better controlled, more culturally sensitive studies refute the idea that poor, African American, and Hispanic American students are brought up in deprived or disadvantaged cultures.

Activities

1. The following are the major contentions of those who believe that cultural disadvantage is an important cause of the educational problems of many students. Ask some of your European American middle-class friends or fellow students to tell you their opinion about which, if any, of these assumptions are characteristic of African American, Hispanic American, or poor students. Ask some of your African American or Hispanic American friends or fellow students from poor backgrounds if they were ever told or believed any of these assumptions.

Parents' communication, teaching, and parenting styles impede children's cognitive development and academic achievement. Their children do not have the linguistic skills necessary to succeed in school. Disadvantaged students have poor auditory discrimination skills. Their poor self-concepts interfere with their achievement in school. They do not aspire or expect to do well in school because their parents do not have high aspirations for them, do not expect them to do well, and do not provide them with acceptable male role models. They have an external locus of control, which has a negative effect on their academic and vocational achievement. Many of their educational and behavior problems are caused at least in part by the absence of a father in the family.

2. Improve your understanding of the problems of children born addicted to substances such as alcohol and drugs by visiting a program that serves them.

References

The following references deal with the effects of poor nutrition and health care on students' behavior and school success.

1. Baumeister, A. A., Kupstas, F., & Klindworth, L. M. (1990). New morbidity: Implications for prevention of children's disabilities. *Exceptionality, 1*, 1–16.

2. Escalona, S. K. (1982). Babies at double hazard: Early development of infants at biological and social risk. *Pediatrics, 70*, 670–675.

3. Food Research and Action Center. (1984). *The Widening Gap: The Incidence and Distribution of Infant Mortality and Low Birthweight in the United States—1978–1982*. Washington, DC: Author.

4. Galler, J. R. (Ed.). (1984). *Human Nutrition: A Comprehensive Treatise: Vol. 5. Nutrition and Behavior*. New York: Plenum Press.

5. Hoy, E. A., Bill, J. M., & Sykes, D. H. (1988). Very low birthweight: A long-term developmental impairment? *International Journal of Behavioral Development, 11*, 37–67.

6. Hughes, D., Johnson, K., Rosenbaum, S., Butler, W., & Simons, J. (1988). *The Health of America's Children: Maternal and Child Health Data Book*. Washington, DC: Children's Defense Fund.

7. Institute of Medicine. (1985). *Preventing Low Birthweight*. Washington, DC: National Academy Press.

8. Kopp, C. B., & Kaler, S. R. (1989). Risk in infancy: Origins and implications. *American Psychologist, 44*(2), 224–230.

9. Lane, J. M., & Johnson, C. L. (1981). Prevalence of iron deficiency. In *Report of the Eighty-Second Ross Conference on Pediatric Research*. Columbus, OH: Ross Laboratories.

10. Lieberman, E., Ryan, K., Monson, R., & Schoenbaum, S. (1987). Risk factors accounting for racial differences in the rate of premature birth. *New England Journal of Medicine, 317*, 743–748.

11. Lozoff, B. (1988). Behavioral alterations in iron deficiency. *Advances in Pediatrics, 35*, 331–360.

12. Lozoff, B. (1989). Nutrition and behavior. *American Psychologist, 44*(2), 231–236.

13. National Center for Clinical Infant Programs. (1986). *Infants Can't Wait: The Numbers*. Washington, DC: Author.

14. National Center for Health Statistics. (1987). *Advance Report of Final Natality Statistics, 1985*. (Monthly vital statistics report, Vol. 36). Washington, DC.

15. R. W. Johnson Foundation. (1983). *A National Collaborative Study*. Princeton, NJ.

16. Shapiro, S., McCormick, M. C., Starfield, B. H., & Crawley, B. (1983). Changes in infant morbidity associated with decreases in neonatal mortality. *Pediatrics, 72*, 408–415.

The following references discuss the prevalence and effects of prenatal substance abuse.

17. Adler, T. (1989). Cocaine babies face behavior deficits. *American Psychological Association Monitor, 20*(7), 14.

18. Archer, L. D. (1987). *Program Strategies for Preventing Fetal Alcohol Syndrome and Alcohol Related Birth Defects.* DHHS Publication No. (ADM) 87–1482.

19. Aronson, M., Kyllerman, M., Sobel, J. G., Sandin, B., & Olegard, R. (1985). Children of alcoholic mothers: Developmental, perceptual, and behavioral characteristics as compared to matched controls. *Acta Paediatrica Scandinavica, 74,* 27–35.

20. Besharov, D. J. (1989). The children of crack, will we protect them? *Public Welfare, 47*(4), 6–11.

21. Besharov, D. J. (1990). Crack children in foster care. *Children Today, 19,* 21–35.

22. Brooks-Gunn, J., & McCarton, C. (1991). *Effects of Drugs In-Utero on Infant Development.* (Report to Congress). Washington, DC: National Institute of Child Health and Human Development.

23. Burkett, B., Yasin, S., & Palow, D. (1990). Perinatal implications of cocaine exposure. *Journal of Reproductive Medicine, 35*(1), 35–42.

24. Chasnoff, I., Landress, H., & Barrett, M. (1990). The prevalence of illicit drug and or alcohol use during pregnancy and discrepancies in mandatory reporting in Pinellas County, Florida. *New England Journal of Medicine, 322,* 1202–1206.

25. Chavin, W., & Kandall, S. R. (1990). Between a rock and a hard place: Perinatal drug abuse. *Pediatrics, 85,* 223–225.

26. Cohen, S. (1985). *The Substance Abuse Problems, Vol II. New Issues for the 1980s.* Redding, CA: Hawthorn Press.

27. Cole, C., Ferara, V., Johnson, D., Jones, M., Schoenbaum, M., Tyler, R., Wallace, V., & Poulsen, M. (1989). *Today's Challenge: Teaching Strategies for Working with Young Children Pre-natally Exposed to Drugs/Alcohol.* Los Angeles: Los Angeles Unified School District.

28. Dow-Edwards, D. L. (1988). Developmental effects of cocaine. *National Institute of Drug Abuse Research Monographs, 88,* 290–303.

29. Finnegan, L. (1989). *Drug Dependency in Pregnancy: Clinical Management of Mother and Child.* Washington, DC: National Institute of Drug Abuse Service Research Monograph Service, U.S. Government Printing Office.

30. Fried, P. A., & O'Connell, C. M. (1987). A comparison of the effects of prenatal exposure to tobacco, alcohol, cannabis, and caffeine on birthsize and subsequent growth. *Neurotoxicology and Teratology, 9,* 79–85.

31. Gittler, J., & McPherson, M. (1990). Prenatal substance abuse. *Children Today, 19,* 3–7.

32. Griffith, D. (1991, May). *Intervention Needs of Children Prenatally Exposed to Drugs.* Congressional testimony before the House Select Committee on Special Education. Washington, DC.

33. Haflon, N. (1989). *Hearing: Born Hooked, Confronting the Impact of Perinatal Substance Abuse.* Select Committee on Children, Youth and Families, U.S. House of Representatives. April 27.

34. Howard, J., Beckwith, L., Rodning, C., & Kropenske, V. (1989). Development of young children of substance-abusing parents: Insights from seven years of intervention and research. *Zero to Three, 9,* 8–12.

35. Kronstadt, D. (1989). *Pregnancy and Cocaine Addiction: An Overview of Impact and Treatment.* San Francisco: Far West Laboratory for Educational Research and Development.

36. Miller, G. (1989). *Hearing: Born Hooked, Confronting the Impact of Perinatal Substance Abuse.* Select Committee on Children, Youth and Families, U.S. House of Representatives. April 27.

37. New York City HRA Office of Management Analysis. (1990). *Report Issued on January 31, 1990.* New York: Author.

38. The New York Times. (1989). *Crack's Toll Among Babies: A Joyless View of Even Toys.* September 17.

39. Petitti, D. B., & Coleman, C. (1990). Cocaine and the risk of low birth weight. *American Journal of Public Health, 80*(1), 25–28.

40. Phillipson, R. (1988). The fetal alcohol syndrome: Recent international statistics. *Australia and New Zealand Journal of Developmental Psychology, 14*(3/4), 211–221.

41. Poulsen, M. (1991). *Schools Meet the Challenge: Educational Needs of Children at Risk Due to Substance Exposure.* Sacramento, CA: Resources in Special Education.

42. Reed, B. (1987). Developing women sensitive drug dependent treatment services: Why so difficult? *Journal of Psychoactive Drugs, 19*(2), 151–164.

43. Rist, M. C. (1990). The shadow children. *American School Board Journal, 177*(1), 19–24.

44. Straus, A. (1981). Neonatal manifestations of maternal phencyclidine (PCP) abuse. *Pediatrics, 66,* 4.

45. Streisstguth, A. P. (1989). *Prenatal Alcohol Exposure and Child IQ, Achievement and Class-*

room Behavior at Age 7. Paper presented at the annual conference of the Society for Research in Child Development, Kansas City, MO.

46. Streissguth, A. P., Clarren, S. K., & Jones, K. L. (1985). Natural history of the fetal alcohol syndrome: A 10-year follow-up of eleven patients. *Lancet, 2*(8446), 85–91.

47. U.S. Department of Health and Human Services, Office of Inspector General. (1990). *Crack Babies.* Washington, DC: Author.

48. U.S. National Center for Health Statistics. (1989). *Advance Report of Final Natality Statistics, 1987.* Vol. 38, No. 3, Supplement, June 29. Washington, DC: U.S. Department of Health and Human Services.

49. Vincent, L. J., Poulsen, M. K., Cole, C. K., Woodruff, G., & Griffith, D. R. (1991). *Born Substance Exposed, Educationally Vulnerable.* Reston, VA: Council for Exceptional Children.

50. Wescott, S. M. (1990). Time to address a preventable tragedy. *Winds of Change, 5*(3), 30–34.

51. Weston, R. R., Ivins, B., Zuckerman, B., Jones, C., & Lopez, R. (1989). Drug-exposed babies: Research and clinical issues. *Zero to Three, 9,* 1–7.

52. Wilson, G. S. (1989). Clinical studies of infants and children exposed prenatally to heroin. *Annals of The New York Academy of Sciences, 562,* 183–194.

53. Zuckerman, B. (1991). Drug-exposed infants: Understanding the medical risk. *The Future of Children, 1*(1), 26–35.

The prevalence and effects of pediatric autoimmune deficiency syndrome is the focus of the following references.

54. Belman, A. L., Diamond, G., Dickson, D., Horoupian, D., Llena, J., Lantos, G., & Rubinstein, A. (1988). Calcification of the basal ganglia in infants and children with acquires immuno-deficiency syndrome. *American Journal of Diseases of Children, 36,* 1192–1199.

55. Belman, A. L., Ultmann, M. H., Horouopian, D., Novick, B. D., Spiro, A. J., Rubinstein, A., Kurtzberg, D., & Cone-Wesson, B. (1985). Neurological implications in infants with acquired immunodeficiency syndrome. *Annals of Neurology, 18,* 560–566.

56. Epstein, L. G., Sharer, L. R., Oleske, J. M., Cannon, E. M., Gouldsmit, J., Bagdon, L., Robert-Guroff, M., & Koenigsberger, M. R.

(1986). Neurological manifestations of HIV infection in children. *Pediatrics, 78,* 678–688.

57. Mays, V. M. (1987). *Epidemiology of AIDS among Ethnic Minorities.* Paper presented at the annual meeting of the American Psychological Association, New York.

58. Task Force on Pediatric AIDS. (1989). Pediatric AIDS and human immunodeficiency virus infection. *American Psychologist, 44*(2), 258–264.

Genetic explanations of ethnic and socioeconomic differences in school outcomes are presented in the references listed next.

59. Agassiz, L. (1850). The diversity of origin of the human races. *Christian Examiner, 49,* 110–145.

60. Blatt, B. (1981). *In and Out of Mental Retardation.* Baltimore: University Park Press.

61. Davenport, C. B. (1911). *Heredity in Relation to Eugenics.* New York: Holt.

62. Eysenck, H. J., (1973). *The Inequality of Man.* London: Temple Smith.

63. Gould, S. J. (1981). *The Mismeasure of Man.* New York: W. W. Norton.

64. Herrnstein, R. J. (1973). *IQ in the Meritocracy.* Boston: Little, Brown.

65. Jensen, A. R. (1971). *A Two-Factor Theory of Familial Mental Retardation.* ERIC ED 060–577.

66. Jensen, A. R. (1974). Interaction of Level I and Level II abilities with race and socioeconomic status. *Journal of Educational Psychology, 66*(1), 99–111.

67. Jensen, A. R. (1981). *Straight Talk about Mental Tests.* New York: Free Press.

68. Latham, G. L. (1987). *Breeding Poverty? Great Issues Lecture.* ERIC ED 293–232.

69. Popenoe P., & Johnson, R. H. (1918). *Applied Eugenics.* New York: Macmillan.

70. Shockley, W. (1971). Models, mathematics, and the moral obligation to diagnose the origins of Negro IQ deficits. *Review of Educational Research, 41*(4), 369–377.

71. Spuhler, J. N., & Lindzey, G. (1967). Racial differences in behavior. In J. Hirsch (Ed.), *Behavior-Genetic Analysis.* New York: McGraw-Hill.

72. Thorndike, E. L. (1931). *Human Learning.* New York: Century.

The fallacy of the meritocracy theory is the subject of these references.

73. Goldberg, A. S. (1974a). *Mystery of the Meritocracy.* Madison, WI: Institute for Research on Poverty, University of Wisconsin.

74. Goldberg, A. S. (1974b). *Professor Jensen, Meet Miss Burks.* Madison, WI: Institute for Research on Poverty, University of Wisconsin.

75. Jencks, C., Smith, M., Acland, H., Bane, M. J., Cohen, D., Gintis, H., Heyns, G., & Michelson, S. (1972). *Inequality: A Reassessment of the Effect of Family and Schooling in America.* New York: Harper & Row.

76. Rumberger, R. W. (1983). The influence of family background on education, learnings, and wealth. *Social Forces, 3,* 755–773.

Arguments and evidence against the genetic explanation of educational disparities are included in the following references.

77. Bronfenbrenner, U. (1972). Is 80% of intelligence genetically determined? In U. Bronfenbrenner (Ed.), *Influence on Human Development.* Hinsdale IL: Dryden.

78. Green, R. B., & Rohwer, W. D. Jr. (1971). SES differences on learning and ability tests in black children. *American Journal of Educational Research, 8*(4), 601–609.

79. Kamin, L. J. (1973). Text of Dr. Kamin's presentation denying that proof exists that IQ test scores are hereditary. *South Today, 4*(8), 1–5.

80. Kamin, L. J. (1974). *The Science and Politics of I. Q.* Hillsdale, NJ: Lawrence Erlbaum.

81. Mensh, E., & Mensh, H. (1991). *The IQ Mythology: Class, Race, Gender, and Inequality.* Carbondale, IL: Southern Illinois University Press.

82. Moore, E. G. J. (1986). Family socialization and the IQ test performance of traditionally and transracially adopted black children. *Developmental Psychology, 22,* 317–326.

83. Moore, E. G. J. (1987). Ethnic social milieu and black children's intelligence achievement. *Journal of Negro Education, 56*(1), 44–52.

84. Persell, C. H. (1981). Genetic and cultural deficit theories: Two sides of the same racist coin. *Journal of Black Studies, 12*(1), 19–37.

85. Scarr, S. (1968). Environment bias in twin studies, *Eugenics Quarterly, 15,* 34–40.

86. Scarr, S. (1971). Race, social class and IQ. *Science, 174,* 1285–1295.

87. Vernon, P. E., & Mitchell, M. C. (1974). Social-class differences in associative learning. *Journal of Special Education, 8*(4), 297–311.

The role of socioeconomic factors in predicting differences in scores on tests of intellectual functioning within ethnic groups is discussed in the following references.

88. Bardouille-Crema, A., Black, K. N., & Feldhusen, J. (1986). Performance on Piagetian tasks of black children of differing socioeconomic levels. *Developmental Psychology, 22*(6), 841–844.

89. Blau, Z. S. (1981). *Black Children/White Children.* New York: Free Press.

90. Hall, V. C., & Kaye, D. B. (1980). Early patterns of cognitive development. With commentary by Sandra W. Scarr. *Monographs of the Society for Research in Child Development, 45*(2), Serial No. 184.

91. Scarr, S. (1981). *Race, Social Class, and Individual Differences in I. Q.* Hillsdale, NJ: Erlbaum.

92. Yando, R., Seitz, V., & Zigler, W. (1979). *Intellectual and Personality Characteristics of Children.* Hillsdale, NJ: Erlbaum.

Research regarding and discussion of the theory of genetically determined ethnic group and socioeconomic differences in Level I and Level II abilities is included in the following references.

93. Bee, H., Barnard, K., Eyres, S., Gray, C., Hammond, M., Speitz, A., Snyder, C., & Clark, B. (1982). Prediction of IQ and language skills from perinatal status, child performance, family characteristics, and mother-infant interaction. *Child Development, 53,* 44–75.

94. Borkowski, J. G., & Krause, A. (1983). Racial differences in intelligence: The importance of the executive system. *Intelligence, 7,* 379–395.

95. Bridgeman, B., & Buttram, J. (1975). Race differences on nonverbal analogy test performance as a function of verbal strategy training. *Journal of Educational Psychology, 67*(4), 586–590.

96. Butcher, H. J. (1972). Comments on Arthur Jensen's "Do schools cheat minority children". *Educational Research, 14*(2), 87–100.

97. Humphreys, L. G., & Dachler, P. (1969a). Jensen's theory of intelligence. *Journal of Educational Psychology, 60,* 419–426.

98. Humphreys, L. G., & Dachler, P. (1969b). Jensen's theory of intelligence: A rebuttal. *Journal of Educational Psychology, 60,* 432–433.

99. Jensen, A. R. (1969). How much can we boost IQ and scholastic achievement? *Harvard Educational Review, 39,* 1–123.

100. Jensen, A. R. (1971). The role of verbal mediation in development. *Journal of Genetic Psychology, 118,* 39–70.

101. Jensen, A. R. (1973a). *Genetics and Education.* New York: Harper & Row.

102. Jensen, A. R. (1973b). *Level I and Level II Abilities in Three Ethnic Groups.* ERIC ED 080–646.

103. Jensen, A. R., & Inouye, A. R. (1980). Level I and Level II abilities in Asian, white, and black children. *Intelligence, 4,* 41–49.

104. Nisbet, J. (1972). Comments on Arthur Jensen's "Do schools cheat minority children?" *Experimental Research, 14*(2), 87–100.

105. Orn, D. E., & Das, J. P. (1972). IQ, socioeconomic status, and short-term memory. *Journal of Educational Psychology, 63,* 327–333.

106. Schubert, J., & Cropley, A. (1972). Verbal regulation of behavior and IQ in Canadian Indian and white children. *Developmental Psychology, 7,* 295–301.

107. Sigel, I. (1982). The relationship between parental distancing strategies and the child's cognitive behavior. In L. Laosa & I. Sigel (Eds.), *Families as Learning Environments for Children.* New York: Plenum.

108. Skanes, G. R., Sullivan, A. M., Rowe, E. J., & Shannon, E. (1974). Intelligence and transfer: Aptitude by treatment interactions. *Journal of Educational Psychology, 66,* 563–568.

109. Vernon, P. (1972). Comments on Arthur Jensen's "Do schools cheat minority children?" *Experimental Education, 14*(2), 87–100.

Publications by proponents of the cultural deprivation theory are listed below.

110. Bacon, M. K., Child, I. L., & Barry, H. (1963). A cross cultural study of correlates of crime. *Journal of Abnormal and Social Psychology, 66,* 291–300.

111. Bandura, A., & Walters, R. H. (1959). *Adolescent Aggression.* New York: Ronald.

112. Bloom, B. S., Davis, A., & Hess, R. (1965). *Compensatory Education for Cultural Deprivation.* New York: Holt, Rinehart & Winston.

113. Bronfenbrenner, U. (1967). *The Psychological Costs to Quality and Equality in Education.* ERIC ED 113–405.

114. Deutsch, C. P. (1964). Auditory discrimination and learning: Social factors. *Merrill-Palmer Quarterly, 10,* 277–296.

115. Deutsch, M. (1960). Minority group and class status as related to social and personality factors in scholastic achievement. *Society for Applied Anthropology,* Monograph No. 2. Ithaca, NY: Cornell University Press.

116. Hess, R. (1970). Social class and ethnic influences on socialization. In P. Hussen (Ed.), *Manual of Child Psychology,* Vol. 2. New York: Wiley.

117. Hunt, J. (1964). The psychological basis for using pre-school environment as an antidote for cultural deprivation. *Merrill-Palmer Quarterly, 10,* 209–248.

118. Jensen, A. R. (1968). Social class and verbal learning. In M. Deutsch, I. Katz, & A. R. Jensen (Eds.), *Social Class, Race and Psychological Development.* New York: Holt, Rinehart & Winston.

119. Lewis, O. (1966). The culture of poverty. *Scientific American, 215,* 19–25.

120. McClelland, D. C. (1961). *The Achieving Society.* New York: Van Nostrand.

121. McCloskey, E. F. (1967). *Urban Disadvantaged Pupils; Characteristics, Environments, Potentials.* Portland, OR: Northwest Regional Educational Laboratory.

122. Miller, W. B., (1958). Lower class culture as a generating milieu of gang delinquency. *Journal of Social Issues, 14*(30), 5–19.

123. Pettigrew, T. F. (1964). *A Profile of the Negro American.* Princeton: Van Nostrand.

The implications of the cultural deprivation theory is the focus of the reference listed below.

124. Banfield, E. (1970). *The Unheavenly City.* Boston: Little, Brown and Company.

Criticism of the concepts culturally deprived, culturally disadvantaged, and educationally disadvantaged and the procedures used with students with these labels is contained in the following references.

125. Adams, M. J. (1986). Teaching thinking to Chapter 1 students. In B. I. Williams, P. A. Richmond, & B. J. Mason (Eds.), *Designs for Compensatory Education: Conference Proceedings and Papers.* ERIC ED 293–913.

126. Bender, P. S., & Ruiz, R. A. (1974). Race and class as differential determiners of underachievement and underaspiration among Mexican-Americans and Anglos. *Journal of Educational Research, 68*(2), 51–55.

127. Bowles, S., & Gintis, H. (1976). *Schooling in Capitalist America: Educational Reform and the Contradictions of Economic Life.* New York: Basic Books.

128. Calfee, R. (1986). Curriculum and instruction: Reading. In B. I. Williams, P. A. Richmond, & B. J. Mason (Eds.), *Designs for Compensatory Education: Conference Proceedings and Papers.* ERIC ED 293–912.

129. Clark, K. B., Deutsch, M., Gartner, A., Keppel, G., Lewis, H., Pettigrew, T., Plotkin, L., & Reissman, F. (1972). *The Educationally Deprived: The Potential for Change.* New York: Metropolitan Applied Research Center.

130. Cummings, S. (1977). Explaining poor academic performance among black children. *Educational Forum, 41*(3), 335–346.

131. Datcher-Loury, L. (1989). Family background and school achievement among low income blacks. *Journal of Human Resources, 24*(3), 528–544.

132. Dolye, W. (1986). Vision and Reality: A reaction to issues in curriculum and instruction for compensatory education. In B. I. Williams, P. A. Richmond, & B. J. Mason (Eds.), *Designs for Compensatory Education: Conference Proceedings and Papers.* ERIC ED 293–918.

133. Goodman, Y. T. (1969). The culturally deprived child: A study in stereotyping. *Integrated Education, 7*(4), 58–63.

134. Grossman, H. (1984). *Educating Hispanic Students: Cultural Implications for Instruction, Classroom Management, Counseling and Assessment.* Springfield, IL: Charles C Thomas.

135. Gurin, P., & Epps, E. (1975). *Black Consciousness, Identity and Achievement.* New York: Wiley.

136. Irvine, J. J. (1991). *Black Students and School Failure*: Policies, Practices, and Prescriptions. New York: Praeger.

137. Irvine, R. W. (1978). The black family and community: Some problems in the development of achievement values. *Negro Educational Review, 29*(3–4), 249–254.

138. Katz, I. (1969). A critique of personality approaches to negro performance, with research suggestions. *Journal of Social Issues, 25*(3), 13–27.

139. Levin, H. M. (1987). *New Schools for the Disadvantaged.* Unpublished manuscript. Stanford, CA: Stanford University.

140. Passow, A. H. (1990). *Enriching Compensatory Education Curriculum for Disadvantaged Students.* New York: ERIC Clearinghouse on Urban Education, Teachers College, Columbia University.

141. Sowell, T. (1976). Patterns of black excellence. *The Public Interest, 43,* 26–58.

142. Staples, R. (1976). *Introduction to Black Sociology.* New York: McGraw-Hill.

143. Sullivan, A. R. (1972). The influence of social processes on the learning abilities of Afro-American School Children: Some educational implications. *Journal of Negro Education, 41*(2), 127–136.

144. Tulkin, S. (1972). An analysis of the concept of cultural deprivation. *Developmental Psychology, 6,* 326–339.

The relative influences of cultural, linguistic, and socioeconomic factors on school achievement are discussed in the following references.

145. Laosa, L. M. (1982). School, occupation, culture, and family: The impact of parental schooling on the parent-child relationship. *Journal of Educational Psychology, 74*(6), 791–827.

146. Laosa, L. M. (1984). Ethnic, socioeconomic, and home language influences upon early performance on measures of abilities. *Journal of Educational Psychology, 76*(6), 1178–1198.

147. Macias, R. F. (1979). *Mexicano/Chicano Sociolinguistic Behavior and Language Policy in the United States.* Unpublished doctoral dissertation. Georgetown University, Washington, DC.

148. Rosenthal, A. S., Milne, A., Ginsburg, A., & Baker, K. A. (1981). *A Comparison of the Effects of Language Background and Socioeconomic Status on Achievement Status among Elementary School Students.* Draft final report, subcontract #b43601 from System Development Corporation under contract #300–75–0332. Washington, DC: U.S. Department of Education.

149. So, A. Y., & Chan, K. S. (1982). *What Matters? The Relative Impact of Language Background and Socioeconomic Status on Reading Achievement.* Los Alamitos, CA: National Center for Bilingual Research.

150. Valencia, R. R., Henderson, R. W., & Rankin, R. J. (1981). Relationship of family constellation and schooling to intellectual performance of Mexican American children. *Journal of Educational Psychology, 73*(4), 524–532.

The following references deal with the low validity of ethnic and socioeconomic profiles in identifying students who do not fit their ethnic and socioeconomic stereotypes.

151. Stodolosky, S. S., & Lesser, G. (1967). Learning patterns in the disadvantaged. *Harvard Educational Review, 37,* 546–593.

152. Trotman, F. K. (1977). Race, IQ, and the middle class. *Journal of Educational Psychology, 69*(3), 266–273.

The following references deal with ethnic and socioeconomic differences in cognitive verbal skills.

153. Adams, J. L., & Ramey, C. T. (1980). Structural aspects of maternal speech to infants reared in poverty. *Child Development, 51,* 1280–1284.

154. Bee, H., Van Egeren, L., Striessguth, A. P., Nyman, B. A., & Leckie, M. S. (1969). Social class differences in maternal teaching strategies and speech patterns. *Developmental Psychology, 1*(6), 726–734.

155. Bernstein, B. (1961). Social class and linguistic development. In A. Halsey, J. Floud, & C. Anderson (Eds.), *Education, Economy and Society.* Glencoe, IL: Free Press.

156. Borduin, C. M., Henggeler, S. W., Sanders-Walls, M., & Harbin, F. (1986). An evaluation of social class differences in verbal and nonverbal maternal controls, maternal sensitivity and child compliance. *Child Study Journal, 16*(2), 95–112.

157. Brice-Heath, S. (1982). Questioning at home and at school: A comparative study. In G. Spindler (Ed.), *Doing Ethnography: Educational Anthropology in Action.* New York: Holt, Rinehart & Winston.

158. Collins, J. (1988). Language and class in minority education. *Anthropology and Education Quarterly, 19*(4), 299–326.

159. Farron, D. C., & Ramey, C. T. (1980). Social class differences in dyadic involvement during infancy. *Child Development, 51,* 254–257.

160. Ford, C. E. (1984). The influence of speech variety on teachers' evaluation of students with comparable academic ability. *TESOL Quarterly, 18*(1), 25–40.

161. Gibson, E., & Levin, H. (1975). *The Psychology of Reading.* Cambridge, MA: MIT Press.

162. Hall, W., & Dore, J. (1980). *Lexical Sharing in Mother-Child Interaction.* Technical Report No. 161. Urbana, IL: University of Illinois at Urbana-Champaign, Center for the Study of Reading.

163. Hall, W., & Tire, W. (1979). *The Communicative Environment of Young Children: Social Class, Ethnic, and Situational Differences.* Technical Report No. 125. Champaign, IL: University of Illinois at Urbana-Champaign, Center for the Study of Reading.

164. Henggeler, S. W., & Tavormina, J. B. (1980). Social class and race differences in family interaction: Pathological, normative, or confounding methodological factors? *Journal of Genetic Psychology, 137,* 211–222.

165. Hess, R. D., & Shipman, V. (1968). Maternal influences upon early learning: The cognitive environment of urban preschool children. In R. D. Hess & R. M. Bear (Eds.), *Early Education.* Chicago: Aldine.

166. Hill, E. H., & Giammatto, M. C. (1963). Social economic status and its relationship to school achievement in elementary school. *Elementary English, 40,* 465–470.

167. Howard, M. J. Jr., Hoops, H. R., & McKinnon, A. J. (1970). Language abilities of children with different socioeconomic backgrounds. *Journal of Learning Disabilities, 3*(6), 328–335.

168. Labov, W. (1972). Academic ignorance and black intelligence. *Atlantic Monthly, 229,* 59–67.

169. Laosa, L. M. (1979). Inequality in the classroom: Observational research on teacher-student interactions. *Aztlan, 8,* 51–66.

170. Loban, W. D. (1963). *The Language of Elementary School Children.* Research Report No. 1. Champaign, IL: National Council of Teachers of English.

171. Piestrup, A. (1973). *Black Dialect Interference and the Accommodation of Reading Instruction in First Grade.* Monograph No. 4. Berkeley, CA: University of California—Berkeley, Language-Behavior Research Laboratory.

172. Rogoff, B., & Gardner, W. (1984). Adult guidance of everyday cognition. In B. Rogoff & J. Lave (Eds.), *Everyday Cognition: Its Development in Social Context.* Cambridge, MA: Harvard University Press.

173. Scheinfeld, D. R. (1983). Family relationships and school achievement among boys of lower-income urban black families. *American Journal of Orthopsychiatry, 53*(1), 127–143.

174. Scott-Jones, D. (1984). Family influences on cognitive development and school achievement. *Review of Research in Education, 11,* 259–304.

175. Simon, H. (n. d.). *Black Dialect Interference and Classroom Interaction.* Unpublished manuscript, University of California—Berkeley, School of Education.

176. Slaughter, D. T., & Epps, W. G. (1987). The home environment and academic achievement of black American children and youth: An overview. *Journal of Negro Education, 56*(1), 3–20.

177. Solomon, D., Hirsch, J. G., Scheinfeld, D. R., & Jackson, J. C. (1972). Family characteristics and elementary school achievement in an urban ghetto. *Journal of Consulting and Clinical Psychology, 39*(3), 462–466.

178. Sroufe, L. A. (1970). A methodological and philosophical critique of intervention-oriented research. *Developmental Psychology, 2,* 140–145.

179. Taylor, J. B. (1983). Influence of speech variety on teachers' evaluation of reading comprehension. *Journal of Educational Psychology, 75*(5), 662–667.

180. Templin, M. C. (1957). *Certain Language Skills in Children: Their Development and Interrelationships.* Minneapolis: University of Minnesota Press.

181. Wilson, K. R., & Allen, W. R. (1987). Explaining the educational attainment of young black adults: Critical familial and extra-familial influences. *Journal of Negro Education, 56*(1), 64–76.

Research on ethnic and socioeconomic differences in auditory discrimination is found in the following references.

182. Baratz, J. A. (1969). A bidialectic task for determining language proficiency in economically disadvantaged Negro Children. *Child Development, 40,* 889–901.

183. Bartel, N. R., Grill, J. J., & Bryen, D. N. (1973). Language characteristics of black children: Implications for assessment. *Journal of School Psychology, 11*(4), 351–364.

184. Bryen, D. N. (1976). Speech-sound discrimination ability on linguistically unbiased tests. *Exceptional Children, 42*(4), 95–201.

185. Clark, A. D., & Richards, C. J. (1964). Auditory discrimination among economically disadvantaged and nondisadvantaged preschool children. *Exceptional Children, 33,* 259–262.

186. Evans, J. S. (1974). Word-pair discrimination and imitation abilities of preschool Spanish-speaking children. *Journal of Learning Disabilities, 7*(9), 49–56.

187. Fowles, B. R., & Kimple, J. A. (1972). Language tests and the "disadvantaged" reader. *Reading World, 11*(3), 183–195.

188. Karger, G. (1970). *The Effect of Black English on the Performance of Lower Class Black Children on the Wepman Auditory Discrimination Test.* Unpublished manuscript. Cambridge,MA: School of Education, Harvard University.

189. Mathewson, G. C., & Pereyra-Suarez, D. M. (1975). Spanish language interference with acoustic-phonetic skills and reading. *Journal of Reading Behavior, 7*(2), 187–196.

190. Oakland, T. D. (1969). Auditory discrimination and socioeconomic status as correlates of reading ability. *Journal of Learning Disabilities, 2,* 32–39.

191. Ralph, J. B. (1965). Language development in socially disadvantaged children. *Review of Educational Research, 35,* 389–400.

192. Ross, H. W. (1979). Wepman Test of Auditory Discrimination: What does it discriminate? *Journal of School Psychology, 17*(1), 47–54.

The relationship between ethnic and socioeconomic background and self-concept is the focus of the references listed below.

193. Arnez, N. (1972). Enhancing the black self-concept through literature. In J. Banks (Ed.), *Black Self-Concept: Implications for Education and Social Science.* New York: McGraw Hill.

194. Banks, J. A., & Grambs, D. (Eds.). (1972). *Black Self-Concept: Implications for Education and Social Sciences.* New York: McGraw-Hill.

195. Baughman, E. E. (1971). *Black Americans: A Psychological Analysis.* New York: Academic Press.

196. Braroe, N. W. (1975). *Indian and White: Self Image and Interaction in a Canadian Plains Community.* Stanford, CA: Stanford University Press.

197. Carter, T. P. (1968). Negative self-concept of Mexican-American students. *School and Society, 96,* 217–219.

198. Coopersmith, S. (1967). *The Antecedents of Self-Esteem.* San Francisco: W. H. Freeman.

199. Deutsch, M. (1960). *Minority Group and Class Status as Related to Social and Personality Factors in Scholastic Achievement.* Society for Applied Anthropology, Monograph 2. Ithaca, NY: Cornell University Press.

200. Douglas, L. A. (1970). Comparative analysis of the relationships between self-esteem and certain selected variables among youth from

diverse racial groups. *Dissertation Abstracts,* 31(2A), 641.

201. Evans, F. B., & Anderson, J. G. (1973). The psychocultural origins of achievement and achievement motivation: The Mexican-American family. *Sociology of Education, 46,* 396–416.

202. Healy, G. W., & DeBlassie, R. R. (1974). A comparison of Negro, Anglo, and Spanish American adolescents' self concepts. *Adolescence, 33,* 15–24.

203. Heaps, R. A., & Morrill, S. G. (1979). Comparing the self-concepts of Navajo and white high school students. *Journal of American Indian Education, 18*(3), 12–14.

204. Hishiki, P. (1969). The self-concepts of sixth grade girls of Mexican-American descent. *California Journal of Educational Research, 20,* 56–62.

205. Ladner, J. (1973). The urban poor. In R. P. Rothman & W. Wilson (Eds.), *Through Different Eyes: Black and White Perspectives on American Race Relations.* New York: Oxford University Press.

206. Larned, D. T., & Muller, D. (1979). Development of self-concept in Mexican American and Anglo students. *Hispanic Journal of Behavioral Sciences. 1*(2), 179–185.

207. Luftig, R. L. (1982), *The Effects of Schooling on the Self-Concept of Native American Students.* ERIC ED 220–227.

208. McDaniel, E. L. (1967). *Relationship between Self-Concept and Specific Variables in a Low-Income Culturally Different Population.* ERIC ED 019 124.

209. Muller, D., & Leonetti, R. (1974). Self-concepts of primary level Chicano and Anglo students. *California Journal of Educational Research, 25,* 57–60.

210. Parry, R. (1982). Poor self-concept and differential academic achievement: An inadequate explanation of school performance of black and Native American children. *Canadian Journal of Native Education, 10*(1), 11–24.

211. Patton, S. M., Walberg, H. J., & Yeh, E. G. (1973). Ethnicity, environmental control, and academic self-concept in Chicago. *American Educational Research Journal, 10,* 85–91.

212. Poussaint, A. R. (1974). Building a strong self-image in the black child. *Ebony,* August, 136–143.

213. Schwartz, A. J. (1969). *Comparative Values and Achievement of Mexican-American and Anglo Pupils.* Occasional Report No. 37. Los Angeles: Center for the Study of Evaluation, University of California—Los Angeles.

214. Trowbridge, N. T. (1973). Self-concept and socioeconomic status in elementary-school children. *American Educational Research Journal, 9,* 525–537.

215. Wells, E. E. (1978). *The Mythical Negative Black Self Concept.* San Francisco: R & E Research Associates.

216. Ziller, R. C., Hagey, J., Smith, M. D. C., & Long, B. H. (1969). Self-esteem: A self-social construct. *Journal of Consulting and Clinical Psychology, 33*(1), 84–95.

217. Zirkel, P. A. (1973). Self-concept and the "disadvantage" of ethnic group membership and mixture. *Review of Educational Research, 41,* 211–225.

218. Zirkel, P. A., & Moses, E. G. (1971). Self-concept and ethnic group membership among public school students. *American Educational Research Journal, 8,* 253–265.

Research that deals with students' level of aspiration is discussed in the following references.

219. Bales, K. B. (1979). The single parent family aspirations and academic achievement. *Southern Journal of Educational Research, 13*(4), 145–160.

220. Castenell, I. A. (1983). Achievement motivation: An investigation of adolescents' achievement patterns. *American Educational Research Journal, 20*(4), 503–510.

221. DeBord, L. W., Griffin, L. J., Clark, M. (1977). Race and sex influences in the schooling processes of rural and small town youth. *Sociology of Education, 42,* 85–102.

222. George, V. D. (1981). Occupational aspirations of talented black and white adolescent females. *Journal of Non-White Concerns in Personnel and Guidance, 9*(4), 137–145.

The following references found that middle-class parents have higher aspirations for their children, and expect and encourage them to attain more education.

223. Baker, D. P., & Entwisle, D. R. (1987). The influence of mothers on the academic expectations of young children: A longitudinal study of how gender differences arise. *Social Forces, 65*(3), 670–694.

224. Brooks, J. S., Whiteman, M., Lukoff, I. F., & Gordon, A. S. (1979). Maternal and adolescent expectations and aspirations as related

to sex, ethnicity, and socioeconomic status. *Journal of Genetic Psychology, 135*, 209–216.

225. Lareau, A. (1987). Social class differences in family school relationships: The importance of cultural capital. *Sociology of Education, 60*, 73–85.

References that found that poor and African-American parents have as high if not higher aspirations for their children are listed next.

226. Goodwin, L. (1976). A critical comment on success-value research. *American Journal of Sociology, 81*, 1151–1155.

227. Kandel, D. B. (1971). Race, maternal authority, and adolescent aspiration. *American Journal of Sociology, 76*(6) 999–1020.

228. Rodman, H., & Voydanoff, P. (1978). Social class and parents' range of aspirations for their children. *Social Problems, 25*, 333–344.

Students' locus of control is the focus of the references listed below.

229. Brown, D., Fulkerson, K. F., Furr, S., & Ware, W. B. (1984). Locus of control, sex role orientation, and self-concept in black and white third- and sixth-grade male and female leaders in a rural community. *Developmental Psychology, 20*(4), 717–721.

230. Cummings, S. (1977). Family socialization and fatalism among black adolescents. *Journal of Negro Education, 46*(1), 62–75.

231. Epps, E. G. (1969). Negro academic motivation and performance:An overview. *Journal of Social Issues, 25*(3), 5–11.

232. Gurin, P., Gurin, G., Lao, R. C., & Beattie, M. (1969). Internal-external control in the motivational dynamics of negro youth. *Journal of Social Issues, 25*(3), 29–53.

233. Knight, G. P., Kagan, S., Nelson, W., & Gumbiner, J. (1978). Acculturation of second- and third-generation Mexican American children: Field independence, locus of control, self esteem, and school achievement. *Journal of Cross-Cultural Psychology, 9*(1), 87–97.

234. Willig, A. C., Harnisch, D. L., Hill, K. T., & Maehr, M. L. (1983). Sociocultural and educational correlates of success-failure attributions and evaluation anxiety in the school setting for black, Hispanic and anglo children. *American Educational Research Journal, 20*(3), 385–410.

The following references discuss the effects of father absence on students' cognitive development and school achievement.

235. Collins, M. A. (1970). Achievement, intelligence, personality, and selected school-related variables in Negro children from intact and broken families attending parochial schools in central Harlem. *Dissertation Abstracts International, 30*, 5280A–5281A.

236. Fowler, P. C., & Richards, H. C. (1978). Father absence, educational preparedness, and academic achievement: A test of the confluence model. *Journal of Educational Psychology, 70*(4), 595–601.

237. Havinghurst, R. J., & Neugarten, B. L. (1967). *Society and Education*. Boston: Allyn & Bacon.

238. Hill, R. (1972). *Strengths of Black Families*. New York: National Urban League.

239. Hoffman, M. L. (1971). Father absence and conscience development. *Developmental Psychology, 4*(3), 400–406.

240. Jaffe, B. D. (1966). The relationship between two aspects of socioeconomic disadvantage and the school success of 8th grade Negro students in a Detroit junior high school. *Dissertation Abstracts International, 27*, 1546A.

241. Kukuk, C. R., Levine, D. U., & Meyer, J. K. (1978). Neighborhood predictors of reading achievement in six big city school districts: A path analysis. *Multiple Linear Regression Viewpoints, 8*(3), 27–43.

242. LeCorgne, L. L., & Laosa, L. M. (1976). Father absence in low-income Mexican-American families: Children's social adjustment and conceptual differentiation of sex role attributes. *Developmental Psychology, 12*(5), 470–471.

243. Lessing, E. E., Zagorin, S. W., & Nelson, D. (1973). WISC subtest and IQ score correlates of father absence. *Journal of Genetic Psychology, 117*, 181–195.

244. Liebow, E. (1967). *Tally's Corner*. Boston: Little, Brown.

245. McAdoo, H. (1977). Family therapy in the black community. *American Journal of Orthopsychiatry, 47*(1), 75–79.

246. Peterson, R. A., DeBord, L., Peterson, C. L., & Livingston, S. K. (1966). *Educational Supportiveness of the Home and Academic Performance of Disadvantaged Boys*. Nashville: Institute on Mental Retardation and Academic Development, George Peabody College for Teachers.

247. Prom-Jackson, S., Johnson, S. T., & Wallace, M. G. (1987). Home environment, talented minority youth and school achievement. *Journal of Negro Education, 56*(1), 111–121.

248. Scanzoni, J. (1971). *The Black Family in Modern*

Society: Patterns of Stability and Security. Chicago: University of Chicago Press.

249. Sciara, F. J. (1975). Effects of father absence on the educational achievement of urban black children. *Child Study Journal, 5,* 45–55.

250. Scott-Jones, D. (1984). Family influences on cognitive development and school achievement. *Review of Research in Education, 11,* 254–304.

251. Solomon, B. (1976). *Black Empowerment.* New York: Columbia University Press.

252. Stack, C. (1975). *All Our Kin: Strategies for Survival in a Black Community.* New York: Harper & Row.

253. Svanum, S., Bringle, R., & McLaughlin, J. E. (1982). Father absence and cognitive performance in a large sample of six-to-eleven-year-old children. *Child Development, 83,* 136–143.

254. Williams, M. (1974). *Community in a Black Pentecostal Church.* Pittsburgh: University of Pittsburgh Press.

255. Willie, C. (Ed.) (1976). *The Family of Black People.* Columbus, OH: Merrill.

The following reference discusses ethnic differences in poverty rates.

256. Baumeister, A. A., Kupstas, F., & Klindworth, L. M. (1990). New Morbidity: Implications for prevention of children's disabilities. *Exceptionality, 1,* 1–16.

Chapter 3

Extrinsic Causes of Ethnic and Socioeconomic Disparities

The previous chapter dealt with the ideas of those who attribute some non–European American and poor students' lack of success in school to the students themselves. Actually, the research described in this and subsequent chapters indicates that many of the causes of their problems in school lie outside of the students. This chapter describes how, with the exception of some excellent bilingual and multicultural education programs, the American educational system provides these students with contextually and culturally inappropriate instruction, and classroom management, counseling and assessment services that do not suit their educational and psychological needs. Many teachers, psychologists, and administrators are prejudiced against non–European American and poor students. School officials have attempted to maintain segregated educational settings by assigning non–European American and poor students to low-ability tracks and groups, and misplacing them in special education programs. When these students realize that both schools and society in general are structured in ways that reproduce ethnic and socioeconomic inequality, many of them become alienated and angry, and they resist the prejudice and hostility they experience by refusing to do their homework, truanting, and dropping out of school.

Contextually Inappropriate Educational Approaches

The educational approaches that predominate in most schools are ill-suited to the context or living conditions of many poor and non–European American students' lives. For example, immigrant and refugee students are especially unlikely to receive the education services they require and likely to do poorly in school (1–7) (see Chapter 5). Too often they do not receive the assistance they require to overcome the culture shock they experience upon entering a new and strange environment. As a result, they may react angrily and aggressively toward teachers and systems they do not understand and cannot easily adjust to, or they may become sullen, depressed, and withdrawn. This is especially true of students who have never attended school because they come from rural areas or internment camps, or grew up in cultures that have no written languages.

Even when their culture shock passes, they need more help than they typically receive to learn how to learn in classes taught in foreign languages and unfamiliar teaching styles. This, too, can interfere with their learning.

Refugee students who suffer the psychological effects of the war, famine, and persecution they experienced at home or in internment camps are most likely to lack the assistance they need to overcome their problems. Educators who work with refugee and immigrant students need skills in instructing students with special needs and managing the special problems these students bring to school, and they need to maintain a high degree of tolerance for behavior that students cannot control while adjusting to their new educational environments.

Like foreign-born students, Native American students who live on reservations live in a region separate from mainstream America where they speak a language other than English. They, too, are ill-prepared to adjust to and profit from the curriculum typically offered in mainstream schools, which encourages beliefs and values which conflict with their communities, and is often taught in a language they do not understand by teachers who are unprepared to succeed with them in schools (8, 9). Like immigrant students, they are susceptible to experiencing culture shock, identity conflicts, and feelings of alienation, confusion, and frustration.

Contextual problems make it difficult for poor non–European American migrant students to actualize their potential for learning (10–16). Attending school irregularly, losing considerable time traveling with their families from job to job, enrolling in numerous schools during the academic year—all contribute to their poor achievement. Lack of a stable home base, inadequate medical care, poverty, and prejudice are examples of other contextual problems that complicate their lives. In addition, although migrant students can be helped by educational programs geared to their needs, school systems that have been designed for students who are permanent members of the community often add to their problems rather than contribute to solving them.

Rural students face many contextual problems (17–27). Those from rural families that rely on seasonal activities such as fishing, agriculture, timber, and so on, may not be able to attend school during certain times of the year. In addition, it is difficult for school systems to provide services to small numbers of students scattered over vast land areas with major transportation problems.

The contextual problems that confront poor homeless students are horrendous (28–45). Many do not have their basic food, clothing, and shelter needs met. They have four times as many health problems and twice as many chronic diseases, but they have less access to medical care and are less able to follow the health regimes prescribed by physicians. They move from place to place and shelter to shelter and attend school erratically.

When one considers the numbers of poor urban, rural, homeless, and migrant students and the large numbers of immigrant and refugee students whose contextual needs are not met by the American educational system, it becomes clear that many students are not receiving an appropriate education. Thus, contextually inappropriate educational approaches contribute significantly to the problems of poor and non–European American students.

Culturally Inappropriate Educational Approaches

In the past, and especially in recent years, an increasing number of individuals have come to believe that schools have not adapted their educational approaches to the cultural needs of their non-European and poor students (46–49, also see Chapter 4). They tend to claim that schools in the United States, like many other aspects of life, have historically served the needs of the European American middle-class majority. They argue that once the European Americans succeeded in wresting control of the territory that presently comprises the United States from the Native Americans and Hispanics who shared it with them, they installed their approach to life from the Atlantic to the Pacific, to Alaska and Hawaii.

That is not to say that other cultures did not continue to survive. However, they survived in a powerless state. Most Native Americans were confined to their reservations, African Americans were subjected to stringent restrictions—first slavery and then segregation—and the Hispanic Americans who inhabited the lands taken from Mexico were considered to be inferior and treated as second-class citizens. For many years, therefore, the European American way of life, including the educational system that developed to serve the needs of the upper-class and middle-class European Americans who had the power and influence to shape it, reigned supreme with no effective challenges to it.

Over the years many events contributed to a change in the status quo. Immigration from Mexico, Puerto Rico, other Latin American countries, China, Japan, the Philippines, and Eastern Europe increased the numbers of persons who were not prepared for or able to adapt easily to the established educational system. Segregation was ended in most areas of American life, including education. The American working class unionized and gained political power. Large numbers of African Americans and Hispanic Americans gained the right to vote. With all of these developments, the demand for educational reform grew louder and louder.

One of these demands was for the modification and elimination of biased programs and programs such as Head Start that some reformers believed attempted to compensate for unreal deprivations or to change students' socioeconomically or culturally determined behavior or learning styles.

> *Child rearing practices not in accord with mainstream values have generally been seen. . . . as unfortunate personal practices that indicate a lack of information or training. Black families in particular have been labelled "pathological", black mothers deficient, and black children deprived.*
>
> *Since the problem is seen to rest with individuals, it is assumed that it is individuals who need to change. Millions of dollars have been expended both to provide*

poor, frequently non–European American, children with educational experiences that their own homes "lack" or to provide poor and minority parents with training that would enable them to raise children "properly." (49, pp. 46–47)

The entire intervention model of Head Start rests on an assumption of linguistic and cognitive deficits which must be remedied if the child is to succeed in school. . . . The theoretical base of the deficit model employed by Head Start programs denies obvious strengths within the Negro community and may inadvertently advocate the annihilation of a cultural system which is barely considered or understood by most social scientists. . . . Education for culturally different children should not attempt to destroy functionally viable processes of the subculture. . . . Head Start has failed because its goal is to correct a deficit that simply does not exist. (46, p. 112, 116, 124, 125)

A second demand was to make education more culturally relevant. Many reformers insisted that school personnel should be sensitized to the importance of educationally relevant ethnic and socioeconomic cultural differences and the special challenges and problems poor students have to deal with because of their economic situations. They wanted educators to be trained to take such differences into consideration when planning school programs and selecting instructional, classroom management, counseling, and assessment techniques for non–European American and poor students.

This belief is still current. It is clearly reflected in the following quotation, which summarizes the results of a national survey of the opinions of experts and parents about the state of the educational services for non–European American students.

The current educational system has a mainstream cultural bias which adversely affects the education of students from minority backgrounds. This bias is manifested in preconceived expectations about children from diverse cultures that are limiting and inaccurate. In addition, lack of awareness, sensitivity and understanding of diverse cultures by school personnel interfere with the education of students and the development of productive relationships with parents. . . . In general, the current instruction curricula, materials/methods and service delivery models are inadequate for meeting the educational needs of children from minority backgrounds. . . . Existing methods are not adequate to correctly assess/ identify students from diverse backgrounds and determine appropriate educational services. (47, pp. 5–7)

The opinion of these experts is supported by a great deal of research evidence. This research is discussed in detail in Chapters 6, 9, 10, and 11. The following two examples illustrate these research findings.

Students from different cultural backgrounds have different learning styles (see Chapter 10). When educators do not adapt their educational approaches to these differences, mismatches between teachers' culturally determined teaching style and students' culturally determined learning styles occur. This can cause students to do poorly in school and to be referred to and accepted into programs for students with learning disabilities and/or cognitive disabilities.

Students from different cultures also have different *behavioral* styles (see Chapter 11). Students who come from different ethnic or socioeconomic backgrounds than their teachers may be viewed as troublesome if they behave in ways that are acceptable in their homes and communities, but not in school (50). (See Chapter 11.)

Prejudice and Discrimination in the Educational System

It has been clear for many years that the behavior of teachers, psychologists, and school administrators toward poor and certain non-European students reflects the biases that exist in the larger society. As a result, these students often fall behind in school and misbehave. In the 1960s, 1970s, and 1980s, research repeatedly documented the prejudice and discrimination that non–European American students experienced in America's schools. To a considerable degree the groups that bore the brunt of this biased approach were those that populated the particular school or school system. For example, Stein reported that in an area with substantial numbers of African American and Puerto Rican American students,

> At every grade level the curriculum is "modified" to the teacher's image of what the child can be expected to do—even in kindergarten where Black and Puerto Rican children are taught to hang up their clothes and "take turns," while white children are taught "numbers and letters." (55, pp. 168–169)

Bennet and Harris cite the following results of their survey of the attitudes of a group of European American teachers to support their conclusion that the European American faculty of the school they studied was rife with prejudice against Black students.

> Many of the teachers would not live in a desegregated neighborhood, did not favor mandatory school desegregation, felt the civil rights movement had done more harm than good, and felt that the problems of prejudice were exaggerated. One-third believed that Blacks and whites should not be allowed to intermarry. Furthermore, the majority of the teachers perceived their white students to be superior intellectually, socially, and in other characteristics related to school achievement. (52, pp. 420–421)

Becker described the attitude of teachers toward the Portuguese American students in a Rhode Island community as follows:

> Teachers' attitudes and behavior reflected stereotypes of the Portuguese student as intellectually inferior, noneducationally oriented, socially backward. . . . The teachers expressed feelings of alienation from their students. . . . When the teach-

ers' feelings about the Portuguese were examined closely, many revealed patterns of racism, ethnocentrism and cultural superiority. . . . There was definite resistance to cultural diversity. (51, p. 4)

Working-class non-European students often are treated in an even more discriminatory manner than their middle-class peers. For example, in his classical study comparing the way teachers treated African American students from different socioeconomic backgrounds, Rist documented how teachers acted out their prejudices against poor students.

When a teacher bases her expectations of performance on the social status of the student and assumes that the higher the social status, the higher the potential of the child, those children of low social status suffer a stigmatization outside of their own choice or will. Yet there is a greater tragedy than being labeled as a slow learner, and that is being treated as one. The differential amounts of control-oriented behavior, the lack of interaction with the teacher, the ridicule from one's peers, and the caste aspects of being placed in lower reading groups all have implications for the future life style and value of education for the child. . . . Given the treatment of poor children from the beginning of their kindergarten experience, for what class strata are they being prepared other than that of the lower class? It appears that the public school system not only mirrors the configurations of the larger society, but also significantly contributes to maintaining them. Thus the system of public education in reality perpetuates what it is ideologically committed to eradicate—class barriers which result in inequality in the social and economic life of the citizenry. (54, pp. 107–108)

Reviews of the educational system done in the 1990s indicate that prejudice and discrimination are very much alive and well. For example, The National Black Child Development Institute described the educational conditions for African Americans in Selma, Alabama, twenty years after the school system was supposedly desegregated as follows:

Selma schools are desegregated, although African American children largely remain in separate classes due to a racially discriminatory tracking system. Children are tracked into three levels, with level I designated as the college preparatory track. . . . Ninety-seven percent of African American children were placed in levels II and III, and African American faculty were not assigned to teach at the higher levels. *[One student reported] "In sixth grade I was next to the top of my class. Yet my sixth grade teacher referred me to level III classes." (53, p. 12)*

Anecdotal evidence suggests that most educators believe that they are not biased against non–European American and poor students, and many researchers have found little or no prejudice or discrimination among the educators they studied (56–63). However, as the research summarized in the next section indicates, many teachers were and continue to be biased.

Biased Expectations

Although a few studies (discussed earlier) failed to find significant ethnic and class differences in educators' expectations for their students, most studies have found such bias. Beginning in preschool and continuing through their college careers, educators and education students tend to expect the European American middle-class students in their classes to do better academically than non–European American and poor students. In addition, they expect European American middle-class students to be more intelligent, even when students' achievement test scores, grades, and school histories would predict otherwise. In experiments in which educators are given the exact same information about students except for their ethnic or socioeconomic backgrounds, they attribute higher academic and intellectual potential to European American students than African American students (64, 65, 68, 69, 71, 76, 79) and Hispanic students (66, 70, 72, 79). They have the same prejudicial expectations for middle-class students in comparison to poor students (65, 73, 75, 76).

All too often teachers have overly optimistic expectations for Asian and Pacific American students (67, 74, 77, 78). Dao offers the following observation.

> *There is an assumption that Asian-Americans, in general, are a model minority. This notion is related to the stereotypic perception that Asian-American families place high priority on education and push their children to succeed in school. . . . Although there have been impressive occupational and educational achievements by Asian-Americans in the past, these achievements should not obscure the changes now occurring in the Asian-American population. . . . The growing and changing Asian-American student population includes many children from families with life and educational experiences vastly different from children from established Asian-American families. Among the Mein and Hmong refugees, for example, the unemployment rate is 90%. Recent immigrant or refugee children from these families face the triple burden of simultaneously learning English and the new school curriculum, adjusting to a new culture, and surviving an impoverished environment. (67, p. 594)*

Educators also maintain prejudicial behavior expectations for non–European American students, especially African Americans, whom they expect to be more disruptive and deviant than European Americans (see Chapter 11).

Biased Evaluation

Although a few studies have not found teacher bias (57, 61), most studies done in the 1970s and 1980s indicate that teachers tend to evaluate African American, Hispanic and poor students' academic performance and behavior in a biased manner (80–85, 88–91). For example, although neither ethnicity nor social class is ever the sole criterion educators use when assigning students to ability groups, teachers often assign non–European American and poor students to lower ability groups than objective data such as test scores would warrant.

Teachers also evaluate African American students' behavior in a biased manner. When teachers evaluate the severity or deviancy of students' behavior problems, they judge the exact same transgressions as more severe or deviant when they are committed by African American male students. They evaluate European American females higher than they evaluate African American females in the areas of responsibility, compliance, persistence, performance, ability, and relationships with others. And African American students who are seen as fun-loving, happy, cooperative, energetic and ambitious by African American teachers are viewed as talkative, lazy, fun-loving, high-strung, and frivolous by their European American teachers.

Teachers also tend to allow their judgments about students' work to be influenced by whether students express themselves in Black English (the English dialect many African Americans speak—especially, but not exclusively, those from poor backgrounds), a working-class dialect (a variety of nonstandard dialects spoken by individuals from poor backgrounds), an Hispanic accent, or standard English (the English used in textbooks, newspapers, television news programs, found in grammar books, and typically used by most middle- and upper-class European Americans). In general teachers incorrectly rate the quality and accuracy of the English of speakers of standard English higher than nonstandard English. More important, even when students' work is identical or of equal quality, teachers judge the oral and written work of students who speak in a black English, Hispanic, or a working-class accent to be poorer than students who speak standard English. African American students who speak "Black English" are also rated lower than those who speak more standard English (58, 60, 61, 63, 64, 66, 68, 69).

As is noted in Chapters 2 and 9, at one time many educators may not have perceived this as a biased approach to evaluation. In the 1960s and early 1970s, researchers typically used European American middle-class students' scores on tests prepared in standard English as the norm to which they compared the scores of students who spoke nonstandard English. As a result, they concluded that Black English and working-class English were inferior to standard English. By the mid-1970s, the results of research studies that did not make that methodological error led most authors to conclude that these varieties of English are actually equally effective and valid forms of communication, and many scholars, especially those from African American backgrounds, were encouraging schools to incorporate Black English into the curriculum rather than attempt to eradicate it.

Black children must be educated to learn and believe that deviation from the normative pattern of standard English is not an indication that they are abnormal. . . . Whites should not become reference points for how Black children are to speak and behave. One's family and community and how one measures up to one's peers should provide some of these reference points. Black children's encounters with the white world should be filtered through a Black frame of reference, which includes the use of Black English. (59, p. 215)

Apparently, many teachers still believe that standard English is superior to other forms of English. That is, instead of correctly viewing Black English, Hispanic, and working-class dialects and accents as different, they view them as deficient, and they continue to allow their beliefs to prejudice their evaluations of students.

There is no reason to assume that the biases found in the studies reported earlier have disappeared. Because they were done in the 1970s and mid- 1980s, however, additional research is needed to determine whether the situation has improved significantly in recent years.

There is also evidence that teachers evaluate Asian and Pacific American students in a biased manner (86, 92, 93). There appear to be three reasons for this. First, believing that all of them are good students, they fail to notice their academic problems (93). As Yao puts it: "Many school teachers share a myth: that all Asian American youngsters are diligent, respectful, intelligent, good students. But teachers should not be dismayed if they find the opposite is true in their classrooms." (93, p. 82).

Second, Asian American students tend to internalize their emotional problems rather than act them out. Even though they may be experiencing serious emotional problems, their suffering is less obvious and less disruptive than that of students who act out their problems. As a result, they are less likely to be noticed by teachers (86). For example, Kim reports that many troubled Asian and Pacific American students

> *resort to passivity and conformity. . . . Their quietness, inconspicuousness, withdrawal, and non-threatening stance in the classroom tend to make them less noticeable. A teacher might not recognize a certain behavioral manifestation of passivity as a sign of poor adjustment. [In addition] Teachers tend to perceive passive Asian American children as being better adjusted to the classroom as compared to passive Caucasian children. (87, pp. 83–84)*

Third, because teachers welcome the quiet unobtrusive behavior of many Asian and Pacific Americans, they often fail to recognize when it may be a sign of problems. Takeuchi points out that "the quiet passive behavior of Asian American students should not be unquestionly encouraged. Rather, it often signifies problems in verbalization needing attention" (78, p. 2).

Teachers' Perceptions of Asian American and European American Students

European Americans	Asian Americans
More extroverted	Less extroverted
Less cheerful	More cheerful
Less emotionally stable	More emotionally stable
Less kind	More kind
Less obedient	More obedient

Continued

**Teachers' Perceptions of Asian
American and European American Students** *(Continued)*

European Americans	Asian Americans
Less disciplined	More disciplined
Less cooperative	More cooperative
Less patient	More patient
More prone to anger	Less prone to anger
Less academically competent	More academically competent
Less able to concentrate	More able to concentrate
Less organized	More organized
Less persevering	More persevering
Less adequate memory	More adequate memory

Biased Treatment

Most, but not all, studies indicate that, in addition to having biased expectations for non–European American and poor students and evaluating them in a discriminatory manner, many teachers also treat them unfairly. The following are some of the discriminatory ways many educators treat African American, Native American, and Hispanic American students (52, 53, 71, 95–97, 99–102, 104–112).

In comparison to European American students, teachers praise African Americans less and criticize them more. The praise teachers give these students is more likely to be routine, rather than feedback for a particular achievement or behavior, and when teachers praise them for a specific behavior, it is more likely to be qualified ("Your work is almost good enough to be put on the board.") or, in the case of females, more likely to be for good behavior than for academic work.

Teachers interact more with European American students than with African Americans, especially males, and give the latter less attention. In comparison to European American students, educators are less likely to respond to African American male students' questions or to direct questions to them. Unlike the preferential treatment many teachers give their brightest European American students, they give bright African American students, especially females, the least attention and criticize them the most. Although European American teachers typically demonstrate considerable concern and interest in European American females' academic work, they pay less attention to African American female students' academic work than to their social behavior. Teachers encourage European American female students in intellectual and academic areas, whereas they encourage and praise African American females in areas involving social skills. In addition, European American females are more likely to receive trusted lieutenant duties and special high-prestige assignments; African American female students' duties typically involve social responsibilities.

Educators tend to use different classroom management techniques with African American and European American students. In general, teachers of classes with high percentages of African American students are more likely to be authoritarian and less likely to use an open classroom approach. Teachers spend more time on the lookout for possible misbehavior by African American students, especially males. When male students misbehave, educators are especially prone to criticize the behavior of African American males and to use more severe punishments, including corporal punishment and suspension, with them, and when females misbehave, teachers treat African Americans more harshly than European Americans.

Grant describes the effect this can have on African American females' perception of the role that is most suitable for them in the following way:

> *The emphasis on black girls' social rather than academic skills, which occurs particularly in white-teacher classrooms, might point to a hidden cost of desegregation for black girls. . . . While such skills assuredly are helpful in high-status adult roles, the lesser attention to black girls' work might diminish motivation for gaining credentials to enter such positions. Black girls' everyday schooling experiences seem more likely to nudge them toward stereotypical roles of black women than toward alternatives. (71, p. 109)*

Teachers relate to Hispanic American students in much the same way as they treat African American students. Although Hispanic American students tend to prefer more positive reinforcement and feedback from their teachers than most European American students (see Chapters 10 and 11), teachers praise them less often and give them less positive feedback when they answer correctly or perform well. Teachers are also less likely to encourage them when they need encouragement, to accept their ideas, and to direct questions to them.

Research about how teachers treat Native Americans is sparse. There is some evidence that teachers and their aides tend to speak to and attend to them less than European American students (102). However, this may be partly the result of the teachers' failure to recognize the nonverbal ways in which Native American students ask for help and attention.

Poor students also receive unfair treatment in school (94, 98, 103, 106). Beginning in primary school, teachers give them less attention and fewer rewards. Educators provide poor students, especially males, fewer social and instructional contacts, but more disciplinary and control contacts. And when they discipline students, teachers in schools that serve predominantly poor students are more likely to endorse or use corporal punishments, verbal punishments, or suspension than teachers in middle-class schools.

Apparent and Real Lack of Bias

Bias against non–European American students and poor students is not quite as pervasive as the preceding summary suggests. African American teachers tend to be less prejudiced than European American teachers toward African American students (71, 108); only some European Americans are biased against non–European American students and poor students; and there is some evidence that the ratio of non–European American to European American teachers on the staff of a school district has an effect on the discriminatory treatment students receive. For example, in one study, a high percentage of African American teachers in a school district was associated with a decrease in the overrepresentation of African American students among students who were disciplined by corporal punishment, suspended, or expelled. There also was a decrease in their dropout rates and their underrepresentation in programs for gifted and talented students, and an increase in their high school graduation rates (114).

At least in some cases, however, the apparent lack of bias against students who belong to a different ethnic group may not be real (108, 110, 113). Many European American and African American teachers are not aware of their biases against students from ethnic backgrounds different from their own. In order to hide their true feelings and attitudes from themselves, some European American and African American teachers may give students a double message without realizing it. They consciously praise students who belong to a different ethnic group more than they do students who share their ethnic background, but they unknowingly treat them negatively by giving them less nonverbal positive attention, maintaining a greater distance from them, and touching them less often.

European American teachers exhibit more unconscious discrimination than African American teachers do. In addition to the negative, nonverbal communication mentioned earlier, they also give African American students less positive feedback when they answer questions correctly and fewer helpful hints when they call on them to answer questions. Simpson and Erickson report:

> *Naturalistic observational studies in the classroom may show overcompensatory behavior on the part of black and white teachers. However, the nonverbal behaviors may indicate a natural preference or comfortableness with students of one's own race. (108, p. 185)*

Implications

Many educators believe that much of the disruptive behavior, inadequate motivation, lack of participation in school, and poor achievement that many poor, and non–European American students demonstrate is caused, at least in part, by the biased evaluations, expectations, and treatment they receive in school. Thus, these problems will not be solved until teachers correct their biased attitudes, beliefs, and treatment of non–European American and poor students.

These educators also believe that teacher bias contributes to the unnecessary suspension of many African American, Hispanic American, and poor students, and their overrepresentation in special education programs for the behaviorally disordered and emotionally disturbed (53, 115–117). They feel that non–European American and poor students will not receive the kind of educational services they deserve until educators behave more democratically and serve the needs of the population as a whole. To their way of thinking, the elimination of teacher prejudice and discrimination is the first and most important step educators can take to ensure that students receive culturally appropriate education services.

Conclusions

Prejudice and discrimination against non–European American and poor students is still rampant. Not all teachers are biased. As was noted earlier, a few studies have found that ethnic and class differences do not influence how educators perceive, judge, and relate to students; those that have uncovered bias did not find that all teachers behaved in a biased manner; and a few studies found that some teachers evaluate and treat opposite-race students better than same-race students. However, when the evidence is considered as a whole, it is clear that teachers' conscious and unconscious prejudice against certain non–European American and poor students influences their relationships with them, their expectations for them, their evaluation of their work, and their choices of which instructional and classroom management techniques to use with them. In turn, these biases affect their students' performance in and attitudes toward school.

SELF-QUIZ: Students' Responses to Prejudice

What is your opinion about the following statement? "In a prejudiced society, students' assertive behavior in school that is aimed at correcting injustices may be positive and acceptable even though teachers and others may find it disruptive, be uncomfortable with it and threatened by it."

Structured Reproduction

As was noted at the beginning of this chapter, schools reproduce the inequalities found in society at large. One of the schools' many missions is to perpetuate the values, ideas, and attitudes of the societies they serve. Because American society does not completely live up to the high ideals it espouses, much of what is transmitted from generation to generation is what actually is, rather than what should be. This applies to ethnic and socioeconomic issues as well as to many other aspects of American life. Because many of the prevailing societal views and values about ethnicity and socioeconomic class are biased, students are exposed to an educational structure that reproduces the ethnic and socioeconomic disparities in outcomes.

Some educators with a neo-Marxist perspective see purpose behind the bias in the schools' structure. They believe it is only one of many biased structures that the European American middle and upper classes, especially males, have set up throughout society to maintain their economic and social power and position. That is, they believe that those who exercise control and power in our society—middle- and upper-class European American males—structure its institutions, including schools, to maintain their special position by reproducing the inequality that serves their interests (118–131). Thus, they use schools to maintain an ethnic, class, and gender division of labor. According to these theorists, schools provide non–European American, poor, and female students with the kinds of educational experiences that maintain them as a source of cheap, though well-prepared, labor, whereas more affluent European males are trained to be the leaders of society. At the same time, schools teach poor, non–European American, and female students to accept the status quo—their economic and social inferiority.

Giroux has described three ways in which schools could be said to reproduce inequality:

> *First, schools provided different classes and social groups with knowledge and skills they needed to occupy their respective places in a labor force stratified by class, race, and gender. Second, schools were seen as reproductive in the cultural sense, functioning in part to distribute and legitimate forms of knowledge, value, language, and modes of style that constitute the dominant culture and its interests. Third, schools were viewed as part of a state apparatus that produced and legitimated the economic and ideological imperatives that underlie the state's political power. (123, p. 258)*

Grant and Sleeter claim that

> *School plays a major role in the culture students develop. Like the family and neighborhood, school affects how students understand and pursue their life chances. It provides an institutional ideology, socializing agents, and an experiential context within which students define and shape the way they think about their personal dreams. The school context, containing social relations defined by race, social class, and gender, can produce a student culture in which young people accept and live out their parents' place in a stratified society, in spite of the school's espoused mission as equalizer and escalator to a better life. (125, p. 19)*

Reproduction theorists criticize the schools for the disparity between the lower level of funding for schools that serve students from poor and non–European American neighborhoods, the use of tracking and ability grouping to separate European American middle-class students from other students, and the use of the community college system to prevent working-class and minority students from enrolling in four-year colleges. They claim that females, especially minority and poor females, are exposed to two separate but related forces in the schools—those designed to maintain middle- and upper-class hegemony over the poor and those designed to maintain male hegemony over females. The following quotation is an example of their point of view. Although it focuses on Native American females' educational experiences in government run schools, it exemplifies what they think about the education many non-European women receive.

> *The government's master plan for Indian women has been to generate an endless stream of domestics, and to a lesser extent, secretaries. The vocational choices for native children in boarding schools have always been sexist: boys do woodworking, car repair, house painting or farmwork; while girls do domestic or secretarial*

work. . . . When we look at the occupations of native women in this country today, it should come as no surprise to find us locked into the nations' female work ghetto employees; it was designed that way. (115, pp. 47–48)

Resistance, Production, and Transformation

Neo-Marxist reproduction theorists also suggest that although students are being exposed to ethnic, socioeconomic, and gender biases in school and society at large, they are also being exposed to ideas and experiences that contradict these biases. These theorists note that egalitarian ideas are available in the media and in the materials students read in school. In addition, many teachers do not believe in the current class, ethnic, and gender biases. Thus, bombarded by conflicting messages, students do not passively accept the biases presented to them. Instead, they are constantly involved in a process of accommodating to some messages and resisting others (132–159).

According to reproduction theorists, especially those with a neo-Marxist perspective, students are alienated, distrustful, angry, and disillusioned about the problems inherent in attending schools that are structured to maintain inequality, but many of them also realize that schools are merely one aspect of a society structured against them. These theorists believe that many students also know that even if they do well in school, a society stratified along class, ethnic, and gender lines will not afford them the same benefits that European American upper-class males receive from succeeding in school. Therefore, instead of acquiescing to the educational system for payoffs they do not believe will be forthcoming, they battle against the system to maintain their own sense of identity.

There are significant ethnic, socioeconomic, and gender differences in how students resolve these contradictions (132, 140, 154). This makes sense when one considers the fact that students from different ethnic, socioeconomic, and gender backgrounds have somewhat different options available to them for resolving the contradictory pressures they experience.

Some students accommodate more than they resist; others actively resist the biased education they receive and the inferior position it threatens to place them in. Some defy schools' ethnic, socioeconomic, and gender biases in nonconstructive ways. They purposefully misbehave in aggressive or sexual ways, tune out their teachers, refuse to do their homework, come late to school, drop out before graduating, decide not to participate in higher education, and so on (133, 134, 146–148, 150, 154).

Other students battle the same forces in constructive ways. They reject the biased ideas they are exposed to. Instead, they assert their own experiences, heighten their own sense of self-identity, and leave school transformed into a new person with a new understanding of their ethnicity, gender, and class and with the knowledge, skills, value, and self-awareness they require to contribute to transforming society (129, 140, 141, 143). Thus, for some students, schools reproduce the stereotypes prevalent in society, whereas in other cases schools actually help students to reject these stereotypes.

Some theorists believe that society and schools are not equally biased against all non-European students. They believe that the European American dominant class differentiates between voluntary immigrants and involuntary, subordinated caste-like groups such as African Americans, Native Americans, Puerto Rican Americans, and Mexican Americans. Voluntary immigrants, according to their way of thinking, are those who chose to come to the United States. Involuntary immigrants are those who were brought here as slaves (e.g., African Americans) or who were incorporated into the United States against their will by conquest (e.g., Native Americans and Mexican Americans). Voluntary immigrants are likely to be accepted into society as equals once they have assimilated, and they tend to be the preferred non–European Americans because they most resemble the original northern European American settlers of the continent. Involuntary groups, however, are unlikely to be accepted as equals, regardless of what they do, for three reasons: the history of their relationship with the dominant European Americans; the myths European Americans have created about their innate inferiority in order to justify the conquest of their land, the eradication of their culture, and the enslavement of their ancestors; and the fact that they do not resemble European Americans in either looks or behavior.

European Americans are willing to accept voluntary immigrants into their country clubs and into some high-status positions, and school personnel are willing to tolerate their cultural differences at least to some degree. Involuntary caste-like groups are not treated as well socially or vocationally, and in school, the cultural differences between them and European Americans are devalued, disliked, and squashed because these groups have been deemed inferior for hundreds of years.

According to these theorists, students from the subordinated groups are less willing to play the educational game according to the rules established by their oppressors. They reject and resist school because of the prejudicial treatment they receive no matter how much they accomplish academically. Their point of view is aptly expressed by Ogbu.

> *All minority children encounter social adjustment and academic learning problems, at least initially. For some minority groups these tend to diminish over time, so that they eventually learn more or less successfully. For some other minority groups the problems tend to persist and may even increase in magnitude and seriousness. . . . The main factor differentiating the more successful from the less successful minorities appears to be the nature of the history, subordination, and exploitation of the minorities, and the nature of the minorities' own instrumental and expressive responses to their treatment which enter in the process of their schooling.*
>
> *[These subordinate minorities] develop a new sense of social identity in opposition to the social identity of the dominant group after they have become subordinated and they do so in reaction to the way that dominant-group members treat them in social, political, economic, and psychological domains. [They] do not really believe that they have an equal chance with white Americans to get ahead through education. They tend to reject or attack the criteria by which aca-*

demic achievement is measured and also the use of educational qualifications or measures as a criterion for employment in some situations.

The relationship between involuntary minorities and white Americans, who control the public schools, characterized by conflict and distrust, contributes to the minorities' social adjustment and academic performance problems. . . . Involuntary minorities do not necessarily accept or interpret school rules of behavior and standard practices in the same way that white people and immigrants do. The latter seem to endorse the rules and standard practices as necessary. . . . Involuntary minorities appear, on the other hand, to interpret the same rules and standard practices as an imposition of the white frame of reference, which does not necessarily meet their educational needs.

[As a result, those involuntary minorities students who are rebelling against the schools] do not work hard, and spend limited time on academic tasks; they avoid taking "hard"/"difficult"/"white" courses; they tend to be satisfied with average grades; although the children may do their homework, they do not routinely study; they do not usually separate academic tasks from their activities; they seem to prefer peer solidarity to schoolwork and easily submit to peer pressures that take them away from their schoolwork; they distrust school authorities with whom they are frequently in conflict; and they have a tendency to resist following school rules and standard practices. (148, pp. 317, 323, 324, 333, 334)

Like those who believe in the cultural difference explanation, those who share Ogbu's point of view want schools to offer culturally relevant and culturally appropriate educational experiences to minorities. However, they also believe that society as a whole must be reformed in ways that give non–European American students confidence that if they succeed in school they will reap the benefits of their success.

Implications

Although neo-Marxist reproduction theorists believe that it is important to eliminate class, cultural, and gender inequities in the schools, their ultimate goal is to transform the very nature of the public schools. Neo-Marxists want teachers to prepare students to resist the reproductive forces of society in more constructive ways and above all to change both the schools and the social and economic structure of the society they serve instead of preparing students to fit into the capitalist status quo (129, 155, 156).

The ultimate purpose of radical pedagogy is not simply one of changing people's consciousness or restructuring schools along more democratic principles; the latter aims are important but are reformist in nature and incomplete when viewed within a radical problematic. At the core of any radical pedagogy must be the aim of empowering people to recognize and work for a change in the social, political, and economic structure that constitutes the ultimate source of class-based power and domination. (122, p. 427)

Criticisms

Many educators are critical of the major assumptions underlying the theory of structured reproduction. Some critics question whether schools are actually structured in ways that reproduce the inequalities found in society at large; many more believe that even if schools do help to reproduce inequality there is no evidence that this is part of a purposeful plan by those in power to maintain the status quo; and many do not agree with the distinction between voluntary immigrants and caste-like groups. For example, Treuba challenges the claim that Mexican Americans are a caste-like group.

> *Ogbu has described "caste-like" groups, and Mexican Americans in particular, as being composed of individuals who live involuntarily in this country, occupy menial positions, and remain at the bottom of the educational and economic ladder, failing to incorporate into mainstream American society. . . . In the case of Mexicans, classified by Ogbu as an exemplary caste-like group, we have obtained recent empirical evidence from studies showing that there is educational progress, an increase in English language proficiency, and upward mobility taking place among the Mexican families in California and Arizona, and that the improvement is incremental across generations over a period of time. (157, pp. 276–277)*

Treuba goes on to explain that the apparent lack of progress of many Mexican Americans in such states as California is not due to their caste-like condition but to the large numbers of recent immigrants who have not had time to be incorporated into the American educational economic and social systems.

> *The overwhelming majority of people who recognize themselves as Mexicans (85%) are either foreign born or first generation U.S. born. . . . High dropout rates are much more characteristic of the Mexican born, who constitute a large proportion of the current Latino population in the state. Dropout rates among the U.S. born Latinos are not much higher than those of all Californians. Comparing the occupational profiles of Mexican born with those of U.S. born, and both with that of all Californians, we find the following distribution: Highly skilled jobs, professional, teacher, manager, technician, sales clerk, account for 5% of Mexican born, 12% of U.S. born Mexican origin, and 27% of all Californians. Service jobs account for 14%, 33%, and 34% respectively. Semi-skilled jobs represent respectively 21%, 20%, and 19%. Farm jobs, 15%, 6%, and 3%. Unskilled, 45%, 29%, and 17%. (157, p. 277)*

Research

There is a great deal of evidence to support the contention that the structure of American schools contributes to the reproduction of ethnic and socioeconomic inequality. Examples of the relevant research follow.

Financing

Local and state governments spend less money on educating poor and non–European American students and provide them with less adequate instructional materials and equipment, especially in the areas of computer technology and science (158–170). Per-pupil expenditures for schools serving students in poor and non-European communities are considerably below those for European American middle-class students. For example, in Kentucky the per-pupil cost ranged from a low of $1,800 to a high of $4,200. In Texas the per capita expenditure on education in the 100 poorest school districts was less than $3,000 compared to the more than $7,000 spent on pupils attending the 100 richest school districts. In New Jersey the gap between the amount of money spent per pupil by the richest and poorest districts was more than $10,000 (165). The per-pupil expenditure for students in New York City, a predominantly non–European American poor student population, was $4,351 compared to $6,605, $6,539, and $5,852 in the three surrounding suburban counties (168). The results of these disparities are reflected in the availability of equipment and materials, especially computers and science laboratory equipment, for academic courses, the availability of nonacademic course offerings, the quality of the educational staff, and so on. Karp describes the effects of the disparities in spending for education in these three states in the following way:

> *These numbers translate into daily injustices for school kids. Princeton's high school science students study in seven modern, well-equipped labs and student athletes can play golf, field hockey and lacrosse in addition to baseball, basketball and football. In Jersey City, middle-school science students have no labs at all while in East Orange, NJ, the track team practices in a second floor corridor. In rural Kentucky, elementary schools have done without music and art teachers. In one poor Texas district students study computer science by pretending to type on an artificial paper replica of a computer keyboard. (165, p. 1, 14)*

Even programs specifically designed to serve poor students are underfinanced. At the height of their financial support in 1980, compensatory educational programs only served 57% of the 9,000,000 eligible students. Since then the program has experienced repeated cutbacks. Even Head Start only reaches 18% of eligible students (159).

Tracking and Ability Grouping

As reported earlier, research confirms that poor and non–European American students are much more likely to be placed in low-track and low-ability groups than are European American middle-class students. Tracking and ability grouping has been justified on the grounds that

> *students learn better when they are grouped with other students who are similar to them academically; that the placement process used to sort students into groups is accurate and fair and, in addition, reflects past achievements and*

innate abilities; that slower students develop more positive attitudes in relation to themselves and their schools if they are not sorted into groups with students who are more capable; that it is easier for teachers to accommodate individual differences in homogeneous groups; that similar students are easier to manage. (172, p. 94)

However, research on these approaches indicates that they typically do more harm than good (169, pp. 171–182). Students placed in low-ability groups do not learn better. After reviewing the research, Lake concluded:

Once in a low track, students rarely switch tracks after grade three. Schools do not help them to move into a higher track. By the end of the primary grades students are set into rigid ability tracks correlating to their race and socioeconomic status. The effects last even longer than the school years. (176, abstract)

In a similar vein, Oakes reported:

The typical ways elementary schools respond to students' performance may help to "fix" students' perceptions of their ability to learn and, over time, may actually exaggerate initial differences among them. . . . At the high school level, whether a student is enrolled in an academic (college-preparatory) or non-academic program has an independent effect on achievement. Students who are initially similar in background and aptitude exhibit increased achievement differences resulting from their placements in higher and lower tracks. . . . Students placed in low-ability groups in elementary school are likely to continue in these tracks in middle schools and junior highs; in senior high they typically are found in non-college-preparatory tracks.

In the data about curriculum paths, course offerings, and track-related classroom differences, we find that the differentiated structure of schools often throws up barriers to achievement and participation of poor and minority students. Measures of ability work against them, which leads to minimal course offerings at their schools and these students' disproportionate placement in groups identified as "slow." Once in these classes, their success seems to be further inhibited by the type of knowledge they are taught and by the quality of the learning experiences that are afforded. (179, pp. 115–116, 118–119)

Students in low tracks and ability groups do not improve their self-esteem. On the contrary, they experience a loss of self-esteem and a worsening of their attitudes towards school.

Students do not receive the instructional approaches and attention they require. In fact, research clearly demonstrates the opposite. Schools spend less money on students in low-ability groups. They are counseled less often. They are exposed to a watered-down curriculum and treated poorly by their teachers, who call on them less often, criticize them more often, praise them less frequently, give them less help and feedback, expect less from them, and so on.

Management problems are typically increased rather than diminished by grouping students into low-ability groups and tracks because students tend to be more disruptive and teachers tend to interrupt the academic work more often to deal with discipline problems. After studying the effects of ability grouping, Eder concluded:

> *Students in low groups were instructed in an environment characterized by disruptions from the teacher as well as from other members. In other words, those students who were likely to have more difficulty learning were inadvertently assigned to groups whose social contexts were much less conducive for learning. (173, p. 159)*

Finally, students are not placed in ability groups in an accurate and fair manner. On the contrary, as noted earlier, non–European American and poor students are often assigned to low-ability groups in a biased manner when objective evaluation of their academic functioning would not justify their placement, and in some cases, ability grouping is used to resegregate students, not to enhance their learning. This topic will be discussed later in this chapter.

Community colleges serve to track students rather than to provide them with the opportunity to achieve their potential (183–187). Research reveals that non–European and poor students are grossly overrepresented in the two-year college system. Many of the programs in which they enroll do not lead to viable occupations. The majority of students drop out before completing their programs. Of those that graduate, few go on to earn degrees at four-year colleges. As a result, the community/two-year college system serves to segregate non–European American students in an educational system that does not typically lead to the completion of a four-year college degree or the attainment of sufficient vocational skills to obtain a high-paying or prestigious job. The following quotations are representative of the conclusions of many of the critics of the community college system.

> *The rise of two year systems in some cities raises the unmistakable impression that such systems were established in order to preserve the status quo and to enable senior institutions to remain inaccessible to minority students. (186, pp. XIII–XIV)*
>
> *The two year college system in the United States is a system of whites, it is controlled and operated by whites, and reserves its major rewards for whites. (184, p. 42)*
>
> *Hispanics have made few appreciable gains in either their participation or achievement in community colleges. The fact remains that few Hispanics earn college credentials, graduate, or transfer to senior institutions. (185, p. 139)*

Socioeconomic-Class Differences in School Structure

A study comparing two comprehensive high schools serving students in both a poor and an affluent neighborhood in the same city, discovered the following differences (166).

	Poor Neighborhood	Middle-Class Neighborhood
Campus	Fenced in, security guards	Open , no security guards
Selection of courses	Students select courses	No choice of courses
Dress code	No dress code	Dress code
Teacher resources invested in	Vocational and general tracks	Academic track
Courses emphasized	Physical education, home economics, industrial arts, business education, special education	Science, math, language arts, fine arts, and foreign languages
Program for mentally gifted minors	Available	None available
Academic courses	Restricted to basic level	Many advanced courses offered
Industrial arts course and apprenticeship programs geared to	Blue-collar jobs	White-collar jobs
Graduates advised to attend	Two-year colleges	Four-year colleges

Resistance, Production, and Transformation

Although there has not been a great deal of research on the topic, the available evidence suggests that many non-European and poor students are alienated, distrustful, angry, and disillusioned about the schools they attend and believe that even if they do well in school, they will not obtain the same benefits that European American upper-class males receive from succeeding in school (188–192). Studies indicate that African American middle school and high school students feel alienated and distrustful about their teachers, the schools they attend, and the American political system (187, 191, 192). Research also suggests that although African American students think that getting a good education is important, many of them do not believe that education necessarily leads to a good job (189, 190). In one study, over 50% of 10- to 15-year-old African American students did not believe that a high school diploma led to a good job (189). Although they did not report specific percentages, the authors of another study observed that many African American male high school students had similar doubts and speculated:

> If African American male youth feel that racism hampers the "cashing in of their educational check," it is probably valid to assume that they will not take full advantage of the educational opportunities that their schools have to offer. (190, p. 12)

There is also evidence that Native American and African American high school graduates do not reap the benefits a high school diploma affords European American students. For example, a recent study indicated that with rare exceptions Native American students who graduated from high school obtained the same "menial or service-industry positions" as dropouts (193).

Conclusions

One may believe that schools *simply reflect* the biases that permeate society, that "education does not create the sexual division of labour, nor the kinds of work available in the labour market, nor the class relationships of society, but it rarely does anything to undermine them" (121, p. 20). Or one may agree that European American middle and upper-class males *purposely* structured schools in ways that reproduce their power in society, that "schools provided different classes and social groups with knowledge and skills they needed to occupy their respective places in a labor force stratified by class, race, and gender" (122, p. 258). Whether the current situation is purposeful or not, it is clear that despite the progress that has occurred in providing equal educational opportunities to all students, the educational systems perpetuate inequality both in school and in the larger society, and cause many students to misbehave, tune out, and drop out.

We currently lack the knowledge to predict which students will accept the prevailing biases more than they resist them and which will resist more than succumb, and we certainly cannot predict the manner in which they will resist.

School Resegregation

Some individuals claim that strict disciplinary measures and ability grouping and tracking are often employed to resegregate desegregated school systems and to reinstitute the unequal educational opportunity that accompanies segregation rather than to improve instruction and classroom management,

> Many school systems remain segregated "even after a court ordered desegregation plan has been fully implemented." Through such practices as unequal application of disciplinary measures, ability grouping and educational placement, minority students continue to receive uneven and unfair treatment. They have been, in effect, resegregated. (194, p. 184)

There is considerable evidence to support this contention (187–210). The use of more severe forms of discipline, ability grouping, and tracking was increased significantly in desegregated school systems, especially in the South during the late 1960s and 1970s (114, 195, 197, 206, 208, 210). Desegregation has also been accompanied by a tendency toward the inflexible administration of strict disciplinary codes and an increased use of corporal punishment and suspensions with African American students (202, 203). For example, during the first year of the desegregation of the Milwaukee school system, of the 22 schools who increased their African American student enrollment, 16 had increases in their suspension rates, and of the 11 schools that experienced a decline in African American student enrollment, 8 also experienced a decrease in their suspension rates (203).

Summary

A number of factors contribute to the poor academic achievement of many non–European American students. Their education is often contextually, culturally, and linguistically inappropriate. Too often teachers, psychologists, and administrators are prejudiced against them. In some cases they are assigned to low-ability tracks and groups in order to maintain segregation. When they realize that both schools and society in general are structured in ways that reproduce ethnic and socioeconomic inequality, many of them resist the prejudice and hostility they experience in nonconstructive ways.

Activities

1. Interview students from different ethnic and socioeconomic backgrounds in the courses you are taking about some of the issues discussed in this chapter. Do their opinions vary with their ethnic or socioeconomic backgrounds?

2. Review the textbooks and other materials your professors assign in the courses you are taking. Do they deal with the diversity issues inherent in the topics they cover? Do they focus exclusively or primarily on European Americans to the exclusion of other ethnic groups?

3. Compare your professors in terms the time they devote to the diversity issues inherent in the courses they teach. Do you find that some professors are more sensitive to and interested in diversity issues than others?

References

The special problems of immigrant and refugee students that are not met by the educational system are discussed in the following references.

1. Cervantes, R. C., Salgado de Snyder, V. N., & Padilla, A. M. (1988). *Post Traumatic Stress Disorder among Immigrants from Central America and Mexico.* Los Angeles: University of California, Spanish Speaking Mental Health Resource Center.

2. Juffer, K. A. (1983). Culture shock: A theoretical framework for understanding adaptation. In J. Bransford (Ed.), *Monograph Series: BUENO Center for Multicultural Education, 4,* 136–149.

3. National Coalition of Advocates for Students. (1988). *New Voices: Immigrant Students in the Public Schools.* Boston: Author.

4. Nguyen, T. P. (1987). Positive self-concept in the Vietnamese bilingual child. In M. Dao (Ed.), *From Vietnamese to Vietnamese American: Selected Articles.* San Jose, CA: Division of Special Education and Rehabilitative Services, San Jose State University.

5. Olsen, L. (1988). *Crossing the Schoolhouse Border: Immigrant Students and the California Public Schools.* San Francisco: California Tomorrow.

6. Padilla, A. M., Lindholm, K. J., Alvarez, M., & Wagatsuma, Y. (1985). *Acculturative Stress in Immigrant Students: Three Papers.* Los Angeles: University of California, Spanish Speaking Mental Health Resource Center.

7. Wei, T. T. D. (1980). *Vietnamese Refugee Students: A Handbook for School Personnel.*, (2nd ed.). ERIC ED 208–109.

These references discuss the unmet educational needs of Native American students.

8. Bureau of Indian Affairs. (1988, March). *Report on B. I. A. Education: Final Review Draft.* Washington, DC: Department of the Interior.

9. Chavez, R. C., Belkin, L. D., Hornback, J. G., & Adams, K. (1991). Dropping out of school: Issues affecting culturally, ethnically, and linguistically distinct student groups. *Journal of Educational Issues of Language Minority Students, 8,* 1–21.

The contextual problems of migrant students are discussed in the following references.

10. Center for Educational Planning. (1989). *Migrant Education Dropout Prevention Project Final Report.* ERIC ED 321–951.

11. Interstate Migrant Education Council. (1987). *Migrant Education: A Consolidated View.* ERIC ED 285–701.

12. Interstate Migrant Secondary Services Program. (1985). *Survey Analysis: Responses of 1070 Students in High School Equivalency Programs, 1984–1985.* ERIC ED 264–070.

13. Johnson, F., Levy, R., Morales, J., Morse, S., & Prokop, M. (1986). *Migrant Students at the Secondary Level: Issues and Opportunities for Change.* ERIC ED 270–242.

14. Lawless, K. (1986). *Neediest of the Needy: Special Education for Migrants. Harvesting the Harvesters,* Book 8. ERIC ED 279–473.

15. Migrant Attrition Project. (1987). *Migrant Attrition Project: Abstract of Findings.* Oneonta, NY: State University of New York at Oneonta.

16. Rasmussen, L. (1988). *Migrant Students at the Secondary Level: Issues and Opportunities for Change.* Las Cruces: New Mexico State University, ERIC/CRESS.

The special problems of rural students are described in the following references.

17. Berkeley, T. R., & Ludlow, B. L. (1991). Meeting the needs of special student populations in rural areas. In A. J. DeYoung (Ed.), *Rural Education: Issues and Practices.* New York: Garland.

18. Brown, D. L. (1989). Demographic trends relevant to education in nonmetropolitan America. In *Rural Education—A Changing Landscape.* Washington, DC: U.S. Department of Education.

19. Helge, D. (1984). The state of the art of rural special education. *Exceptional Children, 50,* 294–305.

20. Helge, D. (1989). *Rural Family-Community Partnerships: Resources.* ERIC ED 320–736.

21. Helge, D. (1991). *Rural, Exceptional, At Risk.* Reston, VA: Council for Exceptional Children.

22. Leadership for Special Education. A Conversation with Robert R. Davila. (1989). *Education of the Handicapped,* September 13, 28.

23. National Council on Disabilities. (1989). *The Education of Students with Disabilities: Where Do We Stand?* Washington, DC: Author.

24. Students at Risk. (1990). *Education Week,* October 19, 26.

25. O'Connor, C., Murr, A., & Wingert, P. (1986). Affluent America's forgotten children, *Newsweek, 107*(22), 20–21.

26. Pollard, K. M., & O'Hare, W. P. (1990). *Beyond High School: The Experience of Rural and Urban Youth in the 1980's.* ERIC ED 326–363.

27. Phelps, M. S., & Prock, G. A. (1991). Equality of educational opportunity in rural America. In A. DeYoung (Ed.), *Rural Education Issues and Practice.* New York: Garland.

These references concern the contextual problems of homeless children and adolescents.

28. Bass, J. L., Brennan, P., Mehta, K. A., & Kodzis, S. (1990). Pediatric problems in a suburban shelter for homeless families. *Pediatrics, 85*(1), 33–38.

29. Bassuk, E. L., & Gallagher, E. M. (1990). The impact of homelessness on children. In N. A. Boxill (Ed.), *Homeless Children: The Watchers and the Waiters.* Binghamton, NY: Haworth.

30. Bassuk, F., & Rubin, L. (1987). Homeless children: A neglected population. *American Journal of Orthopsychiatry, 57*(2), 279–286.

31. Bowen, J. M., Purrington, G. S., Layton, D. H., & O'Brien, K. (1989). *Educating Homeless Children and Youth: A Policy Analysis.* Paper presented at the annual conference of the American Educational Research Association, San Francisco.

32. Eddowes, A., & Hranitz., J. R. (1989). Education children of the homeless. *Childhood Education: Infancy through Early Adolescence, 65*(4), 197–200.

33. Friedman, L., & Christiansen, G. (1990). *Shut Out: Denial of Education to Homeless Children.* ERIC ED 320–987.

34. Heflin, L. J., & Rudy, K. (1991). *Homeless and in Need of Special Education.* Reston, VA: Council for Exceptional Children.

35. Miller, D. S., & Linn, E. H. B. (1988). Children in sheltered homeless families: Reported health status and use of health services. *Pediatrics, 81*, 668–673.

36. Rafferty, Y., & Rollins, N. (1989a). *Learning in Limbo: The Educational Deprivation of Homeless Children.* Long Island City: Advocates for Children of New York.

37. Rafferty, Y., & Rollins, N. (1989b). *Homeless Children: Educational Challenges for the 1990's.* ERIC ED 325–589.

38. Rescoria, L., Parker, R., & Stolley, P. (1991). Ability, achievement and adjustment in homeless children. *American Journal of Orthopsychiatry, 61*(2), 210–220.

39. Rivlin, L. G. (1990). Home and homelessness in the lives of children. In N. A. Boxill (Ed.), *Homeless Children: The Watchers and the Waiters.* Binghamton, NY: Haworth.

40. Rosenman, M., & Stein, M. L. (1990). Homeless children: A new vulnerability. In N. A. Boxill (Ed.), *Homeless Children: The Watchers and the Waiters.* Binghamton, NY: Haworth

41. Russell, S. C., & Williams, E. U. (1988). Homeless handicapped children: A special education perspective. Children's Environments Quarterly, 5(1), 3–7.

42. Schumack, S. (Ed.). (1987). *The Educational Rights of Homeless Children.* ERIC ED 288–915.

43. Stronge, J. H., & Helm, V. M. (1990). *Residency and Guardianship Requirements as Barriers to the Education of Homeless Children and Youth.* ERIC ED 319–845.

44. Stronge, J. H., & Tenhouse, C. (1990). *Educating Homeless Children: Issues and Answers.* Bloomington, IN: Phi Delta Kappa Educational Foundation.

45. Wright, J. D. (1990). Homelessness is not healthy for children and other living things. In N. A. Boxill (Ed.), *Homeless Children: The Watchers and the Waiters.* Binghamton, NY: Haworth.

The effects of cultural differences is dealt with in the following references.

46. Baratz, S. S., & Baratz, J. C. (1975). Early childhood intervention: The social science basis of institutional racism. In *Challenging the Myth: The Schools, the Blacks, and the Poor.* Cambridge, MA: *Harvard Educational Review,* Reprint Series No. 5, pp. 111–132.

47. Federal Regional Resource Center. (1991). *Exploring the Education Issues of Cultural Diversity.* Lexington, KY: Interdisciplinary Human Development Institute, University of Kentucky.

48. Hurn, C. J. (1985). *The Limits and Possibilities of Schooling: An Introduction to the Sociology of Education,* (2nd ed.). Boston: Allyn and Bacon.

49. Lubeck, S. (1988). Nested contexts. In L. Weis, *Class, Race, and Gender in American Education.* Albany, NY: State University of New York Press, pp. 46–47.

The following reference discusses reasons why students may get into trouble in school for behaving in ways that are acceptable in their communities.

50. Grossman, H. (1984). *Educating Hispanic Students: Cultural Implications for Instruction, Classroom Management, Counseling and Assessment.* Springfield, IL: Charles C Thomas.

Examples of the opinions of writers in the 1970s, 1980s, and 1990s about prejudice in schools are found in the following references

51. Becker, A. (1980). *The Role of the School in the Maintenance and Change of Ethnic Group Affiliation.* ERIC ED 259–052.

52. Bennett, C., & Harris, J. J. (1982). Suspension and expulsion of male and black students: A case study of the causes of disproportionality. *Urban Education, 16*(4), 399–423.

53. National Black Child Development Institute. (1990). *The Status of African American Children: Twentieth Anniversary Report.* Washington, DC.

54. Rist, R. C. (1971). Student social class and teacher expectations: The self fulfilling prophecy in ghetto education. In *Challenging the Myths: The Schools The Blacks and the Poor.* Cambridge, MA: *Harvard Educational Review.* Reprint Series No. 5.

55. Stein, A. (1971), Strategies for failure. In *Challenging the Myths: The Schools The Blacks and*

the Poor. Cambridge, MA: *Harvard Educational Review.* Reprint Series No. 5.

The following references describe studies that did not find teacher bias.

56. Flynn, T. M. (1983). IQ tests and placement. *Integrated Education, 21,* 124–126.
57. Heller, E. J. (1985). Pupil race and elementary school ability grouping: Are teachers biased against black children? *American Educational Research Journal, 22*(4), 465–483.
58. Huebner, E. S., & Cummings, J. A. (1986). Influence of race and test data ambiguity upon school psychologists' decisions. *School Psychology Review, 15*(3), 410–417.
59. Jaeger, R., & Freijo. T. (1975). Race and sex as concomitants of composite halo in teachers' evaluative ratings of pupils. *Journal of Educational Psychology, 67*(2), 226–237.
60. Matuszek, P., & Oakland, T. (1979). Factors influencing teachers' and psychologists' recommendations regarding special class placement. *Journal of School Psychology, 17*(2), 116–125.
61. Moacdieh, C. (1981). *Grouping for Reading in the Primary Grades: Evidence on the Revisionist Theory.* ERIC ED 200–938.
62. Tobias, S., Zibrin, M., & Menell, D. (1983). *Special Education Referrals: Failure to Replicate Student—Teacher Ethnicity Interaction.* ERIC ED 224–221.
63. Wiley, M., & Eskilson, A. (1978). Why did you learn in school today? Teachers' perceptions of causality. *Sociology of Education, 51,* 261–269.

The references listed below describe teachers' biased expectations for students.

64. Beady, C. H., & Hansell, S. (1980). *Teacher Race and Expectations for Student Achievement.* ERIC ED 200–695.
65. Bennet, C. I. (1979). The effects of student characteristics and task performance on teacher expectations and attributions. *Dissertation Abstracts International, 40,* 979–980-B.
66. Campos F. (1983). *The Attitudes and Expectations of Student Teachers and Cooperating Teachers Toward Students in Predominantly Mexican American Schools: A Qualitative Data Perspective.* ERIC ED 234–026.
67. Dao, M. (1991). Designing assessment procedures for educationally at-risk Southeast Asian-American students. *Journal of Learning Disabilities, 24*(10), 594–601, 629.

68. Derlega, V., Wang, P., & Colson, W. (1981). *Racial Bias in Expectancies and Performance Attributions.* Unpublished manuscript. Norfolk,VA: Old Dominion University.
69. Dusek, J. B., & Joseph, G. (1983). The bases of teacher expectancies: A meta-analysis. *Journal of Educational Psychology, 75,*(3), 327–346.
70. Figueroa, R. A., & Gallegos, E. A. (1978). Ethnic differences in school behavior. *Sociology of Education, 51,* 289–298.
71. Grant, L. (1984). Black females' "place" in desegregated classrooms. *Sociology of Education, 57,* 98–110.
72. Matute-Bianchi, M. E. (1986). Ethnic identities and patterns of school success and failure among Mexican-descent and Japanese-American students in a California high school: An ethnographic analysis. *American Journal of Education, 95*(1), 233–255.
73. Metheny, W. (1979). *The Influences of Grade and Pupil Ability Levels on Teachers' Conceptions of Reading.* ERIC ED 182–713.
74. Mizokawa, D. T., & Morishima, J. K. (1979). *Education for, by, and of Asian/Pacific Americans. I.* ERIC ED 199–355.
75. Ogbu, J. U. (1978). *Minority Education and Caste: The American in Cross-Cultural Perspective.* New York: Academic Press.
76. Smith, J. A. (1979). Ascribed and achieved student characteristics in teacher expectancy: Relationship of socioeconomic status to academic achievement, academic self-concept, and vocational aspirations. *Dissertation Abstracts International, 40,* 959–960-B.
77. Sue, S., & Kitano, H. H. L. (1973). Stereotypes as a measure of success. *Journal of Social Issues, 29*(3), 83–98.
78. Takeuchi, S. M. (1972). *Verbal Skills and the Asian American Student.* ERIC ED 097–395.
79. Wilkerson, M. A. (1980). The effects of sex and ethnicity upon teachers' expectations of students. *Dissertation Abstracts International, 41,* 637-A.

The following references discuss bias in teachers' evaluations of students.

80. Davis, S. A. (1974). *Students' SES as Related to Teachers' Perceptions and Ability Grouping Decisions.* ERIC ED 090–487.
81. DeMeis, D., & Turner, R. (1978). Effects of students' race, physical attractiveness, and dialect on teachers' evaluations. *Contemporary Educational Psychology, 3,* 77–86.

82. Eaves, R. (1975). Teacher race, student race, and the behavior problem checklist. *Journal of Abnormal Child Psychology, 3*(1), 1–9.

83. Elliot, S. N., & Argulewicz, E. N. (1983). The influence of student ethnicity on teachers' behavior ratings of normal and learning disabled children. *Hispanic Journal of Behavioral Sciences, 5*(3), 337–345.

84. Granger, R. E., Mathews, M., Quay, L. C., & Verner, R. (1977). Teacher judgements of communication effectiveness of children using different speech patterns. *Journal of Educational Psychology, 69*(6), 793–796.

85. Haller, E. J., & Davis, S. A. (1980). Does socioeconomic status bias the assignment of elementary school students to reading groups? *American Educational Research Journal, 17*(40), 409–418.

86. Ishi-Jordan, S. (1992). *Effects of Students' Racial or Ethnic Background on Teacher Expectations and Intervention Selection for Problem Behaviors.* Paper presented at the Topical Conference on Cultural and Linguistically Diverse Exceptional Children. Minneapolis, MN.

87. Kim, Y. J. (1983). Problems in the delivery of the school-based psycho-educational services to the Asian immigrant children. *Journal of Children in Contemporary Society, 15*(3), 81–89.

88. Marwit, K., Marwit, S., & Walker, E. (1978). Effects of student race and physical attractiveness on teachers' judgements of transgressions. *Journal of Educational Psychology, 70,* 911–915.

89. Scheinfeld, D. R. (1983). Family relationships and school achievement among boys of lower-income urban black families. *American Journal of Orthopsychiatry, 53*(1), 127–143.

90. Taylor, J. B. (1983). Influence of speech variety on teachers' evaluation of reading comprehension. *Journal of Educational Psychology, 75*(5), 662–667.

91. Tobias, S., Cole, C., Zibrin, M., & Bodlakova, V. (1981). *Bias in the Referral of Children to Special Services.* ERIC ED 208–637.

92. Wong, M. G. (1980). Model students? Teachers' perceptions and expectations of their Asian and white students. *Sociology of Education, 53,* 236–246.

93. Yao, E. L. (1987). Asian-immigrants students—Unique problems that hamper learning. *NASSP Bulletin, 71*(503), 82–88.

Bias in teacher-student interactions is the focus of the following references.

94. Appleford, B., Fralick, P., & Ryan, T. J. (1976). *Teacher-Child Interactions as Related to Sex, Socio-Economic Status and Physical Attractiveness.* ERIC ED 138–869.

95. Barba, L. (1979). *A Survey of the Literature on the Attitudes Toward the Administration of Corporal Punishment in Schools.* ERIC ED 186–538.

96. Bickel, F., & Qualls, R. (1981). *The Impact of School Climate on Suspension Rates in the Jefferson County Public Schools.* Paper presented at the annual meeting of the American Educational Research Association, Boston.

97. Buriel, R. (1983). Teacher-student interactions and their relationship to student achievement: A comparison of Mexican-American children. *Journal of Educational Psychology, 75*(60), 889–897.

98. Friedman, P. (1976). Comparison of teacher reinforcement schedules for students with different social class backgrounds. *Journal of Educational Psychology, 68,* 286–293.

99. Glackman, T., Martin, R., Hyman, I., McDowell, E., Berv, V., & Spino, P. (1980). *Corporal Punishment in the Schools As It Relates to Race, Sex, Grade Level and Suspensions.* Philadelphia: Temple University, National Center for the Study of Corporal Punishment in the Schools.

100. Grant, L. (1985). Race-gender status, classroom interaction, and children's socialization in elementary school. In L. C. Wilkinson & C. B. Marrell (Eds.), *Gender Influences in Classroom Interaction.* New York: Academic Press.

101. Grossman, H., & Grossman, S. (1994). *Gender Issues in Education.* Needham, MA: Allyn and Bacon.

102. Guilmet, G. M. (1979). Instructor reaction to verbal and nonverbal styles: An example of Navajo and Caucasian children. *Anthropology and Education Quarterly, 10,* 254–266.

103. Hamilton, S. (1983). The social side of schooling. *Elementary School Journal, 83,* 313–334.

104. McGhan, B. R. (1978). *Teachers' Use of Authority and Its Relationship to Socioeconomic Status, Race, Teacher Characteristics, and Educational Outcomes.* ERIC ED 151–329.

105. Moody, C. D., Williams, J., & Vergon, C. B. (1978). *Student Rights and Discipline: Policies, Programs and Procedures.* ERIC ED 160–926.

106. Moore, W. L., & Cooper, H. (1984). Correlations between teacher and student back-

ground and teacher perception of discipline problems and disciplinary techniques. *Psychology in the Schools, 21,* 386–392.

107. Richardson, R. C., & Evans, E. T. (1991). *Empowering Teachers to Eliminate Corporal Punishment in the Schools.* Paper presented at the annual conference of the National Black Child Developmental Institute. Washington, DC.

108. Simpson, A. W., & Erickson, M. T. (1983). Teachers' verbal and nonverbal communication patterns as a function of teacher race, student gender and student race. *American Educational Research Journal, 20*(2), 183–198.

109. Stevens, L. B. (1983). *Suspension and Corporal Punishment of Students in the Cleveland Public Schools, 1981–1982.* Cleveland, OH: Office of School Monitoring and Community Relations.

110. Taylor, M. (1979). Race, sex and the expression of self-fulfilling prophecies in a laboratory teaching situation. *Journal of Personality and Social Psychology, 37*(6), 897–912.

111. Washington, V. (1982). Racial differences in teacher perception of first and fourth grade pupils on selected characteristics. *Journal of Negro Education, 51,* 60–72.

112. Woolridge, P., & Richman, C. (1985). Teachers' choice of punishment as a function of a student's gender, age, race and I.Q. level. *Journal of School Psychology, 23,* 19–29.

Apparent and real lack of bias and their effects are the focus of the following references.

113. Feldman, R., & Donohoe, L. (1978). Nonverbal communication of affect in interracial dyads. *Journal of Educational Psychology, 70*(6), 979–986.

114. Meier, K. J., Stewart, J. Jr., & England, R. E. (1989). *Race, Class, and Education: The Politics of Second-Generation Discrimination.* Madison, WI: University of Wisconsin Press.

115. Office for Civil Rights. (1982). *1980 Elementary and Secondary School Civil Rights Surveys.* Washington, DC: U.S. Department of Education.

116. Office of Civil Rights. (1987). *Elementary and Secondary School Civil Rights Survey, 1986. National Summaries.* ERIC ED 304–485.

117. Plata, M., & Chinn, P. C. (1989). Students with handicaps who have cultural and language differences. In R. Gaylord-Ross (Ed.), *Integration Strategies for Students with Handicaps.* Baltimore: Brookes.

References that discuss the role of schools in the reproduction of inequities in society are listed here.

118. Apple, M., & Weis, L. (Eds.). (1983). *Ideology and Practice in Schools.* Philadelphia: Temple University Press.

119. Bowles, S., & Gintes, H. (1977). *Schooling in Capitalist America.* New York: Basic Books.

120. Connell, R. W. (1989). Curriculum politics, hegemony, and strategies of social change. In H. A. Giroux & R. I. Simon (Eds.), *Popular Culture, Schooling and Everyday Life.* Granby, MA: Bergin & Garvey.

121. Deem, R. (1978). *Women and Schooling.* Boston: Routledge Kegan Paul.

122. Giroux, H. A. (1981). Hegemony, resistance, and the paradox of educational reform. In H. A. Giroux, A. N. Penna, & W. F. Pinar, *Curriculum & Instruction: Alternatives in Education.* Berkeley, CA: McCutchan.

123. Giroux, H. A. (1983). Theories of reproduction and resistance in the new sociology of education: A critical analysis. *Harvard Educational Review, 53*(3), 257–293.

124. Giroux, H. A., & Penna, A. N. (1988). Social education in the classroom: The dynamics of the hidden curriculum. In H. A. Giroux (Ed.), *Teachers as Intellectuals: Toward a Critical Pedagogy of Learning.* Granby, MA: Bergin & Garvey.

125. Grant, C. A., & Sleeter, C. E. (1988). Race, class, and gender and abandoned dreams. *Teachers College Record, 90*(1), 19–40.

126. Irvine, J. J. (1989). *Black Students and School Achievement: A Process Model of Relationships among Significant Variables.* ERIC ED 310–220.

127. Kelly, G., & Nihlen, A. (1982). Schooling and the reproduction of patriarchy: Unequal workloads, unequal rewards. In M. Apple (Ed.), *Culture and Economic Reproduction in Education.* Boston: Routledge Kegan Paul.

128. Valli, L. (1986). *Becoming Clerical Workers.* Boston: Routledge Kegan Paul.

129. Weiler, K. (1988). *Women Teaching for Change: Gender, Class & Power.* Granby, MA: Bergin & Garvey.

130. Witt, S. H. (1979). Native women in the world of work. In T. Constantino (Ed.), *Women of Color Forum: A Collection of Readings.* ERIC ED 191–975.

131. Wolpe, A. (1981). The official ideology of education for girls. In M. McDonald, R. Dale, G. Esland, & R. Fergusson, (Eds.), *Politics,*

Patriarchy and Practice. New York: Falmer Press.

The following references deal with student resistance to school.

132. Anyon, J. (1984). Intersections of gender and class: Accommodation and resistance by working class and affluent females to contradictory sex-role ideologies. *Journal of Education, 166*(1), 25–48.

133. Arnot, M. (1982). Male hegemony, social class and women's education. *Journal of Education, 164*(1), 64–89.

134. Bouie, A. (1981). *Student Perceptions of Behavior and Misbehavior in the School Setting: An Exploratory Study and Discussion.* San Francisco: Far West Laboratory for Educational Research and Development.

135. Comer, J. P. (1990). What makes the new generation tick? *Ebony,* October, 34–38.

136. Ford, D. Y. (1991). *Self-Perceptions of Social, Psychological, and Cultural Determinants of Achievement among Gifted Black Students: A Paradox of Underachievement.* Unpublished doctoral dissertation, Cleveland: Cleveland State University.

137. Ford, D. Y. (1992). The American achievement ideology and achievement differentials among preadolescent gifted and nongifted African American males and females. *Journal of Negro Education, 61*(1), 45–64.

138. Fordham, S. (1988). *Racelessness as a strategy in Black students' school success: Coping with the burden of "acting White."* Urban Review, 20, 176–207.

139. Fordham, S., & Ogbu, J. U. (1986). Black students' school success: Coping with the "burden of acting white." *Urban Review, 18*(3), 176–203.

140. Fuller, M. (1980). Black girls in a London comprehensive school. In R. Deem (Ed.), *Schooling for Women's Work.* Boston: Routledge and Kegan Paul.

141. Gaskell, J. (1985). Course enrollment in high school: The perspective of working class females. *Sociology of Education, 58*(1), 48–59.

142. Gibson, M. A. (1987). The school performance of immigrant minorities: A comparative view. *Anthropology and Education Quarterly, 18*(4), 262–275.

143. Kessler, S., Ashenden, R., Connell, R., & Dowsett, G. (1985). Gender relations in secondary schooling. *Sociology of Education, 58*(1), 34–48.

144. Matute-Bianchi, M. E. (1986). Ethnic identities and patterns of school success and failure among Mexican-descent and Japanese-American students in a California high school: An ethnographic analysis. *American Journal of Education, 95*(1), 233–255.

145. MacLeod, J. (1987). *Ain't No Makin' It: Leveled Aspirations in a Low-Income Neighborhood.* Boulder, CO: Westview.

146. Nieto, S. (1992). *Affirming Diversity: The Sociopolitical Context of Multicultural Education.* New York: Longman.

147. Ogbu, J. U. (1986). The consequences of the American caste system. In U. Meisser (Ed.), *The School Achievement of Minority Children: New Perspectives.* Hillsdale, NJ: Erlbaum.

148. Ogbu, J. U. (1987). Variability in minority school performance: A problem in search of an explanation. *Anthropology & Education Quarterly, 18*(4), 312–334.

149. Ogbu, J. U. (1990). Minority education in comparative perspective. *Journal of Negro Education, 59,* 45–57.

150. Simon, R. (1983). But who will let you do it? Counter-hegemonic possibilities for work education. *Journal of Education, 165*(3), 235–256.

151. Suarez-Orozco, M. M. (1987). Becoming somebody: Central American immigrants in the United States. *Anthropology and Education Quarterly, 18*(4), 287–299.

152. Weis, L. (1985). *Between Two Worlds: Black Students in an Urban Community College.* Boston: Routledge and Kegan Paul.

153. Weis, L. (1985). Excellence and student class, race and gender cultures. In P. Altbach, G. Kelly, & L. Weis (Eds.), *Excellence in Education: Perspective on Policy and Practice.* Buffalo: Prometheus Press.

154. Willis, P. (1981). Cultural production is different from cultural reproduction is different from social reproduction is different from production. *Interchange, 12*(2/3), 48–68.

The references listed below include suggestions for preparing students to change both schools and society.

155. Hartsock, N. (1979). Feminist theory and the development of revolutionary strategy. In Z. Eisenstein (Ed.), *Capitalist Patriarchy and the Case for Socialist Feminism.* New York: Monthly Review Press.

156. Lather, P. (1984). Critical theory, curricular transformation and feminist mainstreaming. *Journal of Education, 166*(1), 49–62.

The following author criticizes the theory that there are voluntary and caste-like groups in the United States.

157. Treuba, H. T. (1988). Culturally based explanations of minority students' academic achievement. *Anthropology and Education Quarterly, 19*(3), 270–287.

The following References deal with the inadequate educational services provided to non-European middle-class students.

158. Ascher, C. (1989). *Urban School Finance: The Quest for Equal Educational Opportunity*. New York: ERIC Clearinghouse on Urban Education.
159. Bastian, A., Fruchter, N., Gittell, M., Greer, C., & Haskins, K. (1986). *Choosing Equality*. Philadelphia: Temple University Press.
160. Becker, H. J. (1986). *Computer Survey Newsletter*. Baltimore: The Johns Hopkins University, Center for the Social Organization of Schools.
161. Center for Social Organization of School. (1983). *School Uses of Microcomputers: Reports from a National Survey*, No. 3. Author.
162. Darling-Hammond, L. (1985). *Equality and Excellence: The Status of Black American Education*. New York: College Entrance Examination Board.
163. Furr, J. D., & Davis, T. M. (1984). Equity Issues and microcomputers: Are educators meeting the challenges? *Journal of Educational Equity and Leadership, 4*, 93–97.
164. Hood, J. F. (1984). *Update on the School Market for Microcomputers*. Westport, CT: Market Data Retrieval.
165. Karp, S. (1991). Rich schools, poor schools & the courts. *Rethinking Schools, 5*(2), 1–15.
166. Mickelson, R. A. (1980). Social stratification processes in secondary schools: A comparison of Beverly Hills High School and Morningside High School. *Journal of Education, 162*(4), 83–112.
167. National Assessment of Education Progress. (1988). *Computer Competence: The First National Assessment*. Princeton: Educational Testing Service.
168. New York City Board of Education (1989). *A New Direction: 1989–1990 Budget Request*. New York.

169. Oakes, J. (1983). Limiting Opportunity: Student race and curricular differences in secondary vocational education. *American Journal of Education*, May, 328–355.
170. O'Brien, E. M. (1989). Texas legislators impatient to solve unfairness of school financing system. *Black Issues in Higher Education, 6*(16), 23.

These references are concerned with the effects of tracking and ability grouping.

171. Brophy, J. (1983). Research on the self-fulfilling prophecy and teacher expectation. *Journal of Educational Psychology, 75*(5), 631–661.
172. Chun, E. W. (1988). Sorting black students for success and failure: The inequity of ability grouping and tracking. *Urban League Review, 11*(1–2), 93–106.
173. Eder, D. (1981). Ability grouping as a self-fulfilling prophecy: A micro-analysis of teacher-student interaction. *Sociology of Education, 54*, 151–162.
174. Gamoran, A. (1986). *The Stratification of High School Learning Opportunities*. Paper presented at the annual meeting of the American Educational Research Association, San Francisco.
175. Goodlad, J. (1984). *A Place Called School*. New York: McGraw-Hill.
176. Lake, S. (1985). *Update on Tracking and Ability Grouping*. ERIC ED 274–708.
177. Lee, V. (1986). *The Effect of Tracking on the Social Distribution of Achievement in Catholic and Public Secondary Schools*. Paper presented at the annual meeting of the American Educational Research Association, San Francisco.
178. Oakes, J. (1985). *Keeping Track: How Schools Structure Inequality*. New Haven: Yale University Press.
179. Oakes, J. (1988). Tracking in mathematics and science education: A structural contribution to unequal schooling. In L. Weis, *Class, Race, and Gender in American Education*. Albany, NY: State University of New York Press.
180. Rosenbaum, J. E. (1980). Track misperceptions and frustrated college plans: An analysis of the effects of tracks and track perceptions in the National Longitudinal Survey. *Sociology of Education, 53*(2), 74–88.
181. Simpson, W. (1990). *Black Male Achievement: Strategies for Ensuring Success in School*. Paper presented at the annual meeting of the National Black Child Development Institute. Washington, DC.

182. Slavin, R. (1986). *Ability Grouping in Elementary Schools: A Best Evidence Synthesis*. Baltimore: The Johns Hopkins University Press.

The results of community colleges are discussed in the following references.

183. Astin, A. W. (1982). *Minorities in American Higher Education*. San Francisco: Jossey-Bass.
184. Moore, W. (1976). Black knight/white college. *Community and Junior College Journal*, 6(7), 18–20, 40–43.
185. Nora, A., & Rendon, L. (1988). Hispanic student retention in community colleges: Reconciling access with outcomes. In L. Weis, *Class, Race, and Gender in American Education*. Albany, NY: State University of New York Press.
186. Olivas, M. A. (1979). *The Dilemma of Access: Minorities in Two Year Colleges*. Washington, DC: Howard University Press.
187. Weis, L. (1983). Schooling and cultural production: A comparison of black and white lived cultures. In M. A. Apple & L. Weis (Eds.), *Ideology and Practice in Schooling*. Philadelphia: Temple University Press.

Alienation among African American students is the focus of the following references.

188. Fisher, S. (1981). Race, class, anomie, and academic achievement: A study at the high school level. *Urban Education*, 16(2), 149–173.
189. Ginsberg, E., Berliner, H. S., & Ostow, M. (1988). *Young People at Risk: Is Prevention Possible?* Boulder, CO: Westview Press.
190. Harris, W. G., & Blanchard, R. (1990). *A Select Group of African American Males' Perceptions of Barriers to Successfully Achieving the Typical Male Familial Role—Implications for Educators*. Paper presented at the annual meeting of the National Association for Multicultural Education, New Orleans.
191. Hirsch, B. J., & Rapkin, B. D. (1987). The transition to junior high school: A longitudinal study of self-esteem, psychological symptomatology, school life, and social support. *Child Development*, 58, 1235–1243.
192. Long, S. (1980). Personality and political revenge: Psychopolitical adaptation among black and white youth. *Journal of Black Studies*, 11(1), 77–104.
193. (1992). Utah researcher blames discrimination for Native American high school dropout rate. *Black Issues in Higher Education*, 9(9), 3.

Techniques for resegregating schools are discussed in the following references.

194. Carter, D. G. (1982). Second-generation school integration problems for blacks. *Journal of Black Studies*, 13(2), 175–188.
195. Children's Defense Fund (1974). *Children Out of School*. Washington, DC: Children's Defense Fund of the Washington Research Project.
196. Cross, D. E., Long, M. A., & Ziajka, A. (1978). Minority cultures and education in the United States. *Education and Urban Society*, 10(3), 263–276.
197. Eyler, J., Cook, B. J., & Ward, L. E. (1983). Resegregation: Segregation within desegregated schools. In C. H. Rossell & W. D. Hawley (Eds.), *The Consequences of School Desegregation*. Philadelphia: Temple University Press.
198. Finn, J. D. (1982). Patterns in special education placement as revealed by the ORC surveys. In K. A. Heller, W. H. Holtzman, & S. Messick (Eds.), *Placing Children in Special Education*. Washington, DC: National Academy Press.
199. Gelb, S. A. (1983). *Special Education and Linguistic Minority Students: The Historical Bases of Discriminatory Practices*. ERIC ED 232–401.
200. Goodale, R., & Soden, M. (1981). *Disproportionate Placement of Black and Hispanic Students in Special Education Programs*. ERIC ED 204–873.
201. Johnson, J. L. (1969). Special Education and the Inner City: A challenge for the future of another means for cooling the mark out? *Journal of Special Education*, 3(3), 241–251.
202. Kritek, W. J. (1979). Teacher's concerns in a desegregated school in Milwaukee. *Integrated Education*, 17(1), 19–24.
203. Larkin, J. (1979). School desegregation and student suspension: A look at one school system. *Education and Urban Society*, 11(4), 485–495.
204. Network of Regional Desegregation Assistance Centers. (1989). *Resegregation of Public Schools: The Third Generation*. Author.
205. Richardson, J. G. (1979). The case of special education and minority misclassification in California. *Educational Research Quarterly*, 4(1), 25–40.
206. Rogers, H. R., & Bullock, C. S. III (1972). *Law and Social Change*. New York: McGraw Hill.

207. Smith, G. R. (1983). Desegregation and assignment for children to classes for the mildly retarded and learning disabled. *Integrated Education, 21*(1–6), 208–211.

208. Smith, M., & Dziuban, C. D. (1977). The gap between desegregation research and remedy. *Integrated Education, 15*, 51–55.

209. Tillman, J. (1991). Wake up! Please don't let your children become special education students. *Black Issues in Higher Education, 8*(16), 31.

210. Trent, W. T. (1981). Expert opinion on school desegregation issues. In W. D. Hawley (Ed.), *Assessment of Current Knowledge about the Effectiveness of School Desegregation Strategies.* Nashville, TN: Institute for Public Policy Studies, Vanderbilt University.

Chapter 4

Educational Approaches for Students from Diverse Ethnic and Socioeconomic Backgrounds

Culturally appropriate education is an accepted goal. Policy statements issued by the federal government and many educational organizations emphasize the importance of multiculturalism. Because there is no legal definition of culturally appropriate education, however, there are many different approaches to providing culturally appropriate educational services aimed at increasing respect for diversity, reducing prejudice, improving interethnic group relations, and resolving cultural incompatibilities between students' styles of learning and behavior and educators' styles of instruction. The lack of a legal definition of culturally appropriate education has also left room for differences of opinion about the desirability and efficacy of these approaches.

This chapter describes various approaches to these problems. It discusses the advantages and disadvantages of the approaches and summarizes the research evidence for their effectiveness. Most important, it assists readers to examine the controversies surrounding them and to develop their own points of view about them.

Increasing Respect for Diversity, Reducing Prejudice, and Improving Interethnic Group Relations

Currently, U.S. schools are plagued by ethnic strife. Many groups of students are alienated from schools that reflect a European American cultural bias. Some educators argue that in times like these, education cannot be culturally appropriate if it does not increase respect for diversity, reduce prejudice and discrimination, and help to eliminate alienation, and improve interethnic group relations.

Many approaches for solving these problems have been suggested. These include discussing the similarities and differences among different ethnic groups, including aspects of students' cultures in the curriculum, taking proactive steps to counter and correct bias and prejudice, and preparing students to emancipate themselves and transform society.

Discussions of Differences and Similarities

An approach to increasing respect for diversity and reducing prejudice that has received considerable support among educators is to teach students that all people have similar needs, desires, and problems, but have different ways of satisfying and solving them. This approach is based on the assumption that when students realize that people who behave differently are actually the same, they will have more respect for the diversity they observe among human beings.

> Children must be provided the concepts and experiences which are necessary to assist them in realizing the extent of the similarities and the nature of the differences in their various human associations. In this manner, children are encouraged to develop an understanding and appreciation of human diversity. (1, p. 4)

Younger students can learn that all people need to eat well but eat different foods and prepare them differently; all humans need to keep warm and protect themselves against the elements but use many different and equally effective ways of accomplishing these goals. Older students can study how people discipline their children, organize themselves into groups, handle interpersonal conflicts, schedule activities, express themselves verbally, nonverbally, and artistically, and so on. In classes that include students from diverse backgrounds, younger children can tell each other what they like to do to have a good time, what their favorite foods are, and the like. Older students can describe how things are done at home: how respect is shown in their families, what is embarrassing and distasteful, how family members relate to each other, how late is late, what happens when children do not do what they are supposed to do, how parents discipline children, and who does the disciplining. They can learn how different students like to have things done at school—whether they prefer a lot or very little teacher supervision and feedback, cooperative or competitive learning environments, lectures or discussions, individual or group work, and so on.

Criticisms

Some educators are not comfortable with this approach because they believe that it is better to focus exclusively on the similarities among people. They want educators to avoid discussing differences among people because they are concerned about the divisive effect it can have on relationships between different groups. The following quotations express this point of view.

When people focus on the differences among themselves they engender conflict and hostility. (2, p. 17)

We are all Americans and as Americans we would do well to be blind to the differences that divide us. (2, p. 17)

Although this is a valid concern, proponents of the approach believe that because students also study the similarities among people they will become decentered and avoid becoming ethnocentric.

My experience in teaching multicultural education courses leads me to believe that an effective way of decentering a person is to use his or her ethnic background as a cross-cultural bridge by showing the parallels between his or her group's experience and that of other ethnic groups. . . . Increasing awareness of such parallels in experiences can, I think, help develop mutual understanding and empathy between different ethnic groups and contribute to the process of depolarization. (3, p. 309)

As seen later in this chapter, the available evidence indicates that discussions of similarities and differences increases appreciation and respect for diversity. There is no evidence that it causes the kinds of problems that concern its critics.

Inclusion of Students' Cultures in the Classroom

Numerous educators who believe that American schools are too monocultural have recommended, if not demanded, that they become more representative of today's pluralistic society. They have documented the lack of inclusion of non–European American cultures in the curriculum and have made a variety of suggestions for how educators can include students' cultures in the classroom (4–6, 8, 9, 11–14). The following quotes typify their reasoning.

Through the omission of information, America's schools have become monocultural environments. They dispense a curriculum centered on western civilization that encapsulates only narrowly the truth, reality, and breadth of human experience. This curriculum reinforces institutional racism by excluding from discourse and from the ethos of the school and the classroom the intellectual thought, scholarship, history, culture, contributions, and experience of minority groups. Schools have become sites for producing and making acceptable myths and ideologies that systematically disorganize and neutralize the cultural identities of minorities. Consequently, schools—where the hearts and minds of children are shaped and controlled—have been dominated for far too long by the attitudes, the beliefs, and the value system of one race and class of people. This is not a politically, socially, morally, or economically justifiable situation in a democratic, multicultural society. (12, p. 90)

All U.S. citizens need to master a common core of shared knowledge. However, the important question is: Who will participate in the formulation of that knowledge and whose interests will it serve? *We need a broad level of participation in the identification, construction, and formulation of the knowledge that we expect all of our citizens to master. Such knowledge should reflect cultural democracy and serve the interests of all of the people within our pluralistic nation and world. (6, p. 126)*

A multicultural approach that has been used by many educators to achieve these goals is to include aspects of students' cultures in the curriculum. They teach units on the foods, clothing, stories, legends, dances, and arts of the major American ethnic groups. They select textbooks and other educational materials that include pictures of and stories about different ethnic groups. They listen to the music of different ethnic groups, discuss and celebrate their holidays, and note their historical and current contributions. On these occasions some educators also encourage students to bring to class things such as pictures, foods, games, photos, jewelry, pets, money, and musical instruments from home.

Some experts note that multicultural education is usually included in special units or only on special occasions. They maintain that although this is a positive first step, multicultural education approaches are more effective when they are included in the ongoing, daily curriculum.

When educators add ethnic heroes and fragmented ethnic content to the curriculum, ethnic heroes and content are assumed to be nonintegral parts of the mainstream U.S. experience. Consequently, it is assumed sufficient to add special units and festivals to teach about ethnic groups and their cultures. Particularly in elementary social studies, ethnic content is taught primarily with special lessons and pageants on holidays and birthdays. Blacks usually dominate lessons during Black History Month or on Martin Luther King's birthday, but they are largely invisible in the curriculum during the rest of the year. (5, p. 533)

Some experts believe that teachers often teach students superficial inaccurate stereotypes. Thus, Pepper advises:

Bias about Indians is often the result of inaccurate information. The realities of American Indian and Alaskan Native life are often oversimplified and distorted. Stylized accounts of Indian life reinforce the "buckskin and feather" and the "Eskimo and igloo" stereotypes. With such instruction, students are certain to develop misguided impressions of Indians. (11, p. 1)

They note that merely celebrating special days, learning about selected heroes, eating ethnic foods, and building tepees and igloos does not help students understand the experiences, attitudes, problems, life-styles, and so on of different groups. They recommend that teachers focus more on these real-life current problems.

Focusing on the strange and exotic traits and characteristics of ethnic groups is likely to reinforce stereotypes and misconceptions. The making of tepees does not reveal anything significant about contemporary American Indian values, cultures, or experiences. It merely adds to the classical Indian stereotype, which is so pervasive on television and in the wider society. Rather than focus on the exotic characteristics of ethnic groups the teacher should emphasize the common needs which all human groups share, such as the need to explain the unknown and the need for artistic expression, and the diverse ways in which American ethnic groups have solved the problems of survival. (9, p. 86)

The infusion of fragmented ethnic content into the curriculum. . . results in the trivialization of ethnic cultures. The study of Mexican-American food or of native American tepees will not help students develop a sophisticated understanding of Mexican-American culture and of the tremendous cultural diversity among native Americans. (5, p. 533)

Criticisms

Although few educators oppose demonstrating respect for cultural diversity in these ways, some believe many teachers go too far. They think that educators overemphasize the importance of the contributions of non–European American groups. They worry that educators do not teach students that American society was founded by European Americans and do not give sufficient attention to their belief that United States owes its greatness to the Anglo-Saxon democratic principles the European settlers brought with them. They also believe that the inclusion all cultures in the curriculum waters it down. For example, in a monograph titled "Pluralism Gone Mad," Thomas argues that

Those who founded this nation wrote some important ideas into our national documents. It is those ideas that must be taught in our schools. . . . It is an ethos that supports diversity with limits. . . . and a set of political principles that distinguishes us from all other nations. . . . The American ethos has sustained us for over 200 years. . . . And it will eventually lead us through the quicksand of pluralism gone mad. . . . as we enter a third century as a free nation, the American ethos of freedom, opportunity, self-reliance, hard-work, adherence to law, respect for individuals, and commitment to rigorous standards will become the norm of our schools. (pp. 27–29)

If the schools are expected to teach the cultures of all groups and the preferences of all political persuasions in our nation, then the curriculum will become so overloaded that little of substance will be accomplished. (14, pp. 16–17)

Other critics of multicultural education have stated that:

"Multicultural education" should not take place at the expense of studies that transcend cultural differences; the truths of mathematics, the sciences, history,

and so on, are not different for people of different races, sexes, or cultures, and for that reason alone their study is liberating. Nor should we further attenuate the study of the traditions of the West. Not only is knowledge of those traditions essential for any evaluation of our own institutions, it is increasingly relevant to our understanding of other nations, which in striking testament to the universality of the values they embody, are rapidly adapting Western practices to their own situations. (10, p. A23)

Multicultural education "promotes cultural relativism instead of teaching students to respect and appreciate the best that has been produced in Western and in other cultures" (7, pp. A13, A22).

Proponents of multicultural education do not accept these criticisms. They believe that many groups besides Western Europeans contributed to the development of the United States; they do not agree that including the contributions of other groups diminishes the importance of the contributions of Western Europeans; and they do not agree that including information about various ethnic groups will lead to a watering down of the curriculum, because they do not expect schools to teach the cultures of all groups. As Suzuki explains:

Of course it would be impossible for any teacher to incorporate the experiences and perspectives of all the ethnic groups—there are more than 300—into the curriculum. I would suggest including at least those groups that are present in significant numbers in the local community, along with a few that may not be present. However, there would still be a massive amount of factual information even on these groups. Since there is little merit in having students memorize a lot of low-level facts about these groups, a conceptual approach that provides a framework for understanding the experiences and perspectives of all the groups would appear to be the most effective strategy. (3, p. 311)

There is little evidence that multicultural approaches have gone too far. The opposite appears to be true. Very little multicultural information is included in elementary and secondary school programs, and, as was noted earlier, what is included tends to be taught during special occasions, not infused into the ongoing curriculum.

Proactive Antibias Curricular Approaches

Acknowledging a variety of cultures in the classroom and discussing why various ethnic and socioeconomic characteristics are equally acceptable demonstrates respect for students' cultural backgrounds. However, these instructional techniques do very little to reduce prejudice, discrimination, and intergroup hostility in the classroom. Some authors maintain that in order to accomplish these goals, educators must take positive steps specifically designed to eliminate the prejudiced and discriminatory treatment students receive in school and help resolve hostility, animosity, and suspicion between students from different cultural backgrounds (15–20). Research supports their position. Taking specific steps to improve students' relationships and perceptions of each other is more effective than merely talking at students or teaching them a unit about prejudice; teaching students about the realities of prejudice in the United States accomplishes more than only including students' cultures in the curriculum; and a schoolwide approach that is designed to influence all students and to change the climate of the school is better than an approach that only involves a single class or group of students.

Eliminating Teacher Bias

Many experts on teacher bias have suggested that teachers should begin by monitoring their own behavior to be sure that they do not model prejudiced attitudes and behavior. Becoming aware of your own prejudices and stereotypic perceptions and behavior is a necessary first step in changing them. However, self-insight alone is insufficient, especially since the very structure of society supports certain biases. Real behavior change requires determined effort over time. The following self-quiz is an example of the biased beliefs people harbor about one ethnic group.

SELF-QUIZ: Beliefs about Native Americans

Pepper maintains that the following myths about Native Americans are commonplace in most textbooks and elementary school curricula. Which if any of them did or do you believe to be true?

1. American Indians and Alaskan Natives are a similar group of people who share a common language and culture and live together in similar places.
2. All American Indians and Alaskan Natives live on reservations.
3. American Indians and Alaskan Natives receive checks from the government because they are Indian.

4. The existing status of American Indians, their people, and their governments is the product of accepted principles of international law and equity.
5. American Indians are a defeated people.
6. The Allotment Act (Dawes Act of 1887) was passed to civilize American Indians by making them private property owners.
7. Thanksgiving is a day of rejoicing that marks the advent of a mutually beneficial relationship between European settlers and Native people. (11, p. 1–2)

Eliminating Curricular Bias

Eliminating the bias found in the curricula materials you will use and in the content of the courses you will teach can help prevent student bias. There are many published guidelines you can refer to for assistance (21–27). This list of sources of bias is a good place to begin.

- Representing certain groups in an unflattering or demeaning manner (Jews are money-mad and stingy, Native Americans are savages, Mexican Americans are lazy, African Americans are on welfare, gang members are African American or Hispanic Americans)

- Overgeneralizations (African American families are always headed by females, Hispanic Americans have many children)
- Omitting non-Europeans altogether or underrepresenting them
- Revisions of the pictures and illustrations in a book to include significant numbers of non–European Americans without changing its content
- Darkening illustrations of people with obvious European facial features to make them appear ambiguous
- Stereotyping in instructional material (presenting non-Europeans in stereotypic roles at work and play, attributing stereotypic personality characteristics, such as studious to Asian Americans and athletic to African Americans)
- Assigning certain ethnic groups traditional and stereotypic roles that imply that they have limited abilities and potential or are less valuable to society (European Americans perform leadership roles, take the initiative, play the key roles in solving problems, give aid and assistance; non–European Americans are their helpers and the recipients of their assistance.)
- Omitting the roles of non-Europeans in history, their contributions to science, and so on
- Describing their cultural heritage from a European American view (presenting only a European American perspective on such issues as wars and other conflicts between groups, calling Native American victories massacres and their defeats battles),
- Presenting problems such as drug abuse, poverty, homelessness, and crime as if they were restricted to non-European communities,
- Including only a few non-Europeans' work in basal readers, literary anthologies, and language arts kits
- Glossing over or ignoring such controversial or troublesome issues as slavery, oppression, poverty, prejudice, injustice
- Setting non-Europeans off in boxes away from the main body of the text, which remains biased and one-sided
- Describing families as two-parent families living in suburban middle-class neighborhoods in which the father goes to work in a suit and the mother stays home
- Employing only middle-class standards of success such as a college degree and working as a professional, executive, or entrepreneur
- Illustrating the final rung on the evolutionary ladder as a European American male

Teaching about Prejudice

Some experts think teachers need to inform students about the facts of racism in the United States if they want them to become less biased. Their point of view is expressed in the following quotations.

The overt goals of multicultural education can be realized only when policy-makers, educators, and communities acknowledge the subtle (and sometimes not so subtle) forms of institutionalized racism that permeate the structures of schools and mediate the interactions between educators and students. In other words, unless it becomes "anti-racist education," "multicultural education" may serve only to provide a veneer of change that in reality perpetuates discriminatory educational structures. (28, pp. 127–128)

Although the beautiful and heroic aspects of our history should be taught, so must the ugly and exclusionary. Rather than viewing the world through rose-colored glasses, antiracist multicultural education forces both teachers and students to take a long, hard look at everything as it was and is. (19, pp. 208–209)

To truly address racism, instruction must enable teachers and students to analyze the inequities in power and economic status that determine race relations. (17, p. 1)

Proponents of antibias curricular approaches have offered teachers the following suggestions (17, 19, 28, 29).

- Make discussions of racism and discrimination an explicit aspect of the curriculum. Do not allow the truth about these problems to be swept under the carpet as something too ugly or un-American for discussion.
- Replace teaching about tepees, igloos, and other out-of-date stereotypes with discussions of real current problems and issues in the lives of different ethnic groups. In the case of Native Americans these issues could include fishing and hunting rights, land claims, self-rule, education and health issues, and the like.
- Introduce pertinent incidents of prejudice and discrimination in the news or their particular field of study into the curriculum on a regular and timely basis.
- Have students examine T.V. programs, movies, magazine articles, and their textbooks for prejudice, bias, and stereotyping.
- Invite guest speakers who perform roles that counteract stereotypes. Talks by African American and Hispanic American lawyers and physicians can reduce students' stereotypes of such groups.
- Eliminate stereotypes by demonstrating to students that whatever the stereotype, there are many exceptions to the rule.

Although it is always important to understand how culture, language, gender and economic class influence such things as learning and communication style, it is equally crucial to understand that these factors are not deterministic. That is, not all Jewish students have an ethos for scholarship, not all African American students have a relational learning style, and not all Asian students are quiet and independent learners. (19, p. 254).

Improving Interethnic Group Relations and Resolving Intergroup Conflicts
There are many approaches to improving interethnic group relations. Many published materials designed to assist educators to improving interethnic group rela-

tions have proven to be effective with older students (30–40). Unfortunately, their effectiveness with young students has not been evaluated.

Teacher-initiated techniques have also been shown to work. These include organizing discussions in which students describe the prejudice that they have suffered, using role-playing activities to help students experience rejection and prejudice, and having students divide into groups on the basis of some arbitrary characteristic—hair color, height, or alphabetical order—and assigning superior and subordinate roles to each group.

Exposing students to the life experiences of the refugee and immigrant students, who are often ridiculed and rejected, helps the other students to understand them and reduces prejudice against them. Themes such as Coming to America, Forced Out, Homeland Histories, and Our Lives have been used to encourage immigrant and refugee students to describe their experiences through art projects, murals, plays, and oral reports. Published materials specifically designed to teach students about the immigrant and refugee experience are also available (35). It is also possible to request guest speakers from such groups as Children of War.

The guest speakers provided by Children of War are children who have been victims of war themselves. They participate in workshops throughout the United States designed to help other students understand the experiences of refugees children and their problems. Many cities have local chapters that can provide service to local schools (31). As noted earlier, teachers can do the same thing by having refugee students in the school describe their experiences in class or as part of an assembly program. The following quote describes the reaction of a student who was exposed to such information.

> *When I first heard other kids stand up and talk about what it is like to grow up in a country at war—like when I first heard Guatemalans coming from their country and having been tortured at such a young age, I thought "Oh, my God, wait a minute! My biggest worry is waking up at 7:00 so I can get to my classes on time! I don't have to think about my family disappearing." It is a tremendous eye-opener to see what life is like for refugees here. It shocked me and my friends into realizing there is more to the world than our own experiences. (31, p. 52)*

Another helpful approach is to encourage interethnic group interaction. Forming interethnic groups in class and at recess and pairing ESL or bilingual classes with regular classes on a weekly or monthly basis to discuss life experiences or engage in multicultural activities have all been used successfully.

Many teachers prefer to avoid dealing with discriminatory incidents or intergroup friction in the form of fights, name-calling, and threats. However, many experts suggest that teachers should handle them head-on. They advise teachers not to merely tell students "We don't call others names in this room," or something to that effect. Rather, they should discuss such occurrences not as isolated incidents, but as a reflection of the society in which students are growing up.

> *Teachers generally avoid discussing such issues as racial name-calling or peer*
> *relationships and how they develop among students. Yet, such issues are often*
> *the more potent aspects of the immediate social reality of students and can be*
> *used by teachers to give students a deeper, more personal understanding of*
> *broader social issues. By personalizing learning in this way, I believe that stu-*
> *dents will gain not only cognitive knowledge, but equally important, they will*
> *also develop greater empathy and sensitivity. (3, p. 313)*

Interethnic group conflicts can be handled within the classroom or by means of various schoolwide entities. Student mediation panels composed of student volunteers who have been trained to mediate intercultural problems among their fellow students have proven successful at resolving the problems of students who are referred to the panel by teachers counselors and others. Interethnic advisory boards/forums made up of students, parents, staff, and community members are another effective way to respond to conflicts (31).

It is also possible to use a case study method to examine how prejudice, discrimination, ethnic conflict, and the like, occur and to discover how they can be avoided and resolved. Educators can prepare cases on their own or use some that are available in the literature as models (41). To develop a case study for use in your classroom consider the following:

- What issues do you want the students to consider?
- How does the situation look from the points of view of the students involved?
- What went wrong?
- What could have been done to avoid the problem?
- What should be done now?

Schoolwide Approaches

Research indicates that the goals of multicultural education cannot be fully achieved in a one-time or one-classroom approach (12, 19, 42). As Nieto points out:

> *The entire "culture" of the school must be changed if the impact of multicultural*
> *education is to be felt, including curriculum and materials, institutional norms,*
> *attitudes and behaviors of teachers and other staff, counseling services, the extent*
> *to which parents are welcome in the school. (19, p. 253)*

Following are some of the many schoolwide programs that are designed to reduce prejudice and discrimination and improve intergroup relations (31).

Project REACH is a year-long, four-phase program that has been used successfully with middle school students (31). In the Human Relationship Skills phase, students complete activities designed to enhance their self-esteem, self-awareness, interpersonal communication skills, and understanding of group dynamics. This is followed by the Cultural Self-Awareness phase, in which students examine their own culture, ethnicity, family history, or community. The third phase, Multicultural Awareness, is based on a set of booklets, the *Ethnic Perspectives* series, that are designed to present American history from diverse ethnic points of view. In the final phase, Cross-Cultural Experience, students engage in dialogue and exchange with students and adults from different ethnic backgrounds.

Research indicates that students who have completed the program have a greater sense of pride and know more about other cultures than students who have not taken the program. They are more accepting of ethnic differences and more interested in learning about students from other backgrounds, and they engage in fewer incidents of putting down other students, name-calling, and ethnic slurs (34, 36).

A World of Difference provides a number of services including community action and school-based programs, one of which is a 40-lesson program for secondary level students on American beliefs and values; prejudice, stereotyping, and discrimination; scapegoating and racism (31). The Green Circle Program provides schools with workshops for students run by trained facilitators who guide students through understanding how they can include rather than exclude certain groups of individuals who appear to be different because of their religion, ethnic background, or disability (31).

Emancipatory and Transformational Approaches

Some educators believe that merely helping students to become informed about racism is not sufficient. They believe that students, especially those who are the victims of prejudice, must also be taught how to resist and combat it. This approach has been labelled emancipatory multicultural education and education for empowerment by its proponents (3, 6, 43–46). (See Chapter 3.)

> *Education for empowerment demands taking seriously the strengths, experiences, strategies, and goals members of oppressed groups have. It also demands helping them to analyze and understand the social structure that oppresses them and to act in ways that will enable them to reach their own goals successfully. . . . Education for empowerment also means teaching students how to advocate effectively for themselves as individuals as well as collectively. (45, p. 6)*

Some educators suggest that resistance is insufficient. To their way of thinking, teachers should prepare students to change the biased discriminatory aspects of society. This approach has been called transformational education and social reconstructionist education (see Chapter 3).

> *A transformative curriculum cannot be constructed merely by adding content about ethnic groups and women to the existing Eurocentric curriculum or by integrating or infusing ethnic content or content about women into the mainstream curriculum. When the curriculum is revised using either an additive or an infusion approach, the basic assumptions, perspectives, paradigms, and values of the dominant curriculum remain unchallenged and substantially unchanged,*

despite the addition of ethnic content or content about women. . . . A curriculum designed to empower students must be transformative in nature and help students to develop the knowledge, skills, and values needed to become social critics who can make reflective decisions and implement their decisions in effective personal, social, political, and economic action. (6, pp. 130–131)

Criticisms

Suggestions for reducing prejudice meet with a mixed reception. Not many educators have gone on record as supporting the prejudiced treatment that non–European American and poor students receive described in Chapter 3. Few educators would disagree that teachers' expectations for students, evaluation procedures, instructional techniques, curriculum materials, and classroom management techniques should be as free from bias as possible. However, there is considerable disagreement about whether schools should expose students to the negative aspects of our country's history and present circumstances—"the ugly realities of systematic discrimination," the "ugly and exclusionary" (discussed earlier). There is also much debate about what role, if any, the schools should play in preparing students to be self-advocates and change agents (see Chapter 3).

SELF-QUIZ: Techniques for Increasing Respect for Diversity, Reducing Prejudice, and Improving Interethnic Group Relations

State which of the following techniques you would be comfortable using.

- Discussing similarities and differences
- Including students' cultures in the classroom
- Eliminating teacher bias
- Teaching about bias against people who are non–European American or poor
- Exposing students to the life experiences of immigrant and refugee students
- Pairing students in ESL and bilingual education programs with students in mainstream education programs
- Meeting discrimination and intergroup conflicts head on
- Preparing students to advocate for themselves
- Preparing students to change society's attitudes and behavior toward them

---

Learning and Teaching Style Incompatibilities

Non–European American and poor students often are unprepared for the instructional techniques they are exposed to in school because their learning and behavior styles do not match their teachers' instructional styles. There are at least four different ways in which educators can handle the incompatibilities and discontinuities between students' cultural characteristics and the norms, expectations, and methods that prevail in most schools. They can *accommodate* their methods to students' cultural characteristics, help students to *assimilate* to the approaches that are typically found in American schools, assist students to become *bicultural,* or *empower* them to resolve their cultural conflicts in their own ways. This chapter examines the arguments for and against each of these approaches. Chapters 9 through 11 describe how educators can implement them when they assess, instruct, and manage students.

Accommodation

Many educators believe that when there are mismatches between their teaching and classroom management styles and students' learning and behavior styles they should adapt or accommodate their educational approaches to their students. This is also the position of many professional organizations.

Criticisms

Nevertheless, many educators have reservations about accommodating to cultural differences. Some of them believe that it is impractical. Others believe that even if accommodation were feasible, it is undesirable. Their reasons are discussed here.

1. *There are no monolithic cultures in the United States.* Some individuals argue that even within such groups as Asian and Pacific Americans, Hispanic Americans, and African Americans, people are so different that it is not possible to accommodate educational techniques to the cultural needs of any ethnic group. This point of view is presented in the following quotation about Hispanic Americans, but it applies to other ethnic groups as well.

> Latin America is composed of developed industrialized countries such as Argentina and Chile and basically under-developed countries such as Bolivia, Honduras, Belize and Panama. Some countries have a strong European cosmopolitan influence, others have an American influence and others are still predominantly Indian. Some have high rates of illiteracy while others have well-developed educational systems which are as fine or better than those found in some states in the U.S. How then can we talk about a Hispanic culture in the U.S. when Hispanics come here from such diverse countries? (2, pp. 9–10)

Other educators grant that there is great variability among members of a particular ethnic group, but they claim that as important as these differences are, there are also many important similarities among the members. As an Hispanic American educator put it: "When I am with a group of fellow Latinos I'm conscious of our differences. Cubanos, Mexicanos, Puerto Riqueños, Colombianos, we are all different. Yet when I find myself among non-Latinos I realize how much alike we Latinos are." (2, p.10).

As will be seen throughout this text, research studies consistently reveal the existence of educationally relevant cultural differences among different ethnic, socioeconomic, and regional groups. Although these characteristics may not apply to all individuals in a particular group, they are common enough so that educators should be alert to the *possibility* that they may be applicable to an individual student.

2. *It is impossible to accommodate educational approaches to the cultural needs of the many culturally different students found in any particular school system or often within a particular classroom.* Many people do not believe that educators can accommodate their methods and techniques to the different cultural groups with whom they work. Some of their reasons are found in the following quotation.

> My school district, the Los Angeles County School District, has over one hundred different language/culture groups. How can anyone be expected to know about all these different cultures, and how can anyone be expected to apply what they do know? From what I have been told during in-service training, what are appropriate teaching technique for one group are inappropriate for another. How can I teach my Anglo students one way, my Latino students a second way, my Vietnamese students a third, my Korean students a fourth way, my Hmong, my Portuguese, etc., at the same time? Impossible! (2, pp. 15–16)

Other educators believe it is possible. They do not agree that each culture requires a unique educational approach. They point out that alternative methods of instructing students, organizing classrooms, and counseling parents are limited. For example, educators can encourage or require their students to work individually or in groups; they can motivate them through the use of competitive games or cooperative settings; they can allow them to work at their own pace or encourage them to work as quickly as possible; they can attempt to develop close personal relationships with them or maintain a "professional distance"; they can correct and criticize them in front of their peers or privately; they can encourage them to discuss controversial issues and express differences of opinion or emphasize similarities of experience and opinion; and they can teach abstract concepts or utilize methods that stress the concrete and learning by doing. Believing that educators are always choosing between alternatives as limited as those listed earlier, proponents of accommodation think educators can easily adapt their methodology to the cultural needs of their students.

There is little research to support either position. We do not know how effective educators can be when they have to accommodate their techniques simultaneously to many different groups in the same classroom (73).

3. *It would not be a good idea for professionals involved in educating non–European American students to use misleading and even prejudiced description of their cultures.* Some people are concerned that when educators attempt to be culturally relevant they will believe misleading and outdated stereotypes about their students' cultures and will adapt their educational practices to these incorrect beliefs. Some teachers do accept outdated or fictionalized versions of their students' cultures and focus on the quaint or unusual aspects of their life-styles. For example, some teachers of Native American students may believe that they still have life-styles like those depicted in Hollywood westerns (59). However, this suggests that educators should take great care to avoid these problems. It does not mean that they should not attempt to learn as much as they can about their students' cultural background.

Many educators are also concerned that educators will fall victim to prejudiced stereotypes of non–European American students. The following statements reflect their view.

> *I believe enough good research has been done to dismiss bigoted stereotypes. . . . I, personally, get very tired of having to defend my culture against the mythical themes of the "hot blooded, lazy, Latin." (2, p. 11)*

As the following quotations indicate, many other educators maintain that one of the most effective ways of combatting such prejudice is to provide educators with accurate descriptions of the cultural characteristics of ethnic groups.

> *Regardless of the benefits that may accrue from public institutions refusing to acknowledge, in public, general descriptions of ethnic traits, it is my conviction that this very refusal has fostered the continued use of incorrect and often unjust stereotypes about ethnic groups. (61, p. 10)*

> *To identify differences related to Afro-Americans is, of course, a controversial issue; regardless of the disclaimers, values of good or bad, inferior or superior, are so ingrained in our society that the issue will still lead to reinforcement of stereotypes. . . . However, if we are to engage in an educational revolution aimed at promoting the success of a larger percentage of the Afro-American population, it is an area that must be explored. (70, p. 238)*

4. *Cultural descriptions can lead to misleading overgeneralizations.* Some educators are concerned that teachers may think that their knowledge of the cultural characteristics of different ethnic groups and socioeconomic classes is sufficient for them to understand an individual student or parent. This concern is expressed in the following statement.

> *There are many common stereotypes of the Hispanic person such as never being on time, being deeply religious, etc. Those who work with Hispanics should be aware of this and guard against a generalized, stereotyped view of those they work with. This is not to say that a specific stereotype (like being deeply religious) may not apply to an individual. Rather, the individual should always be dealt with as a unique human being who may or may not exhibit certain attitudes, habits, and beliefs.*

> *A list of over-general attributes which describe certain socioeconomic sub-groups of Hispanics such as the poor who may be more apt to have certain problems in school or the Indian who may be more apt to believe in La Llorona will not make educators more sensitive. Educators must recognize that children come to us*

from an infinitely varied array of backgrounds and not assume that all Hispanic students come from poor or Indian backgrounds. (2, p. 12)

The possibility of overgeneralization is an ever-present danger. However, as the following statement indicates, many people believe that despite this possibility, educators should be aware of the cultural traits that may characterize their students.

It is important for educators to be aware of our culture just so long as they refrain from thinking that we are all exactly alike. Just as knowing one Anglo would not enable a Hispanic to know all Anglos, so too knowing a few Hispanic students does not enable an Anglo educator to "know" all Hispanic students either as a group or individually. (2, p. 13)

5. *To treat some students differently than others is discriminatory.* Some critics of the accommodation position argue that because all people are basically the same they should be treated the same. Not to do so, in their opinion, is unfair and discriminatory.

Proponents of the accommodation position disagree. They grant that human beings are basically the same; they prefer success to failure, praise and recognition to criticism or condemnation, and acceptance and attention to rejection and inattention. However, those who believe in accommodation maintain that people's behavior in these situations is influenced by different cultural veneers. They have different criteria for success; they find different forms of praise and recognition rewarding; they differ in terms of when, where, why, and how they are willing to accept criticism or condemnation; and they express acceptance and rejection in their own culturally determined ways. Therefore, if teachers expect all individuals to behave the same way or interpret everyone's behavior from a single culturally determined point of view, they may fail to respond to the unique needs of many of their ethnic minority students.

In addition, the result of treating all students the same may be that those who do not fit the model used by their teachers are treated in a discriminatory manner: "When teachers ignore students' race and claim that they treat all children the same, they usually mean that their model of the ideal student is white and middle-class." (57, p. 54)

For example, Hilliard (55) advises that educators who believe in providing students the same instructional techniques, classroom management approaches, and so on, have the mistaken notion that they are treating the students equally and being fair to them. However, they are not treating all students the same, but are dealing with some students in a culturally appropriate manner and others in a biased manner. Hilliard suggests that there is a more valid way of treating students the same, which is to provide all students with culturally appropriate educational approaches. According to him, although this may make it appear that students are being treated differently, they are actually being treated the same and in a nondiscriminatory manner.

6. *Treating groups of students differently can result in lower expectations and standards for some non–European American groups, and it can lead European Americans to retaliate against those whom they believe are given preferential treatment.* Anecdotal evidence that needs updating suggests that these are valid concerns (59, 73). In an attempt to be culturally relevant, some well-meaning educators do lower their standards for students. For example, Thomas reports that

> *A young man whom I taught in senior high school is now attending a predominantly black college. He has an English teacher who happens to be white and who constantly tells blacks of the hard work whites at a nearby university receive. She further informs them (blacks) that she is not going to give work that is "too difficult"—that they need not worry. . . . Such conduct is demeaning and, indeed, criminal on the part of the teacher, for blacks do not need missionaries to pity them; they need teachers to instruct them. (73, p. 320)*

Kleinfeld reports the following conversation between a teacher whom she labels a cultural relativist and a Native American student.

> *After class, an Indian girl came up to the teacher and told her that she had been sick and had missed the last test. "What should I study for it," she asked. "Don't worry," the teacher replied. "I'll make up a special test for you and you'll do well on it." "But I don't know what to study." "Don't worry," repeated the teacher. "I'll make it special for you. You'll do well." (59, p. 271)*

Kleinfeld also found that many European American students do resent the special treatment Native Americans receive from some teachers: "White students resent the easier assignments, tests, and grading system used exclusively for the Indians. They often take it upon themselves to redress the inequity" (59, p. 271).

There probably are many teachers like the ones just described who reduce their standards for non–European American students and cause other students to express their resentment in nonconstructive ways. However, these teachers are not following the advice of educators who caution them to maintain realistic standards for non–European American students and not expect them to behave in an antisocial manner or to achieve less than others while they educate them in a culturally appropriate manner (55).

Assimilation

A great many educators believe that the best way to deal with cultural incompatibilities in students' learning styles, behavior styles, and communication styles is for students to assimilate to the school's European American culture. The reasons they typically cite for believing that assimilation should be the ultimate goal are discussed here.

1. *Students will learn more effectively if they assimilate to the learning and behavior styles that prevail in schools.* Many educators believe that for non-European stu-

Accommodation: An Example of a Culturally Compatible Educational Approach

Hawaiian students are often perceived as lazy and uninvolved by teachers who are unaware of the cultural incompatibilities that these students experience in school. In school, teachers constantly supervise students, set rules, make assignments, and regulate the classroom's resources. On the other hand, at home when a Hawaiian parent wants something done, he or she tells the children to do it and lets them organize themselves and take care of it. When teachers act more like Hawaiian parents by withdrawing from supervising students and assuming that they will act responsibly, Hawaiian students involve themselves in the classroom activities. An approach that has been used successfully to make the classroom routines more culturally compatible and involve Hawaiian students in classroom activities includes the following.

- The teacher models a routine or task and explains the procedure.
- The teacher instructs the students to perform the desired task, then withdraws as quickly as possible from supervising the group.
- The teacher lets the group determine how the task will be done, who the leader will be, who will perform which aspects of the task, and so on.
- The teacher does not interfere in order to impose her or his own cultural values about such things as fair play, sharing the workload equally, and so on (58).

dents to actualize their potential in school "they must aspire to enter the middle class, adopt the middle-class lifestyle, and use the middle-class value standard as a reference to judge their own behavior." (71, p. 20).

There is little evidence to support this hypothesis. In fact, there is evidence that among some non-European groups those who are most likely to be well-adjusted and to succeed both academically and vocationally are not those who reject their ethnic identity, but rather those who identify with their own ethnic group (49–51, 58, 60, 63, 64, 69, 71, 72, 74, 75, 76, 78).

The reasons for this have not been well studied. Some possible explanations are:

- Students who have not assimilated bring the positive aspects of their cultures to the educational situation.
- Students who assimilate may substitute the poor attitudes toward school that characterize many European American students for the positive attitudes that prevail in their original culture.
- Students who maintain their cultural identity have more self-esteem and self-confidence than those who reject their cultural background.
- In comparison to monocultural students, bicultural students have a larger repertoire of learning strategies and coping techniques to apply to the tasks and challenges of school
- Students who are attempting to assimilate may experience conflicts with their parents as well as identity conflicts, resentment, anger, and, rebelliousness, all of which can interfere with students' learning (discussed later).

2. *Schools should not accommodate their expectations and approaches to those of disadvantaged/inferior non–European American cultures.* Some educators believe that schools should not accommodate to the cultural needs of non–European American students because the European American culture is superior to other cultures. Instead, schools should encourage non–European American students and their parents to give up those cultural characteristics which have held back the progress of their native countries or ethnic groups. The following quotation exemplifies this point of view.

> *People come to this country to better themselves. If their native cultures are so great, why did they have to immigrate? If they aren't willing to accept the values that have helped the United States have the largest economy and the highest standard of living then they should return to the countries from which they came and settle for the limited opportunities they provide. (anonymous)*

The idea that some cultures, especially the African American, Hispanic American, and Native American cultures, are inferior, deprived, or disadvantaged was discussed at length in Chapter 2 and rejected.

3. *Non–European American students and their families should adapt to the mainstream culture in the schools because people living in the same country should all speak the same language, follow the same laws and share the same morality.* This idea is embodied in the following statements.

> *We cannot survive as a culture with different laws for different people. Everyone must pay taxes, serve in the army, respect private property and the rights of others regardless of where they were born or what religion they profess. (2, p. 13)*

> *Pluralism in our society has produced a moral climate that tells everyone to establish a sense of what is right and wrong* for you. *This trend has a way of blurring the limits of a moral code. In the educational arena this trend has produced a no-fault morality and relativistic values. . . . Schools, if they are to survive, must protect and articulate moral standards, ethical behavior, and historical principles of social cohesion. It is their function to teach the common beliefs that unite us as a free nation. (14, pp. 15–16)*

These concerns are based on the incorrect assumption that people who favor pluralistic approaches believe in complete cultural relativism. Pluralists typically recommend that diversity should be balanced against higher and universal values (3, 19, 54, 66). Two examples of this position follow.

> *Because each cultural group proceeds from a different context, we can never reach total agreement on the "best" or most appropriate ways in which to lead our lives. . . .*

> *Nevertheless, it should also be stressed that above and beyond all cultures there are human and civil rights that need to be valued and maintained by all people.*

These rights guarantee that all human beings are treated with dignity, respect, and equality. Sometimes the values and behaviors of a group so seriously challenge these values that we are faced with a dilemma to reject it or to affirm the diversity it represents. If the values we as human beings hold most dear are ultimately based on extending rights rather than negating them, we must decide on the side of those more universal values. (19, pp. 278–279)

I believe in a form of cultural pluralism in which universal and particularistic values would be dialectically balanced against each other. In particular, I believe that the universal values of equality, freedom, and democracy, which are among the most important values that have been promulgated under the concept of common school, should be balanced against the particularistic values associated with the maintenance of cultural diversity. But the freedom of an individual must be restrained to the extent that it imposes detrimentally on the freedom of others. Unfortunately, this two-sided nature of cultural pluralism is rarely underlined and, as a consequence, it is sometimes misunderstood as licence for runaway ethnicity, rather than as a way of avoiding such ethnocentric behavior. (3, pp. 300–301)

The contention that accommodating to cultural differences in the classroom necessarily leads to having two or more national languages and different laws for different cultural groups is also incorrect. Instructing students in their native languages while they learn English, permitting them to work at their own pace, developing the kinds of interpersonal relationships with them that make them feel comfortable, allowing them to choose whether to behave competitively or cooperatively, and so on, does not necessarily lead to adopting two or more national languages, moral codes, or sets of laws.

4. *Adapting educational approaches to students' cultural characteristics does not prepare them to function effectively in the mainstream European American–dominated society.* Educators who support this position argue that the real world is not nearly as tolerant or as flexible as some educators would like it to be. They maintain that because employers and others require individuals to conform to mainstream expectations and norms, accommodating to students' culturally influenced behavior patterns, learning styles, communication styles, concepts of punctuality, and so on, dooms the students to be uncompetitive and disadvantaged in the real world.

There is some truth to this concern. Americans do live in an imperfect society. Despite federal and state laws against discrimination, too many people with supervisory and administrative power over others continue to expect and insist that those over whom they have influence conform to their culturally determined standards. However, does that mean that educators should prepare their students to acquiesce to the prejudiced attitudes of these individuals? Who has the right to decide whether students should be encouraged and helped to submit to such abuse, or to fight it—the students' teachers or the students themselves? (See "Empowerment").

Criticisms

Critics of the assimilation position offer the following reasons for preferring alternative solutions to cultural incompatibilities (47, 48, 52, 53, 61, 65, 77).

- Many students do not want to replace their values, attitudes, learning and behavior styles, and so on, with those of the European American middle-class. Requiring them to do so can cause them to become angry, resentful, suspicious, and rebellious, and to tune out their teachers or drop out of school.
- If students believe that their culture is inferior or agree that they should change their culturally determined ways of functioning, they may suffer a loss of self-esteem and self-confidence.
- Even if students want to change, it may be too difficult to accomplish, because it is no easy task to change one's life-style and values. Thus, Longstreet maintains that,

    There is a limited capability within each of us to modify the ethnic traits we absorb as children. We may change our accent or the way we smile but we cannot, intellectually or emotionally, change the multitude of traits that would have to be altered to change our basic ethnicity. (61, p. 20)

- Even if students succeed in changing, their efforts can create serious problems and unwanted side effects. When non–European American students act in ways that are less natural to them than to European American middle-class students, who were brought up from their earliest years to behave in these ways, they can become tense and nervous, and they may experience the guilt shame, and anxiety that often results from rejecting one's culture.
- Students may experience identity conflicts if they are exposed to conflicting pressure from home and community and the schools.
- Students who assimilate may suffer the loss of friendship and outright hostility from peers who accuse them of trying to be "coconuts, oreos, or bananas" (brown, black, or yellow on the outside and white on the inside). This is especially likely to happen if there is movement within the students' culture toward increasing the group's cultural pride or if there is a history of conflict and oppression between the students' ethnic group and the European American power structure.

    An African American high school student who lived in a poor neighborhood and attended a predominantly white middle-class preparatory school described the experience this way.

    When trying to live in two different worlds, one is in peril of not belonging to either of them. . . . Being put in a position of changing one's character every morning and afternoon to adapt to two different worlds endangers one's identity. (65, p. 337)

- There is little reason to assume that assimilation can work. It has been tried for years with very little success. This concern was expressed quite some time ago by one of the pioneers in the field of multicultural education.

  Schools' past efforts to acculturate culturally different children have failed miserably. These children as a whole are still not being educated, and the school system cannot continue to ignore its ethical, legal, moral, and professional responsibilities to accommodate children as they are. It is highly presumptuous for any school system to assume the responsibilities of acculturating children when the potential emotional consequences of forced acculturation are so pernicious. If most educators realized the way in which they risk the mental health of culturally different children by insisting on acculturating them, they would look more favorably on their potential role in developing a culturally pluralistic society. (48, p. 555)

Assimilation: An Example of a Less Stressful Approach to Changing Students

Papago parents teach their children through nonverbal means such as modeling, gesturing, and economical speech. In school, children are expected to be verbal. At home and in their community, Papago children enjoy considerable autonomy. They are not rebuked by adults for interfering with their work or conversations nor forced to bow to the wishes of their elders. Because children are raised with few limitations on their freedom, they are not accustomed to being controlled, reprimanded, or punished by adults. In school, Papago children are expected to conform to many rules and procedures, and they are exposed to punitive consequences if they do not.

Papago preschool teachers whose goal was to prepare Native American students to transit to European American schools did so without creating undue stress for them. For example, the teachers respected and accepted the students' desire not to participate and recite in class. They allowed children to learn by doing and by observing how their teachers did things. However, they also explained how things should be done. They combined activities that involved physical activities with those that involved verbal activities, such as dancing and singing simultaneously, and they exposed them to the behavior that would eventually be required of them by presenting them with activities designed to entice them into improving their verbal skills and self-assertive classroom participatory behavior.

Teachers taught students to conform to school rules and procedures, but because students were unaccustomed to so many limitations on their freedom, teachers did not use consequences to enforce rules. Instead they repeatedly reminded students what was expected of them and patiently waited for them to conform. In these ways teachers helped students to gradually acculturate to the school's culture without unduly confronting the culturally determined learning and behavior styles they brought with them to school. As Macias describes the teachers' approach:

Teachers continuously present their students with experiences which are typical of mainstream education and which necessitate the child's adjustment to culturally different ways of behaving and learning. Yet, of most importance, these same teachers act to mitigate the discontinuity of the necessary preschool experiences and ensure that the child's appreciation of his own culture is not eroded. (62, p. 378)

Biculturalism

Since the 1970s some educators have been rejecting both accommodation and assimilation (67, 68). They disagree that the school's way is best; they do not think that schools can accommodate to an unlimited number of cultural differences; and they do not believe that non–European American students should be required to choose between the ways of their family and the way school officials expect them to function. They propose a third alternative—biculturalism. Instead of having to choose between maintaining the values, beliefs, and practices of the home and rejecting the mainstream culture of the schools, or rejecting the culture of their home and adopting the school culture, students can identify with and accept both cultural systems and use each in appropriate situations.

There are two different bicultural approaches. Some educators who favor biculturalism believe that although neither the school's culture nor the students' culture is superior, the school's culture is more appropriate in school and the students' culture is more appropriate at home and in their neighborhoods. Thus, they recommend that teachers prepare students to function one way at home and another way at school. Other educators view biculturalism as a process of mutual accommodation. They maintain that teachers should expect students to assimilate to only some of their procedures while they also accommodate to some aspects of their students' culture. Proponents of this form of biculturalism do not believe that students must leave all of their cultural characteristics at the doorstep of the school building—only those that conflict with the effective operation of the educational process (19, 68).

Nieto's conception of biculturalism is an example of this approach.

> *Mutual accommodation means accepting and building on students' language and culture as legitimate expressions of intelligence and as the basis for their academic success. On the part of students and families, it means accepting the culture of the school in such areas as expectations about attendance and homework and learning the necessary skills for work in school. (19, p. 259)*

Proponents of mutual accommodation believe that both school and students are enriched by it. Teachers expand their repertoires of instruction and classroom management techniques, and bicultural students acquire a second way to react to challenges and tasks. Thus, they are able to adapt their approaches to the requirements of the situation (e.g., being cooperative or competitive, assertive or nonassertive, as needed).

In actual practice, this second approach to biculturalism differs from the first only in the degree to which teachers accommodate to students' cultural characteristics or require students to assimilate to the school's culture. It does allow for some accommodation on the part of the school, but it still requires students and their parents to acknowledge that the school's way is necessary if not superior in some areas.

Criticisms

Some educators see problems associated with both of these bicultural approaches. They do not believe either one is as fair as it appears at first glance. They ask why only one cultural perspective has to predominate at all in schools that serve a pluralistic society and why the European American way should be the accepted way in school. They assert that although teachers may think they are communicating to students that neither the school's way or their home's way is more desirable, by stating that the European American way is best for even some school situations, they are communicating that it is also the better way. Critics also maintain that both bicultural approaches can place students in conflict situations if students' parents and friends do not believe that there should be only one cultural perspective in school or that the European American way is the best approach in any areas of the educational settings.

Empowerment

Some educators believe that the assimilation, accommodation, and bicultural models create problems for students because they are too teacher-directed. They prefer to empower students to choose how to resolve their cultural conflicts (45). This approach involves exposing students to the fact that there are various ways they may function, educating them about the possible advantages and disadvantages of each one, and helping them to select the solution that they themselves favor.

Criticisms

Many educators who appreciate the good intentions of those who wish to empower students to make important decisions for themselves question whether the approach can work. They doubt that teachers can be neutral and impartial regarding students' choices, especially when the values involved are important to the teacher, they wonder whether teachers can avoid communicating their preferences to students, and they ask if teachers can accept students' choices that interfere with the smooth progress of their class or rights of others.

Critics of the empowerment approach are also skeptical about students' abilities to make reasonable choices. They point out that until students reach adolescence, they are not mature enough to evaluate the alternatives among which they must choose. Critics also worry about the results of allowing even the best-prepared students to choose for themselves. They find it difficult to believe that students who are relative strangers to the United States can appreciate the ramifications of different alternatives. They ask whether adolescents can project themselves into the future and imagine how employers might react if as a result of choosing to remain true to their cultural backgrounds these students were unable or unwilling to engage in competitive behavior, to work at the same pace as others, to acknowledge their mistakes and errors, to discuss difficult interpersonal issues without a mediator, to accept public criticism, and so on.

Critics also point out that the empowerment approach may have only a limited positive effect on students' identity problems. It may help teachers avoid placing students in conflict situations by not pressuring them to choose one cultural value over another. However, it will not help students avoid identity conflicts if the choices they would like to make conflict with those that their parents or peers prefer.

Research

Educators cannot accommodate completely to students' learning styles (79, 84). The subject matter and skills to be learned by students impose a certain amount of structure on the teaching situation, and educators' personalities also influence the instructional styles that they can comfortably and effectively use with students. As a result, it is necessary for students to assimilate to at least some of the unfamiliar approaches to which they are exposed in school. Thus, a bicultural approach is the most likely outcome of educators' attempts to facilitate students' adjustments to new and unfamiliar classroom situations.

Within these limitations, research has consistently indicated that educators can enhance students' learning and success in school by accommodating their instructional techniques to students' communication, learning, and motivational styles (73, 80–84). As is noted in Chapter 5, expecting students to assimilate to European American middle-class values and methods too rapidly places additional stress on them and creates identity conflicts. There is little evidence regarding the effectiveness of the empowerment approach.

Individual Differences

In actual practice educators do not use the same approach with each and every case of cultural incompatibility that occurs in their classes. Their responses to each situation depend on such factors as the importance they place on the particular cultural incompatibility or issue involved, the effect their students' behavior has on the classroom environment, and the attitude of the students or their parents toward the particular cultural trait. For example, with many exceptions, educators are probably more likely to accommodate their approaches to students who feel uncomfortable in competitive situations or who prefer to work independently rather than in groups. These culturally influenced learning styles do not seriously impede the progress of the group as a whole.

Educators may be a little less likely to accommodate to students who work at a slow pace, request a great deal of feedback and direction, express their needs only in extremely subtle, indirect ways, or resist admitting they don't know or understand something. These culturally influenced learning styles do not impede the progress of the group, but they do require extra work and sensitivity on the teacher's part. Educators are probably least likely to accommodate to students who prefer to settle differences with their peers by fighting or students who think it is better to be assertive and aggressive than compliant and conforming. These behaviors seriously interfere with the rights of others and tend to impede teachers' ability to manage the class.

Some educators may be less willing to accommodate to cultural differences that go against their deeply held beliefs. Educators who prefer students to function in androgynous rather than gender stereotypical ways may be less willing than those who are comfortable with gender stereotypic roles to empower students to choose their own solutions to cultural-conflicts when students' cultures encourage males to act like men and females to be ladies.

Educators may refrain from encouraging the children of Hispanic migrant workers to function biculturally if they and their parents do not plan to stay in the United States. They may also avoid attempting the assimilation and bicultural approaches with African American and Native American students who do not believe that European American values and life-styles are desirable.

Historically, American Indians have resisted acculturation and assimilation more than any other ethnic group. What this means is that by retaining traditional values and beliefs that are important to them, a natural conflict is set up in the classroom that must be handled by children of a very sensitive age. (56, pp. 45–46)

SELF-QUIZ: Critical Incidents

This self-quiz is designed to provide you with some insight into the approaches you may use to resolve diversity issues. First describe how you think the teacher involved should handle each of the following critical incidents. Then disregard the description of the teacher's point of view. Instead, put yourself in the teacher's place, imagine what your viewpoint would be, and state how you would deal with the problem. Then decide which of the alternatives (assimilation, accommodation, biculturalism, empowerment) best describes each of your solutions.

If you prefer a number of different approaches to the incidents, try to determine the factors that led you to select the particular approaches you would use in each critical incident.

1. A second-grade Filipino student who has been brought up to respect and depend on adult authority figures appears to be unable or unwilling to make choices such as selecting a book to bring home from the school library, choosing a partner, and selecting which learning center to work at during free time without his teacher's guidance. The teacher feels that one of the educator's roles is to help young children learn to function more independently.

2. A parent who is representing the parents of all four of the Chinese American students in a third-grade class asks the teacher not to require their children to express their opinions in class because they are in school to learn what the teacher knows. He tells the teacher that Chinese Americans believe that children should be taught to respect the k nowledge and opinions of adults, and he adds that it is not a good idea for children to discuss their per-students should be participants in the

Continued

SELF-QUIZ: Critical Incidents   *Continued*

learning process, not merely banks into which teachers deposit information. The teacher also thinks that presenting problems and having students share their opinions about them is an effective technique for developing students' critical thinking skills.

3. After hearing a seventh-grade student tell his classmate that he would "get him" after school for what he said about his mother, the teacher tells the two students they should settle their arguments without fighting. The teacher reminds them that fighting is against the rules, and warns them that if they fight after school they will get into trouble. The student who did the threatening answers that his parents expect him to stand up for himself, especially when someone says something derogatory about his family.

4. An eleventh-grade student in a predominantly poor neighborhood school complains that his teacher is too tough on him. He accuses the teacher of being insensitive to the students in the class because the teacher gives them too much homework, and he insists that as long as he does okay on tests he should not be marked down every time he does not complete an assignment because he has to work after school to earn money for the family expenses. Although the teacher realizes that the student is telling the truth, the teacher also feels that teachers in urban schools should expect as much from their students as teachers in more affluent suburban schools do. In the teacher's opinion, to expect less of students is to condemn them to life as second-class citizens.

Summary

Many educators believe that increased respect for diversity, improved interethnic group relations, and a reduction in prejudice should be included among the outcomes of culturally appropriate education. However, there is much disagreement about how best to accomplish these goals.

Educators may employ at least four approaches to resolve cultural incompatibilities between students' learning and behavioral styles and educators' instructional and classroom management styles. They can accommodate to students' cultural characteristics, require students to assimilate to the teacher's educational techniques, assist students to become bicultural, or empower them to resolve their cultural conflicts in their own ways. Since each approach has its advantages and disadvantages, educators should examine and evaluate their ways of handling cultural incompatibilities.

Activities

1. Ask a few of your fellow students to answer the self-quiz on techniques for increasing respect for diversity, reducing prejudice, and improving interethnic group relations. If possible, include persons from different backgrounds. How do your responses compare to theirs? Are all of your responses similar? Do you notice any differences in the responses of individuals from different background?

2. Administer a quiz similar to the one on Native Americans about other ethnic groups to some of your friends or fellow students. What kinds of misconceptions do they have about these other groups?

3. Ask some of your friends or fellow students whether they believe that studying the characteristics of different ethnic groups is helpful or should be avoided. Ask them if they think it is possible to adapt educational approaches to cultural differences.

4. Ask some of your fellow students which of the four approaches for dealing with cultural incompatibilities they would prefer to use in their classes. Do their preferences match yours? Do students from different backgrounds have similar preferences?

5. Ask a few of your fellow students to respond to the four critical incidents listed previously. Include people from different backgrounds. How do your responses compare to theirs? Are all of your responses similar? Do you notice any differences in the responses of individuals from different background?

References

These references are concerned with discussions about differences and similarities among people.

1. Glimps, B., & Hicks, J. (1983). *Planning for a Culturally Sensitive Program in the Preschool Setting.* ERIC ED 230–009.
2. Grossman, H. (1984). *Educating Hispanic Students: Cultural Implications for Instruction, Classroom Management, Counseling, and Assessment.* Springfield, IL: Charles C Thomas.
3. Suzuki, B. H. (1984). Curriculum transformation for multicultural education. *Education and Urban Society, 16,* 294–322.

The following reference documents the omission of non–European American holidays, contributions, values, and so on, in texts and other reading materials.

4. Knafle, J. D., Rodriguez-Brown, F. V., & Budinsky, M. (1991). Values in American and Hispanic children's readers. *Journal of Educational Issues of Language Minority Students, 8,* 53–70.

These references discuss the pros and cons of including students' cultures in the classroom.

5. Banks, J. A. (1987). Social studies, ethnic diversity, and social change. *Elementary School Journal, 87*(5), 531–543.

6. Banks, J. A. (1991). A curriculum for empowerment, action, and change. In C. Sleeter (Ed.), *Empowerment Through Multicultural Education.* Albany: State University of New York Press.
7. Heller, S. (1989). Press for campus diversity leading to more closed minds, say critics. *Chronicle of Higher Education, 36,* A13, A22.
8. Loridas, L. (1988). *Culture in the Classroom: A Cultural Enlightenment Manual for Educators.* ERIC ED 303–941.
9. Mendenhall, P. T. (1982). Bicultural school organization and curriculum. In R. Barnhardt (Ed.), *Cross-Cultural Issues in Alaskan Education,* Vol. II. Fairbanks: University of Alaska, Center for Cross-Cultural Studies.
10. National Association of Scholars. (1989). Is the curriculum biased? A statement by the National Association of Scholars. *Chronicle of Higher Education, 36,* A23.
11. Pepper, F. C. (1990). *Unbiased Teaching about American Indians and Alaska Natives in Elementary Schools.* Charleston, WV: ERIC/CRESS.
12. Pine, G. J., & Hilliard, A. G., III. (1990). Rx for racism: Imperatives for America's schools. *Phi Delta Kappan, 71*(8), 593–600.

13. Sleeter, C. E., & Grant, C. A. (1988). *Making Choices for Multicultural Education.* Columbus, OH: Merrill.

14. Thomas, M. D. (1981). *Pluralism Gone Mad.* Bloomington, IN: Phi Delta Kappa Educational Foundation.

The following references stress the importance of proactive antibias and antiracism approaches.

15. Banks, J. A. (1988). *Multiethnic Education: Theory and Practice,* (2nd ed.). Boston: Allyn and Bacon.

16. Brandt, G. L. (1986). *The Realization of Anti-Racist Teaching.* London: Falmer Press.

17. Mitchell, V. (1990). *Curriculum and Instruction to Reduce Racial Conflict.* New York: Teachers College, Columbia University, ERIC Clearinghouse on Urban Education.

18. Moultry, M. (1988). *Multicultural Education Among Seniors in the College of Education at Ohio State University.* ERIC ED 296–634.

19. Nieto, S. (1992). *Affirming Diversity: The Sociopolitical Context of Multicultural Education.* New York: Longman.

20. Olneck, M. R. (1990). The recurring dream: Symbolism and ideology in intercultural and multicultural education. *American Journal of Education, 98*(2), 147–174.

The following references offer guidelines, checklists, and suggestions for detecting prejudice and bias in curricular materials and instructional techniques.

21. Banks, J. A. (1984) *Teaching Strategies for Ethnic Studies.* Boston: Allyn and Bacon.

22. California State Department of Education. (1988). *Ten quick ways to analyze children's books for racism and sexism.* Sacramento, CA: Author.

23. California State Department of Education. (n.d.). *Standards for Evaluation of Instructional Materials with Respect to Social Content.* Sacramento: Author.

24. Cotera, M. P. (1982). *Checklists for Counteracting Race and Sex Bias in Educational Materials.* ERIC ED 221–612.

25. Ferguson, H. (1987). *Manual for Multicultural Education.* Yarmouth, ME: Intercultural Press.

26. National Education Association. (n.d.) *How Fair Are Your Children's Books?* Washington, DC: Author.

27. Office of Intergroup Relations. (1977). *Guide for Multicultural Education: Content and Context.* Sacramento: California State Department of Education.

The following describe techniques for increasing respect for diversity and reducing prejudice, animosity, and alienation, and their effectiveness.

28. Cummins, J. (1988). From multicultural to anti-racist education: An analysis of programmes and policies in Ontario. In T. Skutnabb-Kangas & J. Cummins (Eds.), *Minority Education: From Shame to Struggle.* Philadelphia: Multilingual Matters.

29. Kanpol, B. (1992). The politics of similarity within difference: A pedagogy for the other. *Urban Review, 24*(2), 105–131.

Programs and approaches to reduce prejudice and improved interethnic and intercultural relationships are described in the following references.

30. Anti-Defamation League of B'nai B'rith. (1986). *The Wonderful World of Difference: A Human Relations Program for Grades K–8.* New York: Author.

31. Olsen, L., & Dowell, C. (1989). *Bridges: Promising Programs for the Education of Immigrant Children.* San Francisco: California Tomorrow.

32. Byrnes, D. A., & Kiger, G. (Eds.). (1992). *Common Bonds: Anti-Bias Teaching in a Diverse Society.* Wheaton, MD: Association for Childhood Education International Publications.

33. Cole, J. (1990). *Filtering People: Understanding and Confronting Our Prejudices.* Philadelphia. New Society Publishers.

34. Howard, G. (1989). Positive multicultural outcomes: A practitioner's report. *Multicultural Leader, 2*(1), 12–16.

35. Jorgensen-Esmaili, K. (1988). *New Faces of Liberty: A Curriculum for Teaching about Today's Refugees and Immigrants.* Berkeley: Graduate School of Education, University of California, Berkeley.

36. Lynch, J. (1987). *Prejudice Reduction and the Schools.* New York: Nichols.

37. Panel of Americans. (1991). *No Dissin' Allowed.* New York: Author.

38. San Francisco Study Center. (n.d.) *Voices of Liberty.* San Francisco: Author.

39. Southern Poverty Law Center. (1991). *Teaching Tolerance.* Montgomery, AL: Author.

40. Teidt, I., & Teidt, P. (1986). *Multicultural Teaching: A Handbook of Activities, Information,*

and Resources. Needham, MA: Allyn and Bacon.

Descriptions of materials that can be employed in a case study approach for dealing with ethnic conflict are included in the following reference.

41. Kleinfeld, J. (1990). *The Case method in Teacher Education: Alaska Models.* Charleston, WV: ERIC/CRESS.

The following reference includes evidence that schoolwide approaches reduce prejudice and improve interethnic group relations in school.

42. Pate, G. S. (1989). Reducing prejudice in the schools. *Multicultural Leader,* 2(20), 1–3.

The works of authors who favor a transformational education or social reconstructionist education multicultural approach are listed here and in Chapter 3.

43. Mullard, C. (1985). Racism in society and school: History, policy, and practice. In F. Rizvi (Ed.), *Multiculturalism as an Educational Policy.* Victoria, Australia: Deakin University Press.

44. Quality Education for Minorities Project. (1990). *Education that Works: An Action Plan for the Education of Minorities.* Cambridge, MA: MIT Press.

45. Sleeter, C. (Ed.). (1991). *Empowerment Through Multicultural Education.* Albany: State University of New York Press.

46. Wood, G. H. (1984). Schooling in a democracy: Transformation or reproduction? *Educational Theory,* 34(3), 219–239.

The following references discuss the different ways students and educators can respond to cultural incompatibilities in school and examine their advantages and disadvantages.

47. Alley, J. (1980). Better understanding of the Indochinese students. *Education,* 101, 111–114.

48. Bernal, E. (1974). A dialogue on cultural implications for learning. *Exceptional Children,* 40, 552–563.

49. Buriel, R. (1984). Integration with traditional Mexican-American culture and sociocultural adjustment. In J. L. Martinez Jr. & R. H. Mendoza, *Chicano Psychology,* (2nd Ed.). Orlando, FL: Academic Press.

50. Buriel, R., & Saenz, E. (1980). Psychocultural characteristics of college bound and non-college bound Chicanos. *Journal of Social Psychology,* 110, 245–251.

51. Cloud, N. (1991). Acculturation of ethnic minorities. In A. M. Ambert (Ed.), *Bilingual Education and English as a Second Language: A Research Handbook* 1988–1990. New York: Garland.

52. Ellis, A. A. (1980). *The Assimilation and Acculturation of Indochinese Children into American Culture.* ERIC ED 213–484.

53. ERIC/CUE. (1985). The social and psychological adjustment of Southeast Asian refugees. *Urban Review,* 17(2), 147–152.

54. Higham, J. (1984). *Send These to Me: Immigrants in Urban America.* Baltimore: The Johns Hopkins University Press.

55. Hilliard, A. G., III (1992). *Language, Culture, and Valid Teaching.* Paper presented at the Topical Conference on Cultural and Linguistically Diverse Exceptional Children., Minneapolis, MN.

56. Hornett, D. M. (1990). Elementary-age tasks, cultural identity, and the academic performance of young American Indian children. *Action in Teacher Education,* 12(3), 43–49.

57. Irvine, J. J. (1991). *Black Students and School Failure: Policies, Practices, and Prescriptions.* New York: Praeger.

58. Jordan, K., Tharp, R. G., & Baird-Vogt, L. (1991). Cross-culturally compatible schooling. In M. Saravia-Shore & S. F. Arvizu (Eds.), *Cross-Cultural Literacy: Ethnographies of Communication in Multiethnic Classrooms.* New York: Garland.

59. Kleinfeld, J. (1975). Positive stereotyping: The cultural relativist in the classroom. *Human Organization,* 34(3), 269–274.

60. Landsman, M., Padilla, A., Clark, C., Liederman, H., Ritter, P., & Dornbusch, S. (1990). *Biculturality and Academic Achievement Among Asian and Hispanic Adolescents.* Paper presented at the annual meeting of the National Association for Bilingual Education, Tuscon.

61. Longstreet, W. S. (1978). *Aspects of Ethnicity.* New York: Teachers College Press.

62. Macias, J. (1987). The hidden curriculum of Papago teachers: American Indian strategies for mitigating cultural discontinuity in early schooling. In G. Spindler & L. Spindler (Eds.), *Interpretive Ethnography of Education: At Home and Abroad.* Hillsdale, NJ: Lawrence Erlbaum.

63. Melville, M. B. (1980). Selective acculturation of female Mexican migrants. In M. B. Melville

(Ed.), *Twice a Minority: Mexican American Women*. St. Louis: Mosby.

64. Morales, R. F. (Ed.). (1983). *Bridging Cultures*. Los Angeles: Asian American Health Training Center.

65. Niera, C. (1988). Building 860. *Harvard Educational Review, 58*(2), 337–342.

66. Patrick, J. L. (1986). Immigration in the curriculum. *Social Education, 50*(3), 172–176.

67. Ramirez, M., & Castenada, A. (1974). *Cultural Democracy, Bicognitive Development and Education*. New York: Academic Press.

68. Saville-Troike, M. (1978). *A Guide to Culture in the Classroom*. Rosslyn, VA: National Clearinghouse for Bilingual Education.

69. Santiseban, D., & Szapocznik, J. (1982). Substance abuse disorders among Hispanics: A focus on prevention. In R. M. Becerra, M. Karno, & J. I. Escobar (Eds.), *Mental Health and Hispanic Americans: Clinical Perspectives*. New York: Grune & Stratton.

70. Shade, B. J. (1982). Afro-American cognitive style: A variable in school success. *Review of Educational Research, 52*, 219–244.

71. So, A. Y. (1987). High-achieving disadvantages students: A study of low SES Hispanic language minority students. *Urban Education, 22*(1), 19–35.

72. Szapocznik, J., Kurtines, W. M., & Fernandez, T. (1979). *Bicultural Involvement and Adjustment in Hispanic American Youths*. ERIC ED 193–374.

73. Thomas, E. W. (1978). English as a second language for whom? *The Crisis, 85*(9), 318–320.

74. Tharp, R. (1989). Psychocultural variables and constants: Effects on teaching and learning in schools. *American Psychologist, 44*(2), 349–359.

75. Torres-Matrullo, C. M. (1980). Acculturation, sex-role values and mental health among mainland Puerto Ricans. In A. M. Padilla (Ed.), *Acculturation: Theory, Models, and Some New Findings*. Boulder, CO: Westview Press.

76. Vigil, J. D. (1982). Chicano high schoolers: Educational performance and acculturation. *Educational Forum, 47*(1), 58–73.

77. Wei, T. T. D. (1980). *Vietnamese Refugee Students: A Handbook for School Personnel*. ERIC ED 208–109.

78. Wong-Rieger, D., & Quintana, D. (1987). Comparative acculturation of Southeast Asian and Hispanic immigrants and sojourners. *Journal of Cross-Cultural Psychology, 18*(3), 345–362.

Limitations on educators' ability to adapt to students' learning styles are discussed in the next reference.

79. Hyman, R., & Rosoff, B. (1984). Matching learning and teaching styles: The jug and what's in it. *Theory into Practice, 23*(1), 35–43.

The following references provide evidence that matching instructional techniques to students' personal characteristics enhances learning.

80. Carbo, M. (1984). Research in learning style and reading: Implications for instruction. *Theory into Practice, 23*(1), 72–76.

81. Dunn, R. (1984). Learning style: State of the art. *Theory into Practice, 23*(1),10–25.

82. Hare, B. R., & Levine, D. U. (1985). Effective schooling in desegregated settings: What do we know about learning style and linguistic differences? *Equity and Choice, 1*(2), 13–18.

83. Mickler, M. L., & Zippert, C. J. (1987). Teaching strategies based on learning styles of adult learners. *Community/Junior College Quarterly, 11*, 33–37.

84. Smith, L. H., & Renzulli. (1984). Learning style preferences: A practical approach for classroom teachers. *Theory into Practice, 23*(1), 44–50.

Chapter 5

Contextually Appropriate Education

The techniques educators use to assess, instruct, and manage students are often designed for middle-class students from stable homes with two native-born, well educated parents who understand how U.S. schools work and have the time and resources to help their children gain the most that they can from their school experiences. Many students do not grow up in these kinds of families. Because the context of their life is different, they do not profit as much from traditional educational approaches.

This chapter discusses the effects of various contextual factors on students' school experiences. It describes the additional problems students may face because of the context of their lives and suggests specific ways in which educators can reduce or even eliminate these potential problems. The following topics are included: immigrant and refugee students, children of illegal immigrants, migrant students, students from cultures that have a history of unequal cross-cultural relationships with European Americans, students in rural and isolated areas, abused and neglected students, and students whose parents are unable to provide them with adequate child care.

Immigrant and Refugee Students

Immigrant and refugee students experience many contextual problems in U.S. schools that interfere with their learning (1–23). When these students do not learn English or subject matter as rapidly as expected, teachers should investigate and attend to the possible contextual causes of their slower-than-expected progress. Too often however, teachers react to their academic difficulties by placing them in low-ability tracks and groups. To avoid these mistakes, teachers should be sensitive to the following potential contextual problems.

> *Immigrant students are clustered along with minority American students in classes which teach the answers to questions on minimum competency exams. So there is very little enrichment, there's very little encouragement for critical thinking or some of the other skills that are so very important for success in later life.*
>
> *Immigrant students tend to become tracked for failure and geared toward low-level jobs. They are steered away from college prep courses. (13, p. 48)*

Culture Shock

When people have to adjust to a culture that is significantly different from their own, they often become confused, anxious, and frustrated because they don't know what is expected of them in different situations. They often cannot solve interpersonal problems and do not know what is and isn't acceptable behavior in the new culture. They may become angry at people whose behavior they can't understand. They can also feel anxious and fearful about not being able to function adequately in the new culture or sad and depressed over the loss of their familiar way of life. All of this disorientation and confusion is called culture shock (1, 9).

Students who immigrate to the United States from other countries can also suffer culture shock in school. They may become angry, anxious, sad, or depressed. Some students may withdraw from their teachers and the other students or act aggressively toward them. These behaviors can lead educators to refer such students to be assessed for the kinds of emotional problems that require special educational services. The plight of the Hispanic American student who suffers culture shock is described here.

> *The very first day in the first grade the Mexican American child starts with a handicap no humane society should place on the shoulders of a mere child. English is the language of the classroom. He speaks no English or he speaks inadequate English. The whole program is designed to make him an Anglo. . . . He doesn't want to become an Anglo or he doesn't know how. . . . The Anglo concepts and values that prevail are unintelligible to him. . . . There is nothing in the atmosphere from which he can draw any comfort. Nothing he can relate to. . . . . He is one scared kid. (21, p. 3)*

The following excerpt from the responses of a Japanese teacher studying in the United States about what a European American teacher should know about the background of a recently arrived Japanese student provides examples of specific differences that can cause immigrant students to experience culture shock in American schools.

A. There is a lot of memorization. . . . Most students would expect a teacher to teach them rather than ask them questions or raise discussions. When I first came here, I expected all the professors to be lecturing us rather than asking us questions. At first, I was very embarrassed; it was hard for me to follow.

Q. Sometimes a problem is created when a teacher picks out a student and corrects him.

A. I think it might cause the student to react in a negative way. He might try to keep to himself. If the teacher corrects mistakes in class, the student might be very embarrassed.

Q. What kinds of other adjustment problems would a Japanese student face?

A. The small daughter of a friend of mine from Japan was having difficulties when she entered school here. When she started to go to school, she used to come back every day, crying. It appears that in her math class, she was doing the math according to the Japanese way. An American student corrected her by saying, "This is not the way." And every time she wrote something, the American boy erased it. Since she could not speak any word of English, she had no way of indicating that she was doing it the Japanese way, she had no way but to cry. The teacher thought that the child was kind of nervous and somewhat strange. (7, pp. 24–27)

Imposing the school's culture on students without regard to the culture they bring with them can cause them to experience even greater degrees of culture shock than they already do. But building bridges between their home culture and the culture of the classroom can help manage the severity of the culture shock they will have to suffer.

Culture brokers have been used successfully to assist non–European American students (recent immigrants, second-generation Americans, and Native Americans, African Americans, and others who are not knowledgeable about the ways of European American schools) to acculturate to unfamiliar school environments (27, 28, 31). Culture brokers are bicultural individuals, usually other students, assistant teachers, paraprofessionals, or parent volunteers who are equally knowledgeable about and comfortable in both the non–European American students' culture and the culture of the school. Although it is not essential, it is helpful for them to have experienced and solved the kinds of problems that face the students they are going to help. Typically they belong to the same ethnic groups as the non–European American students; however, some people believe that European Americans who are very familiar with a particular non–European American culture can also serve as culture brokers.

Culture brokers help bridge the gap between the school's and non–European American students' culture by performing three roles: "translators of the academic subculture to the student's ethnic subculture, translators of the student's ethnic subculture to the academic subculture, and role models" (27, pp. 122–126). As translators to students' subcultures, they teach students which behaviors are appropriate in various situations, explain the possible motivations behind European Americans' actions or their reactions to the students' behavior, and so on. As translators to the academic subculture, they help students' teachers and peers understand and appreciate their feelings, attitudes, motives, and behavior. As models, they demonstrate the appropriate behavior necessary to be successful in the new culture. The following statement by a Peruvian American student with an African American, European American, and Native American background illustrates the usefulness of a cultural broker.

> My first day in school I didn't understand anything at all. I didn't speak English, I didn't understand the Black students. I didn't understand the white students and there were hardly any Latinos. I was real scared. Then they assigned me a buddy. She was Black and Latino like me and she was in the eighth grade too. I went to all of her classes with her and never went anywhere during recess, lunch, or any time without her.
>
> She told me that the other students were trying to figure out what I was, Black, Latino or what. I looked like I could be Black but didn't speak or act Black. She helped me understand things. She taught me what to do when people started up with me. She taught me how to do things right in school. And she explained why the Black kids acted that way.
>
> Little by little I learned how to act in school. I even learned how to be Black. Now I can act Latino, Black or White. (24)

Cultural assimilators have also helped students who are unfamiliar with American school practices to understand and adjust to them. Cultural assimilators typically consist of a series of problematic situations with a number of alternate ways of behaving in the situation or perceiving the situation. Students choose which alternative is one they would follow or how they would perceive

---

Cultural Assimilator (26)

The following scenarios are examples of items included in cultural assimilators.

What should you do?

- You are sitting in the classroom talking with classmates when the teacher enters the room. The teacher gives out papers to the class and you don't get one.
- The teacher is talking to the class, and you didn't understand part of his lecture.
- You are talking to a friend, and you want to end the conversation because you are in a hurry.
- Your teacher gave you a homework assignment that you aren't able to do. It's due the next day.

How should you feel?

- You see a classmate walking toward you. You stop and say hello. Your classmate smiles, says "Hello, how are you," and continues walking.

Why do people behave that way?

- A man gets on the bus and goes all the way to the back to get a seat by himself, even though there is a seat next to you.
- One of your women teachers sometimes sits on her desk when teaching, wears slacks to class, and often talks with students informally after class.

the situation. Then they discuss each alternative's advantages and disadvantages, appropriateness or inappropriateness, accuracy or inaccuracy in America (25, 26, 29, 30).

Including aspects of the student's home culture in the classroom by putting up pictures of the student's native country, arranging for classroom demonstrations of the cooking, music, or dancing of the student's place of birth, and discussing the student's country of origin can make the classroom environment a little less strange and help smooth the student's transition. Tolerating symptoms of culture shock in the classroom when they occur, as long as they are not too disruptive, will avoid putting extra pressure on students to adjust faster than they are able to. Providing alternatives when the activity of the moment is not appropriate, can sometimes prevent them from having unpleasant experiences. For example, some students may not be ready for coed recreational activities, competitive games, or showering nude in front of others. You can make other options available to them. Providing alternative foods and snacks to replace what the students are unaccustomed to eating or are prohibited by religious beliefs from eating can show your concern and respect for them and their customs. Such sensitivity also avoids placing students in a conflict situation.

Identity Conflicts

Many immigrant students may experience identity conflicts during the acculturation process if they are pressured at home and in their community to maintain the traditional values of their culture and at the same time are pressured at school to accept new cultural values (32–34). Some students adopt the culture of the school and try to abandon the traditions of their families. If they do this, they may be punished by their parents and suffer from feelings of guilt and shame. Other students may reject the pressures of school and satisfy their parents, but by doing so, they risk getting into trouble with their teachers and school administrators (34).

> *The immigrant child lives between two cultures—that of the family, and that of the mainstream society. He is thus exposed to the conflicting values of home, peer group, school, to clashing definitions of the good life, and to the tug and pull of competing loyalties.(Rudolf Vecoli, Director, Immigrant History Research Center, University of Minnesota, St. Paul) (13, p. 21)*

> *He is living in two worlds. During the day, he is American. He is trying to "Americanize himself." He is trying to fit in. He has a lot of peer pressure to deal with. And when he comes home at night, he is Haitian. And that is very hard. He has two different sets of rules to follow. (Reine Leroy, Intergroup Relations Representative, Dade County Public Schools, Florida) (13, p. 21)*

A Chinese American high school student who immigrated to the United States when she was ten years old expressed her identity conflict in this way.

> *I don't know who I am. Am I the good Chinese daughter? Am I an American teenager? I always feel I am letting my parents down when I am with my friends*

*because I act so American, but I also feel that I will never really be an American.
I never feel really comfortable with myself anymore. (33, p. 30)*

Some non–European American students born in the United States are
brought up by parents who want them to assimilate totally to the culture of the
school. Many others are torn between conflicting messages and pressures regarding the right and wrong ways to live their lives. The school's role in exacerbating
Hispanic American and Indian American students' identity conflicts is described
in the following statements.

*Cultural conflicts between home and school cause youth to either choose one or
the other. This causes conflicts in personality, adjustment, etc. He needs to act
one way at school and when he gets home, uses a different language and a different set of cultural values. If the school allowed him to be himself, he wouldn't
have the problem. (32, p. 122)*

*The more schools pressured Punjabi children to conform to prevailing norms for
behavior, the more tightly their parents supervised their behavior and advised
against too much social contact with nonPunjabi peers. Punjabi parents defined
"becoming Americanized" as forgetting one's roots and adopting the most dis-
paraged traits of the majority group, such as young people making decisions on
their own without parental counsel, leaving their families at age 18 to live independently, dating, dancing, and friendship between the sexes.*

*Parents constantly admonish their young that they will dishonor themselves,
their families, and their community if they adopt the values and behaviors of
majority peers. (8, p. 269)*

You can reduce the severity of your students' identity conflicts by not pressuring them to do things the way you are used to having them done. Examples of
such pressure could include calling on students who do not volunteer or feel comfortable speaking up in class, asking students to state publicly whether they agree
with the previous speaker, or requiring students to admit their mistakes and apologize for them verbally when their culturally determined ways are just as
effective.

The techniques for reducing culture shock described earlier—such as including students' language, heritage, and cultural values in the curriculum and using
teaching styles that are familiar to students—reduce pressure on students to
choose between assimilating completely at the expense of their original cultures
or rejecting the school's culture in order to maintain their own. Educators can use
many different activities to demonstrate their respect for students' cultural heritages. For example, students can prepare multicultural calendars that include the
important dates in the history of students' countries of origin and the holidays
celebrated in their native countries, and they can present written, oral and videotaped reports to their classmates and write and perform in skits on themes such as
Coming to America, What Do I Miss?, Forced Out, Homeland Histories, and so

on. Teachers can also include literature and films about immigrants in their curricula.

A large number of published materials are available to educators. These include descriptions of educational programs that have proven to be effective approaches for immigrant and refugee students, curriculum guides for teaching about immigrant and refugee students, lists of books suitable for students about immigrants and refugees, and lists of films, videos, and so on (35–40).

As one person, your influence on your students' identity conflicts is limited; a schoolwide approach initiated and encouraged by school administrators can accomplish much more. As Sleeter and Grant have put it, "If one wants children to learn to value America's cultural diversity . . . it is not enough simply to tell children that these should be valued. The whole environment of the school must be teaching this" (40, p. 150). Still, it would certainly benefit your students for you to do whatever you personally can to help them avoid identity conflicts.

Language and Teaching Style Differences

Having to adjust to a new language and an unfamiliar teaching style can be traumatic for some students. Wei (22) describes some of the difficulties Vietnamese students often experience in American schools where they are taught in a language foreign to them and in an unfamiliar teaching style.

> There are three categories of educational difficulties that the Vietnamese child must face: (I) different learning styles and classroom activities; (2) a change in the student–teacher relationship; and most of all (3) the language barrier.
>
> Differences in learning style and classroom activities. *The Vietnamese educational system promotes a passive type of learning where the students learn by listening, watching, and imitating their teachers. The open type of classroom common in many American schools is perceived by the Vietnamese as confusing and disorganized. Since Vietnamese students are used to a lecture method, team teaching and active class participation are uncommon and strange to many of them. They are not used to group activities and do not know how to react. Independent projects or library research are foreign to them, and they need to be guided with patience.*
>
> The student-teacher relationship. *The American teachers' friendliness and informality are shocking to the Vietnamese students and hard for them to accept. The absence of honorific terms in the English language compounds the problem and makes the Vietnamese students feel uneasy and uncomfortable when talking with their teachers. They are reluctant to ask questions in class because such behavior seems aggressive and disrespectful to them. Their confusion is increased when, to their surprise, their teachers reward such behavior in class.*
>
> *Since they are not accustomed to talking in front of the class, they are shy and uncomfortable when asked to do so in the American classroom. They do not volunteer answers because they have been taught to be modest. If they need help, they probably will not ask for it.*

The language barrier. *The language problem can be very acute when there is only one or very few Vietnamese students in the school. The lack of communication or understanding between the child and the school authority can cause a small misunderstanding to grow into a large emotional or discipline problem. I remember a woman principal who asked me if a little boy in a kindergarten class knew Kung Fu because of his uncontrolled strength. Being the only Vietnamese in the school, he was totally confused and bewildered with no one to turn to for help. His tension had built to an explosive limit. Once explanations were given to him in Vietnamese, he was a changed child.*

The language barrier also limits the child's social contacts with American peers. A high school teacher was concerned when a Vietnamese boy changed from being friendly and cooperative to being antisocial. A talk with the boy revealed that he did not know enough English to communicate with his peers, and as a result, he was slowly withdrawing from them. He was frustrated because he could not say "maybe later" or "not at this time" when he was asked to join in an activity. His abrupt responses seemed rude to his classmates, further frustrating him, and in effect, discouraging other social interaction.

Many of the directions and explanations in the American classroom are verbal. . . . You can imagine the tremendous amount of self-control and self-discipline that a non-English-speaking child must maintain in order to keep quiet and not disturb others. He can rely only on visual clues. These are not always dependable and mean that the child will always be one step behind the others. This causes his/her reactions and behavior to be out of place." (22, p. 13–14)

Research indicates that instructing students for part of the day in their native languages while they are learning English as a second language helps them adjust better to attending schools where almost every transaction is in English (8). (See Chapter 6.) The Bilingual Education Act of 1988 provides that limited English proficient students may be instructed bilingually for three years and up to five years if needed in order to bridge the transition from their native language to English. When bilingual education is not a viable option, students can be placed in programs that combine sheltered English instruction, in which basic English is used to teach students their academic subjects, and English as a second language instruction to improve their advanced English skills. Although not as desirable as bilingual education, these programs are preferable to merely submerging non-English proficient students in regular classes taught in English, in which they either swim or sink (see Chapter 6).

A Chinese American Student's Reaction to Being Taught in a Strange Language

I started to hate myself when I failed to answer the teacher's questions . . . because I couldn't express my answers in English. Then I began to hate everything in the world, including my parents because they took me to this country. (13, p. 25)

Adapting your instructional and classroom management techniques to the learning styles of these students while they acquire the skills necessary to learn in U.S. classrooms can enhance their learning, (see Chapter 11). It may also reduce the likelihood that students will be frustrated, angry, anxious, or resentful in class.

Previous Educational Experiences

The educational experiences of immigrant students vary greatly. Some have attended school before they arrive in the United States. Many others are too young to have participated in the educational programs of their countries of origin. Immigrant students from industrialized countries such as Taiwan and Korea typically have very different school experiences than those who come from Haiti, El Salvador, Laos, and Cambodia. Their experiences in a nonindustrialized environment may not provide them with the knowledge they require here.

Preschool immigrant students are exposed to their own rich culture instead of the cultural experiences that most mainstream educators and school administrators expect and value. As a result, they may begin school already behind because they don't know what their teachers expect them to know about the alphabet, numbers, colors, and places, even though they know a great deal about other areas not included in the traditional curriculum. If their teachers don't capitalize on what these students do know, they may soon fall even further behind. Then, frustrated by trying to produce at the level of the other students, they may act out their anger by behaving in ways that are disruptive to other students, or they may give up trying, withdraw, and tune out their teachers.

Differing school experiences of immigrant children are described in the following quotation.

> Some have been exposed to one hour a day of political indoctrination as their sole education, while others have put in eight-hour school days, six days a week covering all major academic areas. . . . There are dramatic contrasts between rural and urban education. For example, in Mexico . . . 75% of those in urban areas finish the 6th grade, compared to only 15% of those in rural areas. In El Salvador most rural areas schools don't go beyond second grade and operate with few materials or trained teachers. . . .
>
> Most students from Southeast Asia in the past decade have had disrupted school histories because of war, and have lived for a period in refugee camps. Depending on the camp's location and who ran it, a student may have had a few hours a day or less of instruction. Most camps had minimal if any books or instructional materials and few educated teachers. (33, p. 21)

Immigrant students who are accustomed to philosophies of life and education far different from those that prevail in the United States may have adjustment problems in school. This may be especially true of students from communist or former communist countries, such as Cuba and the former Soviet Union, who have been taught ideas about economics, history, international relationships, interpersonal relationships, and so on, that are very different from those included in the courses taught in American schools (14, 19). Students whose educational experience has had the focus described here may have considerable difficulty dealing with the ideas and ideals presented to them in the United States.

> *Three important objectives of present Cuban education are to determine the types of crimes that "American imperialism" has committed in different parts of the world, to explore the many advantages of socialism over capitalism and to recognize other people's struggles against imperialism around the world. (19, p. 37)*

As was just noted, immigrant students' academic readiness skills and knowledge will be different from those of most students in their classes. If they have not attended school prior to coming to the United States, they will lack a great deal of knowledge and skill that children acquire in school; if they attended school irregularly, there will be huge gaps in what they know and can do; and even if they attended regularly, they will not have learned many of the things that are included in the curriculum of the typical U.S. school.

It is therefore essential to provide these students with a curriculum that is as individualized to their needs as possible. This can be done by starting at the student's current level of functioning, including the concepts and skills the student has acquired, being on the lookout for and filling in gaps, and using teaching techniques that complement the student's learning styles.

Conflicting Demands

Immigrant students often are faced with demands that conflict with those of the schools they attend. If they are the only one in the family who can speak some English, they may have to interpret for their parents during school hours at meetings with community agencies; if they are the oldest child, they may have to care for their siblings instead of attending school; and if they came to the United States on their own as unaccompanied minors, they may have family back home who are dependent on them.

> *At quite an early age . . . children serve as interpreters for their parents and help their families confront many adult tasks. For example, if their tenement has no heat in the winter, the school child who knows English might be the one to place a telephone call . . . these immigrant children face much more responsibility and pressure than the average American school child. (13, p. 21)*

> *A lot of people, 13–14-year-old boys for example, that have come into the United States alone, by themselves, or just with a friend, are supposed to come and stay at a parent's or relative's house. But they know that they have sisters, they have brothers, they sometimes have parents that are waiting for them to support them. . . . And they cannot do it by attending school. (13, p. 27)*

It is important to take these conflicting demands into consideration when working with immigrant students. As much as possible, teachers should try to relieve students of as much of their outside burdens as possible. Teachers can assist families to obtain interpreters and child care services so that their students may be free to attend class. They can help parents understand that in the United States it is difficult for children to succeed in school unless they attend regularly.

When students are caught between conflicting demands despite their teachers best efforts, teachers can also adjust their expectations and demands to their students' realities. Adapting schedules, deadlines, and work loads to students' outside schedules can also be helpful.

Encouraging or pressuring students to avoid and resist outside demands on their time can be counterproductive, however. In many cases such pressure exacerbates the conflict in their lives without providing them with ways of solving their dilemmas.

Impoverished Living Conditions

Many immigrants and most refugees arrive in the United States with few economic resources to support them. As a result, many of them move into relatively impoverished environments, which can seriously impede their ability to succeed in school. Many do not find employment. Many of those that do earn very low wages. As a result, immigrants are much more likely to live below the poverty level (4). Too often parents do not have the financial resources to provide children with an adequate diet, health care, sleeping arrangements, materials necessary to progress in school, and so on. The home environment is often too crowded and noisy for students to prepare their lessons. As To explains:

> *Immigrants tend to settle in relatively deteriorating areas of inner cities where educational facilities are already poor and heavily used. In the absence of sufficient additional assistance, the influx of immigration adds an almost unbearable burden on the resources of the school. The home living condition of immigrant children is equally a serious drawback in terms of learning environment. Many of these immigrants live in crowded houses and apartments occupied by more than one family. The children may have no quiet place at home to do their homework or to study. (20, p. 7)*

In order to succeed with students who are living in impoverished conditions, it is important for teachers to adapt their methods and expectations to these students' realities. A section on homeless students includes many suggestions for accomplishing this.

Native American and Rural Students

Native American students who grow up on reservations and attend schools run by and designed for European American students are in a position that is somewhat analogous to that of immigrant students (41–43). Like foreign-born students, they live in a region separate from mainstream America where they speak a language other than English, and they are ill-prepared to adjust to and profit from the education typically offered in mainstream schools. This is especially true if the curriculum is culturally irrelevant, encourages beliefs and values that conflict with those of their communities, and is taught by teachers who are unfamiliar with their culture and unable to speak their native languages.

Rural children who migrate to urban areas often have similar experiences (44–48). For example, the following problems have tended to characterize many Appalachian students and their families who have moved to urban northern cities.

> *Appalachian youth are less likely to seek, or readily accept, school personnel support such as sponsorship or encouragement by a particular teacher or counselor. . . . They are less likely to participate in school activities.*
>
> *Youth do not identify with their schools especially in junior and senior high school, since most youth are placed in an unfamiliar neighborhood. . . . Familism requires that family situations take priority over education. . . . High absenteeism is at least in part a result of youth being needed at home to help care for siblings and household matters. The traditional migration process, in the three to five years after initial settlement in urban areas. . . can mean moving several times to find satisfactory neighborhoods, jobs, schools, doctors, and shopping areas. . . . Parents may encourage students into career/practical skills and vocational classes rather than college preparatory or advanced placement classes. . . . Class differences cause Appalachian youth to feel "looked down on" and the lack of attention given to Appalachian culture only adds to a defeated self-image. Differences in language, dress, and values are seen by other classes as deficiencies or inferiority. (46, pp. 99–101)*

Other students can suffer similar problems, albeit to a lesser degree. For example, students who move from middle America to the coasts, or from the South to the North or vice versa, and students who are bussed from one ethnic neighborhood to another may experience many of the problems of immigrant-like students.

Rural Students in Urban Schools

To say that Appalachians are poorly served by urban public schools is an understatement. Ethnographic studies of teaching and learning in urban primary and secondary schools have documented the biases of social class and ethnicity faced by urban Appalachian students. These biases are manifest in such routine practices as grouping children for instruction in reading and mathematics, segregating them by perceived ability, retaining students in grade, and administering Ritalin to young children labeled as hyperactive. (44, p. 125)

Illegal/Undocumented Immigrants

Although the children of illegal immigrants are entitled to a free education, they are not always afforded their rights (49–52). They are less likely to receive them because their parents are reluctant to take an active or assertive role with governmental agencies such as schools. Padilla describes the plight of the undocumented immigrant family vis-à-vis employers and community authorities in the following manner.

> *They are considered to be a menace to the country since they are here illegally; cannot find employment that is more than subsistence level and which is long and back breaking and for which they are frequently cheated out of wages; find it next to impossible to obtain needed health or social services because of fear of deportation if they have to admit to being here illegally . . . and are essentially powerless to counter discriminatory behaviors directed against them. (51, p. 3)*

As an attorney who advocates for children reported,

> *One way or another, vigilante principals and people who are misinformed are asking kids for their papers and denying them access to schooling on the basis that they do not have them, or refuse to produce them. (Peter Roos, Attorney, Multicultural Education Training and Advocacy [META], San Francisco) (13, p. 41)*

Enforcement of immigration laws can also interfere with students' education. A child advocate reported that

> *There appears to be a pattern developing with INS (Immigration and Naturalization Service) focusing their attention around school sites. Last spring . . . the school was a site for an immigration raid. Approximately 10 parents were arrested . . . they were taking their children there . . . of course, after that . . . many went down and pulled their children out of school for several weeks. (Audrey Yamagata Noji, Commissioner, Orange County Human Relations, California) (13, p. 64)*

Another child advocate stated that

> *INS harassment also affects the drop-out rate . . . you may have a child who is born in the United States, whose father is undocumented [but] the mother is here legally, born in the U.S. The INS apprehends the father, and the family moves. They're pulled out of school for six months and re-enter again. (Gilberto Cardenas, Tomas Rivera Center, San Diego, California) (13, p. 64)*

Since many undocumented immigrants live in fear of being discovered and deported, educators can avoid requesting information about students' immigration status or documents related to immigration questions and can assure students and their families that their immigration status is confidential.

Refugee Traumatic Experiences

Refugee students who have experienced war, famine, persecution, and other forms of suffering in their native lands or internment camps prior to coming to the United States bring to school additional problems that can interfere with their functioning. The following are some descriptions of the problems such experiences can create for students (53, 54).

> *Vietnamese students came to the United States not only as immigrants to this new land, but also as refugees. Immigrants leave their homeland on their own volition, with many possibilities of motivation for the move, whereas refugees have "no choice but to leave or to suffer." Refugees are in fact "driven away from their homeland"—they are "pushed out."*
>
> *Studies have shown that this type of forced migration and the experience of being uprooted involuntarily causes more psychological problems to refugees than to immigrants. With this in mind, an educator must be concerned about the mental well-being of students who have lived in conditions of violence and socio-political turmoil before coming to this country. Such students have been exposed to loss, extended violence, prolonged threat, and terrorization. They may have witnessed violence inflicted to members of their family or to close friends. Their exodus to this country has been paved with dangers and life threatening situations such as poverty, starvation, drowning at sea, rape, murder, piracy, life in a refugee camp, and the possibility of the separation of the family. (15, p. 1)*

Describing school life in Central America, a Salvadorian American has stated:

> *There are countless situations where children . . . were in the classroom where their teachers . . . were killed by armed people in different countries in Central America. And that is something that definitely affects a kid's performance and the overall ability for them to adapt into the school system. (Oscar Chacon, National Co-Coordinator, Comite El Salvador, Cambridge, Massachusetts, National Advisory Panel) (13, p. 22)*

Life in Cambodia for school children has been described this way:

> *Many teachers were executed . . . schools were destroyed and children sent to live on "work farms" often separated from their families . . . almost half the population died, either by starvation, disease, execution, or the war. (David Gilbert, Researcher, San Francisco) (13, p. 22)*

> *I remember teaching a spelling lesson to mostly Cambodian youngsters, and I was using a hangman game. One youngster said to me, "You know, that is how my parents died." (33, p. 66)*

Teachers, psychologists, and other professionals need to be aware of the contextual causes of refugee students' problems. When they are not, they may fail to give students the help they need.

Educators can make the class a safe haven for students who have suffered the traumatic experiences that cause families to leave their homelands precipitously. Students who do not yet feel secure in their new surroundings, who are frightened by physical aggression or threats of aggression, or even verbal conflicts among students, may need to feel that their teachers will protect them from being caught up in these events. If they are unable to handle discussions of themes such as war, starvation, crime, and so on, they may need to be allowed to engage in another activity or leave the class until the discussions have terminated.

Students who have survived the ordeals of refugee camps by becoming hard and tough and engaging in activities that in this country would be considered delinquent require understanding when they continue to behave in these ways in school. Although educators should not accept the behavior patterns refugee students acquired to survive terrible situations, they should not view the students as bad or punish them. A more appropriate and fairer approach would be to explain that although their behavior may have been necessary while they were refugees, because their situation in the United States is different they no longer need to behave that way.

Prejudice

Brought up in fairly homogeneous societies, many immigrant students get their first taste of ethnic prejudice when they begin to attend the American school system. Rural students who migrate to urban areas and Native American students who leave their reservations to attend schools run by and attended by European Americans also are often treated in a prejudiced manner. Students who experience prejudiced treatment from other students may form self-protective gangs, and their antagonisms may affect the way they function in school. If they also receive prejudiced treatment from teachers and/or other school personnel they may react in the ways described in Chapter 3.

Immigrant and immigrant-like students should not have to suffer experiences like those just described. The previous chapter includes many suggestions for eliminating prejudice in schools.

Strengths

Although it is true that immigrant and refugee students experience many contextual problems that can interfere with their functioning in school, they also have unique strengths that teachers can use in the classroom (8, 55).

Those that leave their native lands to emigrate to the United States tend to be the active strivers and survivors—those who are best prepared to make sacrifices for their family's future. The strengths needed to make the decision to leave and to survive the leaving stand them in good stead in the United States.

Prejudice in the Schools

American students always picked on us, frightened us, made fun of us and laughed at our English. They broke our lockers, threw food on us in cafeteria, said dirty words to us, pushed us on the campus. Many times they shouted at me "Get out of here, you Chink, go back to your country." Many times they pushed me and yell on me. I've been pushed, I had gum thrown on my hair. I've been hit by stones, I've been shot by air gun. I've been insulted by all the dirty words in English. All this really made me frustrated and sad. (Reported by a Chinese American limited English proficient student)

The Americans tell us to go back to our own country. I say we don't have a country to go back to. I wish I was born here and nobody would fight me and beat me up. They don't understand. I want to tell them if they had tried to cross the river and were afraid of being caught and killed and lost their sisters, they might feel like me. (Reported by a Cambodian American student) (33, pp. 34–35)

In school, Punjabi teenagers are told they stink, directly by white students and indirectly by their teachers. They are told to go back to India. They are accused of being illegals. They are physically abused by the majority students, who spit at them, refuse to sit by them in class or on buses, crowd in front of them in line, stick them with pins, throw food at them and worse. They are labelled troublemakers if they defend themselves. . . . They are criticized for their hairstyle, their diet, and their dress. They are faulted because they place family ahead of individual interests, defer to the authority of elders, accept arranged marriages, and believe in group decision making. (8, p. 268)

In addition, compared to many native-born students, immigrant and refugee students and their parents are more likely to view education as the major and often only way for them to improve their vocational and economic status, to repay their parents for the sacrifices they made to bring them to this country, and to help those family members left behind, and they appreciate the opportunity (often denied their parents in their native countries) to obtain an education (8, 55). For example, Suarez-Orozco describes the attitudes of Central American immigrants and refugees in the following manner.

Universally, informants reported that schooling was the single most significant avenue for status mobility. It is important to note that the majority of my parent-informants had been pushed out of school in their native lands. Some could not afford the luxury of schooling in remote rural areas of Central America. Others had to face hard physical labor at an early age to contribute to the family's income. The parents were mostly laborers and semiskilled laborers. The current opportunities open to their children in the new land were seen by many parents in contrast to their own experiences in Central America. . . . As one Salvadorean informant succinctly put it, "Here is what you know, there is who you know."

Most of the Central American students I came to know well were keenly aware of the degree of parental sacrifice involved in getting out of the country of origin. . . . Students saw their parents become janitors, maids, busboys, and in some cases, take two jobs so they could go to school to receive the education the parents themselves never had.

The majority of my informants had one or more members of their nuclear family still residing in a war-torn Central American nation. Most of my informants worked about four hours a day, commonly after school, to help their relatives and those left behind with remittances. . . . Schooling efforts in the new land were framed in reference to a wish to "rescue" those relatives still in Central America. (55, pp. 291–292)

Identifying Immigrant, Immigrant-Like, and Refugee Students

Educators who work with refugee and immigrant students, Native American students who have grown up on reservations, and rural students in urban areas should adapt their educational approaches to the context of their students' lives. They also need to accept a certain amount of problematic behavior that students cannot control while they are adjusting to their new educational environments.

Although almost all of the students discussed in this section experience at least some of the problems just described, none of them experience all of these problems. In addition, you may have students in your class who are no longer experiencing many of these problems, especially if they have had time to acculturate to the American system. It is therefore important to understand the particular circumstances and contextual problems of each of your students and to treat them as individuals. The following information may help you to individualize your approaches to the particular needs of individual students.

Immigrant students who have spent the first four, five, or more years of their lives somewhere else require a number of years to acculturate to the way things are done in the United States, even if they and their parents want to learn the new ways as quickly as possible. Thus, if a student from another country hasn't been here at least for a few years, you can assume that her classroom functioning will be affected by at least some of the problems described earlier. If the student has recently arrived and is just beginning to attend school, you can also anticipate that she will experience some degree of culture shock. The same would apply to many other students who have to adjust to unfamiliar school environments, including Native American students, rural students in urban schools, and students who attend schools that serve children and youth from a different socioeconomic class.

Students' cumulative folders should include the information you need to determine where they were born and how long they have been in this country. Their folders may also contain information about whether they attended school prior to coming to the United States and, if so, the kind of school experiences they had. This is extremely important for refugee students, who may have spent two, three, four, or more years in refugee camps where there were no schools, and for students from rural areas in developing countries, where schooling may not have been compulsory or even available. If students' cumulative folders do not contain this information, you should be able to obtain it from the students themselves (if they are old enough), or their parents or guardians.

You can obtain some information about your Native American or rural students from their cumulative folder. However, you may have to rely on the students themselves, their parents, and sometimes agencies that are working with the students for most of the information you need.

Unequal Cross-Cultural Relationships

The history of the relationship between the students' groups and the group the teacher represents, usually the dominant culture, can affect a student's classroom behavior and success in school (12). Students who have personally experienced prejudice, oppression, rejection, or abuse by European Americans, or who have been brought up to anticipate and be wary of such treatment, may be suspicious of the teacher's motives. They may reject the teacher's friendship, act provocatively and disrespectfully, or rebel against the teacher's authority. This certainly could apply to African American and Hispanic American students who have first- or second-hand experience of the discriminatory treatment described in Chapter 3.

Other groups of students may also be suspicious of and hostile toward their teachers. The history of the relationships between Native Americans and the oppressive European American immigrants to this country, the current relationships between the two groups, and the discriminatory treatment Native American students experience in school give them good reason to be critical of and suspicious of European Americans in general and European American teachers in particular. Some Vietnamese American students have been told by their parents to be wary of European Americans, who betrayed them by withdrawing from the war and leaving behind many Vietnamese people who fought alongside them and supported them. As a result of the damage Korean American businesses suffered in Los Angeles in 1992, some Korean American students may harbor resentments against African Americans.

Growing up Indian in White America entails learning legends about historical atrocities committed by whites against Indians as well as personally experiencing white prejudice and discrimination in daily encounters. (43, p. 18)

An individual teacher may not merit such feelings on the part of his or her students, but their existence in the students' attitudes can adversely affect how they function in class and in school. Students who are alienated, hostile, and suspicious of another group, especially the dominant society and its institutions and organizations, can bring this hostility to school. They may disbelieve and reject out of hand much of what they are taught in class. For example, even at a young age, they may already disbelieve the concept "your friend, the police officer." As they progress through the grades, they may reject both their teachers' and the textbooks' interpretations of U.S. and world history, (for example the role of Christopher Columbus, the causes of the Civil War, or the desirability of U.S. intervention in Central America) as well as the standard explanations of how the U.S. economic and political systems function. Their opinions about the best way to solve the current issues facing The United States and the world may be at odds with those of their teachers. They may believe, sometimes with justification, that their teachers are insensitive to their cultural needs and indifferent, or even prejudiced, toward them. As a result, they may be suspicious of their teachers' motives.

Although some students keep their feelings to themselves in class, many others—especially the older ones—act them out. In doing so, they may repeatedly challenge their teachers' statements and demonstrate a lack of respect and disregard for their teachers' authority by not following rules, acting bored, making sarcastic and provocative comments, and purposely disrupting the class. Some students may withdraw from what they consider to be an irrelevant and prejudiced education by tuning their teachers out, arriving late, and cutting class. These students may function the same way in your class regardless of whether you merit their reactions because of what you represent to them, at least until they get to know and trust you.

If you have alienated students in your class or if you are the recipient of their anger, resentment, and distrust of the system, tell them that you understand how they feel and why they might feel that way, but explain how things are different in your classroom. If students act out their anger or resentment in class, explain that because you understand their feeling you can accept their behavior as long as they do not seriously disrupt the class. But make it clear that, although you understand how they feel, they will not be allowed to interfere with other students' right to learn. When students withdraw from classroom participation, tune you out, come late, cut classes, and so on, explain that there are better ways of expressing their feelings and solving the problem than denying themselves an education.

Earn their trust and confidence by utilizing a multicultural approach when you instruct students and manage their behavior (see Chapters 10 and 11), and advocate for their rights when they are mistreated or victimized by prejudice.

It is also important to correct any misperceptions students' families may have about you and develop positive relationships with them before it becomes necessary to solve problems and resolve issues. Communicating the positive accomplishments of their children, inviting them to visit the class and to participate in class events, and seeking their input and feedback about your curriculum can help establish a relationship of mutual respect and confidence. (See Chapter 4 for a detailed discussion of techniques for dealing with suspiciousness and alienation.)

Migrant Students

As was noted in Chapter 1, migrant students drop out is the highest rate of any group in the United States (60, 62, 65). Even while they are attending school they often perform poorly because of both the contextual aspects of their lives and the school system's inability or unwillingness to provide them with a contextually appropriate education (56–70). Dyson has described some of the unique contextual problems migrant students must deal with.

Imagine the problems a migrant child must face as he shifts from one school to another—perhaps as many as three times a year. Very often the migrant child does not use English as the primary language; he is not accepted readily by his

SELF-QUIZ: Contextual Problems

List and compare the possible contextual problems that each of the following students may be experiencing. Although there is insufficient information to really understand them, it is possible to be sensitive to potential problems they may be facing because of the context of their lives.

Martín is a 5-year-old Hispanic American student in a bilingual kindergarten program who has learned very little during the seven months he has been in school. He was born in a rural town in Mexico and came to the United States with his parents when he was three. Very little is known about Martin's parents because they resist providing information to school authorities. However, it is known that both parents speak only Spanish.

Jaime is a 12-year-old full English proficient Nicaraguan American student who came to this country when he was seven months old. After spending three years in a bilingual program, he was transitioned to the regular English program.

Jewel is a 14-year-old, eighth-grade African American student. Because she was previously held back in the third grade and is in danger of failing again, she has been referred for evaluation for possible learning disabilities. She lives in a predominantly poor African American neighborhood. Her parents both dropped out of high school when they were sixteen and seventeen.

Rashid is a 9-year-old African American student who has been a behavior problem since kindergarten. He lives in a predominantly middle-class African American neighborhood. His parents are both college graduates.

Hoa is a 6-year-old Vietnamese American student who came to this country when she was four years old. She comes from a rural area. After escaping from Vietnam by boat she was kept in a camp for refugees for 17 months before coming to the United States.

Mai is an English proficient 13-year-old Vietnamese American student. She was born in the United States. Both of her parents were born in Vietnam and came here when the U.S. forces left Vietnam in the 1970s. She is doing well in all of her subjects except mathematics.

classmates because he is "different"; educational approaches and textbooks tend to vary from school to school; and many times instructors are not willing to bother with a student who will be in the classroom only a few weeks. (59, p. 1)

The negative results of these problems are all too prevalent.

Inevitably this constant interruption of learning, lack of continuity, absence from school during travel time, and often blatant discrimination by local communities and school personnel all contribute to migrant students falling behind . . . and getting disinterested in an educational system which cannot provide the needed continuous education. (66, p. 4)

These problems can be ameliorated to a considerable degree by educational programs geared to the needs of migrant students. Unfortunately, schools often add to students' problems rather than contribute to solving them. As Dyson puts it, "It is an unfortunate but undeniable reality that our educational system has been developed for, and geared toward, the permanent community resident" (59, p. 1).

Helping Migrant Students

The following suggestions for adapting educational approaches to the context of migrant students' lives appear repeatedly in the literature (57–63, 68–70). Educators would do well to incorporate as many of them as possible in their classrooms.

- Utilize a multicultural approach to make the classroom more relevant to students and to help students bridge the gap between their experiences and the culture of the school (see Chapter 4).
- Include English as a second language instruction, sheltered English approaches, and bilingual paraprofessionals to facilitate limited English proficient students' academic learning and their acquisition of English language skills (see Chapter 6).
- Because migrant students tend to be characterized by inconsistent enrollment and attendance in a number of different schools, do not assume that students have been receiving the education assistance they need or that they have even attended school on a regular basis.
- Identify and help students with the academic problems students experience because of their irregular school attendance.
- Provide students with successful role models by inviting individuals who have escaped from the vicious cycle many migrant families are caught in to be guest speakers, tutors, and so on.
- Help students become acquainted with the community, the services the community offers, and how their life can be improved by making use of those services. Field trips can be especially useful.
- Provide students with opportunities to learn career and vocational skills other than farmwork that will increase their employability.
- Encourage and assist parents to become involved in their children's education. Research indicates that even if parents are unable to help students with their schoolwork because they themselves have not attended or succeeded in school, children will learn more and have better attitudes about school if their parents are interested in the children's education and discuss it with them (60).
- Help parents develop a portfolio of documents such as birth certificates, previous school records, individualized educational plans, and the like. Since many students will transfer from school to school, their parents should have copies of the documents the students need to obtain the educational services they require.

Rural Students

The rural communities that students call home cannot and should not be stereotyped. Students may be living on remote islands, in rural farming areas, deserts,

Arctic villages, Native American reservations, isolated mountainous regions, and so on. Economically they may come from well-off, stable farming communities or economically depressed mining towns. Their communities may be connected to each other and to a large urban area by good roads that are open all year, their connecting roads may be impassible during the winter, or their only means of transportation to other areas may be by plane. Despite these important variations, there are some important contextual factors that educators who work with students in rural areas should be aware of (71–89).

Although students in rural schools face economic and social strains at least as difficult as those confronting students who attend inner city schools, their problems receive far less attention than those of urban students (76, 87). As was noted in Chapter 1, the dropout rate for rural students, between 40% and 50%, is more than twice the national average.

Research indicates that rural students experience many more problems and are exposed to many more adverse conditions than nonrural students (72, 76, 80, 84). However, educators are often unaware of these students, contextual problems. In one study they scored significantly poorer than nonrural students on 34 of 39 risk and problems factors (76). In comparison to nonrural students, rural students are twice as likely to come from poor families. They are significantly more likely to have illiterate parents, to be children of substance abusers, and to be victims of child abuse; they have lower self-esteem; and they have a greater tendency to be substance abusers, to experience depression, and to attempt suicide. As one researcher has stated: "It is apparent that the image of rural children leading wholesome, trouble-free lives compared with youth in more crowded settings is in need of revision" (76, p. 3).

Contextual Problems

Transportation difficulties in getting to remote locations, vast distances between population groups, impassable roads during inclement weather, and low population density make it difficult to provide education services to some students. Loss of farming, mining, timber, coal, and gas jobs has led to exacerbation of poverty. This has lowered an already small tax base for education and other services, and it limits what local governments can provide. As a result, although rural communities expend a greater percentage of their local resources on education, they are less able to afford technological tools such as computers, interactive television, and so on, that could help them overcome the logistics problems mentioned earlier.

Remoteness, poverty, and the unavailability of the many amenities found in urban areas make it difficult to attract and keep adequate numbers of qualified, well-trained professionals. The scarcity of prenatal care programs and nutrition programs that result from the lack of human resources leads to a high level of the kinds of biomedical problems that increase the number of children and youth with learning problems. Children from rural families that rely on seasonal activities such as fishing, agriculture, timber, and so on, may not be able to attend school during certain times of the year. Inconsistent attendance makes it especially difficult for educators to do what is necessary to help students actualize their potential.

Motivational Factors

Low self-esteem; high rates of poverty; low levels of parental education; parental encouragement to accept jobs that do not require a college education, to join the military, or to attend a trade school rather than a college; and a scarcity of jobs that require higher education have combined to keep the educational and vocational aspirations of rural students at a very low level (73, 81, 85, 87). In fact, rural youth who remain in rural areas as adults have the lowest educational aspirations of American youth (73).

Contextual, Motivational, and Cultural Strengths

Educators should also be aware of the contextual and cultural strengths that exist in rural communities (75, 76, 79). These include a tendency to trust their neighbors, close nuclear and extended family ties, a sense of community that leads rural citizens to aid their neighbors, and a strong sense of personal accountability. As Marrs puts it, "Rural Americans take pride in helping each other solve problems; they know each other, are aware of needs and resources, and are willing to share what they have if their neighbors need it" (80, p. 361).

Appropriate Education Services for Rural Students

The following suggestions for providing appropriate education services to students in rural areas have been made by experts in the field (75, 78, 89–103).

1. *Involve students' parents and their extended families in the education process as fully as possible* Especially when human resources are in short supply, parents can serve as volunteers in class and tutors at home. Since rural parents often tend to avoid authority figures in the schools, it is especially important to establish a positive rapport with parents through social contacts, nonthreatening social events, or meetings. Providing free child care and starting off with a meal can increase parent willingness to cooperate with educators.

2. *Use creative means to solve communication/transportation problems in isolated areas.* Use the community's informal communication network and enlist the support of the important people in the community to get your message across. These people may be the cooperative extension worker or the gas station attendant at the one regional gas station who speaks to everyone in the community, a well-respected church member, and so on. Work closely with other agencies and personnel—such as home health agents, county demonstration workers, public health workers, bookmobile librarians, and utility meter readers—who visit families.

3. *Augment the qualified professional personnel available with trained paraprofessionals if funds are available and with trained community volunteers and students' parents.* In rural areas, individual concerned community members, social clubs, librarians, local small business persons, church groups, volunteer fire departments, 4-H clubs, Chambers of Commerce, veterans groups, and other organizations are all good sources of human resources to augment the efforts of paid professionals and paraprofessionals. Although volunteerism has declined in urban areas, Kirmer and colleagues have reported: "Recruiting volunteers is not a problem in rural America. The main problem is keeping them busy" (96, p. 366).

4. *Employ technology to reach and teach rural students.* Current education practices that are based on communication among individuals working in comparatively close contact are less effective in rural settings. Technological tools such as videodiscs and videotapes, interactive television, instructional television, computers, and CB radio can improve instruction and enhance communication.

Middle-Class, Affluent, Suburban Students

Many educators tend to overlook the contextual problems facing students who grow up in middle-class, affluent suburbs. Contrary to the view presented in many basal readers, television programs, magazine articles, and education textbooks, children and youth who live in middle-class, affluent suburbs often lead lives that are far from idyllic. In some cases, their parents are too involved in their own careers to provide their children with the supervision, support, attention, and affection they need. Parents who are concerned that if their children do not get into the right preschool they will not be in the track that leads to acceptance by the right college and eventually to the right career may have great difficulty accepting their children for who they are. As a result, these parents may pressure their children when they are older to study more than they can, learn faster than they are able, and earn higher grades than they are capable of obtaining.

Students who live in aggregate families in which three or four parents share custody over them may find themselves living disjointed, unstable lives. Unless they have duplicates of all the education support materials they require at both of their homes, whether or not they can complete a particular assignment may depend in part on which home they are living in during a particular week. If they spend some nights of the week in one home and the remainder of the nights in another, they may forget to bring all of their school materials and books with them when they go from one to another.

Growing up in more affluent circumstances, they may have more money at their disposal to abuse drugs, alcohol, cars, and so on. They may have the money to spend their time in amusement arcades instead of attending school, and they may have more expensive electronic games at home to tempt them away from their schoolwork.

For these and other reasons, educators should be as concerned about possible contextual problems among their more affluent students as they are about any other groups of students.

Inadequate, Neglectful, and Abusive Child Care

Some students do not receive adequate child care. Through no fault of their own, very poor students' parents are often unable to provide them with the same nutrition and medical care that their more advantaged peers receive, and many of them cannot give their children the financial support they need to succeed in school.

Students do not have to be poor to suffer inadequate child care. Many middle-class and upper-class parents do not adequately care for children. Divorced parents may use students as pawns in their battles with each other. As was noted in Chapter 2, regardless of their ethnic or socioeconomic background, parents who abuse drugs and alcohol are often unable to care for their children while they are under the influence of these substances, and they may be unable to care for their children financially and psychologically even when they aren't under the influence if their lives are consumed by drug problems. In some cases the inadequate care students receive amounts to neglect or abuse.

Neglect and Abuse

The number of abused and neglected children and youth has risen precipitously in recent years. Although about 2 million cases of child abuse and neglect are officially reported annually, conservative estimates suggest that the number of children and adolescents that actually suffer abuse and neglect is two to three times that number. Thus, between 10% and 15% of the student population suffers from maltreatment (106). Whether this reflects a real increase in the prevalence of these problems or merely a greater willingness to report them is somewhat unclear. However, it is clear that far too many students suffer the effects of neglect and psychological, physical, and sexual abuse.

Although neglected children have many problems, those who suffer actual abuse are much worse off. Fink and Janssen have described the effects of abuse on adolescents as follows:

> *Systematic abuse causes significant dysfunction in intellectual, emotional, developmental, and motoric ability. Systematic abuse creates substantial "at risk" conditions among adolescents for psychological, interpersonal, academic, medical, and legal problems. Self-image, motivation, personal satisfaction, and success in the workplace are negatively impacted. Systematic maltreatment is an experience that dominates and delimits personal competence and effectiveness. (106, p. 32)*

Abused students tend to demonstrate serious behavior problems in school. However, the form their problems take depends on how they react to the abuse. Those who act out against others tend to be aggressive and abusive toward others. If they have been sexually abused, they may abuse others sexually or at least act out sexually. Those who turn away from others are likely to reject friendly overtures from others and withdraw from interpersonal relationships.

In general, whatever the outward manifestations of their problems they tend to mistrust others, especially adults. They have a low self-concept. In comparison to nonabused students, they are more likely to develop conduct and emotional problems, to abuse drugs and alcohol, to lack the motivation and energy necessary to succeed in school, and to misunderstand and be suspicious of the behavior and intentions of others.

Their tendency to misperceive others makes it especially necessary for teachers to be careful when selecting classroom management techniques for them. Because they have been maltreated in the past, they are less able to tolerate any kind of negative consequences, even mild ones. Students who have been locked up alone may have extreme difficultly coping with time out in an isolated area. Corporal punishment can have disastrous repercussions especially with students who have been physically abused.

Abused students may experience authoritative teachers who take charge of their classrooms as abusive, and they may even experience praise as a manipulative attempt to control them.

Students who have been sexually abused may be threatened by friendly and warm teachers. They may recoil from any form of physical contact no matter how innocent. Some of them may imagine that their teachers are on the verge of abusing them.

To avoid these potential problems and to help students overcome them, educators need to know which, if any, of their students have been victims of abuse or neglect. Although others may be the source of such information, educators are often the first persons to suspect and report possible cases of child abuse and neglect to the appropriate authorities. Every state has passed laws that require educators to report observations that lead them to suspect the possibility of child abuse. Because most teachers need additional training to be able to identify the signs of possible child abuse (109), it is important that they seek such training from their school districts or teacher preparation programs. Educators can also avail themselves of some of the material currently available to improve their level of competency (105, 111–113).

You can help students who are known to have been abused in a number of ways (104, 108, 110, 114–116). Begin by maintaining a classroom climate that makes abused students feel comfortable and secure. Determine whether students have actually suffered any of the potential negative results of child abuse that interfere with their cognitive functioning, powers of attention and concentration, ability to relate positively to others, and so on. Follow up your assessment by utilizing education techniques to deal with these negative results and by avoiding techniques like the ones mentioned earlier that can be inappropriate with abused students.

Identifying Neglected and Abused Students

The following physical and behavioral symptoms should alert educators to the possibility of child abuse and the need for additional investigation. However, they may also be caused by other problems.

Physical Abuse

- Unexplained cuts, bruises, burns, fractures, and welts
- Wary of adult contact
- Apprehensive when other students cry
- Aggressiveness or withdrawal
- Resists going home
- Fear of parents
- Reports abuse by parents

Physical Neglect

- Consistent hunger
- Poor hygiene
- Inappropriate dress
- Consistent lack of supervision
- Unattended physical or medical problems
- Abandonment
- Begging or stealing food
- Early arrival and late departure from school
- Constant fatigue, listlessness, or falling asleep in class
- Alcohol or drug abuse

- Delinquency
- Reports of parental neglect

Sexual Abuse

- Difficulty in walking or sitting
- Torn or stained clothing
- Pain or itching in genital area
- Venereal disease
- Pregnancy
- Unwilling to change for gym, withdrawal, fantasy, or infantile behavior
- Bizarre, sophisticated, or unusual sexual behavior, preoccupations, or knowledge
- Poor peer relationships
- Running away
- Reported sexual abuse

Emotional Maltreatment

- Speech disorders
- Lag in physical development
- Failure to thrive
- Sucking, biting, rocking
- Antisocial, destructive behavior
- Sleep disorders
- Compulsions, phobias, obsessions
- Behavior extremes—compliant, passive, demanding, aggressive
- Mental or emotional developmental lag
- Attempted suicide

As a teacher you are entrusted with a real treasure—a child's spirit. It can grow and flourish or it can be crushed. For the abused child, the school may be the only avenue of escape, a place where s/he can feel safe. Your classroom can support the child's needs if you:

Promote an accepting environment in your classroom.
Be warm and loving.
Create an individualized program for the maltreated child.
Give the maltreated child additional attention wherever possible. (116, p. 3)

When it is desirable or necessary to discuss students' abusive experience with them, reassure them that it is not their fault, they are not in trouble, have not done anything wrong, and are not bad persons because of the actions of others. Avoid asking prying questions and making judgmental statements about the adults who abused them. If students describe their abusive experiences, do not appear shocked, surprised, or horrified. Report your discussion in a timely manner to the person who has been legally designated by the school administration.

Homeless Children and Youth

Estimates of the number of homeless children, including those who have run away from home, range from 272,773 to 3,000,000 (123, 124, 142). Homeless children live on the streets, in cars, in public places such as railway terminals and subway stations, in abandoned buildings, or in tent cities. The luckier ones live in welfare hotels or shelters. The plight of homeless children and youth is horrendous (117–159). In comparison to those who live in homes, homeless students have more developmental delays, emotional problems, behavior disorders, and sleep disorders. They are more likely to be aggressive and noncompliant, shy and withdrawn, anxious, tired, and restless. They have greater difficulty forming relationships with others. They are also more likely to exhibit symptoms associated with stress and low self-esteem. Studies indicate that approximately 50% of them are clinically depressed, over 50% have contemplated suicide, and from 31% to 50% of them need psychiatric evaluation. Although they have four times as many health problems and twice as many chronic diseases, they have less access to medical care and are less able to follow the health regimes prescribed by physicians.

Many homeless children and youth are actually runaways. Between 1,000,000 and 1,500,000 children and youth run away from home each year (145). These children and youth suffer a great many problems (130, 142, 146, 155, 157). Prior to running away they may have suffered severe maltreatment including physical and sexual abuse (see the previous section). In comparison to children and youth who live at home, they are more likely to engage in self-destructive behavior, to abuse drugs and alcohol, to have medical and psychological problems, to attempt suicide, to be involved in illegal activities such as stealing, selling drugs, and prostitution in order to obtain money, to be the victims of abuse, and to have serious school problems.

The McKinney Homeless Assistance Act of 1987 and the 1990 amendments to the Act require school districts to operate outreach programs to identify homeless and runaway children and youth; to enroll them in school even if they do not have the proper documents, prior school records, proof of residency, inoculations, and so on; to provide them with materials such as paper, pens, books, and the like; and to establish free educational programs that meet their needs (138, 139). However, the contextual problems that confront homeless children interfere with their schooling. In addition to the reasons mentioned earlier, the homeless may not attend school because they cannot afford public transportation, they do not have proper clothing, they smell bad due to a lack of bathing facilities, or they are afraid of being rejected by their peers. As a result, from 28% to 43% of them do not even attend school. According to Heflin and Rudy,

> *The combination of physical, psychological, intellectual, and behavioral outcomes of homelessness for children and youth may make it difficult for them to achieve in school. . . . A variety of legal, financial, bureaucratic, social, and familial barriers serve to effectively exclude homeless children and youth from accessing educational opportunities. (133 p. 15, 17)*

Very few states have developed specialized programs that meet the needs of runaway and homeless students. This is particularly true of high school–age adolescents (146, 159).

To be effective, educators have to adapt their approaches to the realities of these students' lives. The following suggestions have been offered by experts in the field.

- *Focus on making sure students' basic needs are met.* Students who are struggling with problems involving transportation to school, food, clothing, sleep, and school supplies are unable to give their all to their studies. Assist students and their families to obtain the social, medical, financial, and other support service they require. Be discreet in order to avoid embarrassing them, and use techniques that empower parents to deal with these agencies in order to strengthen their child-care role and foster more positive parent-child relationships. However, if necessary, advocate for families who meet with resistance from service agencies.
- *Provide students a safe environment in which they can feel secure, relax their guard, act their age, and be themselves.* Runaway and homeless students often have learned to distrust adults who may have been unable or unwilling to care for them. They may be on their guard against anticipated disappointments, rejections, and abuse, and they may have had to assume adult-like responsibilities before they were ready to do so.
- *Assign students personal space.* Since homeless and runaway students are unlikely to have space of their own—their own room, closet, bed, place at a dinner table and so on—providing them with a space in their classroom that they can call their own and mark with symbols of their identity can improve their sense of self-worth and stability.
- *Assess students' skills, knowledge, abilities, and strengths and weaknesses in great detail.* Although this is desirable for all students, it is especially important for students who attend school irregularly, enroll in many different schools, and often do not complete assignments when they do attend.
- *Encourage students to become autonomous and independent so that they come to believe that they can be in control of their own lives.* Runaway and homeless students' living conditions tend to lead them to develop an external locus of control.

- *Maintain the kinds of flexibility necessary to incorporate students into your program for whatever amount of time they are able to attend.* Allowing students to progress at their own pace, individualizing their assignments, using modules, and computerized instruction are tools that can provide needed flexibility.
- *Encourage and assist students to attend your program even when it becomes difficult for them to do so.* Do not penalize students who are unable to attend, complete assignments, and so on, because of contextual problems.
- *Help runaways, students living alone, and the parents of homeless children to develop a portfolio of documents such as birth certificates, previous school records, individualized educational plans, and the like.* Like migrant students, they or their parents should have copies of the documents they need to obtain the educational services they require.
- *Work closely with other agencies that are assisting your students and their families.* Collaborative efforts are more effective than individualistic uncoordinated approaches.

A number of model educational programs designed for homeless students have been described in the literature (126, 159). Although most of these programs were developed with the needs of younger children in mind, they shed light on the ways in which both school districts and individual teachers can serve all homeless students.

Problems of Adolescence

As any adolescent psychology textbook will certify, adolescence is an especially difficult developmental phase. The problems that many adolescents face can seriously impact their functioning in school.

Dealing with their emergent sexual drives, deciding who they are and who they want to be, becoming independent and self-reliant, and making decisions that will effect their whole lives can consume much of teenage students' interest and energy. At times, even for the best of students, these issues can be more important and pressing than attending to and completing school work.

Approximately one million teenagers in the United States become pregnant each year (160). Although some teenage parents are or become dropouts, many continue in school. Adolescent parents who are also students have to balance and juggle the responsibilities of bringing up children and the demands of school. Without additional help, may of them are likely to fail and drop out.

Many teenagers have to deal with the temptations and results of substance abuse (164–168). Some adolescents who are members of violent gangs, neo-Nazi skinhead organizations, satanical societies, and other such groups, bring their attitudes and preoccupations with them to school. Students who bring such problems to school may have a difficult time learning and behaving appropriately.

To be effective with adolescents who have these kinds of problems, educators need to be sensitive to the potential difficulties that adolescents bring with them to school. They should be able to identify particular students with such problems, and they should have the skills necessary to adapt their expectations and teaching strategies to their students' difficulties and to help them to obtain the additional outside assistance they may require. Space does not permit a discussion of these topics here, but they are dealt with in the references at the end of the chapter (160–170).

Contextual Versus Cultural Factors

Educators sometimes incorrectly attribute some of their students' contextually influenced attitudes, behavior, and problems to cultural factors. For example, children of migrant workers have difficulty succeeding in school because they miss a great deal of school time while they are traveling from place to place and they attend various schools in which they have to cope with different curricula, expectations, procedures, teaching and classroom management styles, and so on. As a result, despite their intense desire to succeed in school they may become discouraged about and give up on education. Teachers who work in schools in which most of their Hispanic American students' parents are migrant workers tend to misperceive their students' *loss* of interest in school as a *lack* of interest in school, and many of them conclude that all Hispanic Americans devalue education. Similarly, because migrant workers and their children who move back and forth across the border between the United States and Mexico may not be motivated to learn English or assimilate to how things are done in the United States, some teachers who have little exposure to other Hispanic Americans may mistakenly believe that for cultural reasons Hispanic Americans in general are disinterested in assimilating or learning English.

Some parents avoid contact with the school because of their illegal status; some cannot afford the child care required to attend school meetings and functions or work two jobs to support their families; others cannot speak English well enough to participate in such functions or even understand the announcements that are sent home. Teachers who are unaware of the role played by these contextual factors may incorrectly attribute some parents' lack of attendance at school functions, open houses, back to school days, and so on, to a culturally influenced lack of interest in their children's education.

Many educators are not aware that many non–European American and poor parents are suspicious about the motives of teachers and school administrators because of the history of an unequal cross-cultural relationship between their ethnic or socioeconomic group and the group to which the educators belong. As a result, teachers may mistakenly assume that these students and their parents are brought up to be suspicious and hostile in general.

Teachers who are not aware of the extent to which racism and structured reproduction have helped to create a huge unemployment problem among African American teenage and adult males are too quick to assume that they are lazy and shiftless because they hang out in the neighborhood during the day. Not aware of many African American males' inability to support a family, they assume that African American males are brought up to avoid marriage and family responsibilities.

Teachers who do not take into account the effects of the trauma, abuse, neglect, and culture shock many Asian and Pacific American refugee students experience can mistakenly attribute their reticence and lack of participation in class to culturally influenced learning and behavior styles. As these examples demonstrate, it is essential that teachers understand the contextual aspects of their students' lives and avoid attributing the effects of contextual factors to cultural factors. This is one way in which they can avoid harmful prejudicial beliefs about students and their cultures.

Summary

Many students are faced with contextual problems that can seriously impede their ability to succeed in school. Immigrant and refugee students, migrant students, students from cultures that have a history of unequal cross-cultural relationships with European Americans, students in rural and isolated areas, abused and neglected students, and students whose parents are unable to provide them with adequate care all need a contextually appropriate education. Educators should adapt their approaches to these students contextual problems and strengths.

Activities

1. Enhance your understanding and appreciation of homeless and runaway students by visiting a local shelter for homeless families or runaway youth.

2. Interview some of your friends or fellow students to determine whether they mistakenly attribute contextual factors to cultural characteristics. You may find the that examples in the section on contextual versus cultural factors are a useful group of items with which to begin your list of questions.

References

The following references describe the problems of immigrant/refugee students and their families.

1. Adler, P. S. (1975). The transitional experience: An alternative view of culture shock. *Journal of Humanistic Psychology, 15*, 13–23.
2. Buell, L. H. (1984). *Understanding the Immigrant Mexican.* San Diego, CA: Los Amigos Research Associates.
3. Carlin, J. E. (1979). The catastrophically uprooted child: Southeast Asian refugee children. In J. D. Call, J. D. Noshpitz, R. L. Cohen, & I. N. Berlin (Eds.), *Basic Handbook of Child Psychiatry,* Vol I. New York: Basic Books.
4. Chan, K. S. (1980). *Limited English Speaking, Handicapped, and Poor: Triple Threat in Childhood.* ERIC ED 247–686.
5. Cloud, N. (1991). Acculturation of ethnic minorities. In A. M. Ambert (Ed.), *Bilingual Education and English as a Second Language: A Research Handbook 1988–1990.* New York: Garland.
6. Eisenbruch, M. (1988). The mental health of refugee children and their cultural develop-

ment. *International Migration Review, 22*(2), 282–300.

7. Geschwind, N. (1974). *Cross-Cultural Contrastive Analysis: An Exploratory Study.* Unpublished masters thesis, University of Hawaii, Honolulu.

8. Gibson, M. A. (1987). The school performance of immigrant minorities: A comparative view. *Anthropology and Education Quarterly, 18*(4), 262–275.

9. Juffer, K. A. (1983). Culture shock: A theoretical framework for understanding adaptation. In J. Bransford (Ed.), *Monograph Series: BUENO Center for Multicultural Education, 4,* 136–149.

10. Lee, E. (1988). Cultural factors in working with Southeast Asian refugee adolescents. *Journal of Adolescence, 11,* 167–179.

11. Mortland, D. A., & Egan, M. G. (1987). Vietnamese youth in American foster care. *Social Work, 32*(3), 240–245.

12. Mostek, K. (1985). *Exploring the Definition of Culture Shock and Second Language Learning in Elementary School—Grades 4–8.* ERIC ED 270–975.

13. National Coalition of Advocates for Students. (1988). *New Voices: Immigrant Students in U.S. Public Schools.* Boston MA: Author.

14. North Carolina Department of Public Instruction. (1983). *Here They Are . . . What Do We Do?* Raleigh, NC: Author.

15. Nguyen, T. P. (1987). Positive self-concept in the Vietnamese bilingual child. In M. Dao (Ed.), *From Vietnamese to Vietnamese American: Selected Articles.* San Jose, CA: Division of Special Education and Rehabilitative Services, San Jose State University.

16. Padilla, A. (1980). Acculturation: Theory, models, and some new findings. *American Association for the Advancement of Science Symposium Series,* No. 39. Boulder, CO: Westview Press.

17. Padilla, A. M., Lindlholm, K. J., Alvarez, M., & Wagatsuma, Y. (1985). *Acculturative Stress in Immigrant Students: Three Papers.* Occasional Paper No. 20. Los Angeles, CA: Spanish Speaking Mental Health Research Center, University of California, Los Angeles.

18. Rumbalt, R., & Ima, K. (1988). *The Adaptation of Southeast Asian Refugee Youth: A Comparative Study.* ERIC ED 299–372.

19. Silva, H. (1985). *The Children of Mariel from Shock to Integration: Cuban Refugee Children in South Florida Schools.* ERIC ED 261–136.

20. To, C. (1979). *The Educational and Psychological Adjustment Problems of Asian Immigrant Youth and How Bilingual-Bicultural Education Can Help.* Paper presented at the annual conference of the National Association of Asian American and Pacific Island Education, San Francisco.

21. Ulibari, S. (1970). *Stereotypes and Caricatures.* Paper presented at the National Education Task Force de La Raza Staff Training Institute. Albuquerque, New Mexico.

22. Wei, T. T. D. (1980). *Vietnamese Refugee Students: A Handbook for School Personnel,* (2nd ed.). ERIC ED 208–109.

23. Westmeyer, J., Neider, J., & Callies, A. (1989). Psychosocial adjustment of Hmong refugees during their first decade in the United States: A longitudinal study. *Journal of Nervous and Mental Disease, 177*(3), 132–139.

Techniques and materials for reducing culture shock are included in the following references.

24. Aranguri-Oshiro, R. (1987). Personal communication.

25. Fiedler, F., Mitchell, T., & Triandis, H. C. (1971). The culture assimilator: An approach to cross-cultural training. *Journal of Applied Psychology, 55,* 95–102.

26. Ford, C. K., & Silverman, A. M. (1981). *American Cultural Encounters.* San Francisco: Alemany Press.

27. Gentemann, K. M., & Whitehead, T. L. (1983). The culture broker concept in bicultural education. *Journal of Negro Education, 52*(2), 118–129.

28. Herzog, J. D. (1972). The anthropologist as broker in community education: A case study and some general propositions. *Council on Anthropology and Education Newsletter, 3,* 9–14.

29. Rosita, A., & Adamopoulos, J. (1976). An attributional approach to culture learning: The culture assimilator. In *Topics in Cultural Learning,* IV. Honolulu: East West Culture Learning Institute.

30. Triandis, H. C. (1975). Culture training, cognitive complexity and interpersonal attitudes. In R. W. Brislin, S. Bochner, & W. J. Lonner (Eds.), *Cross-Cultural Perspectives on Learning.* Beverly Hills, CA: Sage.

31. Wyatt, J. D. (1978–1979). Native involvement in curriculum development: The Native teacher as cultural broker. *Interchange: A Journal of Educational Studies, 9,* 17–28.

Identity conflicts of immigrant students are discussed in the following references.

32. Grossman, H. (1984). *Educating Hispanic Students: Cultural Implications for Instruction, Classroom Management, Counseling, and Assessment.* Springfield, IL: Charles C Thomas.

33. Olsen L. (1988). *Crossing the Schoolhouse Border: Immigrant Students and the California Public Schools.* San Francisco, CA: California Tomorrow.

34. Ramirez, M., & Castaneda, A. (1974). *Cultural Democracy, Bicognitive Development and Education.* New York: Academic Press.

Suggestions for helping immigrant and refugee students adjust to and succeed in school and lists of books, materials, films, and so on that are concerned with immigrants and refugees are listed here.

35. California Tomorrow. (1989). *Bridges: Promising Programs for the Education of Immigrant Children.* San Francisco: Author.

36. Chang, H. N. (1990). *Newcomer Programs: Innovative Efforts to Meet the Educational Challenges of Immigrant Students.* San Francisco: California Tomorrow.

37. Friedlander, M. (1991). *The Newcomer Program: Helping Immigrant Students Succeed in School.* Washington, DC: National Clearinghouse for Bilingual Education.

38. Jorgensen-Esmaili, K. (1988). *New Faces of Liberty: A Curriculum for Teaching about Today's Refugees and Immigrants.* Berkeley, CA: Graduate School of Education, University of California, Berkeley.

39. National Council of La Raza. (1986). *Beyond Ellis Island: Hispanics—Immigrants and Americans.* Washington, DC: Author.

The importance of schoolwide approaches to multiculturalism is the focus of the following reference.

40. Sleeter C. E., & Grant, C. A. (1988). *Making Choices for Multicultural Education: Five Approaches to Race, Class, and Gender.* Columbus, OH: Merrill.

These references describe the experiences of Native American students in nonNative American settings.

41. Bureau of Indian Affairs. (1988). *Report on B. I. A. Education: Final Review Draft,* (March). Washington, DC: Department of the Interior.

42. Chavez, R. C., Belkin, L. D., Hornback, J. G., & Adams, K. (1991). Dropping out of school: Issues affecting culturally, ethnically, and linguistically distinct student groups. *Journal of Educational Issues of Language Minority Students, 8,* 1–21.

43. Lin, R. (1987). A profile of reservation high school girls. *Journal of American Indian Education, 26*(2), 18–28.

The adjustment problems of rural students in urban settings is the focus of the following references.

44. Obermiller, P. J., Borman, K. M., & Kroger, J. A. (1988). The Lower Price Community School: Strategies for social change from an Appalachian street academy. *Urban Education, 23*(2), 123–132.

45. Maloney, M. E., & Borman, K. M. (1987). Effects of schools & schooling upon Appalachian children in Cincinnati. In P. J. Obermiller & W. W. Philliber (Eds.), *Too Few Tomorrows: Urban Appalachians in the 1980's.* Boone, NC: Appalachian Consortium Press.

46. McCoy, C. B., & McCoy, H. V. (1987). Appalachian youth in cultural transition. In P. J. Obermiller & W. W. Philliber (Eds.), *Too Few Tomorrows: Urban Appalachians in the 1980's.* Boone, NC: Appalachian Consortium Press.

47. Swift, D. (1988). *Preparing Rural Students for an Urban Environment.* Las Cruces, NM: ERIC/CRESS, New Mexico State University.

48. Vaughn, D., & Vaughn, P. R. (1986). *Preparing Rural Students for an Urban Work Environment.* ERIC ED 270–243.

The special difficulties facing illegal immigrants/refugees are documented and discussed in the references listed next.

49. Carrera, J. W. (1989). *Education Undocumented Children: A Review of Practices and Policies.* Las Cruces, NM: ERIC/CRESS, University of New Mexico.

50. Gardner, C., & Quezada-Aragon, M. (1984). *Undocumented Children: An Ongoing Issue for the Public Education System.* Las Cruces, NM: ERIC/CRESS, New Mexico State University.

51. Padilla, A. M. (1987). Human rights in the human service of Central Americans. *Spanish Speaking Mental Health Research Center,* Spring, 1–4.

52. Stepick, A. & Portes, A. (1986). Flight into despair: A profile of recent Haitian refugees

in South Florida. *International Migration Review*, *20*(2), 329–350.

The stress experienced by refugees from countries engaged in civil wars is the focus of the following references.

53. Cervantes, R. C., Salgado de Snyder, V. N., & Padilla, A. M. (1988). *Post-Traumatic Stress Disorder among Immigrants from Central America and Mexico*. Occasional Paper No. 24. Los Angeles: Spanish Speaking Mental Health Research Center, University of California, Los Angeles.
54. Padilla, A. M. (1987). Post traumatic and psychosocial stress: The Central American experience. *Spanish Speaking Mental Health Research Center*, Spring, 5–6.

The strengths of immigrant and refugee students are described in the following reference.

55. Suarez-Orozco, M. M. (1987). Becoming somebody: Central American immigrants in the United States. *Anthropology and Education Quarterly*, *18*(4), 287–299.

Migrant students and their families are discussed in the following references.

56. Baca, L., & Harris, K. (1988). Teaching migrant exceptional children. *Teaching Exceptional Children*, *20*, 32–35.
57. Center for Educational Planning. (1989). *Migrant Education Dropout Prevention Project Final Report*. ERIC ED 321–951.
58. Chavkin, N. F. (1991). *Family Lives and Parental Involvement in Migrant Students' Education*. Las Cruces, NM: ERIC/CRESS, New Mexico State University.
59. Dyson, D. D. (1983). *Migrant Education: Utilizing Available Resources at the Local Level*. Las Cruces, NM: ERIC/CRESS, New Mexico State University.
60. Henderson, A. (1987). *The Evidence Continues to Grow: Parent Involvement Improves Student Achievement*. ERIC ED 315–199.
61. Herrington, S. (1987). How educators can help children of the road. *Instructor*, *97*, 36–39.
62. Interstate Migrant Education Council. (1987). *Migrant Education: A Consolidated View*. ERIC ED 285–701.
63. Interstate Migrant Secondary Services Program. (1985). *Survey Analysis: Responses of 1070 Students in High School Equivalency Programs, 1984–1985*. ERIC ED 264–070.

64. Johnson, F., Levy, R., Morales, J., Morse, S., & Prokop, M. (1986). *Migrant Students at the Secondary Level: Issues and Opportunities for Change*. ERIC ED 270–242.
65. Lawless, Ken. (1986). *Neediest of the Needy: Special Education for Migrants. Harvesting the Harvesters*, Book 8. ERIC ED 279–473.
66. Mattera, G. (1987). *Models of Effective Migrant Education Programs*. Las Cruces, NM: ERIC/CRESS, New Mexico State University.
67. Migrant Attrition Project. (1987). *Migrant Attrition Project: Abstract of Findings*. Oneonta, NY: State University of New York at Oneonta.
68. Rasmussen, L. (1988). *Migrant Students at the Secondary Level: Issues and Opportunities for Change*. Las Cruces, NM: ERIC/CRESS, New Mexico State University.
69. Salerno, A. (1991). *Migrant Students Who Leave School Early: Strategies for Retrieval*. Las Cruces, NM: ERIC/CRESS, New Mexico State University.
70. Simich-Dudgeon, C. (1986). *Parent Involvement and the Education of Limited-English Proficient Students*. ERIC ED 279–205.

The special problems inherent in providing educational services to rural students are described in the following references.

71. Berkeley, T. R., & Ludlow, B. L. (1991). Meeting the needs of special student populations in rural areas. In A. J. DeYoung (Ed.), *Rural Education: Issues and Practices*. New York: Garland.
72. Brown, D. L. (1989). Demographic trends relevant to education in nonmetropolitan America. In *Rural Education—A Changing Landscape*. Washington, DC: U.S. Department of Education.
73. Cobb, R. A., McIntire, W. G., & Pratt, P. A. (1989). Vocational and educational aspirations of high school students: A problem for rural America. In R. Quaglia (Ed.), *Research in Rural Education*, *6*(20), 123.
74. Helge, D. (1984a). The state of the art of rural special education. *Exceptional Children*, *50*, 294–305.
75. Helge, D. (1989). *Rural Family-Community Partnerships: Resources*. ERIC ED 320–736.
76. Helge, D. (1991). *Rural, Exceptional, At Risk*. Reston, VA: Council for Exceptional Children.
77. Joe, J. R. (1988). Governmental policies and disabled people in American Indian commu-

nities. *Disability, Handicap, and Society*, 3(3), 253–262.

78. Leadership for Special Education. (1989). A conversation with Robert R. Davila. *Education of the Handicapped*, September 13, 28.

79. Marrs, L. W. (1984a). A bandwagon without music: Preparing rural special educators. *Exceptional Children*, 50(4), 334–342.

80. Marrs, L. W. (1984b). Should a special educator entertain volunteers? Independence in rural America. *Exceptional Children*, 50(4), 361–366.

81. McGranahan, D. A. (1988). Rural workers at a disadvantage in job opportunities. *Rural Development Perspectives*, 4, 7–12.

82. National Council on Disabilities. (1989). *The Education of Students with Disabilities: Where Do We Stand?* Washington, DC: Author.

83. National Rural Studies Committee. (1989). Percentage of rural poor exceeds urban rate: Program mix needed to ameliorate conditions. *Rural Postscript*, 7.

84. O'Connor, C., Murr, A., & Wingert, P. (1986). Affluent America's forgotten children, *Newsweek*, 107(22), 20–21.

85. O'Hare, W. P. (1988). *The Rise of Poverty in Rural America*. ERIC ED 302–350.

86. Phelps, M. S., & Prock, G. A. (1991). Equality of educational opportunity in rural America. In A. DeYoung (Ed.), *Rural Education Issues and Practice*. New York: Garland.

87. Pollard, K. M., & O'Hare, W. P. (1990). *Beyond High School: The Experience of Rural and Urban Youth in the 1980's*. ERIC ED 326–363.

88. Students at Risk. (1990). *Education Week*, October 19, 26.

Techniques for providing appropriate services in rural areas are the focus of the following references.

89. Baker, B. O. (1991). Technological delivery systems and applications for K–12 instruction in rural schools. In A. J. DeYoung (Ed.), *Rural Education: Issues and Practices*. New York: Garland.

90. ERIC/CRESS (1987). *Interactive Distance Learning Technologies for Rural and Small Schools: A Resource Guide*. Charleston, WV: Author.

91. Exceptional Children (1984). Rural special education services, activities, and products. *Exceptional Children*, 50(4), 368–369.

92. Gear, G. H. (1984). Providing services for rural gifted children. *Exceptional Children*, 50(4), 326–331.

93. Helge, D. (1984b). Models for serving rural students with low-incidence handicapping conditions. *Exceptional Children*, 50(4), 313–324.

94. Helge, D. (1984c). Technologies as rural special education problem-solvers. *Exceptional Children*, 50(4), 351–359.

95. Hofmeister, A. M. (1984). Technological tools for rural special education. *Exceptional Children*, 50, 344–349.

96. Kirmer, K., Lockwood, L., Mickler, W., & Sweeney, P. (1984). Regional rural special education programs. *Exceptional Children*, 50(4), 306–311.

97. Luhman, A., & Fundis, R. (1989). *Building Academically Strong Gifted Programs in Rural Schools*. Charleston WV: ERIC/CRESS.

98. McIntosh, D. K., & Raymond, G. I. (1988). Training special education teachers in rural areas: A viable model. *Rural Special Education Quarterly*, 9(1), 2–5.

99. Miller, B. (1991). *Teaching and Learning in the Multigrade Classroom: Student Performance and Instructional Routines*. Charleston WV: ERIC/CRESS.

100. Oliver, J. P., & Howley, C. (1992). *Charting New Maps: Multicultural Education in Rural Schools*. Charleston WV: ERIC/CRESS.

101. Olmstead, K. (1989). *Touching the Past, Enroute to the Future: Cultural Journalism in the Curriculum of Rural Schools*. Charleston WV: ERIC/CRESS.

102. Sherwood, T. (1989). *Nontraditional Education in Rural Districts*. Charleston WV: ERIC/CRESS.

103. Theobald, P. (1992). *Rural Philosophy for Education: Wendell Berry's Tradition*. Charleston WV: ERIC/CRESS.

The following references discuss the educator's role in helping students who have been abused.

104. Broadhurst, D. (1986). *Educators, Schools and Child Abuse*. Chicago: National Committee for the Prevention of Child Abuse.

105. Caplan, P., Watters, J., White, G., Parry, R., & Bates, R. (1984). Toronto multi-agency child abuse research project: The abused and the abuser. *Child Abuse and Neglect: The International Journal*, 8, 343–351.

106. Fink, A. H., & Janssen, K. N. (1990). *Abused/ Neglected Adolescents: Programming for Their*

Educational Needs. Paper presented at the National Conference on Adolescents with Behavior Disorders, Miami, FL.

107. Fink, A. H., & Janssen, K. N. (1992). The management of maltreated adolescents in school settings. *Preventing School Failure, 36*(3), 32–36.

108. Hurwitz, B. D. (1985). Suspicion: Child abuse. *Instructor, 94*(4), 76–78, 81, 125.

109. McIntyre, T. (1990). The teacher's role in cases of suspected child abuse. *Education and Urban Society, 22*(3), 300–306.

110. National Center on Child Abuse and Neglect (1984). *The Educator's Role in the Prevention and Treatment of Child Abuse and Neglect.* Washington, DC: U.S. Department of Health and Human Services, Administration for Children, Youth, and Families, Children's Bureau.

111. National Clearinghouse on Child Abuse and Neglect. (1991a). *Curricula.* Washington, DC: Author.

112. National Clearinghouse on Child Abuse and Neglect. (1991b). *Prevention Programs: Training Materials.* Washington, DC: Author.

113. Ohman, L. (1988). The NEA: Professional organization and advocate for teachers. In A. Maney & S. Wells (Eds.), *Professional Responsibilities in Protecting Children: A Public Health Approach to Child Sexual Abuse.* New York: Praeger.

114. Shaman, E. J. (1986). Prevention programs for children with disabilities. In M. Nelson & K. Clark (Eds.), *The Educator's Guide to Preventing Child Sexual Abuse.* Santa Cruz, CA: Network Publications.

115. Warger, C. L., Tewey, S., & Megivern, M. (1991). *Abuse and Neglect of Exceptional Children.* Reston, VA: Council for Exceptional Children.

116. Wolverton, L. (1988). *Teaching the Abused Migrant Child: What's a Teacher to Do?* Las Cruces, NM: ERIC/CRESS, New Mexico State University.

These references concern the educational problems of homeless and runaway children and adolescents.

117. Bass, J. L., Brennan, P., Mehta, K. A., & Kodzis, S. (1990). Pediatric problems in a suburban shelter for homeless families. *Pediatrics, 85*(1), 33–38.

118. Bassuk, E. L., & Gallagher, E. M. (1990). The impact of homelessness on children. In N. A. Boxill (Ed.), *Homeless Children: The Watchers and the Waiters.* Binghamton, NY: Haworth.

119. Bassuk, F., & Rosenberg, L. (1988). Why does family homelessness occur? *American Journal of Public Health, 78,* 783–788.

120. Bassuk, F., & Rosenberg, L. (1990). Psychosocial characteristics of homeless children and children with homes. *Pediatrics, 85,* 257–261.

121. Bassuk, F., & Rubin, L. (1987). Homeless children: A neglected population. *American Journal of Orthopsychiatry, 57*(2), 279–286.

122. Bowen, J. M., Purrington, G. S., Layton, D. H., & O'Brien, K. (1989). *Educating Homeless Children and Youth: A Policy Analysis.* Paper presented at the annual conference of the American Educational Research Association, San Francisco.

123. Burns, S. (Ed.). (1991). Homelessness demographics, causes and trends. *Homewords, 3*(4), 1–3.

124. Cavazos, L. F. (1990). *U.S. Department of Education Report to Congress on the Education for Homeless Children and Youth Program for the Period October 1, 1988 through September 30, 1989.* Washington, DC: U.S. Department of Education.

125. Children's Defense Fund. (1988). *What Every American Should Be Asking Political Leaders in 1988: About Children and the Future, about Leadership and Vision, about National Values and Priorities.* Washington, DC: Author.

126. Eddowes, E. A. (1993). Education of younger homeless children in urban settings. *Education and Urban Society, 25*(4), 381–393.

127. Eddowes, E. A., & Hranitz, J. R. (1989). Educating children of the homeless. *Childhood Education: Infancy through Early Adolescence, 65*(4), 197–200.

128. Ely, L. (1987). *Broken Lives: Denial of Education to Homeless Children.* Washington, DC: National Coalition for the Homeless.

129. Faber, E., McCoard, D., Kinast, C., & Baum-Falkner, D. (1984). Violence in families of adolescent runaways. *Child Abuse and Neglect, 2*(3), 173–192.

130. Friedman, L., & Christiansen, G. (1990). *Shut Out: Denial of Education to Homeless Children.* ERIC ED 320–987.

131. Gewirtzman, R., & Fodor, I. (1987). The homeless child at school: From welfare hotel to classroom. *Child Welfare, 66*(3), 237–245.

132. Hall, J. A., & Maza, P. L. (1990). No fixed address: The effects of homelessness on families and children. In N. A. Boxill (Ed.), *Home-*

less Children: The Watchers and the Waiters. Binghamton, NY: Haworth.

133. Heflin, L. J., & Rudy, K. (1991). *Homeless and in Need of Special Education.* Reston, VA: Council for Exceptional Children.

134. Jackson, S. (1989). *The Education Rights of Homeless Children.* Cambridge, MA: Center for Law and Education.

135. Kayne, A. (1989). *Annotated Bibliography of Social Science Literature Concerning the Education of Homeless Children.* Cambridge, MA: Center for Law and Education.

136. Layzer, J. I., Goodson, B. D., & deLange, C. (1986). Children in shelters. *Children Today, 15,* 6–11.

137. Linehan, M. F. (1989). Homeless children: Educational strategies for school personnel. *PRISE Reporter, 21*(2), 1–2, insert.

138. Stewart B. McKinney Homeless Assistance Act of 1987, P.L. 100–77.

139. Stewart B. McKinney Homeless Assistance Amendment Act of 1990, PL 100–77.

140. Mihaly, L. K. (1991). *Homeless Families: Failed Policies and Young Victims.* Washington, DC: Children's Defense Fund.

141. Miller, D. S., & Linn, E. H. B. (1988). Children in sheltered homeless families: Reported health status and use of health services. *Pediatrics, 81,* 668–673.

142. National Network of Runaway and Youth Services. (1988, January). *Preliminary Findings from the National Network's Survey of Runaway and Homeless Youth.* Testimony before the House Subcommittee on Human Resources.

143. Neiman, L. (1988). A critical review of resiliency literature and its relevance to homeless children. *Children's Environments Quarterly, 5*(19), 17–25.

144. Palenski, J. E., & Launer, H. M. (1987). The "process" of running away: A redefinition. *Adolescence, 22*(86), 347–362.

145. Powers, J. L., Eckenrode, J., & Jaklitsch, G. (1988). *Running Away from Home: A Response to Adolescent Maltreatment.* ERIC ED 296–228.

146. Powers, J. L., & Jaklitsch, B. (1993). Reaching the hard to reach: Educating homeless adolescents in urban settings. *Education and Urban Society, 25*(4), 394–409.

147. Rafferty, Y., & Rollins, N. (1989). *Learning in Limbo: The Educational Deprivation of Homeless Children.* Long Island City, NY: Advocates for Children of New York.

148. Rafferty, Y., & Rollins, N. (1990). *Homeless Children: Educational Challenges for the 1990's.* ERIC ED 325–589.

149. Rescoria, L., Parker, R., & Stolley, P. (1991). Ability, achievement and adjustment in homeless children. *American Journal of Orthopsychiatry, 61*(2), 210–220.

150. Rivlin, L. G. (1990). Home and homelessness in the lives of children. In N. A. Boxill (Ed.), *Homeless Children: The Watchers and the Waiters.* Binghamton, NY: Haworth.

151. Rosenman, M., & Stein, M. L. (1990). Homeless children: A new vulnerability. In N. A. Boxill (Ed.), *Homeless Children: The Watchers and the Waiters.* Binghamton, NY: Haworth.

152. Russell, S. C., & Williams, E. U. (1988). Homeless handicapped children: A special education perspective. *Children's Environments Quarterly, 5*(1), 3–7.

153. Schumack, S. (Ed.). (1987). *The Educational Rights of Homeless Children.* ERIC ED 288–915.

154. Stronge, J. H., & Helm, V. M. (1990). *Residency and Guardianship Requirements as Barriers to the Education of Homeless Children and Youth.* ERIC ED 319–845.

155. Stronge, J. H., & Tenhouse, C. (1990). *Educating Homeless Children: Issues and Answers.* Bloomington, IN: Phi Delta Kappa Educational Foundation.

156. Waxman, L. D., & Reyes, L. M. (1987). *A Status Report on Homeless Families in America's Cities: A 29-City Survey.* ERIC ED 296–018.

157. Witt, V. (Ed.), (1988). *Children's Defense Budget: FY 1989. An Analysis of Our Nation's Investment in Children.* Washington, DC: Children's Defense Fund.

158. Wright, J. D. (1990). Homelessness is not healthy for children and other living things. In N. A. Boxill (Ed.), *Homeless Children: The Watchers and the Waiters.* Binghamton, NY: Haworth.

159. Zeldin, S., & Bogart, J. (1990). *Education and Community Support for Homeless Children and Youth: Profiles of Fifteen Innovative and Promising Approaches.* (Contract LC No. 89089001). Washington, DC: U.S. Department of Education.

Teenage parents in school is the focus of the following references.

160. Brindis, C. (1990). Reducing adolescent pregnancy. *Family Life Educator, 9*(1), 3–63.

161. Kleinfeld, A., & Young, R. (1989). Risk of pregnancy and dropping out of school

among special education adolescents. *Journal of Social Health, 59*(8), 359–361.

162. LaFazia, M. (1988). *Washington Alliance Concerned with School Aged Parents.* Washington, DC: U.S. Department of Health and Human Services, Office of Human Services.

163. Muccigrosso, L., Scavarda, M., Simpson-Brown, R., & Thalacker, B. E. (1991). *Double Jeopardy: Pregnant and Parenting Youth in Special Education.* Reston, VA: Council for Exceptional Children.

These references are concerned with substance abuse among school-age youth.

164. Allison, K., Leone, P. E., & Spero, E. (1990). Alcohol and drug use among adolescents: Social context and competency. In P. E. Leone (Ed.), *Understanding Troubled and Troubling Youth.* Newbury Park, CA: Sage.

165. Beamer, S., Timmreck, T., & Butterworth, D. (1991). Effectiveness of drug intervention groups in high school settings. *High School Journal, 75*(1), 59–72.

166. Friedman, A. S., Glickman, N., & Utada, A. (1985). Does alcohol and drug use lead to failure to graduate from high school? *Journal of Drug Education, 15*, 353–364.

167. Leone, P. (1991). *Alcohol and Other Drugs: Use, Abuse, and Disabilities.* Reston, VA: Council for Exceptional Children.

168. United States General Accounting Office. (1990). *Drug Education: School-Based Programs Seen as Useful But Impact Unknown.* Gaithersburg, MD: Author.

The references below discuss deviant adolescent subcultures.

169. Clark, C. M. (1992). Deviant adolescent subcultures: Assessment strategies and clinical interventions. *Adolescence, 27*(106), 283–293.

170. Steck, C. M., Anderson, S. A., & Boylin, W. M. (1992). Satanism among adolescents: Empirical and clinical considerations. *Adolescence, 27*(105) 901–914.

$$Chapter \quad 6$$

Communicatively Appropriate Education

In a pluralistic society such as ours, students come to school speaking different languages and dialects and using different verbal and nonverbal communication styles. This chapter discusses how educators can take these differences into account when they instruct and assess students.

Limited English Proficiency

As was noted in Chapter 1, the limited English proficient (LEP) population is the fastest growing in the United States. It is probable that almost 8 million American youngsters have a non-English background, either because they were born elsewhere or because they grew up in the United States in a home where another language was spoken. More than 3 million of these students scored in the lowest 20% on tests of English proficiency. More than 5 million scored in the lower 40%. Whichever of these two figures one uses, it is clear that millions of students are not proficient enough in English to function in English-only classes without considerable difficulty (1).

The appropriate instructional services required by LEP students has been the subject of a number of court decisions and federal laws. In 1974, in Lau v. Nichols, the Supreme Court unanimously decided that schools must provide special assistance to LEP students in the form of linguistically appropriate educational services (3).

The Bilingual Education Act defines these services (2). Schools may satisfy the requirement that LEP students receive linguistically appropriate services by providing students with instruction in their native language (bilingual education), English as a second language (ESL) , sheltered English (also called structured English), or a combination of these approaches. These alternate ways of providing linguistically appropriate education services are discussed in this section. However, it should be noted that many LEP students are not being taught by any of these approaches.

Bilingual Education

In the not too distant past, many people argued that the best way to work with LEP students was to immerse them in English as quickly and as completely as possible. Now we know from research that English immersion programs are less desirable than teaching students subject matter in their native languages (bilingual education) while they are also learning English as a second language (4, 6, 8). There are three main reasons for this.

1. Although it takes only a year or two for students to become proficient enough in a second language to carry on everyday conversations—basic interpersonal communication skills (BICS)—it usually takes at least five years to reach the level of proficiency in a second language that is required to learn subject matter—cognitive academic learning proficiency (CALP) (5). Thus, if students are instructed in subject matter too soon in a second language they will not be able to benefit optimally from such instruction.

A bilingual educator put it this way:

> *The fact is, it takes time to learn English. But we cannot forgo learning other content areas while they're in the process of acquiring English. Put a child in a class for a year or two to learn English and meanwhile forget learning math, forget art, forget social studies. I don't think we can do that. (7, p. 57)*

A principal of a school designed to prepare immigrant students for the regular school in their area stated:

> *We know that the kind of English we are talking about is not just fluency, being able to converse, being able to make small talk. We are talking about academic English . . . the English you need to evaluate, criticize, voice your opinion. That kind of English requires a lot of study and requires a certain amount of cultural literacy in the American context. It takes time to acquire it. We know for a fact that what these kids most need is time—time in the school system. (7, p. 64)*

2. There is considerable evidence that switching students from their native language to a new language before they have acquired CALP can stunt their language development in either language. However, once students have acquired CALP in one language they are able to transfer their understanding of the logic and rules of language to the learning of a second language (5, 7). Thus, students taught in their native language until they have developed "languageness" read better and learn more in school than those who are immediately taught in second language.

3. Rejecting students' native languages can alienate students and lead them to develop poor self-concepts.

Although bilingual education is the preferable approach, it is not a practical alternative for many school districts because they lack bilingual education personnel and/or are faced with providing services to LEP students in many different languages. This is an especially difficult problem for school districts that serve a linguistically diverse population—such as the Los Angeles School District, which serves students who speak over one hundred different languages. As a result, a number of school districts have opted for ESL or sheltered English programs for their LEP students.

English as a Second Language

In recent years the art of teaching students a second language has become much more of a science. As a result, educators are now achieving a great deal of success in ESL programs. Unfortunately, only a limited number of teacher preparation programs train teachers to use ESL techniques. Therefore, this option is not readily available to many students and school districts.

Sheltered English/Structured Immersion

In a sheltered English/structured English approach students are taught subject matter in a modified/controlled English vocabulary at their level of English comprehension. Teachers omit difficult words and forms, explain new vocabulary words, often in students' native languages, and employ as many nonverbal gestures, audiovisual aids, and other materials as possible. Gersten and Woodward describe the approach in the following manner.

> *With structured immersion all instruction is done in the commonly used language of the school . . . However,* all instruction is conducted at a level understood by students. *Superficially, structured immersion may seem similar to what the U.S. court outlawed in 1974; that is, a sink-or-swim approach for those not proficient in the language of the dominant culture. But there is a critical difference: teachers do not assume that the children understand English. Difficult new words are pretaught, sometimes using the child's native language. (11, p. 75)*

Research indicated that students improve their second language proficiency and learn subject matter in well-planned sheltered English programs staffed by trained teachers (9–12). However, very few LEP students are enrolled in sheltered English programs.

English Submergence

As was noted earlier, many LEP students are not in bilingual education, ESL, or sheltered English programs. Thus, many LEP students without CALP, and often BICS, English fluency are submerged in the regular classes and are taught in English without regard to their linguistic needs. Submerged in English without the skills necessary to profit from the instruction they receive, they are at risk for

---

ESL Programs Versus Submergence Programs

Compare the experiences of the following three students. A student in an English submergence program reported:

> *I just sat in my classes and didn't understand anything. Sometimes I would try to look like I knew what was going on, sometimes I would just try to think about a happy time when I didn't feel stupid. My teachers never called on me or talked to me. I think either they forgot I was there or else wished I wasn't. I waited and I waited, thinking someday I will know English. (7, p. 62)*

Two other students made the following comparison between their experiences in ESL and a regular class taught in English.

> *My ESL teacher helped me a lot in my first year here. I could relax there. I wasn't afraid. . . . In my other classes I was always confused and lost and I didn't want to ask anything because of my bad English. (7, p. 62)*

> *My first school I didn't want to go, just to stay home. When I went I just sat there and didn't understand anything . . . . No one talked to me and I couldn't say anything. I didn't know what was going on. My second school had an ESL teacher who taught me from the ABC's and helped me learn many more things. (7, p. 62)*

---

joining the ranks of students who tune out their teachers, cut classes, and drop out before graduating from high school.

Dialectal Differences

In the past, many educators believed that the English dialect spoken by many poor African American students (Black English/Ebonics), the dialects spoken by Native Americans, Hispanic Americans, Hawaiian Americans, and certain regional dialects spoken by poor European Americans such as the ones spoken in Appalachia (mountain English) and in the greater New York City Metropolitan Area (New Yorkese) interfered with learning to read and write standard English correctly. Critics of nonstandard dialects also believed that many of them were inferior forms of English and should be eradicated. Today, as was noted in Chapter 2, experts tend to consider dialect variations to be linguistic differences rather than linguistic deficiencies. Nevertheless, they still disagree about how to handle them in school.

Legal Aspects

Since the 1970s schools have had to provide students with linguistically appropriate educational services that take into account the students' nonstandard English dialects. In 1972, the Equal Educational Opportunities Act stated that

Standard English

Although the term "standard English" is used in this text, some people question whether there is a such a thing as standard English. They point out that so-called standard English is not the English dialect spoken in many regions of the United States or by many ethnic groups or poor people. They suggest that the term be replaced by one that avoids the connotation that it is the standard by which other dialects should be judged and the implication that it should be the preferred dialect. The term "American English" has been offered as a substitute. However, it too has many problems.

No state shall deny equal educational opportunity to an individual by . . . the failure by an educational agency to take appropriate action to overcome language barriers that impede equal participation by its students in its instructional program. (13)

In 1979 a U.S. District Court judge ruled in favor of 15 African American students who claimed that they were denied an equal education because their school did not take their nonstandard English dialect into account. Although this ruling only affected schools within the jurisdiction of the court, it has set a national tone. Judge Joiner, the presiding judge reflected the knowledge of the day in his ruling.

The court does not believe that language differences between "Black English" and standard English to be a language barrier in and of itself.

   The unconscious but evident attitude of teachers toward the home language of the plaintiffs causes a psychological barrier to learning by the student. . . . The child who comes to school using the "Black English" system of communication and who is taught that this is wrong loses a sense of values related to mother and close friends and siblings, and may rebel at efforts by his teacher to teach reading in a different language.

   If a barrier exists because of the language used by the children in this case, it exists not because the teachers and students cannot understand each other, but because in the process of attempting to teach the students how to speak standard English the students are made somehow to feel inferior and are thereby turned off from the learning process. (14, pp. 18, 26, 36, 41–42)

The court required the school district to help the teachers of the plaintiff children at the King School to identify children speaking "Black English" and the language spoken as a home or community language in order to use that knowledge in teaching such students how to read standard English. However, the court did not provide guidelines for how teachers should use their knowledge of Black English to teach students. As a result, two very different educational approaches are being employed in schools to deal with mismatches between the English dialects spoken by many students and the oral and written English used by their teachers and found in almost all textbooks and curriculum materials: bidialectalism and appreciation.

Speaking

Bidialectalism

Many individuals believe that speakers of nonstandard dialects should be taught to express themselves in standard English as well as their nonstandard dialects and to use each form when it is appropriate for a given situation. The objectives of bidialectal programs, although expressed in various ways, usually include the following:

1. *To create an awareness of the need for "functional flexibility"' in oral communication (i.e., the ability to use language for varying purposes)*
2. *To develop an understanding of the education, social and economic ramifications of unproductive communication skills, and*
3. *To provide opportunities to develop and practice the alternative style of communication (i.e., mainstream English) while not eradicating the importance and function of "home language." (22, p. 211)*

Three reasons are typically cited in support of bidialectalism.

1. *Although nonstandard English dialects are not substandard, they interfere with students' academic progress* (15, 22). The evidence regarding this contention is mixed. Most studies have found that speakers of nonstandard dialects do not have difficulty learning to read (18, 30–40, 43, 44). Some researchers have reported findings that indicate that Black English and Native American English dialect speakers have difficulty learning to read standard English (34, 45). However, the cause of the relationship between reading difficulty and nonstandard dialect usage that has been observed in some studies is unclear. Although some educators believe that these results indicate that nonstandard dialects interfere with learning, three other explanations have been offered.

Students of nonstandard English dialects tend to be from poor backgrounds. It is the many factors associated with having a poor background, not the students' nonstandard dialects, that account for their lack of progress in reading. Support for this hypothesis lies in the fact that within the various groups that speak nonstandard dialects (such as African Americans, Hawaiian Americans, and so on), nonstandard dialects are much more prevalent among poor than middle-class students.

Educators' prejudiced attitudes against certain nonstandard English dialects interfere with students' learning. As was noted in Chapters 2 and 3, teachers of nonstandard English speakers, especially those who believe standard English to be a more desirable or correct version of English, tend to believe that students do not understand something if they cannot explain it in standard English. They think that students who do not speak standard English are less intelligent; they have lower academic expectations for them; they evaluate both their oral and written work to be worse than comparable work of students speaking standard English; and they are more likely to disapprove of them.

Teachers spend too much time correcting students' dialectal vocabulary, grammatical, and pronunciation "errors." There is considerable evidence that many teachers focus on dialect differences that are not true errors, rather than concentrating their efforts on improving students higher-level skills, and relate to them in unproductive ways (36, 37, 41, 42, 46). The following description illustrates how insistence on standard English speech can interfere with good teaching.

> *A sixth-grade math teacher was quite disturbed because his students referred to the concept of lowest common denominator as "breaking it down more smaller." The students obviously understood the concept and had demonstrated, on the chalk board and in class and homework papers, that they could apply the concept to solve math problems. The teacher kept correcting the students because his perception was, "These kids obviously don't know how to arrive at lowest common denominators." When queried as to how, then, were the students able to solve problems involving the concept, his explanation was, "You can't do anything if you don't know the right word for it."*
>
> *The teacher's solution was to waste the next few days drilling his students on the spelling and textbook terminology of various mathematical operations that they already knew how to perform! (41, p. 89)*

On balance the evidence does not support the contention that students' nonstandard dialects interfere with their learning. As Padak has commented, "one need not speak a dialect in order to understand it" (27, p. 150).

2. *Competency in oral standard English is necessary for students to learn to write standard English.* Although it is true that nonstandard forms of English intrude in students' writing when they are first learning to write standard English, most experts in the field agree that it is not necessary for students to be able to speak standard English in order to write standard English. They point out that many nonstandard English speakers can write standard English; they note that the longer students remain in school, the fewer nonstandard English forms intrude in their writing (21); and they remind us that writing is not speech written down.

> *Learning to write standard English does not mean first learning to speak it. . . . Forcing Chicanos to change their way of speaking English in order to learn to write makes no more sense than forcing an east Texas child or a child from Boston or the Bronx to drop their speech peculiarities and replace them with midwestern English so that they can learn to write. (62, p. 25)*

3. *Standard English is necessary for vocational success and in other areas in which non-standard dialect speakers are branded as uneducated and ill-prepared* (19, 23, 29). The following quotation typifies this line of thinking.

> *There are many dialects in every language, but the standard form is that which is acceptable for purposes of state, business, or other everyday transactions. It is the official language of the country, and anyone who is successful in that country uses it. Those who use the nonstandard language are forever relegated to the most menial jobs and stations in life. . . . If blacks are prepared to accept the hypothesis of "Black English," then they ought to be prepared to accept the relegation to "Black" jobs. If their preparation is second class, their lives will be second class. (30, pp. 318, 320)*

It is true, as was noted in Chapter 3, that many members of our society are prejudiced against certain nonstandard English dialects. However, many educators believe the solution to the problem is to combat discrimination, not accommodate and acquiesce to it. As Dean and Fowler suggested quite some time ago:

> *Previously, people who have applied for a job have been judged on clothing and hair styles. These discriminations have been lessened by change of public opinion. Then, people were judged on the color of their skin or their sex. These prejudices, while still present, are being lessened with the "help" of legislation. . . . Yet proponents of bidialectalism state that a person must speak standard English to be hired for a "good job". . . . White middle-class society has reexamined its values in the previously mentioned areas of hair style, clothing, race and sex. Surely that society can have its eyes opened once again. (17, pp. 305–306)*

Moreover, many individuals believe that schools have an important role to play in correcting discrimination against nonstandard English dialects. On the other hand, many individuals have pointed out that community attitudes are difficult if not impossible to change quickly, and they argue that schools should prepare students to succeed in the meantime.

Those who believe that students should be taught to be able to communicate in standard English in appropriate situations have offered the following guidelines and principles (22, 42, 47–51, 53, 55–57, 59, 64).

- Motivate students to want to become bidialectal. Employ age-appropriate motivational techniques. The older students are, the more they can appreciate the advantages, value, and importance of becoming bidialectal.
- Correct students' misperceptions that standard English is the "white man's" language
- Avoid creating resistance among students. For example, do not correct students. Instead, discuss alternative acceptable ways of saying the same things in different situations.

- Concentrate on those dialect characteristics that are most stigmatized by the community and most hamper success. For example, nonstandard grammar (double negatives, nonagreement of subject and verb, "them" for "those") is viewed much more negatively than nonstandard pronunciation (51).

Many techniques have been employed to help students become bidialectal. Techniques vary depending on the point of view of the educators.

The most common approach is the method of contrastive analysis. In this method students are taught to use both standard and nonstandard forms for expressing same ideas in both dialects and to identify when to use each one (22, 31, 42, 47, 53, 57, 59, 64). In some cases audio- and videotaping has been used to help students experience the difference in their language. Typically this approach involves seven steps.

1. Identify nonstandard dialect speakers. This is usually done informally, but some instruments are available (59).

2. Explain that there are different dialects.

3. Contrast and teach the differences. Lists and descriptions of dialect differences for a number of dialects are available (69–74). Very young children may not be mature enough to recognize, label, and contrast dialect differences.

4. Teach students to distinguish between home English and school and work English and to use the most appropriate one for a given situation.

5. Drill them in substituting standard forms for nonstandard ones.

6. Provide students with opportunities to practice standard forms in class.

7. Evaluate the results. This last step can be done informally or by using a formal instrument (67).

Research indicates that contrastive analysis increases students' use of standard English in the classroom; little data is available about its effects on students' language usage outside of school.

Some educators use the ESL instructional techniques that were developed to assist limited English proficient students to teach nonstandard dialect speakers to speak standard English (66). However, many educators object to the use of a method designed to teach non-English speakers with students who speak English, albeit in a nonstandard dialect.

> *English as a second language is a must for those who have just entered this country; however, I find it distressing when the term is applied to English for my Black brethren who have been in this English-speaking country for generations. (30, p. 318)*

Many educators stress the importance of helping students to resolve their ambivalence and resistance to standard English and increasing their motivation to learn and use it (54, 63, 68). Unlike limited English proficient students, who need to learn English in order to survive in the United States, nonstandard English speakers already speak English. They often have no felt need to learn a second English dialect that is different from the English spoken and accepted by their family, friends, and neighbors, and they often resent teachers' attempts to make them do so.

Educators have used discussions about the advantages of using standard English on the job to increase students' understanding of the economic importance and value of speaking standard English. Role-playing job interviews in which students speak standard and nonstandard English and the class is asked to judge which applicant would be hired have also been tried. Exposing students to the speech of celebrities from their background who speak standard English, and inviting successful non-European business persons who speak standard English to deliver the message that Black English does not open many doors in our society have all been used in this endeavor. An African American female teacher has described how she used herself as a model for her Black English dialect speakers. Her rationale for doing so follows.

> As the students' teacher, I assumed the students perceived me to be competent with status and having control over the learning resources. As a Black person, I assumed these Black students would view me as being similar and would identify with me. As a seemingly successful person, I assumed the students would view my success, in part, the result of my being able to speak standard English. (63, p. 106)

Changing the attitude of all of the students in a class so that they are no longer resistant to and support a bidialectal approach and then having students engage in cooperative learning activities designed to improve their bidialectal skills can be effective (54). Another technique is to expose students to the example of people who changed their way of speaking and profited from the change. Reading *Pygmalion* or *My Fair Lady*, or watching the movies made from these plays and discussing the lessons they teach, illustrate this approach.

Some individuals believe that exposing students to public criticism by correcting their dialects in front of others and teaching standard English are too confronting to students and create unnecessary resistance. They believe less confrontational methods such as reading literature in standard English aloud to students and including works by non–European American writers are more effective means for increasing students' understanding of and ability to use standard English.

Despite the fact that many teachers are currently trying to make students bidialectal, research suggests that attempts to teach nonstandard English speakers to speak standard English have backfired.

> The teaching of standard English to all learners is an implicitly and explicitly stated goal of the American school. Yet the national performance of the American school in teaching standard English to nonstandard speakers is dismal. On almost every reported measure at the national or state level, children from non-

standard English speaking communities achieve lower competency levels in the language of education than children who come from standard English speaking communities. The result has been an overplacement of nonstandard English speaking children in special education classes, speech-language pathology clinical services, and compensatory education classes, and an underplacement of these children in classes for talented and gifted students. . . . In addition this failure has contributed to diminished student self-esteem, lowered teacher expectations, and discipline problems. (29, p. 156)

In addition, the limited research available leaves a number of urgent questions unanswered.

- Is there any value to teaching students to speak standard English besides avoiding discrimination in the community?
- Does encouraging students to speak standard English also encourage the community to continue to discriminate against nonstandard English speakers?
- Should school officials or the students themselves decide whether they should become bidialectal?
- Can all students learn a second dialect through the approaches offered in school?
- What student characteristics foster or impede second dialect learning?
- Which are the most effective approaches to second dialect teaching?
- Which techniques work best with which students?
- What negative side effects accompany schools' attempts to make students bidialectal?
- What are the best ways to avoid these unwanted effects?

Appreciation

Many educators reject the bidialectal approach. They believe that as long as students can understand spoken and written standard English, they should be allowed or even encouraged to express themselves in their own dialects in any and all situations (17, 53). The appreciation approach has been described as follows:

Teachers who employ this approach accept the fact of linguistic equality of the two dialects (standard and Black) and believe that the Black dialect is a competent form of communication. There are no drills to bring out contrasts or comparison between Black and standard English. Teachers, instead, look for additional techniques to bring out the verbal facility that is already present—not merely the potential of verbal ability. . . . This requires special consideration in the language arts—allowing students to use their own dialects or accents without correction in reading, by the teachers dictating oral spelling tests in both dialects if found helpful . . . by accepting Black dialect grammar in written composition, etc. (17, p. 305)

Proponents of the appreciation approach to dialect differences offer the following reasons for their position.

1. *Efforts to teach students to speak standard English do not work.* There is considerable evidence that although highly motivated individuals can learn standard English if they are given intensive instruction and interact on a frequent basis with standard English speakers, the way students are taught to speak standard English in school does not produce an increase in the frequency or correctness of students use of standard English in the classroom, much less outside of school (16, 20, 25; also discussed earlier). As Labov and Harris state it,

> *Underlying grammatical patterns of standard English are apparently learned through "meaningful" and intensive interaction with those who already use standard English grammar, not simply by exposure in the mass media or in schools. (25, p. 22)*

2. *Dialect speakers who are required to speak standard English become less fluent and have difficulty expressing themselves.* The proposition has not been researched very well. However, there is some evidence to support it (29).

3. *Teaching students standard English before they are completely fluent in their original dialects stunts their language development.* In the words of Kochman, switching from one dialect to another "does not develop the child's ability to use language beyond what he is already capable of doing. . . . It is concerned with *how* the child says something rather than *how well* he says it." (24, p. 91)

There is no research regarding this supposition.

4. *It is not possible to encourage students to learn a second dialect without also communicating that their way of speaking is less desirable.* As an English teacher put it:

> *No matter how carefully I explained my purpose and assured them that I was not judging their parents, grandparents, race, or culture . . . my students still resented my correcting them although most of the time they accepted my corrections in good humor. (28, p. 49)*

5. *Acceptance and appreciation of nonstandard dialects by schools and teachers improves students' self-esteem.*

> *Black children must be educated to learn and believe that deviation from the normative pattern of standard English is not an indication that they are abnormal. They must be helped to understand that these negative social and psychological views have resulted and can continue to result in low self-esteem, identity crisis, and self-hatred. An appreciation of Black habits, values, and goals is essential for Black children to develop a positive Black self-identity. The issue of Black English is a "good" place to start. Whites should not become reference points for how Black children are to speak and behave. (53, p. 215)*

6. *Teaching standard English to nonstandard dialect speakers is a form of political and cultural subjugation.* Non-standard English-speaking students and their teachers often have different perceptions of the implications of standard English. Teachers tend to view it as a way to learn more effectively and get ahead in the real world; students often view it as talking white, denying their heritage, and giving in to the European American power structure (26, 41). These individuals tend to believe that the solution to dialectal inequality can only be achieved by eliminating the power differential in society.

> *If one culture possesses hegemony over the other, the less-powerful culture generally adopts the language of the more powerful but not without serious consequences for and potential danger to the harmonious relationship between the two groups. For even as the less-powerful speech community is expanding its linguistic repertoire to incorporate the language of the predominant group, simultaneously its loyalty to the mother tongue and native culture is intensified. . . . In the school setting, the linguistic norms and cultural context of white America prevail and the speech norms and cultural identity of the Black community are forced to give sway to those of the more powerful cultural group. (41, pp. 88–89)*

Proponents of appreciation favor activities that instill pride in students about their language and further their language development. High on the list of recommended activities are studying audio and video tapes of well-known nonstandard dialect speakers, reading plays and novels written in nonstandard dialects, and encouraging students to write nonstandard dialect fiction.

Writing

Teaching dialect speakers to write standard English has been the focus of considerable research and discussion. Anecdotal evidence suggests that few people believe that it is unnecessary to teach nonstandard dialect speakers to write standard English. In fact, many educators who favor the appreciation approach to oral language support a bidialectal approach to written language. They believe students should be encouraged to speak any way they prefer, but they should be taught to write in standard English.

Anecdotal evidence suggests that most teachers currently follow this approach. However, research is needed to determine whether this is actually the case.

Some authors have advised teachers to use written English rather than oral English to teach standard English skills because it does not subject students to public scrutiny and it is more effective (26, 51).

> *Writing provides the means through which black students can experience language and develop alternative mechanisms for using it effectively. . . . Unlike speech, the writing process is slow paced and requires deliberate thinking and planning. Extensive revision and editing allows the student to focus on vocabulary, grammar, and syntactical problems as well as those in content and organization. Because there are no gestures or other nonverbal expressions to help communicate ideas, the written language must be shaped and fashioned so that it alone can convey the intended message. (26, p. 168)*

The references at the end of the chapter provide additional information about techniques for teaching standard English writing skills to nonstandard dialect speakers (18, 50, 52, 57, 58, 60, 61). However, research indicates that the instructional techniques used to teach standard English writing skills are no more effective than those used to teach oral skills (18, 54). This is probably because in most schools students do not write enough to learn the necessary skills; writing a few sentences or filling out blank spaces in work books is insufficient.

SELF-QUIZ

What is your opinion about the following statement? Do you believe that students should be encouraged to speak and/or write in standard English because of the prejudices of society, especially employers? Or do you feel that it is society's obligation to clean up its act?

Language is personal and private; therefore, offering instruction to "improve" speech indicates criticism not only of the language but also of the person. However, since the "real world" is judgmental and critical, we do students a great disservice by continuing to ignore this serious issue. (65, pp. 22–23)

Communication Style

Mismatches between students' and teachers' communication styles can impair students' learning in much the same way as mismatches between students' and teachers' language proficiency. They make it difficult for educators to understand what their students are telling them about how the students feel or think, and sometimes they lead to misunderstandings. For example, teachers who are unaware of students' culturally influenced communication styles may mistakenly believe that the students are shy, insecure, disrespectful, and so on, and students who are unfamiliar with their teachers' communication styles may not be able to distinguish when their teachers are serious and when they are joking. Therefore, to communicate effectively with students, educators should be aware of the communication style differences between them and their students. The following are some examples of typical communication style differences. The references at the end of the chapter provide more in-depth information (75–93).

Formal Versus Informal Communication

Although all cultures have rules that people are expected to follow when they communicate with each other, the expectations of some cultures are much more flexible than others. Some groups expect strict adherence to communication conventions in certain situations—such as when children are addressing parents and other adults or when subordinates are communicating with those who have more status and/or power. Other cultures are much more relaxed and informal about communication codes. Strict codes of communication may be designed to show respect for others, to avoid open demonstrations of conflict and disagreement, or to avoid causing individuals to "lose face."

The communication styles of Hispanic Americans and some Asian and Pacific American groups tend to be much more formal than either the African American or European American communication styles.

> *Because one of the ways in which Hispanics demonstrate their respect for each other is through the maintenance of certain formal conventions like the use of the formal usted rather than the informal tu in conversation, Hispanics may mistake an Anglo's less formal approach to interpersonal relationships as a sign of disrespect. (81, p. 130)*

> *In Asian cultures the communication interaction is very structured and predictable. . . . The individual's status in the situation will define the role that he or she is expected to play in communication. These roles are usually defined by tradition and are often highly formalized. For communication to proceed smoothly, each participant must behave in the expected manner by using verbal and nonverbal behaviors appropriate to one's role. (88, p. 46)*

Emotional Versus Subdued Communication

When people communicate, are they expected to be considerate of other people's sensibilities—their reactions to what is communicated to them and how it is communicated? Or are the right of individuals to express their feelings, regardless of how it might affect others, considered more paramount? Some cultures protect individuals' rights to express their feelings and require their members to learn to tolerate, accept, and deal with the expression of intense feelings. Cultures that are more concerned with protecting people's sensibilities expect feelings to be communicated in a subdued way. African Americans and European Americans tend to be very different in this regard.

> *Whites want social interaction to operate at an emotionally subdued level. To realize this goal they first establish the rule that expressive behavior shall be subdued, which develops sensibilities capable of tolerating only relatively subdued outputs. . . . Black cultural norms desire levels of public interaction that are more emotionally intense. Consequently they allow individuals to express themselves at the level at which feelings are felt. (86, p. 117)*

Although students are allowed to protest the decisions of their teachers, they are expected to do so in an acceptable manner. Because of communication style differences, when African American students express their positions passionately, European American teachers who tend to value cool-headed reasoning may perceive these expressions as being beyond the bounds of acceptability (86).

Direct Versus Indirect Communication

Do people express themselves directly, openly, and frankly, or do they speak indirectly and politely in order to maintain smooth interpersonal relationships? Should teachers be indirect or frank when they have to criticize students' work or behavior?

As the following quotes about Southeast Asian Americans and Filipino Americans indicate, many Asian and Pacific American groups shun European American frankness.

> *American straightforwardness is considered at best impolite if not brutal. In Indochina, one does not come directly to the point. To do so is, for an American, a mark of honesty and forthrightness while a person from Indochina sees it as a lack of intelligence or courtesy. (90, p. 6)*

> *The (Filipino) student will sometimes employ a mediator in communicating with the teacher. While this procedure may appear strange to the Anglo teacher, the child may have had numerous experiences at home with difficult-to-approach adults which have required the services of a mediator. This may be especially true if the teacher is held in high esteem. (82, p. 19)*

If educators use an indirect approach in order to tell students when they want them to do something, will the students who are accustomed to a more direct approach understand that they are actually expected to comply? For example, African American students and students from poor backgrounds who are accustomed to being told directly what they should and should not do may not understand just how serious their teachers are when they are spoken to in an indirect manner (75).

Poetic and Analogous Communication

Some groups use a more poetic communication style or explain things by means of analogies rather than clear and concise terms and relationships. When teachers and students use different communication styles, there is the real possibility of miscommunication between them. Educators who prefer direct expression may also mistakenly think that some African American and Hispanic American students who use a more poetic and analogous speech pattern are "beating around the bush," that they cannot think straight, or that they have communication problems (81).

Honesty

Cultures have very different ideas about exactly what is honest communication and even whether honest communication is desirable. No culture expects people to be completely honest. Other issues besides honesty, such as the relative importance placed by the culture on maintaining one's honor or one's face, avoiding disagreement and conflict, avoiding personal responsibility, and so on, influence a group's opinion about how honest communication should be. In fact, in some cultures when people communicate it is more important to maintain smooth interpersonal relationships than to tell the truth. For example,

> *Falsehood carries no moral stricture for a Cambodian, Laotian, or Vietnamese. The essential question is not whether a statement is true or false, but what the intention of the statement is. Does it facilitate interpersonal harmony? Does it indicate a wish to change the subject? Hence, one must learn the "heart" of the speaker through his/her words. (90, pp. 6, 7)*

Even within cultures, subgroups have different attitudes about honest communication. In the European American culture, although some individuals feel that people should take responsibility for, pay the price for, and stand up for one's actions, many politicians believe that it is appropriate to use such techniques as damage control, spin control, and plausible deniability to color the truth and even hide it from the voters .

In some cultures, a promise to do something or to comply with an expectation may not be meant literally. If a refusal would lead to an awkward or uncomfortable interpersonal moment or insult a person, especially someone in a position of authority, a promise may be little more than a way of maintaining smooth interpersonal relationships. Thus, some students do not have the slightest intention of complying with a behavior plan they have agreed to or a contract they have signed.

Responses to Guilt and Accusations

When individuals are accused of doing the wrong thing, how do they express guilt and remorse or proclaim their innocence? European American students tend to express guilt by lowering their eyes and avoiding eye contact. When they are falsely accused, they may issue vigorous denials. Kochman describes the European American reaction in the following way: "If they are innocent, they issue a vigorous and defensive denial—especially if the charge is serious. If they are guilty and are not trying to pretend otherwise, their response is subdued and embarrassed" (86, p. 93).

As was noted earlier, African American students lower their eyes as a sign of respect, not as an admission of guilt, and they do not experience the same need to proclaim their innocence by emotional statements when they are not guilty. Because European Americans and African Americans respond differently when they admit or deny guilt, they can each assume the other has communicated guilt when he or she has not.

Educators who do not know that African American students tend to avoid direct eye contact with authority figures or elders as a sign of respect and submission, may judge their students' behavior by their own standards—which is exemplified by the expression, "Look me in the eye, and tell me the truth." When

African American students avert their eyes while being confronted about their behavior, teachers may misinterpret their lack of eye contact as indicating insincerity and guilt.

> *When whites ... issue a vigorous and defensive denial—the kind that whites often use when they feel falsely accused—blacks consider this a confirmation of guilt since they believe only the truth would have been able to produce a protest of such intensity. (86, p. 92)*

Themes Discussed

All cultures have unwritten rules about what should or should not be talked about and with whom. Because teachers and students may have culturally determined different expectations about what students should be willing to discuss with their teachers or their peers, it is important to know what students are and are not comfortable discussing. Here are some examples of themes that some students may be reluctant to discuss with teachers.

Needs

In some cultures people are so sensitive to others' needs that it is unnecessary for individuals to be open and direct about their needs. Thus, it is important to ask whether individuals from a student's cultural background express their needs openly or expect others to be sensitive to their feelings and problems. This is especially true for Hispanics.

> *Mexican American children seldom ask for help. Their socialization has accustomed them to the expectation that their needs will be noticed and help provided without its having to be asked for. This type of socialization results in children learning to be sensitive to the needs and feelings of others. (91, p. 15)*

> *Educators should be tuned into these subtle expressions of need. They should not assume that because Hispanic students have not expressed a need for help or understanding in a direct and forthright manner, they do not need special attention or consideration. (81, p. 96)*

Admission of Errors and Mistakes

Do people admit when they are wrong or have made a mistake? Students who have difficulty accepting responsibility for their errors and mistakes or apologizing to others for cultural reasons may be misperceived as defiant or stubborn.

In Spanish-speaking countries, language forms make it easy for people to avoid accepting responsibility for their mistakes. An Hispanic American educator explained it this way:

> *Let's pretend I missed the plane which brought me to this conference. Maybe it was my fault, and maybe not. Perhaps my husband turned off the alarm. Or perhaps my car would not start. But whatever rationalization I use, if I express*

> *myself in English it is my fault. The only way I can express what happened in English is to say "I missed the plane." So I think it would be better to express myself in Spanish. That way I don't have to feel guilty about what happened. I simply say, "El avion me dejó."' That means the plane left me. . . . If I were to drop this glass, some of you would say to yourselves, "She dropped the glass," implying that I'm clumsy. Others of you would say, "se cayo el vaso." Somehow the glass managed to slide out of my hand and break itself. (84, pp. 6–7)*

Should students be required to admit that they made a mistake or to apologize for something they did? Would that make students lose face? Perhaps students should learn to verbally accept both responsibility for and the consequences of their behavior, but some students may be willing to accept the consequences of their behavior whereas they resist admitting their responsibility to others. In such cases, it may be more effective to permit them to avoid having to admit their errors and mistakes.

Disagreement, Unwillingness, and Inability

Are people expected to say when they are unwilling or unable to do something? Are they likely to express disagreement? When people say they, too, feel or believe as others do or that they will do something, do they mean it? Or is this just their way of avoiding an unpleasant moment?

> *In the midst of a great cultural emphasis on harmony and respect in Japan one speaker will rarely directly contradict another or even answer a question with a direct "no." Even in situations in which Americans can perceive "nothing personal" to be conveyed by a "no" answer, the Japanese will usually find one of at least 16 different ways of saying "no" without using the literal equivalent. (79, p. 47)*

> *Hispanics often find themselves in difficulty if they disagree with an Anglo's point of view. To them, direct argument or contradiction appears rude and disrespectful. On the surface they seem agreeable, manners dictating that they do not reveal their genuine opinion openly unless they can take time to tactfully differ. (81, p. 131)*

Can teachers count on students to do the things they commit themselves to do? Some students are brought up to believe that not following through on promises and saying something that is not so are acceptable behavior when doing so contributes to interpersonal harmony or helps someone save face. When students do not fulfill a contract, do they think of it as lying or irresponsible behavior? Or do they believe that their behavior is appropriate?

> *An American who is not familiar with the Filipino culture might become annoyed when a Pilipino speaker says he or she will "try to come" and does not appear for the appointment. . . . The American probably does not know that when the Pilipino speaker says "I'll try" he or she usually means one of the following:*

1. "I cannot do it, but I do not want to hurt feeling by saying no." 2. "I would like to, but I am not sure you really want me to come. Please insist that I do." 3. "I will probably come, but I will not say yes because something may prevent me from coming. I have no control over what may happen." (77, pp. 32–33)

Will students be able to ask questions or request help when they do not understand something?

A Japanese youth.... Will not insult the teacher's efforts by saying, "I don't understand." Will nod politely even while not understanding and attribute the difficulty to his or her own lack of diligence. (75, p. 19)

Facts Versus Feelings

Many cultural groups frown on displays and discussions of feelings but expect their members to discuss matters of fact. For this reason, when students have problems it is important to know whether they are as comfortable discussing feelings such as resentment, anger, shame, guilt and the like, as facts.

In the USA as well as in northern European cultures and many oriental groups, the expression of emotion is limited. Southern European cultures and some Latin American groups seem to permit the incredible in this matter of expressing emotions. (87, p. 4)

Sensitive and Controversial Topics

What are the sensitive subjects that people shy away from? Depending on the group, topics such as politics, sex, religion, finances, and so on, may be acceptable or unacceptable topics of conversation.

East Indian American students would not respond or give opinions about the existence of god because they are afraid of being rude and offensive to anyone (maybe even the teacher) with their opinions. They are taught not to be this way.... On the other hand European American students felt totally comfortable discussing this question.... As a matter of fact, they felt they were being totally honest and straightforward in letting everyone know how they felt about the issue. (93, p. 2)

How well do individuals have to know each other and what kind of relationship do they have to have in order to be able to discuss sensitive or intimate topics? When and under what circumstances will students be willing to discuss sensitive topics with their teachers? In some cultures people will discuss sensitive issues only with family members and extremely close friends.

Affection

Do people demonstrate affection easily? Do they do so verbally or physically? Would students welcome or reject their teachers' display of affection? What are the acceptable ways teachers can express their affection for students? Is a pat on the back, an arm on the shoulder, and so on, acceptable, or are displays of affection limited to verbal statements? Although many students welcome physical touching, it is "taboo" behavior in some cultures. For example, the Hispanic American culture encourages more physical displays of affection than the European American culture does.

> *Hispanics tend to show affection and acceptance through touching. Friends are likely to kiss when they meet. Males are likely to hug each other or pat each other on the back as well as shake hands. And it is not unusual for people to hold others by the arm or place their hands on their shoulders when conversing. Therefore, educators should utilize physical contact when expressing approval and acceptance of their Hispanic students, especially the young ones. (81, p. 97)*

Group Processes

How do groups arrive at decisions and resolve disagreements? Do groups have leaders? Do leaders make decisions or lead the group to arrive at their own decisions? Are differences of opinion discussed openly, or are they side-stepped? Would students be comfortable participating in the decision-making process, or would they prefer to have decisions made by their teachers? Would they feel comfortable expressing opinions and feelings that differ from others in the group? Would they be able to participate in discussions of controversial issues or feel comfortable about deciding group issues by a public vote? Students who have been trained to avoid public conflicts and disagreements may be unable to participate in discussions of controversial issues, express opinions that are different from a previous speaker, or even vote on what the group should or should not do.

The following quotes describe ways in which group process as practiced in Asian American and Hispanic American groups can often differ from the typical European American approach.

> *Because being a member of a group is so important, the ability to work harmoniously with a group is highly valued. . . . The goal of group problem solving is to reach consensus, not to compete for acceptance and approval of one's idea or position at the expense of others in the group. Directness and forthrightness are not valued, and people who display these traits are considered to be rude and impolite. (87, p. 47)*

> *When a group of Hispanics disagree they may resolve the issue by continuing to discuss it until it becomes apparent that a consensus has been reached without polling the group or calling for a vote . . .*

> *This is much better than bringing out the differences of opinion among people by requiring them to take a stand—stand up and be counted, show which side you're on, etc. This can increase conflict and often does. (81, pp. 100–101)*

How many people speak at a time? European Americans expect that even in group situations only one person will speak and the others will wait their turn and listen. This is not true of all cultures.

> *In Arab countries and in many Latin American ones, conversations are invitations for everybody to join. (87, p. 4)*

> *In a heated discussion, blacks frequently make their points whenever they can enter the discussion. Deference is given to the person who considers his or her point most urgent. Turn-taking is the style of whites, who usually raise their hands to be recognized. Teachers find Black students impolite, aggressive, and boisterous when they cut off another student or fail to restrain themselves so that every student can have a turn to talk. (83, p. 29)*

Many European Americans expect groups to function quietly. However, African Americans, Mediterranean Americans, and Hispanic Americans are comfortable with much higher levels of what may seem like noise to European Americans.

Conflict Resolution

Are conflicts faced and dealt with in a straightforward manner or swept under the table? Should teachers bring conflicts between students into the open to resolve them? At home, are youngsters who disagree allowed or encouraged to argue and/or fight it out, or are they required to settle their differences peacefully and shake hands and make up? Is it better to intervene when students have conflicts or permit them to settle their conflicts themselves? Should students be required to shake hands and "make friends"? African American students are brought up to settle their conflicts in a much more open manner than many European American middle-class students and teachers. Teachers' intolerance of their behavior contributes to their being mislabelled behavior disordered.

Turn Taking

The length of time a person must wait to begin to respond or to introduce a new topic after another person has completed a statement varies with different cultures. Students from cultures that require longer pauses may feel left out or blocked out of classroom discussions because others who are used to shorter pauses take the floor before they do (75).

Nonverbal Communication

Nonverbal and verbal communication are different in a number of important respects. Unlike verbal communication, some of the ways people communicate nonverbally are universal. Frowns, smiles, and grimaces, for example, tend to mean the same thing in all groups. Other nonverbal communications—such as

---

SELF-QUIZ: Communication Style

People are not always comfortable with the way others communicate. For example, some individuals feel uncomfortable when people speak their mind in an emotional or frank manner; others find subdued or indirect expression difficult to understand and overly polite. State your preferences, if you have any, about the following aspects of people's communication styles. Do you feel more comfortable with one than the other? Do you think one is preferable to the other. Would you attempt to change those aspects of students' communication styles that you feel are less desirable or acceptable?

In general, are you more comfortable when students speak their minds in an emotional, passionate, excited, spontaneous manner or in a subdued, calm, controlled manner?

Do you prefer direct, open, and frank communication with students or indirect, polite communication?

Would you rather students communicate their feelings, opinions, values, judgments, and so on, directly, factually, and frankly, or indirectly in order to protect people's face or honor or to maintain smooth interpersonal relationships?

Do you prefer that students express their needs directly and openly or would you rather that they do so indirectly?

Would you rather that students admit their mistakes, accept responsibility for their actions, and apologize when they have wronged someone, or would you be satisfied if they are contrite and sorry without admitting so to others?

When students disagree with others or are unwilling or unable to do something, would you rather that they say so directly or indirectly?

Are you more comfortable with confronting and resolving conflicts directly, or do you prefer to avoid them as much as possible?

---

how people signal agreement, disagreement, disapproval, come here, and good-bye—are specific to a particular group.

People have much more conscious control over their verbal than their non-verbal communication. As a result, at times individuals who choose to hide their real feelings, attitudes, opinions, and so on, by verbal miscommunication actually communicate their true reactions nonverbally, often without realizing that they are doing so.

When people make decisions about how another person feels or thinks through her or his verbal messages, they usually can tell you what exactly it was that the individual said that led them to the conclusions they reached. When they arrive at such decisions because of an individual's nonverbal communication, however, they are often unaware of the nonverbal messages on which they based their conclusions.

Although dictionaries are available for almost every verbal language, there are no dictionaries of nonverbal communication that people can turn to when they are unsure of what another person is communicating. This is unfortunate, because people's nonverbal communication can be an even more important clue to their thoughts, feelings, and attitudes than their actual words.

Because of the differences between verbal and nonverbal communication, lack of familiarity with an individual's nonverbal communication can lead to many miscommunication problems. The first step in avoiding such miscommunication is to become sensitive to the differences in people's nonverbal styles. Unfortunately, many educators are unaware of the cultural differences in students' nonverbal communication styles. This section provides some examples of these differences and how they influence teacher–student relationships. More detailed discussions of the topic are found in the references.

Emotion

Cultures differ in how people are expected to express their emotions. In some Asian and Pacific cultures, students laugh or giggle when they are embarrassed. Some cultures bring up males and females to express their feelings differently. For example, in some groups only males can express anger: Females never talk sharply or snap at others. When they are angry, they smile, and their voices becomes softer.

Because cultures differ in how they express emotions and feelings, educators cannot always judge what students are feeling by referring to how they themselves behave when they are upset, embarrassed, angry, and so on. To understand their students' feelings, they need to be sensitive to the subtle, and often not so subtle, clues that are obvious to those who are able to recognize them.

Defiance

European Americans typically express anger and defiance by silent stares. African Americans roll their eyes, and many Asian and Pacific Americans force a smile when they are angry. As Johnson explains, among African Americans, especially females,

> *Rolling the eyes is a non-verbal way of expressing impudence and disapproval of the person who is in the authority role and of communicating every negative label that can be applied to the dominant person. . . . Often white teachers (who are in an authority role and who have contact with Black children) will miss the message communicated by Black children when they roll their eyes. (85, pp. 18, 57)*

African American (and Hispanic American) females will also stand with their hand or hands on their hips when they are angry or defiant. Johnson advises that "Most Black people know to 'cool it' when Black women take this stance. The non-verbal message communicated when a Black female takes this stance is: 'I'm really mad, now. You better quit messing with me.'" (85, p. 57).

Submissiveness

How do students express their respect for authority? In some cultures, looking an adult in the eye is a sign of respect and submission. In other cultures, avoiding eye contact communicates the same message. As a result, teachers may misinterpret the nonverbal messages communicated by students from other cultural backgrounds. The ways African American, Asian and Pacific American, Hispanic American, and other non–European American students are taught to show respect and submission typically differ from how European American students are expected to behave. As a result, European Americans often misinterpret the lack of eye contact among their non–European American students. For example,

> *Asians generally tend to use repeated head nodding, avoidance of direct eye contact, and minimal spontaneous verbalization, and to refrain from making critical comments, as a way of showing deference toward an authority figure. (88, p. 49)*

> *Occasional avoidance of eye contact by Oriental children may be classified as submissive behavior . . . such avoidance of eye contact provides others with a distorted image of an Oriental child—as being timid, shy, insecure, suspicious, undependable, and lacking self confidence. (93, p. 69)*

> *Avoidance of eye contact by a Black person communicates "I am in a subordinate role and I respect your authority over me," while the dominant culture member may interpret avoidance of eye contact as "Here is a shifty, unreliable person I'm dealing with." (85, p. 18)*

The way some African American males walk away from a reprimand can also reveal whether they have accepted it or not.

> *If the young Black male walks away in a natural manner then the reprimand was received positively; if he walks away with a "pimp strut" it means that the young Black male has rejected the reprimand and in fact is non-verbally telling the authority person to "go to hell." (85, p. 19)*

In some cultures a youngster may behave submissively, but grumble about the fact that they have to comply; in other cultures grumbling would be a sign of severe disrespect (80).

Physical Contact

In comparison to European Americans, non–European American groups are more likely to touch each other in many different situations. Differences between European Americans and Haitian and Hawaiian Americans and their implications are described in the following quotations.

> *Haitian children are very physical . . . we use our hands. . . . If a child wants to speak, instead of saying: "Hi, Johnny," he will touch the other child automatically. (Olga Bzdyk, Director, Head Start Program, Homestead, Florida) (89, p. 62)*

> *Children will often simply lay a friendly hand on an adult they are trying to reach, rather than make a verbal approach. For Western teachers such touching on the part of Hawaiian youngsters can cause discomfort and is often not under-*

stood, leaving the teacher with a vague sensation of being pawed at or hung on, and the child with a feeling of having been ignored.

One part of the body not commonly touched by Hawaiians is the head, which is considered tabu throughout Polynesia. . . . By contrast, one of the few touching gestures which is natural and comfortable for Westerners is a friendly pat on the head or tousling a youngster's hair. . . . Although not on a conscious level, Hawaiians react quite negatively to such behavior, with emotions ranging from a vague feeling of discomfort to resentment and anger and a feeling of physical violation. (76, p. 2)

Agreement and Disagreement

How do people communicate yes and no, agreement and disagreement, willingness and unwillingness, and so on?

There is a marked tendency on the part of Westerners to feel that the meaning of head-nods are universal, up-and-down to mean "yes" and side-to-side to mean "no." . . . Hawaiians raise their eyebrows to say "yes", sometimes simultaneously jerking the head back slightly and lowering the corners of the mouth. (76, p. 4)

Beckoning

European Americans call others with their finger or upturned palms. In some cultures this is a sign of disrespect or is used only for dogs. For example, among Hawaiian Americans,

In beckoning someone, the finger is never used nor the upright hand. Both these gestures to the Hawaiians are extremely abrupt and rude. People are called to come by placing the hand sideways, palm facing the center of the body, and beckoning with the hand in that position. (76, p. 4)

A similar problem can occur with Filipino American students.

The familiar "come here" gesture made by curling the forefinger in an upward manner becomes a frightening "you have done something wrong" signal to the Pilipino child. Pilipinos, as well as some other Asian groups, use a palm down sign to indicate "come here," which is often confused with the Anglo gesture "go back." (82, p. 19)

Summary

Students speak many different languages and dialects and use different communication styles. Linguistically appropriate education services for LEP students should include bilingual education, ESL, or sheltered English approaches. Unfortunately, a great many LEP students are placed in English submersion programs. Although students who speak nonstandard dialects can learn to read and write standard English without learning to speak standard English, many educators insist on teaching standard speech to them. Educators who understand their students' communication styles can communicate effectively with them.

Activities

1. Observe and listen to your peers in class. Do you notice any of the dialect and communication style differences described in this chapter? How sensitive are you to these differences?

2. Interview some nonstandard English dialect speakers about their experiences in school. Did/do their dialects interfere with their learning? How did/do their teachers and/or professors react to their dialects?

3. Ask some of your friends or fellow students from different ethnic and socioeconomic backgrounds to describe their communication styles in terms of the characteristics included in this chapter. To what extent do their communication styles conform to the stereotypes reported earlier? Ask them to rate their acculturation to the European American middle-class mainstream culture. Is there a relationship between their type and level of acculturation and their communication style preferences?

References

This reference discusses the large number of limited English proficient students in the United States.

1. Woodrow, K. A. (1988). *Measuring Net Immigration to the United States: The Emigrant Population and Recent Emigration Flows.* Paper presented at the annual meeting of the Population Association of American, New Orleans.

The following references deal with the legal definition of linguistically appropriate education for LEP students.

2. Bilingual Education Act of 1968.
3. Lau *v.* Nichols (1974). 414 U.S. 563.

Bilingual education approaches are the focus of the following references.

4. Crawford, W. (1991). *Bilingual Education: History, Politics, Theory, and Practice.* Trenton, NJ: Crane.

5. Cummins, J. (1984). *Bilingualism and Special Education: Issues in Assessment and Pedagogy.* San Diego, CA: College Hill Press.
6. Cummins, J. (1989). *Empowering Minority Students.* Sacramento, CA: California Association for Bilingual Education.
7. Olsen, L. (1988). *Crossing the Schoolhouse Border: Immigrant Students and the California Public Schools.* San Francisco: California Tomorrow.
8. Willig, A. (1985). A meta-analysis of selected studies on the effectiveness of bilingual education. *Review of Educational Research, 55,* 269–317.

References that discuss sheltered English approaches and their effectiveness are listed next.

9. Chamot, A. U., & O'Malley, J. M. (1986). *A Cognitive Academic Language Learning Approach: An ESL Content-Based Curriculum.* Rosslyn, VA: National Clearinghouse for Bilingual Education.

10. Crandall, J. (Ed.). (1987). ESL *Through Content Area Instruction: Mathematics, Science, Social Studies.* Englewood Cliffs, NJ: Prentice Hall.
11. Gersten, R., & Woodward, J. (1985). A case for structured immersion. *Educational Leadership*, 43(1), 75–79.
12. Northcutt, M., & Watson, D. (1986). *Sheltered English Teaching Handbook.* San Marcos, CA: AM Graphics & Printing.

Legal requirements regarding nonstandard English dialects is the focus of the following references.

13. Equal Educational Opportunities Act of 1972.
14. Martin Luther King Junior Elementary School Children *v.* Ann Arbor School District Board of Education, 451 F. Supplement 1324 (Michigan 1978); 463 F. Supplement 1027 (Michigan 1978); No. 7–71861, Slip Op. (Michigan, July 12, 1979).

Various approaches to dialect differences are the focus of the following references.

15. Adler, S. (1987). Bidialectalism: Mandatory or elective? *Asha*, 29(1), 41–44.
16. Ash, S., & Myhill, J. (1983). *Linguistic Correlates of Interethnic Conflict.* Philadelphia: University of Pennsylvania, Linguistics Laboratory.
17. Dean, M. B., & Fowler, E. D. (1974). An argument for appreciation of dialect differences in the classroom. *Journal of Negro Education*, 43(3), 302–309.
18. Farr, M. (1986). Language, culture, and writing: Sociolinguistic foundations of research on writing. In E. Z. Rothkopf (Ed.), *Review of Research on Education*, No. 13, 195–223.
19. Ferguson, A. M. (1982). A case for teaching standard English to Black students. *English Journal*, 71(3), 38–40.
20. Graff, D., Labov, W., & Harris, W. (1983). *Testing Listeners' Reactions to Phonological Markers of Ethnic Identity: A New Method for Sociolinguistic Research.* Paper presented at the annual meeting of the New Ways of Analyzing Variations in English, Montreal.
21. Groff, P. (1980). Black English and the teaching of spelling. In J. Schwartz (Ed.), *Teaching the Linguistically Diverse.* New York: New York State English Council.
22. Harris-Wright, K. (1987). The challenge of educational coalescence: Teaching nonmainstream English-speaking students. *Journal of*

Childhood Communication Disorders, 11(1), 209–215.
23. Hochel, S. S. (1983). *A Position Paper on Teaching the Acquisition of the Mainstream Dialect in Kindergarten and Elementary School.* ERIC ED 238–060.
24. Kochman, T. (1969). Culture and communication: Implications for Black English in the classroom. *Florida Foreign Language Reporter*, Spring/Summer, 89–92, 172–174.
25. Labov, W., & Harris, W. (1983). *De facto Segregation of Black and White Vernacular.* Paper presented at the annual meeting of the New Ways of Analyzing Variations in English, Montreal.
26. Lipscomb, D. (1978). Perspectives on dialects in Black students' writing. *Curriculum Review*, 17(3), 167–169.
27. Padak, N. D. (1981). The language and educational needs of children who speak Black English. *Reading Teacher*, 35(2), 144–151.
28. Simmons, E. A. (1991). Ain't we never gonna study no grammar? *English Journal*, 80(8), 48–51.
29. Taylor, O. L. (1986). A cultural and communicative approach to teaching standard English as a second dialect. In O. L. Taylor (Ed.), *Treatment of Communication Disorders in Culturally and Linguistically Diverse Populations.* San Diego, CA: College Hill Press.
30. Thomas, E. W. (1978). English as a second language—For whom? *The Crisis*, 85(9), 318–320.
31. Wolfram, W., Detwyler, J., & Adger, C. T. (1992). *All About Dialects: Instructors Manual.* Washington, DC: Center for Applied Linguistics.
32. Wood, B. S., & Curry, J. (1969). Everyday talk and school talk of the city Black child. *Speech Teacher*, 18(4), 282–296.

The following references shed light on the relationship between nonstandard dialects and reading.

33. Anastasiow, N. J., Levine-Hanes, M., & Hanes, M. L. (1982). *Language & Reading Strategies for Poverty Children.* Baltimore: University Park Press.
34. Barth, J. L. (1979). Nonstandard English and native students: When is a difference a disability? *British Columbia Journal of Special Education*, 3(4), 357–363.

35. Bougere, M. B. (1981). Dialect and reading disabilities. *Journal of Research and Development in Education, 14*(4), 67–73.
36. Collins, J. (1988). Language and class in minority education. *Anthropology and Education Quarterly, 19*(4), 299–326.
37. Dandy, E. B. (1988). *Dialect Differences: Do They Interfere?* ERIC ED 294–240.
38. Gibson, E., & Levin, H. (1975). *The Psychology of Reading.* Cambridge, MA: MIT Press.
39. Lass, B. (1980). Improving reading skills: The relationship between the oral language of Black English speakers and their reading achievement. *Urban Education, 14*(4), 437–447.
40. Levine-Hanes, M., & Hanes, M. L. (1979). *Developmental Differences in Dialect, Function Word Acquisition and Reading.* Paper presented at the annual meeting of the International Reading Association, Atlanta.
41. McGinnis, J., & Smitherman, G. (1978). Sociolinguistic conflict in the schools. *Journal of Non-White Concerns in Personnel and Guidance, 6*(2), 87–95.
42. Pflaum, S. W. (1978). Minority student language and reading acquisition. In S. E. Pflaum-Connor (Ed.), *Aspects of Reading Education.* Berkeley, CA: McCutchan.
43. Simons, H. (n.d.). *Black Dialect Interference and Classroom Interaction.* Berkeley, CA: School of Education, University of California.
44. Sims, R. (1976). What we know about dialects and reading. In P. D. Allen & D. J. Watson (Eds.), *Findings of Research in Miscue Analysis: Classroom Implications.* Urbana, IL: National Council of Teachers of English.
45. Strand, C. M. (1979). *Bidialectalism and Learning to Read.* Unpublished doctoral dissertation. Ann Arbor: University of Michigan.
46. Washington, V. M., & Miller-Jones, D. (1989). Teacher interaction with nonstandard English speakers during reading instruction. *Contemporary Educational Psychology, 14*(3), 280–312.

Techniques for helping students acquire bidialectal skills are described in the following references.

47. Adler, S. (1979). *Poverty Children and Their Language.* New York: Grune & Stratton.
48. Anderson, E. (1989). *Students' Language Rights.* ERIC ED 311–959.
49. British Columbia Department of Education. (1981). *English as a Second Language/Dialect Resource Book for K-12.* Victoria BC: Author.
50. Brooks, C. (Ed.). (1985). *Tapping Potential: English Language Arts for the Black Learner.* Urbana, IL: National Council of Teachers of English.
51. Christian, D. (1987). *Vernacular Dialects in U.S. Schools.* ERIC Digest. ERIC ED 289–364.
52. Cronnell, B., (Ed.). (1981). *The Writing Needs of Linguistically Different Students. Proceedings of a Research Practice Conference Held at the Southwest Regional Laboratory for Educational Research and Development.* ERIC ED 210–932.
53. Davis, B. G., & Armstrong, H. (1981). The impact of teaching Black English on self-image and achievement. *Western Journal of Black Studies, 5*(3), 208–218.
54. Eubanks, I. M. (1991). Nonstandard dialect speakers and collaborative learning. *Writing Instructor, 10*(3), 143–148.
55. Farr, M., & Daniels, H. (1986). *Language Diversity and Writing Instruction.* New York: ERIC Clearinghouse on Urban Education, Institute for Urban and Minority Education.
56. Kizza, I. (1991). *Black or Standard English: An African American Student's False Dilemma.* ERIC ED 342–008.
57. Koenig, L. A., & Biel, C. D. (1989). A delivery system of comprehensive language services in a school district. *Language, Speech, and Hearing Services in Schools, 20*(4), 338–365.
58. Larson, D. A. (1989). "Snow White" and Language Awareness. *Journal of Teaching Writing, 6*(1), 171–179.
59. Love, T. A. (1991). *A Guide for Teaching Standard English to Black Dialect Speakers.* ERIC ED 340–248.
60. Morris, R. W., & Louis, C. N. (1983). *"A Writing of Our Own." Improving the Functional Writing of Urban Secondary Students. Final Report.* ERIC ED 241–668.
61. Nembhard, J. P. (1983). A Perspective on teaching Black dialect speaking students to write standard English. *Journal of Negro Education, 52*(1), 75–82.
62. Penfield, J. (1982). *Chicano English: Implications for Assessment and Literary Development.* ERIC ED 255–050.
63. Reed, D. F. (1983). Helping Black high school students speak standard English. *English Journal, 72*(2), 105–108.
64. Reynoso, W. D. (1984). *Standard English Acquisition.* ERIC ED 246–693.
65. Robbins, J. F. (1988). Employers' language expectations and nonstandard dialect speakers. *English Journal, 77*(6), 22–24.

66. Schierloh, J. M. (1991). Teaching standard English usage: A dialect-based approach. *Adult Learning, 2*(5), 20–22.

67. Shipley, K. G., Stone, T. A., & Sue, M. B. (1983). *Test for Examining Expressive Morphology*. Tucson, AZ: Communication Skill Builders.

68. Taylor, H. (1991). Ambivalence toward Black English: Some tentative solutions. *Writing Instructor, 10*(3), 121–135.

The following references provide descriptions of differences between standard English and some nonstandard dialects.

69. Owens, R. E. (1988). *Language Development*. Columbus, OH: Merrill.

70. Hemingway, B. L., Montague J. C. Jr., & Bradley, R. H. (1981). Preliminary data on revision of a sentence repetition test for language screening with Black first grade children. *Language, Speech, and Hearing Services in Schools, 12*, 145–152.

71. Labov, W. (1972). *Language in the Inner City: Studies in Black English Vernacular*. Philadelphia: University of Pennsylvania Press.

72. Labov, W. (1974). *The Study of Nonstandard English*. Urbana, IL: National Council of Teachers of English.

73. Wolfram, W. A., & Christian, D. (1975). *Sociolinguistic Variables in Appalachian Dialects*. Arlington, VA: Center for Applied Linguistics.

74. Wolfram, W. A., & Fasold, R. W. (1974). *The Study of Social Dialects in American English*. Englewood Cliffs, NJ: Prentice Hall.

These references describe differences in verbal and nonverbal communication styles.

75. Wolfram, W., & Adger, C. T. (1993). *Language Differences Across Dialects*. Baltimore: Baltimore City Public Schools.

76. Anthony, A. P. (n.d.). *Hawaiian Nonverbal Communication: Two Classroom Applications*. Honolulu: University of Hawaii at Manoa, Department of Indo-Pacific Languages.

77. Boseker, B. J., & Gordon, S. L. (1983). What Native Americans have taught us as teacher educators. *Journal of American Indian Studies, 22*(3), 20–24.

78. California State Department of Education. (1986). *Handbook for Teaching Pilipino-Speaking Students*. Sacramento: Author.

79. California State Department of Education. (1987). *Handbook for Teaching Japanese-Speaking Students*. Sacramento: Author.

80. Goodwin, M. H. (1990). *He-Said-She-Said: Talk as Social Organization Among Black Children*. Bloomington, IN: Indiana University Press.

81. Grossman, H. (1984). *Educating Hispanic Students: Cultural Implications for Instruction, Classroom Management, Counseling, and Assessment*. Springfield, IL: Charles C Thomas.

82. Howells, G. N., & Sarabia, I. B. (1978). Education and the Pilipino Child. *Integrated Education, 16*(2), 17–20.

83. Irvine, J. J. (1991). *Black Students and School Failure: Policies, Practices, and Prescriptions*. New York: Praeger.

84. Jaramillo, M. L. (1973). *Cautions When Working with the Culturally Different Child*. ERIC ED 115–622.

85. Johnson, K. R. (1971). Black kinetics: Some nonverbal communication patterns in the Black culture. *Florida Reporter*, Spring/Fall, 17–20, 57.

86. Kochman, T. (1981). *Black and White Styles in Conflict*. Chicago: University of Chicago Press.

87. Leggio, P. (n.d.). *Contrastive Patterns in Nonverbal Communication Among Different Cultures*. Trenton: Office of Equal Opportunity, New Jersey State Department of Education.

88. Matsuda, M. (1989). Working with Asian parents: Some communication strategies. *Topics in Language Disorders, 9*(3), 45–53.

89. National Coalition of Advocates for Students. (1988). *New Voices: Immigrant Students in U.S. Public Schools*. Boston: Author.

90. Nguyen, L. D. (1986). Indochinese cross-cultural adjustment and communication. In M. Dao & H. Grossman (Eds.), *Identifying, Instructing and Rehabilitating Southeast Asian Students with Special Needs and Counseling Their Parents*. ERIC ED 273–068.

91. Rodriguez, J. (n.d.). *An In-Service Rationale for Educators Working with Mexican American Students*. Stanford, CA: Chicano Fellow, Stanford University.

92. Sra, D. (1992). *A Comparison of East Indian American and European American Students*. San Jose, CA: Unpublished manuscript, San Jose State University, Division of Special Education.

93. Yao, E. L. (1979). Implications of biculturalism for the learning process of middle-class Asian children in the United States. *Journal of Education, 16*(4), 61–72.

$C\ h\ a\ p\ t\ e\ r$ *7*

Causes of Gender Disparities

As was noted in Chapter 1, males and females have very different experiences in school. Depending on their ethnic and socioeconomic background, they choose different courses, participate in different extracurricular activities, aspire to different careers and occupations, and earn different scores on standardized achievement tests. Male students tend to score higher than females in the upper ranges of tests of advanced mathematics skills, but they do not perform as well as females in language arts and basic computational skills.

Depending on their ethnic background, girls tend to be less self-confident than boys in situations that are in the "male domain" (such as mathematics and physics courses), in competitive situations, and when they lack objective information about how well they have done or can do. They react less positively than boys to difficult and challenging situations; they are less likely to take risks and perform less adequately than boys following failure or the threat of failure; they are more likely to attribute their poor performance to lack of ability rather than lack of effort or motivation; and they tend to seek the assistance and approval of adults more than boys do. Males are more likely to get into trouble for behavior problems, to be disciplined by their teachers, and to be suspended from school.

This chapter examines the causes of gender differences in students' academic achievement, school participation, and behavior. Chapter 8 discusses techniques educators can employ to solve these problems.

Biological Predispositions

Many people believe that biology is a major cause of the gender differences observed in school. Physiological factors that are thought to contribute to these differences include dissimilarities in females' and males' hormonal systems and the lateralization and specialization of their right and left brains.

Hormonal Differences

Some researchers have proposed that the higher levels of male hormones such as testosterone make males more active, assertive, and aggressive (1, 4–6, 11–13, 16,

21). They suggest that teachers are intolerant of the male behavior patterns these hormonal differences create and overreact to their students' behavior.

It is true that males exhibit more behavior problems and get into more trouble in school than females (22–26). There also is evidence that teachers, especially females, tend to be less tolerant of male behavior patterns (27–29), and use more punitive management techniques with males (30, 31). However, these facts do not answer the question of whether teachers should be more tolerant of male behavior patterns or whether males' aggressive, assertive, and active behavior is caused by hormonal rather than cultural differences.

Research indicates that males and females do have different levels of testosterone and that this does affect their levels of activity and aggression and their emotional reactions (1, 4–6, 11–13, 16). It is not clear, however, whether the higher levels of testosterone observed in males *cause* them to behave more assertively and aggressively than females or merely *predispose* them to do so when environmental conditions encourage them to behave in these ways.

Lateralization and Specialization

A number of researchers believe that male-female differences in verbal achievement are largely due to differences in the age at which and the extent to which their brain's right and left hemispheres become specialized in mathematical and verbal functioning (3, 11). Although there are many different theories about exactly how cerebral specialization may cause gender differences, one that is more widely accepted than others is based on the fact that hemispheric specialization in certain functions such as verbal, visual-spatial, and mathematical reasoning occurs earlier in females than in males. This theory proposes that early development of females' brains and their greater hemispheric specialization provides them with a head start that improves their verbal functioning.

Research results regarding gender differences in hemispheric specialization are not entirely consistent. On balance, considerable evidence of differences in cerebral lateralization between males and females exists (3, 7–10, 14, 15, 17–20). Researchers have found that hemispheric specialization in females begins earlier, perhaps as early as three months of age, and develops to a greater degree. However, research has not yet established a direct causal relationship between these physiological differences and the ages at which the genders acquire initial language skills or their scores on tests on verbal skills (3). More research is needed before we can consider the biological explanation for this gender disparity to be proven.

Predisposition Versus Determinism

Educators disagree about the extent to which hormonal and lateralization/specialization differences make gender disparities inevitable. Some think that they cause definite gender differences in behavior and learning; many others view them not as a complete determiner of how individuals behave, but as one of several interacting influences. In this view, aptly expressed by Maccoby and Jacklin in 1974, behavior differences that have a biological base can still be modified by environmental events.

> We suggest that societies have the option of minimizing, rather than maximizing, sex differences through their socialization practices. A society could, for example, devote its energies more toward moderating male aggression than toward preparing women to submit to male aggression, or toward encouraging rather than discouraging male nurturance activities. In our view, social institutions and social practices are not merely reflections of the biologically inevitable. A variety of social institutions are viable within the framework set by biology. It is up to human beings to select those that foster the life styles they most value. (11, p. 374)

Although research since 1974 has provided considerable information about the possible biological bases of gender differences, we still are relatively ignorant about which gender differences have a biological component. In addition, very little research has been conducted to determine the extent to which biological factors cause versus merely predispose males and females to function differently, whether some biological predispositions are more resistant to change than others, and the psychological costs, if any, people pay when they behave in ways that contradict their biological predispositions.

Conclusions

The possibility that male-female differences in hormonal levels and brain specialization and lateralization contribute significantly to differences in their academic success and behavior is basically unsubstantiated. It is also possible that as society and the education it provides students become less sexist, male-female differences in students' attitudes, behavior, academic achievement, and so on, will decrease, and as we learn more about non–European American and non-middle-class students we will find that many of the male-female differences observed among European American middle-class students do not apply to other ethnic groups and socioeconomic classes. As a result, the need to question whether biological factors contribute to gender differences will diminish.

We do not know whether some physiological predispositions are more resistant to change than others, nor do we know the psychological costs, if any, people pay when they behave in ways that contradict their physiological predispositions. Therefore, when educators react to students' gender-specific behaviors that may have a physiological component, they have little to guide them regarding either the extent to which such behavior can be changed or the possible costs involved in attempting to eliminate the behavior completely rather than modify it.

Differential Reinforcement

Everyday life experiences confirm that males and females learn gender-stereotypic roles in part because they tend to be rewarded for behaving differently (playing with different toys, communicating in different styles, settling arguments differently, enrolling in different courses, participating in different sports, and so on) and negatively reinforced for behaving similarly (boys crying about bruises and scrapes, girls playing in an active, boisterous manner, and the like). In addition, considerable research evidence supports this explanation. Although different ethnic and socioeconomic groups may not all share the same ideas about the sex roles children should learn, parents tend to reward their children for behaving in ways that they feel are gender-appropriate and punish them for behaving in ways that they feel are gender-inappropriate (11, 32–35). Teachers also use rewards and punishments to modify their students' behavior, although they differ about the kinds of behavior they want students to exhibit.

Children, even toddlers and preschoolers, also reinforce each other for behaving in gender-stereotypical fashion (36–39). Children in general and males in particular reward each other for playing with the right toys, in the right way, and with the right sex, and for relating to each of the sexes in acceptable ways.

Differential reinforcement affects students' behavior, but only to a limited degree. Students' parents, teachers, and peers cannot decide for them what they will think and how they will behave.

Constructivism: Cognitive Awareness and Modeling

Children voluntarily adopt some gender-stereotypical ways of behaving without having to be rewarded (11, 40–47). They become aware of and identify with their gender, and then copy behavior they believe is gender-appropriate. In fact, as their conceptual abilities develop, they construct increasingly more elaborate schemes of gender-appropriate behavior and proceed to match their behavior to their constructs.

Maccoby and Jacklin describe the process in the following way:

> A child gradually develops concepts of "masculinity" and "femininity," and when he has understood what his own sex is, he attempts to match his behavior to his conceptions. His ideas may be drawn only very minimally from observing his own parents. The generalizations he constructs do not represent acts of imitation, but are organizations of information distilled from a wide variety of sources. (11, pp. 365–366)

There is ample evidence that adults, including parents, model gender-specific behavior and communicate gender-specific expectations to children and youth, which children tend to copy (16, 40–58). Considerable evidence also suggests that children as young as two and three years of age develop constructs of appropriate male and female behavior and tend to bring their behavior into line with these constructs (37, 40).

Structured Reproduction

As was noted in the previous chapter, reproduction theorists claim that schools purposely perpetuate the values, ideas, and attitudes European American middle- and upper-class males have set up throughout society to maintain their economic and social power and position. That is, they believe that those who exercise control and power in our society—middle and upper-class European American males—structure its institutions, including schools, to maintain their special positions by reproducing the inequality that serves their interests (59–65). According to these theorists, schools provide females and others with the kinds of educational experiences that maintain them as a source of cheap, though well-prepared, labor while more affluent male students are trained to be the leaders of society. At the same time, schools teach females and others to accept the status quo—their economic and social inferiority.

Resistance, Production, and Transformation

Although students are exposed to gender and class biases in school and society at large, they are also exposed to ideas and experiences that contradict these biases (66–75). Nonsexist ideas have become more frequent in the media and in the materials students read in school. Many teachers and parents do not adhere to society's stereotypic gender, ethnic, and socioeconomic expectations for children and adolescents. Since they are given conflicting messages, students accept some and resist others.

Some students accept most of the stereotypic messages they receive. Many others do not. They understand that schools are structured to maintain gender inequality, and they know that even if they do well in school, a society stratified along gender lines will not afford them the same benefits that males, especially European American upper-class males, receive from succeeding in school. Therefore, instead of acquiescing to the educational system for payoffs they do not believe will be forthcoming, they strive to maintain their own sense of identity.

As was noted in Chapter 3, some students accommodate more than they resist; others actively resist the biased education they receive and the inferior position it threatens to place them in. Some defy schools' gender and socioeconomic biases in nonconstructive ways (67, 68, 72–75). Other students battle the same forces in constructive ways. They reject the biased ideas to which they are exposed. Instead, they gain a sense of self-identity and a better understanding of their gender and class, and begin to contribute to transforming society (63, 69–71).

Conclusions

Biology, differential reinforcement, modeling, cognitive awareness, and structured reproduction all interact in undetermined ways to lead a given individual to behave in a particular way in a specific situation. These factors can contribute to gender differences; however, they do not make male and female students behave differently. Physiological factors only predispose or incline the genders to act in dissimilar ways. Students can modify and channel their biological predispositions. Differential reinforcement, cognitive awareness and modeling, and educational structures reproduce gender stereotypes, but they can also produce students with new perspectives on gender issues.

The School's Role

This section examines the school's role in the creation and maintenance of gender differences in students' achievement and participation in school.

Administrative Imbalance

Although females comprise the majority of classroom teachers, they are grossly underrepresented in administrative positions (76–79). In 1990 eighty-three percent of the nation's school principals and superintendents were male and the majority of these, 75%, were European American males (79). Thus, the current situation, especially in elementary schools, is no different than the situation described by Frazier and Sadker in 1973: "Elementary school is a woman's world, but a male captain heads the ship" (77, p. 96).

What message does this situation communicate to students? Many authors believe that it teaches them that males, especially European American males, are and should be the authorities (76–79).

Curriculum Materials

Although curriculum materials such as textbooks, readers, and biographies that students currently use are not as sexist as the materials used in classes in the 1960s and 1970s, they continue to introduce society's gender biases into the school's structure (80–91). The disparity in the number of pictures of males and females has been reduced. The stereotypic portrayal of females as nurses and secretaries has been largely eliminated, and working females are engaged in many more occupations. The preponderance of male characters in basal readers has been reduced by eliminating male characters from many stories and replacing them with nonhuman characters such as talking trees or animals without sex roles.

However, many problems still exist. For example, authors and publishers still use male pronouns to describe individuals whose gender is unknown and man for all people. The use of nonhuman characters in basal readers avoids the appearance of sexism, but it does not increase the number of female characters or stories about females. In fact, stories about males still greatly outnumber stories about females in students' readers in the higher grades and in the biographies found in school libraries. In most of the material students read, fathers still work and mothers still stay home. At home, mothers do domestic chores such as taking care of children and cooking; fathers build and repair things. When parents work outside the home, they are still described as involved in gender-stereotypic jobs, but to a lesser degree. Males are depicted as engaged in three times as many different occupations as females, and fathers are the executives, professionals, scientists, firefighters, and police officers. Males participate in a variety of different athletic activities; females are involved primarily in sports that have traditionally been considered female sports.

Females are described as overemotional, dependent, concerned about their appearance, and watching others do things. Males are depicted as actively involved in solving problems and doing adventurous things. Females are still portrayed as receiving help and males as helping them.

In math books, boys learn to count by driving cars, flying planes, and engineering trains, but girls learn to count by jumping rope, measuring cloth, and following cooking recipes. Males are still the scientists in science materials. Although the number of pictures of males and females is about equal in history textbooks, only 5% of their text deals with female experiences, and when females' roles in history are included in the 5% of the text devoted to female experiences, women whose contributions fulfill the more acceptable traditional female role are described almost to the exclusion of feminists or those who were involved in feminist issues.

Computer software is also biased against females. As Woodill puts it: "Much of computer software has been designed by males for males, as shown by the predominance of male figures in programs, computer ads, and on the software packaging" (91, p. 55). Although changes have occurred, curriculum materials are in general still quite sexist.

Teacher Attention, Feedback, Evaluation, and Expectations

Teachers tend to create and maintain gender differences in school through the attention and feedback they give students, how they evaluate them, and the expectations they communicate to them. Chapter 3 described the adverse effects of teachers' biased expectations and evaluations. This section focuses on the harm done to students by gender bias in teacher attention and feedback.

Beginning in preschool, boys receive more attention from their teachers (11, 92–109). One reason boys receive more attention is that teachers spend more time disciplining them for misbehavior (103, 109, 124). Much of the difference, however, is due to the fact that teachers demonstrate a clear bias in favor of male participation in their classes. Teachers are more likely to call on males when students volunteer to recite and when they call on nonvolunteers. When students recite, teachers are also more likely to listen to and talk to males. They also use more of their ideas in classroom discussions and respond to them in more helpful ways (105).

The pattern of giving more attention to males is especially clear in science and mathematics classes. Beginning in preschool grades, teachers ask males more questions and give them more individual instruction, acknowledgment, praise, encouragement, corrective feedback, opportunities to answer questions correctly, and social interaction (92, 100–102, 108). In mathematics classes, they wait longer for males to answer questions before calling on someone else. They reward females for performing computational skills and males for higher-level cognitive skills, demonstrate more concern about giving males remedial help, and expect males to be more interested in math and better at solving math problems (137) .

Gender differences do not favor males in all subjects. In reading, a course traditionally seen as in the female domain, teachers tend to spend more time instructing and attending to females (102, 107).

How do females interpret their teachers' apparent disinterest in them? No one knows for sure. However, Boudreau's conclusion about the probable interpretation students put on the message teachers give them may be correct: "The idea conveyed to girls is, although subtle, quite clear. What boys do matters more to teachers than what girls do" (94, p. 68).

Teachers also provide males and females different kinds of attention. Again the differential treatment favors males. Teachers give boys more praise and attention for high levels of achievement and correct responses (95–97, 99, 111). In fact, teachers give high-achieving girls the least amount of attention, praise, and supportive feedback and the largest number of disparaging statements compared to low-achieving girls and all boys (86, 111). They praise girls more for neatness, following instructions exactly, and raising their hands. Even when they give the wrong answer, girls are often praised for raising their hands and volunteering (110, 114). Many teachers avoid criticizing girls' responses even when they are wrong (114). This is unfortunate because girls learn better when they receive corrective feedback (112).

There is some evidence that these biases are more characteristic of European American teachers than African Americans (115). This may be one more example of the fact that "Blacks are less gender-typed and more egalitarian than whites" (113, p. 61).

What are teachers telling their female students by relating to them in these ways? Are they communicating that they do not expect their female students to be able to perform well in academic areas? Are they implying that they do not believe the females can respond correctly? Are they saying that they feel females are too fragile to be criticized? Any and all of these explanations are possible in the absence of research data.

How do female students interpret their teachers' behavior? A probable answer is that, with the exception of courses in the "female domain," they are still getting the message that teachers do not expect them to do as well as boys.

Research, which needs updating, suggests that teachers have different academic expectations for females and males (93, 116–122). Although they do not expect males and females to have different achievement levels in school, they view high achievement as a masculine characteristic and low achievement as feminine. They believe that courses such as physics are more appropriate for students with masculine characteristics. In mathematics classes they assign females to lower ability groups than their achievement would warrant. These differences can affect students' self-confidence about their academic ability and their motivation to succeed in school.

As was noted in Chapter 3, the message African American females receive is even more destructive (123–126). Teachers, especially European American teachers, perceive and treat African American females in an even more biased manner than European American females (123, 125, 126). Their teachers seem to be telling them that all they are good for is the stereotypic roles such as housekeepers, maids, child care providers, and so on, that European Americans have historically assigned to African American females.

Gender and ethnic differences in teacher attention, feedback, expectations, and evaluations can have other negative effects on students (127–130). These differences may help to explain why girls are more likely than boys to react poorly to failure or the threat of failure and to attribute their poor performance to lack of ability rather than lack of effort. They may also contribute to females' high anxiety during testing situations, and they may be one reason why European American females think such subjects as mathematics and science are less important to them and enroll in fewer math and science courses.

Courses and Activities

Many teachers believe that some courses belong in the male domain and others in the female domain (134). For example, teachers and counselors tend to reward boys more than girls for learning math. They encourage boys to enroll in math and science-related courses and discourage girls from taking advanced courses such as calculus and physics, and boys from enrolling in such "feminine" courses as languages and home economics. Many teachers and counselors believe that higher education and certain careers and occupations are more appropriate for one sex or another, and vocational education teachers often harass female students enrolled in nontraditional vocational courses (131–133, 136).

Students receive sexist messages about participation in physical education activities. Schools tend to provide different sports experiences for males and females (135–137). Many schools, especially at the middle and high school level, continue to have separate physical education classes for boys and girls. The schedule for female teams' practice is often determined by when males are not using the facilities, and coaches of male teams are paid more than those coaching female teams. Girls are almost routinely excluded from contact sports such as football, rugby, and soccer, and boys are discouraged from participating in girls' activities such as dancing, skipping rope, and using the balance beam. When students persist in pursuing activities reserved for the opposite sex they are often labeled tomboys or sissies.

Gender Segregation/Separation

Studies done in the late 1970s and middle 1980s revealed that some teachers discouraged male-female interaction. Instead of encouraging mixed-gender groups, some teachers assigned different chores to boys and girls. For example, girls put things in order while boys moved furniture. Teachers separated boys and girls when assigning seats or areas to hang up clothes and when forming study and work groups and committees (134, 138, 139). Lockheed and Harris reported a particularly pernicious management approach:

> *In classrooms, assignment to mixed-sex seating adjacencies or groups often is used as a punishment designed to reduce student interaction instead of as a learning technique designed to foster cooperative interaction. (139, p. 276)*

It is unclear how many teachers engaged in these practices in the past and whether teachers continue to do so now. Research is needed to determine if these practices continue and if they are widespread.

Encouragement of Behavior Differences

Although all teachers want their students to be well-behaved, according to research that was conducted in the 1970s to middle 1980s they appear to have different standards for males and females. Beginning in preschool, teachers tend to encourage gender-stereotypic behavior (94, 140–144). Teachers praise boys more than girls for creative behavior and girls more than boys for conforming behavior. Boys are rewarded for functioning independently, whereas girls are rewarded for being obedient and compliant. Boudreau believes this form of discrimination harms females: "The pattern of reinforcement that young girls receive may lead them to stake their sense of self-worth more on conforming than personal competency" (94, p. 73).

To the extent that these results are still current, teachers who encourage these gender differences can certainly cause problems for girls in situations that require creativity, assertiveness, or independence.

There is also evidence that teachers accept different kinds of inappropriate behavior from males and females without disciplining them for misbehaving. Huffine, Silvern, and Brooks found that kindergarten teachers discipline males and females for different kinds of misbehavior. They report that

> *Aggression in boys is acceptable while in girls it is not. The reverse seems to be true of disruptive talking. Teachers expect and/or accept talking from girls, at least much more so than from boys. Thus, the stereotypic behaviors, aggressiveness and loquacity, may be acquired and/or maintained by the differential teacher responses to these behaviors. (142, p. 34)*

Intolerance of Male Behavior Patterns and Biased Classroom Management Techniques

As was noted previously, educators, especially female educators, tend to be less tolerant of "male-typical" behaviors. African American males are especially likely to suffer the consequences of teachers' intolerance. Many African American males, and females as well, express their emotions much more intensely than most European Americans. When European American teachers observe African American males behaving aggressively and assertively, they tend to assume that the students are much angrier or upset than they actually are. Attributing a level of anger to African American students that would be correct for European American students who behaved in a similar way, teachers become uncomfortable, even anxious, and concerned about what they incorrectly anticipate will happen next. As a result, they intervene when no intervention is necessary. If teachers appreciated the cultural context of African American males' seemingly aggressive behavior toward others and understood that such behavior is unlikely to cause the physical fight or whatever else they expect to occur, they would be less likely to have to intervene to make themselves feel more at ease in the situation. This, in turn, would lessen the likelihood that African American males would get into trouble needlessly.

Teachers tend to reprimand males more often than females and differently as well (29–31, 94, 142). They tend to speak briefly, softly, and privately to girls but publicly and harshly to boys. With younger children they tend to use physical methods like poking, slapping, grabbing, pushing, squeezing, and so on, with boys, and negative comments or disapproving gestures and other forms of non-verbal communication with girls (142). Teachers are more likely to use even harsher disciplinary techniques, such as corporal punishment and suspension, with poor, African American, and Hispanic American males than with middle-class European American males (26, 29, 142, 145–148).

This is unfortunate, because public and harsh reprimands and physical forms of discipline and severe punishments can cause students to react rebelliously to punishments that they feel are too harsh for their "crimes." This may help to explain why males get into trouble in school and why males from poor backgrounds and some non–European American backgrounds tend to get into even more trouble than European American middle-class students (22–26).

Conclusions

The data just presented clearly indicate that schools play an important role in the formation and maintenance of students' stereotypic views of gender roles. As Meece puts it,

> Schools have been slow in adapting to recent changes in the social roles of men and women. As a result, schools may be exposing children to masculine and fem-

inine images that are even more rigid and more polarized than those currently held in the wider society. Furthermore, the school setting does not seem to provide children with many opportunities to perform behaviors not associated with their gender. Therefore, schools seem to play an important role in reinforcing rigid gender distinctions. (113, p. 67)

SELF-QUIZ: Critical Incidents

It is not always easy to apply a set of principles to a real-life situation when some of the principles that apply to a specific situation appear to lead to apparently contradictory solutions to the problem. Describe how you think teachers should handle each of the following critical incidents.

1. After raising her hand repeatedly to volunteer answers to her teacher's questions without being called on, a fifth-grade student complains that her teacher is unfair because the teacher always calls on the boys to answer the difficult questions. The teacher does not believe she is correct.
2. An African American tenth-grade male in a predominantly poor neighborhood school

tells his teacher in no uncertain terms to get off his case and stop telling him about the value of a high school diploma. He insists that a high school diploma does not help African Americans. The teacher tells the student he is wrong. The next day the student brings in some articles which confirm that African American males who graduate high school do not earn significantly more than those who do not.

3. A teacher overhears two seniors say they plan to protest the prejudice they experienced in school by wearing some outlandish clothes to the graduation ceremony rather than the conservative clothes and cap and gown prescribed by the school administration.

Summary

Many factors contribute to the gender differences observed in school. Males and females are biologically predisposed to function differently. Males and females are reinforced for behaving differently, and they learn different roles by observing adults behaving in gender-stereotypical ways. Further, they are exposed to gender-biased information. Society is structured in ways that promote gender differences. For the present, we are unable to determine which combination of factors contribute to a particular gender difference, how these factors interact to produce the differences, and the relative amount of influence each factor exercises in the case of any particular difference. We also do not know why some individuals conform to these gender stereotypes and others do not. Much more research is needed before scientific answers can be provided to these important questions.

Schools play a significant role in creating and maintaining gender differences. Gender bias exists in the textbooks students use, the unequal amounts of attention and different kinds of feedback and encouragement they receive from their teachers, the gender segregation they experience, and so on. Although these factors tend to reproduce gender differences, substantial numbers of students resist their influences to varying degrees.

Students belong to ethnic groups, socioeconomic classes, and gender groups. Bias against students in school occurs as a result of the interplay between the ways in which teachers relate to students in terms of these three characteristics. Bias against any group of students for any reason is undesirable and should be eliminated.

Activities

1. Compare how your professors relate to different groups of students. You can study almost any aspect of their teaching. For example, count the number of times they call on students who volunteer, the number of times they praise students' contributions, and so on. Then compare the results for different groups of students such as males and females and European Americans and non–European Americans.

2. Interview males and females from different ethnic and socioeconomic backgrounds in the courses you are taking about some of the issues discussed in this chapter. What are their opinions about the origins of gender differences? Do students opinions vary with their gender, ethnic, or socioeconomic backgrounds?

3. Review the textbooks and other materials your professors assign in the courses you are taking. Are they free from gender bias? Do they deal with the gender issues inherent in the topics they cover? Do they focus exclusively or primarily on European Americans to the exclusion of other ethnic groups?

4. Compare the amount of time your professors devote to the gender issues inherent in the courses they teach. Do you find that some professors are more sensitive to and interested in gender issues than others?

References

The following references present evidence that some gender differences in students' behavior in school and academic achievement may have a physiological base.

1. Frankenhaeuser, M., von Wright, M. R., Collins, A., von Wright, J., Sedvall, G., & Swahn, C. G. (1978). Sex differences in psychoneuroendocrine reactions to examination stress. *Psychosomatic Medicine, 40*(4), 334–343.
2. Grossman, H., & Grossman, S. (1994). *Gender Issues in Education.* Needham, MA: Allyn and Bacon.
3. Halpern, D. F. (1986). *Sex Differences in Cognitive Abilities.* Hillsdale, NJ: Erlbaum.
4. Jacklin, C. N., Maccoby, E. E., & Doering, C. H. (1983). Neonatal sex-steroid hormones and timidity in 6–18-month-old boys and girls. *Developmental Psychobiology, 16,* 163–168.
5. Jacklin, C. N., Maccoby, E. E., Doering, C. H., & King, D. R. (1984). Neonatal sex-steroid hormones and muscular strength in boys and girls in the first three years. *Developmental Psychobiology, 17,* 301–310.
6. Jacklin, C. N., Wilcox, K. T., & Maccoby, E. E. (1988). Neonatal sex-steroid hormones and intellect abilities of six-year-old boys and girls. *Developmental Psychobiology, 21,* 567–574.

7. Kimura, D. (1980). Sex differences in intra-hemispheric organization of speech. *Behavior and Brain Sciences, 3,* 240–241.

8. Kimura, D. (1983). Sex differences in cerebral organization for speech and praxic functions. *Canadian Journal of Psychology, 37,* 19–35.

9. Kimura, D. (1985). Male brain, female brain: The hidden difference. *Psychology Today, 19,* 50–58.

10. Levy, J., & Gur, R. C. (1980). Individual differences in psychoneurological organization. In J. Herron (Ed.), *Neuropsychology of Left-Handedness.* New York: Academic Press.

11. Maccoby, E. E., & Jacklin, C. N. (1974). *The Psychology of Sex Differences.* Stanford, CA: Stanford University Press.

12. Maccoby, E. E., & Jacklin, C. N. (1980). Sex differences in aggression: A rejoinder and reprise. *Child Development, 51,* 964–980.

13. Marcus, J., Maccoby, E. E., Jacklin, C. N., & Doering, C. H. (1985). Individual differences in mood: Their relation to gender and neonatal sex steroids. *Developmental Psychobiology, 18,* 327–340.

14. McGlone, J. (1980). Sex differences in human brain asymmetry: A critical survey. *Behavioral and Brain Sciences, 3,* 215–263.

15. McKeever, W. F. (1987). Cerebral organization and sex: Interesting but complex. In S. U. Philips, S. Steele, & C. Tanz (Eds.), *Language, Gender, and Sex in Comparative Perspective.* Cambridge, England: Cambridge University Press.

16. Parsons, J. E. (Ed.). (1980). *The Psychobiology of Sex Differences and Sex Roles.* Washington, DC: Hemisphere Publishing.

17. Ray, W. J., Newcombe, N., Semon, J., & Cole, P. M. (1981). Spatial abilities, sex differences and EEG functioning. *Neuropsychologia, 19,* 719–722.

18. Seward, J. P., & Seward, G. H. (1980). *Sex Differences: Mental and Temperamental.* Lexington, MA: Lexington Books.

19. Shucard, D. W., Shucard, J. L., & Thomas, D. G. (1987). Sex differences in the pattern of scalp-recorded electrophysiological activity in infancy: Possible implications for language development. In S. U. Philips, S. Steele, & C. Tanz (Eds.), *Language, Gender, and Sex in Comparative Perspective.* Cambridge, England: Cambridge University Press.

20. Springer, S. P., & Deutsch, G. (1981). *Left Brain, Right Brain.* New York: W. H. Freeman.

21. Susman, E. J., Inoff-Germain, G., Nottel-mann, E. D., Loriaux, D. L., Cutler, G. B., & Chrousos, G. P. (1987). Hormones, emotional dispositions, and aggressive attributes in young adolescents. *Child Development, 58,* 1114–1134.

References that indicate that males exhibit more behavior problems and get into more trouble in school than females are included next.

22. Center, D. B., & Wascom, A. M. (1987). Teacher perceptions of social behavior in behaviorally disordered and socially normal children and youth. *Behavior Disorders, 12*(3), 200–206.

23. Duke, D. L. (1978). Why don't girls misbehave more than boys in school? *Journal of Youth and Adolescence, 7*(2), 141–157.

24. Epstein, M. H., Cullinan, D., & Bursuck, W. D. (1985). Prevalence of behavior problems among learning disabled and nonhandicapped students. *Mental Retardation and Learning Disability Bulletin, 13,* 30–39.

25. Ludwig, G., & Cullinan, D. (1984). Behavior problems of gifted and nongifted elementary school girls and boys. *Gifted Child Quarterly, 28*(1), 37–39.

26. National Black Child Development Institute. (1990). *The Status of African American Children: Twentieth Anniversary Report.* Washington, DC.

The following references detail differences in teachers' tolerance for male and female behavior patterns.

27. Fagot B. I. (1985). Beyond the reinforcement principle: Another step toward understanding sex roles. *Developmental Psychology, 21,* 1097–1104.

28. Marshall, J. (1983). Developing antisexist initiatives in education. *International Journal of Political Education, 6,* 113–137.

29. Woolridge, P., & Richman, C. L. (1985). Teachers' choice of punishment as a function of a student's gender, age, race, and IQ level. *Journal of School Psychology, 23,* 19–29.

Teachers' use of different management techniques with the sexes is discussed in the following references.

30. Eccles, J. S., & Blumenfeld, P. (1985). Classroom experiences and student gender: Are there differences and do they matter? In L. C. Wilkinson & C. B. Marrett (Eds.), *Gender Influences in Classroom Interaction.* New York: Academic Press.

31. Fagot, B. I., & Hagan, R. (1985). Aggression in toddlers: Responses to the assertive acts of boys and girls. *Sex Roles, 12*(3), 341–351.

These references document that parents reinforce children for behaving in gender-stereotypical ways.

32. Block, J. H. (1984). *Sex Role Identity and Ego Development.* San Francisco: Jossey-Bass.
33. Fagot, B. I. (1978). The influence of sex of child on parental reactions to toddler children. *Child Development, 49,* 459–465.
34. Lewis, M., & Weintraub, M. (1979). Origins of early sex-role development. *Sex Roles, 5*(2), 135–153.
35. O'Brien, M., & Huston, A. C. (1985). Development of sex-typed play behavior in toddlers. *Developmental Psychology, 21*(5), 866–871.

The following references deal with the reinforcement of gender-appropriate behavior by toddlers and preschoolers.

36. Fagot, B. I. (1977). Consequences of moderate cross-gender behavior in preschool children. *Child Development, 48,* 902–907.
37. Fagot, B. I. (1985). Beyond the reinforcement principle: Another step toward understanding sex roles. *Developmental Psychology, 21,* 1097–1104.
38. Lamb, M. E., Easterbrook, A. M., & Holden, G. W. (1980). Reinforcement and punishment among preschoolers: Characteristics, effects, and correlates. *Child Development, 51,* 1230–1236.
39. Lamb, M. E., & Roopnarine, J. L. (1979). Peer influences on sex-role development in preschoolers. *Child Development, 50,* 1219–1222.

The following references discuss the role of cognitive awareness and modeling in children's sex-role acquisition.

40. Andersen, E. S. (1978). *Learning to Speak with Style: A Study of the Socio-Linguistic Skills of Children.* Unpublished doctoral dissertation. Stanford University.
41. Bem, S. L. (1983). Gender schema theory and its implication for child development: Raising gender aschematic children in a gender schematic society. *Signs, 8,* 598–616.
42. Bem, S. L. (1985). Androgyny and gender schema theory: A conceptual and empirical integration. In T. B. Sonderegger (Ed.), *Nebraska Symposium on Motivation: Psychology of Gender.* Lincoln: University of Nebraska.

43. Busey, K., & Bandura, A. (1984). Influence of gender constancy and social power on sex-linked modeling. *Journal of Personality and Social Psychology, 47*(6), 1292–1302.
44. Eagly, A. H. (1987). *Sex Differences in Social Behavior: A Social-Role Interpretation.* Hillsdale, NJ: Lawrence Erlbaum.
45. Fagot, B. I. (1985). Changes in thinking about early sex-role development. *Developmental Review, 5,* 83–98.
46. Hargreaves, D. J., & Colley, A. M. (1987). *The Psychology of Sex Roles.* New York: Hemisphere Publishing.
47. Weintraub, M., Clemens, L. P., Sockloff, A., Ethridge, T., Gracely, E., & Myers, B. (1984). The development of sex role stereotypes in the third year: Relationships to gender labeling, gender identity, sex-typed toy preference, and family characteristics. *Child Development, 55,* 1493–1503.

The role of parents' behavior, expectations, and beliefs in fostering gender differences in students' confidence about their academic abilities and in their choice of academic courses is discussed in the references listed next.

48. Baker, D. P., & Entwisle, D. R. (1987). The influence of mothers on the academic expectations of young children: A longitudinal study of how gender differences arise. *Social Forces, 65,* 670–694.
49. Bempechat, J. (1990). *The Role of Parent Involvement in Children's Academic Achievement: A Review of the Literature Trends and Issues.* No. 14. New York: ERIC Clearinghouse on Urban Education, Institute for Urban and Minority Education.
50. Eccles, J., Adler, T. F., & Kaczala, C. M. (1982). Socialization of achievement attitudes and beliefs: Parental influences. *Child Development, 53,* 310–321.
51. Eccles, J., & Jacobs, J. E. (1986). Social forces shape math attitudes and performance. *Signs, 11,* 367–389.
52. Eccles, J., Kaczala, C. M., & Meese, J. L. (1982). Socialization of achievement attitudes and beliefs: Classroom influences. *Child Development, 53,* 322–339.
53. Entwisle, D. R., & Baker, D. P. (1983). Gender and young children's expectations for performance in arithmetic. *Developmental Psychology, 19*(2), 200–209.
54. Entwisle, D. R., & Hayduk, L. A. (1982). *Early Schooling.* Baltimore: The Johns Hopkins University Press.

55. Jacobs, J., & Eccles, J. (1985). Gender differences in math ability: The impact of media reports on parents. *Educational Researcher, 14*(3), 20–25.

56. Parsons, J. E., Adler, T. F., & Kaczala, C. M. (1982). Socialization of achievement attitudes and beliefs: Parental influences. *Child Development, 53*, 310–321.

57. Parsons, J. E., Kaczala, C. M., & Meese, J. L. (1982). Socialization of achievement attitudes and beliefs: Classroom influences. *Child Development, 53*, 322–339.

58. Yee, D. K., & Eccles, J. S. (1988). Parent perceptions and attributions for children's math achievement. *Sex Roles, 19*(5/6), 317–333.

References that discuss the role of schools in the reproduction of inequities in society are listed next.

59. Connell, R. W. (1989). Curriculum politics, hegemony, and strategies of social change. In H. A. Giroux & R. I. Simon (Eds.), *Popular Culture, Schooling and Everyday Life.* Granby, MA: Bergin & Garvey.

60. Grant, C. A., & Sleeter, C. E. (1988). Race, class, and gender and abandoned dreams. *Teachers College Record, 90*(1), 19–40.

61. Kelly, G., & Nihlen, A. (1982). Schooling and the reproduction of patriarchy: Unequal workloads, unequal rewards. In M. Apple (Ed.), *Culture and Economic Reproduction in Education.* Boston: Routledge Kegan Paul.

62. Valli, L. (1986). *Becoming Clerical Workers.* Boston: Routledge Kegan Paul.

63. Weiler, K. (1988). *Women Teaching for Change: Gender, Class & Power.* Granby, MA: Bergin & Garvey.

64. Witt, S. H. (1979). Native women in the world of work. In T. Constantino (Ed.), *Women of Color Forum: A Collection of Readings.* ERIC ED 191–975.

65. Wolpe, A. (1981). The official ideology of education for girls. In M. McDonald, R. Dale, G. Esland, & R. Fergusson (Eds.), *Politics, Patriarchy and Practice.* New York: Falmer Press.

These references deal with student resistance to school.

66. Anyon, J. (1984). Intersections of gender and class: Accommodation and resistance by working class and affluent females to contradictory sex-role ideologies. *Journal of Education, 166*(1), 25–48.

67. Arnot, M. (1982). Male hegemony, social class and women's education. *Journal of Education, 164*(1), 64–89.

68. Connell, R. W., Dowsett, G. W., Kessler, S., & Aschenden, D. J. (1982). *Making the Difference.* Boston: Allen and Unwin.

69. Fuller, M. (1980). Black girls in a London comprehensive school. In R. Deem (Ed.), *Schooling for Women's Work.* Boston: Routledge and Kegan Paul.

70. Gaskell, J. (1985). Course enrollment in high school: The perspective of working class females. *Sociology of Education, 58*(1), 48–59.

71. Kessler, S., Ashenden, R., Connell, R., & Dowsett, G. (1985). Gender relations in secondary schooling. *Sociology of Education, 58*(1), 34–48.

72. Ogbu, J. U. (1987). Variability in minority school performance: A problem in search of an explanation. *Anthropology & Education Quarterly, 18*(4), 312–334.

73. Simon, R. (1983). But who will let you do it? Counter-hegemonic possibilities for work education. *Journal of Education, 165*(3), 235–256.

74. Thomas, C. (1980). *Girls and Counter-School Culture.* Melbourne Working Papers. Melbourne, Australia.

75. Willis, P. (1981). Cultural production is different from cultural reproduction is different from social reproduction is different from production. *Interchange, 12*(2/3), 48–68.

Administrative imbalance is the focus of the following references.

76. Fennema, E., & Ayer, M. J. (Eds.). (1984). *Women and Education: Equity or Equality?* Berkeley, CA: McCutchan.

77. Frazier, N., & Sadker, M. (1973). *Sexism in School and Society.* New York: Harper & Row.

78. Lockheed, M. E. (1984). Sex segregation and male preeminence in elementary classrooms. In E. Fennema & M. J. Ayer (Eds.), *Women and Education: Equity or Equality?* Berkeley, CA: McCutchan.

79. SUNY study finds school management still white male dominated. (1990). *Black Issues in Higher Education, 7*(5), 23.

The following references provide evidence that gender bias in curriculum materials has been reduced but not eliminated.

80. Cooper, P. (1989). Children's literature: The extent of sexism. In C. Lont & S. Friedly

(Eds.), *Beyond Boundaries: Sex and Gender Diversity in Education.* Fairfax, VA: George Mason University Press.

81. Cooper, P. (1987). Sex role stereotypes of stepparents in children's literature. In L. Stewart & S. Ting-Toomey (Eds.), *Communication, Gender and Sex Roles in Diverse Interaction Contexts.* Norwood, NJ: Ablex.

82. Dougherty, W., & Engel, R. (1987). An 80s look for sex equality in Caldecott winners and honors books. *Reading Teacher, 40,* 394–398.

83. Heinz, K. (1987). An examination of sex occupational role presentations of female characters in children's picture books. *Women's Studies in Communication, 11,* 67–78.

84. Hitchcock, M. E., & Tompkins, G. E. (1987). Basis readers: Are they still sexist? *Reading Teacher, 41*(3), 288–292.

85. Nilsen, A. P. (1987). Three decades of sexism in school science materials. *School Library Journal, 34*(1), 117–122.

86. Purcell, P., & Stewart, L. (1990). Dick and Jane 1989. *Sex Roles, 22*(3/4), 177–185.

87. Tetreault, M. K. T. (1985). Phases of thinking about women in history: A report card on the textbook. *Women's Studies Quarterly, 13*(3/4), 35–47.

88. Timm, J. (1988). *Cultural Bias in Children's Storybooks: Implications for Education.* Paper presented at the annual meeting of the American Educational Research Association, New Orleans.

89. Vaughn-Roberson, C., Thompkins, M., Hitchcock, M. E., & Oldham, M. (1989). Sexism in basal readers: An analysis of male main characters. *Journal of Research in Childhood Education, 4,* 62–68.

90. White, H. (1986). Damsels in distress: Dependency themes in fiction for children and adolescents. *Adolescence, 21,* 251–256.

91. Woodill, G. (1987). Critical issues in the use of microcomputers by young children. *International Journal of Early Childhood, 19*(1), 50–57.

The references listed next deal with gender differences in teacher attention.

92. Becker, J. (1981). Differential treatment of males and females in mathematics classes. *Journal of Research in Mathematics Education, 12,* 40–53.

93. Benz, C. R., Pfeiffer, I., & Newman, I. (1981). Sex role expectations of classroom teachers, grades 1–12. *American Educational Research Journal, 18*(3), 289–302.

94. Boudreau, F. A. (1986). Education. In F. A. Boudreau, R. S. Sennott, & M. Wilson (Eds.), *Sex Roles and Social Patterns.* New York: Praeger.

95. Brophy, J. E. (1985). Interaction of male and female students with male and female teachers. In L. C. Wilkinson & C. B. Marrett (Eds.), *Gender Influences in Classroom Interaction.* New York: Academic Press.

96. Brophy, J. E. (1986). Teaching and learning mathematics: Where research should be going. *Journal for Research in Mathematics, 17,* 323–346.

97. Eccles, J. S., & Blumenfeld, P. (1985). Classroom experiences and student gender: Are there differences and do they matter? In L. C. Wilkinson & C. B. Marrett (Eds.), *Gender Influences in Classroom Interaction.* New York: Academic Press.

98. Fennema, E., & Peterson, P. L. (1985). Autonomous learning behavior: A possible explanation of gender-related differences in mathematics. In L. C. Wilkinson & C. B. Marret (Eds.), *Gender Influences in Classroom Interaction.* New York: Academic Press.

99. Fennema, E., & Peterson, P. L. (1986). Teacher student interactions and sex-related differences in learning mathematics. *Teaching and Teacher Education, 2*(1), 19–42.

100. Fennema, E., Reyes, L., Perl, T., Konsin, M., & Drakenberg, M. (1980). *Cognitive and Affective Influences on the Development of Sex-Related Difference in Mathematics.* Symposium presented at the annual meeting of the American Educational Research Association, Boston.

101. Gore, D. A., & Roumagoux, D. V. (1983). Wait-time as a variable in sex-related differences during fourth-grade mathematics instruction. *Journal of Educational Research, 76*(5), 273–275.

102. Leinhardt, G., Seewald, A. L., & Engel, M. (1979). Learning what's taught: Sex differences in instruction. *Journal of Educational Psychology, 71*(3), 432–439.

103. Lockheed, M. (1982). *Sex Equity in Classroom Interaction Research: An Analysis of Behavior Chains.* Paper presented at the annual meeting of the American Educational Research Association, New York City.

104. Minuchin, P. P., & Shapiro, E. K. (1983). The school as a context for social development. In P. Mussen, & E. M. Hetherington (Eds.),

Handbook of Child Psychology, Vol. 4, (4th ed.). New York: Wiley.

105. Morrison, T. L. (1979). Classroom structure, work involvement and social climate in elementary school classrooms. *Journal of Educational Psychology, 71,* 471–477.

106. Morse, L. W., & Handley, H. M. (1985). Listening to adolescents: Gender differences in science classroom interaction. In L. C. Wilkinson & C. B. Marrett (Eds.), *Gender Influences in Classroom Interaction.* New York: Academic Press.

107. Pflaum, S., Pascarella, E., Boswick, M., & Auer, C. (1980). The influence of pupil behaviors and pupil status factors on teacher behaviors during oral reading lessons. *Journal of Educational Research, 74,* 99–105.

108. Putnam, S., & Self, P. A. (1988). *Social Play in Toddlers: Teacher Intrusions.* ERIC ED 319–529.

109. Stake, J., & Katz, J. (1982). Teacher-pupil relationships in the elementary school classroom: Teacher gender and student gender difference. *American Educational Research Journal, 19,* 465–471.

The following references deal with gender differences in teacher feedback.

110. Dweck, C. S., Davidson, W., Nelson, S., & Enna, B. (1978). Sex differences in learned helplessness: The contingencies of evaluation feedback in the classroom, an experimental analysis. *Developmental Psychology, 14*(3), 208–276.

111. Frey, K. S. (1979). *Differential Teaching Methods Used with Girls and Boys of Moderate and High Achievement Levels.* Paper presented at the annual meeting of the American Educational Research Association, Minneapolis.

112. Hodes, C. L. (1985). Relative effectiveness of corrective and noncorrective feedback in computer assisted instruction on learning and achievement. *Journal of Educational Technology Systems, 13*(4), 249–254.

113. Meece, J. L. (1987). The influence of school experiences on the development of gender schemata. *New Directions for Child Development, 38,* 57–73.

114. Parsons, J. E., Kaczala, C. M., & Meese, J. L. (1982). Socialization of achievement attitudes and beliefs: Classroom influences. *Child Development, 53,* 322–339.

115. Simpson, A. W., & Erickson, M. T. (1983). Teachers' verbal and nonverbal communication patterns as a function of teacher race, student gender, and student race. *American Educational Research Journal, 20,* 183–198.

Gender differences in academic expectations are discussed in the following references.

116. Bem, S. (1977). On the utility of alternative procedures for assessing psychological androgyny. *Journal of Consulting and Clinical Psychology, 45,* 196–205.

117. Bernard, M. (1979). Does sex role behavior influence the way teachers evaluate students? *Journal of Educational Psychology, 71,* 553–562.

118. Casserly, P. L. (1975). *An Assessment of Factors Affecting Female Participation in Advanced Placement Programs in Mathematics, Chemistry, and Physics.* Washington, DC: National Science Foundation.

119. Dusek, J. B., & Joseph, G. (1983). The bases of teacher expectancies: A meta-analysis. *Journal of Educational Psychology, 75,* 327–346.

120. Hallinan, M. T., & Sorensen, A. B. (1987). Ability grouping and sex differences in mathematics achievement. *Sociology of Education, 60*(2), 63–72.

121. Luchins, E. (1976). *Women Mathematicians: A Contemporary Appraisal.* Paper presented at the annual meeting of the American Association for the Advancement of Science, Boston.

122. Phillips, R. (1980). Teachers' reported expectations of children's sex roles and evaluation of sexist teaching. *Dissertation Abstracts International, 41,* 995–996-A.

Ethnic differences in the ways teachers perceive and relate to students is the focus of the following references.

123. Grant, L. (1984). Black females' "place" in desegregated classrooms. *Sociology of Education. 57,* 98–110.

124. Grant, L. (1985). *Uneasy Alliances: Black Males, Teachers, and Peers in Desegregated Classrooms.* Paper presented at the annual meeting of the American Educational Research Association, Chicago.

125. Pollard, D. (1979). Patterns of coping in Black school children. In A. W. Boykin, A. Franklin, & F. Yates (Eds.), *Research Directions of Black Psychologists.* New York: Russel Sage.

126. Washington, V. (1982). Racial differences in teacher perception of first and fourth grade pupils on selected characteristics. *Journal of Negro Education, 51,* 60–72.

The following references deal with the adverse results of gender differences in teacher attention, feedback, and expectations.

127. Brush, L. R. (1980). *Encouraging Girls in Mathematics: The Problems and the Solutions.* Boston: Abt Associates.

128. Eccles, J., Adler, T. F., Futterman, R., Goff, S. B., Kaczala, C. M., Meece, J., & Midgley, C. (1983). Expectations, values, and academic behavior. In J. T. Spence (Ed.), *Perspectives on Achievement and Achievement Motivation.* San Francisco: W. H. Freeman.

129. Fox, L., Brody, L. A., & Tobin, D. (Eds.). (1980). *Women and the Mathematical Mystique.* Baltimore: The Johns Hopkins University Press.

130. Fennema, E., & Sherman, J. (1977). Sex-related differences in mathematics achievement, spatial visualization, and affective factors. *American Educational Research Journal, 14,* 51–71.

The following references describe how teachers and other school personnel foster sex differences in the courses and activities students choose.

131. Farris, C. (1982). *Sex Fair Knowledge, Attitudes, and Behaviors of Vocational Educators: A Research Report.* Utica, NY: SUNY College of Technology.

132. Hopkins-Best, M. (1987). The effects of students' sex and disability on counselors' agreement with postsecondary career goals. *School Counselor, 35*(1), 28–33.

133. Parmley, J. D., Welton, R. F., & Bender, M. (1980). *Opinions of Agricultural Teachers, School Administrators, Students and Parents Concerning Females as Agriculture Students, Teachers and Workers in Agriculture.* ERIC ED 209–488.

134. Roberts, E. J. (Ed.). (1980). *Childhood Sexual Learning: The Unwritten Curriculum.* Cambridge, MA: Ballinger.

135. Schaffer, K. F. (1981). *Sex Roles and Human Behavior.* Cambridge, MA: Winthrop.

136. Stockard, J., Schmuck, P. A., Kemper, K., Williams, P., Edson, S. K., & Smith, M. A. (1980). *Sex Equity in Education.* New York: Academic Press.

137. Tavris, C., & Wade, C. (1984). *The Longest War: Sex Differences in Perspective,* (2nd ed.). New York: Harcourt Brace Jovanovich.

Gender segregation and separation is the focus of the following articles.

138. Guttenberg, M., & Gray, H. (1977). Teachers as mediators of sex-role standards. In A. Sargent (Ed.), *Beyond Sex Roles.* St. Paul, MN: West.

139. Lockheed, M. E., & Harris A. M. (1984). Cross-sex collaborative learning in elementary classrooms. *American Educational Research Journal, 21*(2), 275–294.

The next references deal with the fact that teachers encourage different behaviors in male and female students.

140. Caplan, P. J. (1977). Sex, age, behavior, and school subject as determinants of report of learning problems. *Journal of Learning Disabilities, 10,* 60–62.

141. Fagot, B. I. (1977). Consequences of moderate cross-gender behavior in preschool children. *Child Development, 48,* 902–907.

142. Huffine, S., Silvern, S. B., & Brooks, D. M. (1979). Teacher responses to contextually specific sex type behaviors in kindergarten children. *Educational Research Quarterly, 4*(2), 29–35.

143. Lamb, M. E., Easterbrook, A. M., & Holden, G. W. (1980). Reinforcement and punishment among preschoolers: Characteristics, effects, and correlates. *Child Development, 51,* 1230–1236.

144. Schlosser, L., & Algozzine, B. (1980). Sex behavior and teacher expectancies. *Journal of Experimental Education, 48,* 231–236.

The following references describe how teachers use different classroom management techniques with various ethnic and socioeconomic groups.

145. Glackman, T., Martin, R., Hyman, I., McDowell, E., Berv, V., & Spino, P. (1980). *Corporal Punishment in the Schools as It Relates to Race, Sex, Grade Level and Suspensions.* Philadelphia: Temple University, National Center for the Study of Corporal Punishment in the Schools.

146. Richardson, R. C., & Evans, E. T. (1991). *Empowering Teachers to Eliminate Corporal Punishment in the Schools.* Paper presented at the annual conference of the National Black Child Developmental Institute. Washington, DC.

147. Stevens, L. B. (1983). *Suspension and Corporal Punishment of Students in the Cleveland Public Schools, 1981–1982.* Cleveland, OH: Office of School Monitoring and Community Relations.

148. Woolridge, P., & Richman, C. (1985). Teachers' choice of punishment as a function of a student's gender, age, race and I. Q. level. *Journal of School Psychology, 23,* 19–29.

Chapter 8

Gender Appropriate Education

Chapters 1 and 3 explored a number of gender inequities such as gender disparities in educational outcomes, gender bias in the treatment of students, and gender
differences in the roles for which schools prepare students. This chapter examines
the advantages and disadvantages of four alternative ways of dealing with these
inequities. Chapters 9 through 11 describe techniques educators can use to implement these four approaches when they select assessment, instructional, and classroom management techniques. The chapter does not take a position about which
of these four alternatives is the most appropriate in relation to any specific gender
difference. Rather, it presents the arguments for and against each approach and
includes exercises that enhance the readers' insight into their own views on gender issues. The chapter also describes the problems gay and lesbian students
experience in and out of school and examines what educators can do to assist students with these problems.

Gender Equity in Education: A Controversial Issue

What is gender equity and how can gender equity be achieved in school? Educators' opinions vary. Some educators equate equity with sameness. Their point of
view is that gender equity is achieved when males and females participate in academic and nonacademic courses and extracurricular activities to the same degree,
their achievement is the same, they are treated the same by their teachers, and
they are prepared for the same societal roles.

Other educators define equity in terms of fairness. Assuming that there are
biologically or culturally based educationally relevant differences between male
and female students, they believe equity requires each gender to be treated in
accordance with its biological make-up and cultural preference. To them, educational equity is achieved when males and females are treated in accordance with
their different needs, when the genders have an opportunity to participate in
whichever courses and activities they prefer and to achieve up to their different
potentials, and when they are prepared for different societal roles.

How teachers define gender equity in school is extremely important because it influences how they perceive their students' behavior, the goals they set for them, and how they relate to them.

Controversial and Noncontroversial Practices

Educators may disagree about the broad issues involved in defining gender equity, but most would probably agree that certain current educational practices are unfair and should be corrected. For example, even though educators disagree about the cause or causes of gender differences and have different comfort levels with the status quo, most would probably agree that teachers should:

- Select textbooks, readers, and biographies that include the contributions of both males and females
- Pay equal attention to all students who volunteer answers or ask questions regardless of their gender
- Call on male and female students equally often
- Provide the same kind and amount of help to all students
- Praise female and male students equally for high achievement, creativity, and effort
- Attribute the cause of students' academic problems accurately
- Be equally attentive to the misbehavior of males and females
- Avoid excessively harsh punishments with all students
- Discourage dependent, helpless, and excessively conforming behavior in all students

However, they probably disagree about whether they should:

- Select textbooks and other reading materials that portray males and females fulfilling nontraditional roles
- Permit males and females to choose to work and play in single-sex groups
- Separate boys and girls for activities such as physical education and sex education
- Assign students to single-sex groups during class to protect females from being dominated by males
- Select male teachers for male students and female teachers for female students
- Encourage students to conform to the same standards of behavior regardless of their ethnic and socioeconomic backgrounds
- Use similar classroom management procedures with males and females
- Utilize the same instructional approaches and assessment procedures with all students regardless of their ethnic and socioeconomic backgrounds.

Positions on Gender Differences

Excluding practices that most educators would probably agree are unfair, the following are the four most common positions that have appeared in the literature regarding controversial gender issues like the ones just listed.

1. *Educators should not treat males and females the same* (8, 9). Educators should prepare the genders to fulfill different societal roles because there are natural, physiological differences between the sexes, and they should accommodate their instructional practices to existing gender differences. This quotation exemplifies the position that teachers should not treat males and females the same:

> *Boys who rise to the top in school often resemble girls in many important ways. . . . Scholastic honor and masculinity, in other words, too often seem incompatible. . . . The feminized school simply bores many boys, but it pulls some in one of two opposite directions. If the boy absorbs school values, he may become feminized himself. If he resists, he is pushed toward school failure and rebellion. (8, pp. 13, 33)*

Do you agree that being a "real boy" is incompatible with being a good student? Do you agree that being a "real boy" in the sense that the term is usually used is a desirable personality characteristic? What is your opinion about the author's concern that schools feminize males?

2. *Educators should cease fostering gender-role differences that are unnatural, outdated, and harmful* (1–4, 6). They should prepare students for the androgynous roles that are increasingly available to them in society. They should also encourage and prepare students to do what is necessary to transform our sexist society into a less sexist one. The following quote is an example of this position.

> *In American society, men are supposed to be masculine, women are supposed to be feminine, and neither sex is supposed to be much like the other. If men are independent, tough, and assertive, women should be dependent, sweet, and retiring. A womanly woman may be tender and nurturant, but no manly man may be so. . . . I have come to believe that we need a new standard of psychological health for the sexes, one that removes the burden of stereotype and allows people to feel free to express the best traits of men and women. . . .*
>
> *Traditional sex typing necessarily restricts behavior. Because people learn, during their formative years, to suppress any behavior that might be considered undesirable or inappropriate for their sex, men are afraid to do "women's work" and women are afraid to enter a "man's world." Men are reluctant to be gentle and women to be assertive. In contrast, androgynous people are not limited by labels. They are able to do whatever they want, both in their behavior and their feelings. (2, p. 32)*

Do you agree that students should be encouraged to become androgynous? If you do, you probably favor discouraging students from accepting and acting out any gender-stereotypic roles, whatever they may be.

> *At the core of any radical pedagogy must be the aim of empowering people to recognize and work for a change in the social, political, and economic structure that constitutes the ultimate source of class-based power and domination. (4, p. 427)*

Do you agree that teachers should prepare students to change society in the ways suggested by the author of this statement?

3. *Educators should decide for themselves whether they want to prepare students to fulfill different gender roles or encourage students to fulfill similar roles* (5). The desirability or lack of desirability of gender roles is something for the individual professional or the group to decide.

> *If we value the higher levels of aggressiveness in males, then schools should encourage aggression, competition, and assertion more in females. This might mean more emphasis on competitive athletics for girls, perhaps beginning in early elementary school, or perhaps even in the preschool years. In the academic classroom, it might mean encouraging reticent girls to speak up more forcefully in debates or to become more competitive about their success in mathematics courses. If, on the other hand, we value the low level of aggressiveness of females, we might seek to reduce the level of aggressiveness in boys, while simultaneously encouraging peaceful cooperation for them. . . . We might want to de-emphasize competitive sports in favor of cooperative sports or noncompetitive ones such as jogging. In the classroom, we would avoid competitively structured learning and work toward cooperatively structured learning. . . . Which of these alternatives is chosen, of course, is a matter of values. (5, pp. 64–65)*

Do you agree that gender roles are inherently neither desirable nor undesirable, but depend on the values of different individuals and societies? If so, does that mean that societies have the right to establish different expectations for their male and female members? Does it also follow that different ethnic and socioeconomic groups have the right to expect the schools to respect their freedom to bring up their children to fulfill the gender roles they believe most appropriate? Or should the greater society determine the gender roles for all the subgroups living within its boundaries?

4. *Educators should empower students to decide for themselves whether to conform to any particular gender role or to be androgynous* (7).

> *To force everyone into the new mold may violate the individual as much as to force them into the older stereotypes. . . . Freedom to choose according to individual need would seem to be the preferred way of dealing with the complex problem of man/woman roles. (7, p. 202)*

Should teachers not involve themselves in shaping their students attitudes about gender roles?

Legal Requirements

Title IX of the Education Amendments Act was designed to correct the biased treatment males and females received in school. Some of the provisions of Title IX that protect students from gender bias also restrict the rights of educators to decide for themselves about how to respond to certain gender issues.

Title IX requires schools to provide equal educational opportunities to all students regardless of gender. As it did in the 1970s and 1980s, Title IX serves as the main legal basis for efforts to eliminate gender-discriminatory educational practices. Its requirements include:

- Students may not be denied admission to schools or subjected to discriminatory admissions practices on the basis of their gender.
- Once admitted, students may not be excluded from participation in, be denied the benefits of, or be subjected to discrimination while participating in any academic, extracurricular, research, occupational training, or other educational program or activity.
- All courses and activities, except human sexuality courses, must be open to all students regardless of their gender. If offered, human sexuality courses must be available to all students, but they can be taught separately to males and females.
- Standards for student participation in physical education activities and ability groupings within these activities must be objective and applied equally to all students regardless of gender. Separate athletic teams may be provided for males and females for contact sports or for other sports when the separation is justified by differences in skills. However, if a school has a contact sport for males only, a noncontact alternative team sport for females must be provided.
- Dress codes must be applied equally to males and females.
- Graduation requirements must be the same for both genders.
- Textbooks and other instructional materials are exempted from Title IX regulations due to potential conflicts with freedom of speech rights guaranteed by the First Amendment and other legislation.

SELF-QUIZ: Critical Incidents

This self-quiz is designed to provide you with some insight into the approaches you may use to resolve gender issues. First, describe how you think the teacher involved should handle each of the following critical incidents, then put yourself in the teacher's place. Disregard the description of the teacher's point of view. Instead, imagine what your viewpoint would

Continued

SELF-QUIZ: Critical Incidents   *Continued*

be and how you would deal with the problem. If you prefer a number of different approaches to the incidents, try to determine the factors that led you to select the particular approaches you would use in each critical incident.

1. The father of a Hispanic American pre-school student comes to school irate because his son told him that the teacher encouraged him to play in the housekeeping/doll house area. He tells the teacher he does not want his son to play "girls' games" or with "girl things." The teacher believes that doll and housekeeping play are important for all children because they foster caring and nurturing qualities in children and androgynous gender roles.

2. A group of second-grade boys does not want some of the girls to join in their game in the schoolyard. The teacher believes students should learn to get along with both genders. The teacher also wants to encourage female students to participate in traditionally male activities and vice versa.

3. A fourth-grade student suggests that the teacher should have a spelling bee with the boys against the girls, as some other fifth-grade teachers do in their classes. The teacher, who feels that the students are already too competitive, wants them to learn to be more cooperative. In addition, the teacher believes in bringing the genders together rather than identifying them as competing groups.

4. One of an educator's best students, an eighth-grade Hispanic American female, informs the teacher that she is not going to continue in the program in high school because she is not planning to go to college. When the teacher asks why, she replies that in her family and culture college is for boys. She says her plans are to finish high school, find a job for a while, get married, have four or five children, and stay home. The teacher believes that females should be encouraged to go on to college so they can have the career and other opportunities a college degree provides.

SELF-QUIZ: Gender Differences

The following incident was reported by a school principal.

Allen attended a parochial school where the playgrounds were segregated by gender. In one playground the girls skipped and jumped rope, in the other, the boys played football. Allen often stood on the sidelines and chatted with several other non-athletic boys. Allen's teacher was concerned and arranged privately with several of the male athletes to include Allen and his friends in the daily

football game. The teacher warned that if they failed to do so, all of the boys in the class would be punished. (32, p. 208)

How do you feel about the gender separation that existed on the playgrounds? What is your opinion about the way the teacher responded to Allen and his friends' behavior? What might have been the teacher's reason for responding in that manner? How would you have responded?

Sexual Orientation

Although adolescents have many problems centered around their emerging sexual drives and sexual orientation, people disagree about whether these topics are fit for discussion in school. Many educators feel they are. However, in general, sexuality and especially sexual orientation is a forbidden subject in many schools, and many individuals and community groups demand that it remain so. For example, only 1 out of 28 school districts boards in the New York City public school system voted to include the approved elementary school curriculum that deals with homosexual orientation in their schools (10).

Problems

Many heterosexual adolescents are concerned about their sexual orientation because of one or two homosexual experiences or fantasies. Although research indicates that there are no innate reasons why lesbian, gay, and bisexual students should have more problems than other students, because of society's homophobic attitudes many of them have a very difficult adolescence (11, 12, 14, 17, 18, 20, 23, 24, 27–29, 31). They experience a great deal of discrimination and prejudice both in and out of school, and they also have a great deal of difficulty adjusting to their sexual orientation.

Because gay and lesbian students are brought up in a homophobic society and have little access to information that portrays lesbians and gays in a positive way, many of them suffer from homophobia and believe they are sick, evil, inferior, and disgusting. These ideas can lead to emotional problems such as depression, shame, and guilt, low self-esteem, and self-hatred or at least ambivalence toward their sexual orientation. In turn, their emotional problems can cause them to drop out of school, abuse substances, and commit suicide. Some homosexual students attempt, usually unsuccessfully, to change their sexual orientation. Most students hide their homosexuality, thereby living in fear that they will be discovered. Kissen describes their plight in the following manner.

> *If, like most gay adolescents, they try to hide their identity, they live in constant fear that someone will discover they are gay. Even if they are successful at concealment, they must live every day as a lie, pretending to be someone they are not, and surrounded by homophobic jokes. . . . Anyone who spends time in a high school is surely aware that homophobia—fear and hatred of gay people—is the last "acceptable" form of bigotry among adolescents. Young people who would not dream of uttering (or would not dare to utter) a racial or religious epithet still unthinkingly toss around "queer" and "faggot," probably the most often heard insults in any high school. (20, p. 2)*

Sometimes the desire to be true to themselves, to feel good about themselves, and to stop hiding significant aspects of themselves from others in order to build a relationship based on honesty and trust leads gay, lesbian, and bisexual students to declare their sexual orientation to others (to come out). When they do, family conflicts and parental rejection can lead them to run away from home and to engage in prostitution. Loss of the friendship of and abuse by their heterosexual peers often follow. Ross-Reynolds offers this description of the problems of a gay and a lesbian student:

> *Andy is a middle-class, White sixteen-year-old who ran away from his family home in Oregon after suffering years of abuse from his father after the man read his son's love letters from another boy. . . . Andy worked in a fast food restaurant in the evenings and attended high school during the day, resolving to complete high school and get his diploma, despite the obstacles caused by the relocation. Instead of a supportive environment at his new school, Andy found his peers hostile and harassing. Openly gay to his classmates and teachers, Andy was mocked during class time by other students, and received no support from teachers. After he was physically assaulted at the bus stop after school Andy felt pushed to the point of either quitting school or demanding action.*
>
> *Nina is a Black fifteen-year-old from Harlem. She had difficulty coping with the rejection she faced in her inner-city high school because she was up front about being a lesbian. . . . Name-calling, harassing notes, and verbal threats of violence, including rape, began to turn an upbeat, cheerful girl into a jumble of dysfunction and misery. As Nina faced the unpleasant task of steeling herself for two more years of such assaults, she found herself moving toward leaving school (29, pp. 444–445).*

Children of gay and lesbian parents can also experience many problems both in and out of school. Students who are brought up by openly gay or lesbian parents are exposed to the same homophobic attitudes as gay and lesbian students. Even though they may be straight, their parents' sexual orientation can expose them to prejudiced treatment in school. Students whose parents come out to them and others after many years of living or pretending to live straight lives have difficult adjustments to make. Like gay and lesbian students, children of gay and lesbian parents need all the help and support they can get in school.

Causes

As was just noted, students who are worried about their sexual orientation and gay, bisexual, and lesbian students need help and understanding, as do all students with serious problems. However, many educators believe that school is not the place to deal with or even discuss differences in sexual orientation. Dunham describes the situation in the schools as follows:

> *While mental health professionals have worked to create positive and meaningful programs for the gay and lesbian population, educational systems have been considerably less eager to recognize and respond to the needs of this minority group.*

Public schools have continued to treat homosexuality as a forbidden subject. (15, p. 3)

Various causes of the current invisibility of gay and lesbian students in the schools have been identified. Some educators think it reflects society's justifiable desire to keep sexual orientation out of the school curriculum. Others who are more critical of the schools attribute the "problem" to homophobic attitudes among educators, their lack of the courage needed to advocate for the rights of gay and lesbian students, and the failure of school personnel to correct many educators' misinformation about the causes and "cures "of homosexuality.

A few school districts have developed projects such as Project 10 in Los Angeles and the Harvey Milk School in New York City that offer special services to homosexual and bisexual students (16, 29). Project 10 provides help to students who remain in their local schools. The Harvey Milk School offers an alternative school setting for those who wish to escape the difficulties inherent in being openly homosexual in a regular high school setting. Both types of programs have their share of critics who believe that homosexual students should be helped to convert to heterosexuality, but the Harvey Milk School has been criticized by supporters of gay and lesbian rights for capitulating to discrimination and homophobia—"ghettoizing" nonheterosexual students, removing them from the mainstream, and providing them with inferior educational opportunities. However, because these programs are rare, for the most part, lesbian, gay, and bisexual students have to rely on the assistance and understanding of individual teachers and counselors.

Solutions

Concerned educators offer the following suggestions for helping students who are concerned about their sexual orientation (13, 14, 21, 26, 29).

- Resist community pressure to avoid relating to the needs of students who are concerned about their sexual orientation.
- Refer students to community agencies and resources where they can obtain assistance.
- Protect students from harassment, criticize such incidents when they occur, and express disapproval of jokes about gays.
- Modify homophobic attitudes. Because values are caught, not taught, teach students to accept each other regardless of sexual orientation by modeling acceptance. Include issues and topics that affect gay and lesbian students in the curriculum (e.g., gay rights and contributions in social studies classes, gay lifestyles in health and psychology courses, and gay and lesbian authors in English courses). Oppose censorship of texts and library material that demonstrate respect for lesbian and gay rights and lifestyles. Dispel myths about people with nonheterosexual orientations. Have students experience the

effects of discrimination and homophobic attitudes on students by role playing. Advocate for students rights. Include homosexual role models.

A healthy socialization process involves positive role models. Ideally, the socialization experiences for gay and lesbian adolescents will include learning from competent gay and lesbian adults. Observing how successful adults develop productive and ethical lifestyles, resolve problems of identity disclosure, obtain support, manage a career, and build relationships can be extremely valuable for teenagers. (17, p. 121)

It will not be easy for educators to carry out these suggestions. As Rofes points out,

Because many educators believe that homosexuality is sick, sinful, or criminal, it is tremendously difficult for them to truly adopt an "objective" stance when addressing gay and lesbian issues in the classroom. . . . By allowing positive treatment of homosexuality in the classroom, teachers are vulnerable to witchhunts by parents and school committees attempting to root out homosexual teachers. In certain parts of the nation, laws have been proposed and successfully passed that forbid positive discussion of homosexuality in public school classrooms. (30, p. 451)

In addition, because "Gay and lesbian adolescents continue to be socialized to conceal their identities—educated to be invisible within the school community and the community at large," (15, p. 5) they are often reluctant to come out—to disclose their sexual orientation to others.

Summary

Some ways that some teachers treat the genders differently are clearly discriminatory or illegal, and some of the current differences in the schools outcomes for males and females are clearly undesirable. Except for these differences, educators disagree about their role vis-à-vis the current gender differences observed among many students. Educators' positions on gender issues include the following: teachers should stop fostering gender differences; they should treat each gender in accordance with their unique, natural, and desirable needs; each educator should decide how she or he wants to deal with gender differences; teachers should empower students to make such decisions for themselves.

Although adolescents have many problems concerning their sexual orientation, sexual orientation is a forbidden subject in many schools. Some educators believe that this is as it should be. Many others fault the schools for failing to help students with their problems. They suggest that educators should modify their own homophobic attitudes and those of their students, protect students from harassment, advocate for homosexual students' rights, include homosexual role

Myths About Gay and Lesbian Students

1. *Effeminate boys and masculine females and those who like to cross-dress or play with toys that are thought of as in the domain of opposite gender grow up to become gay and lesbian.* Research indicates that although some gay and lesbian students are more likely to exhibit cross-gender behaviors when they are children and adolescents, many do not, and many children who exhibit these behaviors do not grow up to be gay or lesbian.

2. *One homosexual experience means that a person is and will be homosexual.* In reality, neither homosexual nor heterosexual experimentation is unusual. Human sexuality exists along a continuum from completely heterosexual to completely homosexual, with many people somewhere in between the extremes but close to the heterosexual end.

3. *Discussing gay and lesbian issues encourages students to become homosexuals.* There is no evidence to support this notion.

4. *Lesbian and gay teachers provide role models that encourage students to become lesbians and gays.* Homosexuality is not caught by observing lesbian and gay models.

5. *Gay and lesbian adults sexually abuse children and recruit them to their life-styles.* Children and adolescents are much more likely to be abused by heterosexual adults.

6. *Homosexuality is a sickness or a disorder.* The American Psychological Association and the American Psychiatric Association both state that it is not a disorder.

7. *Homosexual behavior is rare in most animal species.* Research indicates that the opposite is true.

8. *Because gays are incapable of establishing long-term relationships they lead lonely isolated lives.* Many gay and lesbian couples enjoy long-term relationships.

9. *Homosexuality is a choice that one makes.* Research indicates that in our society most homosexuals at first reject their homosexuality and resist thinking of themselves as homosexuals (19, 25, 30).

models and issues and topics that affect gay and lesbian students in the curriculum, oppose censorship of texts and library material that demonstrate respect for lesbian and gay rights and life-styles, and dispel myths about people with non-heterosexual orientations. In today's environment, this will not be easy for educators to accomplish.

SELF-QUIZ: Gay and Lesbian Sexual Orientations

1. What is your opinion about the following statement?

   In a democratic country no citizen should be forced to live under the fear of homophobia. Fear is unhealthy for the individual and our democracy. . . . We need not endorse particular private sexual acts to protect the civil rights of all citizens. (22, p. 285)

2. Should sexual orientation issues be included in the curriculum? Should educators discuss their students sexual orientation problems with students?

3. What should educators do when community organizations and parents prefer or demand policies that conflict with their views of whether and how to deal with sexual orientation issues and problems?

Activities

1. Ask some of your fellow students to respond to the critical incidents presented earlier. Do you notice any gender or ethnic differences in their responses?

2. How knowledgeable are your fellow students about Title IX? Make up and administer a short quiz to them. Do you notice any gender differences in the extent of their knowledge?

3. Ask some gay or lesbian students whether they have experienced any of the problems described in this chapter. Ask them if any of their teachers knew about their sexual orientation, how the teachers reacted to the information, and how they would have prefered them to have reacted.

4. Administer a questionnaire based on the myths about homosexuality to some of your fellow students. Do they believe the prevalent myths or do they know the facts? Do you notice any gender differences in their beliefs?

References

The following references discuss various positions on gender differences in school.

1. Becker, J. B. (1986). Influence again: An examination of reviews and studies of gender differences in social influence. In J. S. Hyde, & M. C. Linn (Eds.), *The Psychology of Gender.* Baltimore: The Johns Hopkins University Press.
2. Bem, S. L. (1983). Traditional sex roles are too restrictive. In G. Leone & M. T. O'Neill (Eds.), *Male-Female Roles: Opposing Viewpoints.* St. Paul, MN: Greenhaven Press.
3. Block, J. H. (1984). *Sex Role Identity and Ego Development.* San Francisco: Jossey-Bass.
4. Giroux, H. A. (1981). Hegemony, resistance, and the paradox of educational reform. In H. A. Giroux, A. N. Penna, & W. F. Pinar. *Curriculum & Instruction: Alternatives in Education.* Berkeley, CA: McCutchan.
5. Hyde, J. S. (1984). Gender differences in aggression. In Hyde, J. S. & Linn, M. C. (Eds.), *The Psychology of Gender: Advances Through Meta-Analysis.* Baltimore: The Johns Hopkins University Press.
6. Jacklin, C. N. (1989). Female and male: Issues of gender. *American Psychologist, 44*(2), 127–133.
7. Schlafly, P. Personal communication, May 1989.
8. Seward, J. P., & Seward, G. H. (1980). *Sex Differences: Mental and Temperamental.* Lexington, MA: Lexington Books.

9. Wardle, F. (1991). Are we shortchanging boys? *Child Care Information Exchange, 79,* 48–51.

Opposition to teaching about sexual orientations is documented in the next reference.

10. Columbia Broadcasting System. (1993, April 4). *Sixty Minutes, The Rainbow Curriculum.* Author.

These references describe the plight of gay, lesbian, and bisexual students and their possible solutions.

11. Benvenuti, A. (1986). *Assessing and Addressing the Special Challenge of Gay and Lesbian Students for High School Counseling Programs.* ERIC ED 279–958.
12. Cates, J. A. (1987). Adolescent sexuality: Gay and lesbian issues. *Child Welfare, 66,* 353–364.
13. Chang, C. L. (1980). Adolescent homosexual behavior and the health educator. *Journal of School Health, 50*(9), 517–521.
14. Coleman, E., & Remafedi, G. (1989). Gay, lesbian, and bisexual adolescents: A critical challenge to counselors. *Journal of Counseling and Development, 68,* 36–40.
15. Dunham, K. L. (1989). *Educated to Be Invisible: The Gay and Lesbian Adolescent.* ERIC ED 336–676.
16. Friends of Project Inc. (1991). *Project 10 Handbook: Addressing Lesbian and Gay Issues in Our Schools. A Resource Directory for Teachers, Guidance Counselors, Parents and School-Based*

Adolescent Care Providers, (3rd ed.) ERIC ED 337–567.

17. Gonsiorek, J. C. (1988). Mental health issues of gay and lesbian adolescents. *Journal of Adolescent Health Care, 9,* 114–122.

18. Hetrick, E. S., & Martin, A. D. (1987). Developmental issues and their resolution for gay and lesbian adolescents. *Journal of Homosexuality, 14*(1/2), 25–42.

19. Hubbard, B. M. (1989). *Entering Adulthood: Living in Relationships.* Santa Cruz, CA: ETR Associates.

20. Kissen, R. M. (1991). *Listening to Gay and Lesbian Teenagers.* ERIC ED 344–220.

21. Krysiak, G. J. (1987). A very silent and gay minority. *School Counselor, 34*(4), 304–307.

22. Lenton, S. M. (1980). A student development response to the gay issue. In F. B. Newton & K. L. Ender (Eds.), *Student Development Practices.* Springfield, IL: Charles C Thomas.

23. Martin, A. D. (1982). Learning to hide: The socialization of the gay adolescent. *Adolescent Psychiatry, 10,* 52–65.

24. Martin, A. D., & Hetrick, E. S. (1988). The stigmatization of the gay and lesbian adolescent. *Journal of Homosexuality, 15*(3), 163–183.

25. Public Broadcasting System. (1993). *Gay By Nature or Nurture.* Author.

26. Powell, R. E. (1987). Homosexual behavior and the school counselor. *School Counselor, 34*(3), 202–208.

27. Remafedi, G. (1987). Adolescent homosexuality: Medical and psychological implications. *Pediatrics, 79*(3), 331–337.

28. Remafedi, G. (1987). Male homosexuality: The adolescent's perspective. *Pediatrics, 79*(3), 326–330.

29. Ross-Reynolds, G. (1982). Issues in counseling the "homosexual" adolescent. In J. Grimes (Ed.), *Psychological Approaches to Problems of Children and Adolescents.* Des Moines: Iowa State Department of Public Instruction, Division of Special Education.

30. Rofes, E. (1989). Opening up the classroom closet: Responding to the educational needs of gay and lesbian youth. *Harvard Educational Review, 59*(4), 444–453.

31. Schneider, M. S., & Tremble, G. (1985). Gay or straight: Working with the confused adolescent. *Journal of Social Work and Human Sexuality, 4,* 631–660.

The incident in the section "Questions for Further Thought and Discussion" was included in the following reference.

32. Hebert, T. P. (1991). Meeting the affective needs of bright boys through bibliography. *Roeper Review, 13*(4), 207–212.

$$Chapter \quad 9$$

Assessment in a Diverse Society

Assessment is an integral part of the educational process. Assessment provides the information educators need to determine whether their students have acquired the knowledge, skills, abilities, and other objectives of the curriculum. If they have not, it helps educators understand why not. Do the students have the potential and motivation to accomplish the objectives? Did the educators use inappropriate instructional or motivational techniques? What additional assistance do the students require? What are their strengths and weaknesses? These are just a few of the many questions assessment helps answer.

Because our society is so diverse, until recently, assessment procedures, particularly standardized tests, were not very accurate when used with many students. The situation has improved somewhat in recent years. Nowadays educators are much more knowledgeable about the bias typically found in the assessment strategies and materials and the harmful effects of biased assessment on students. New, less-biased procedures and materials have been developed. However, the sad fact is that many school districts do not use these approaches.

This chapter describes how inattention to students' ethnic, socioeconomic, linguistic, contextual, and gender characteristics can bias the results of assessments. It examines various alternative solutions educators and others can employ when they assess students. It describes how educators can avoid biased and discriminatory assessment by adapting their assessment procedures to their students' characteristics and selecting appropriate nonbiased/nonsexist assessment materials and procedures.

Student Characteristics

This section describes some of the many differences among students that require adaptations in the assessment process to avoid bias and describes and evaluates suggestions for adapting the assessment process to these differences. As was noted in Chapter 1, it is important to avoid overgeneralizations and stereotypical statements about students. The ethnic, socioeconomic, and gender differences discussed in this chapter are meant to sensitize assessors to differences that may possibly characterize students, not to encourage them to judge students by their ethnic background, name, skin color, or gender.

Familiarity with the Assessment Process

Not all students are accustomed to being assessed, especially in a one-to-one situation. Students who are unfamiliar with assessment procedures often become anxious when they are assessed (1–6). Research indicates that a small amount of anxiety can motivate students to do their best when they are assessed; but too much anxiety can interfere with their performance (4).

> *The way many standardized tests are composed and given do, in fact, elicit or at least allow strong debilitating motivational dynamics such as test anxiety to operate. Such motivational test bias will cause many children to perform well below their optimal level of functioning in the test situation, thereby invalidating their results if one is interested in what the children have learned, as opposed to whether they can demonstrate that learning under heavy testing pressure. (4, p. 4)*

Immigrant and refugee students who have never been assessed, especially on a one-to-one basis, are likely to be anxious during the assessment process (2, 3, 5). There is also considerable evidence that African American and poor students are more anxious in assessment procedures than European American and middle-class students (1, 4, 6)

> *Some Hispanics come from countries where students are seldom assessed individually as they are in the United States. The strangeness and unfamiliarity of this situation may make Hispanic students anxious to the point that their anxiety interferes with their ability to demonstrate their achievement and potential. (3, p. 175)*

Students come to the assessment process with different test-taking skills. Their test-wiseness, their capacity to utilize the characteristics and format of an assessment procedure or the assessment situation to solve the problems included in an assessment procedure, affects their ability to perform up to their actual level. Students who have not acquired test-taking skills (such as when to ask the assessor for clarification or assistance, when to work fast, when to guess and to skip difficult items, how to rule out items in multiple choice items that are obviously meant to mislead or entrap students, how to mark an answer sheet, and so on) may be unable to demonstrate what they actually know and can do.

> *Many Native American Indian students fail to exhibit successful test-taking behaviors due to a multiplicity of underlying causes. Cultural beliefs in some*

tribes may bar competitive behaviors in an academic setting. The student may underestimate the seriousness of the test or fail to adopt a successful response strategy which may involve selective scanning for known items, techniques of using partial information to guess correct answers, or efficient time use. (9, p. 3)

Research has consistently indicated that improving students' test-taking skills, including those of African American, Hispanic American, Native American, and poor students also improves their scores on assessment procedures (7, 8, 10–16). Five to fourteen hours of instruction time spread out over five to seven weeks appears to be the effective range of instructional time needed to improve students' test-wiseness. Ten hours has been recommended by a number of researchers.

Some educators disagree with this approach. They feel it is unethical and misleading to teach test-taking skills to students. Others argue that because students who lack test-taking skills are unable to demonstrate what they can do and what they know, improving their skills through training makes results of assessment more accurate and less biased. Haladyna and colleagues suggest that there are ethical and unethical ways to prepare students for standardized tests (11). Some of the approaches they consider unethical include modifying the curriculum to match the test, teaching students the actual items in the test, and practicing alternate forms of the test. Examples of approaches they believe to be ethical include teaching test-taking skills and motivating students to want to perform their best.

SELF-QUIZ: Test-Wiseness

Were you a test-wise student when you were younger? Which if any techniques did your teachers employ to improve your test-taking skills? Which techniques would you employ to improve your students' test-taking skills? Which techniques do you think are unethical?

Motivation

All students are not equally motivated to do their best when they are assessed. Some students may not realize that the assessment being conducted is designed to evaluate them. This is especially true of Hispanic American, Native American, and Southeast Asian American students, who come from cultures where they are not evaluated in the same way (3, 20). In fact, some Native American students who have not been exposed to a great deal of testing in reservation schools tend to view a test as a game. As a result, they do not try to do as well as they might if they understood the significance of the situation (20).

Many European American females, particularly those from less affluent and working-class backgrounds, have mixed feelings about and are uncomfortable with success in courses or occupations traditionally thought of as being in the male domain. This applies to a lesser degree to African American females (see

Chapter 10). There is also evidence that some African American students, especially males, are motivated to avoid success in school or at least are not motivated to try to succeed (see Chapters 3 and 11). Students who are not motivated to succeed in school may be equally unmotivated to perform their best on school-related assessments. Therefore, it may be necessary for assessors to motivate such students to try their best. If this fails, they should at least take students' lack of motivation into consideration when they interpret and report the results they obtain.

Students' motivational styles also affect their motivation to succeed. Assessors who are aware of students' motivational styles can utilize their knowledge to increase students' motivation to maximize their performance. For example, students who are brought up to view their family as their main reference point when evaluating themselves are more likely to respond positively to statements such as if they do their best during the assessment their family will be proud of them and it will reflect positively on their families and communities. This may be an especially effective approach with Hmong Americans, who have extremely strong loyalty to their kinship group, as the following description indicates. The Hmong believe that

> *A person exists as a member of a specific kin group. . . . The fate of the group determines its individual members' status and identities. People think of themselves as a collective group with an identity and responsibility. Individuals' actions determine the status of the kin group by reflecting on its honor and on the public respect the group can command. Thus a person's achievements are important insofar as they reflect on her or his extended family, and, in turn, affect the well-being of its members. (21, pp. 6–7)*

In comparison to European American students, Hispanic Americans are also brought up to have a greater loyalty to their families and communities.

> *Hispanics have a strong identification with and loyalty to their family and community. As a result, Hispanic students may be highly motivated to do things that have significance for their families, friends, and community. (3, p. 38)*

When attempting to motivate students to do their best when they are assessed, it is also helpful to know whether individual recognition or anonymity is stressed in their culture. Some students try to do their best if they anticipate that their achievement will be recognized publicly, others when they are assured that their anonymity will be preserved. Many non-European students and some European Americans, especially females, have difficulty with public recognition. An Hispanic American educator reported: "When I was a student, I was tremendously embarrassed any time I was singled out. I would have preferred my recognition in private" (3, p. 87).

Are students brought up to behave cooperatively or to compete with others? Would students respond better to competitive or cooperative motivating techniques during the assessment process? Chamberlain and Medinos-Landurand point out that

In American society, students who do not value or are not skilled in competition are at a serious disadvantage in the testing process. These students do not understand or accept the concept of doing their "best" and working to do better than others during a test. (18, p. 118)

As the following quotations indicate, Hispanic Americans, Hawaiian Americans, and Native Americans, among others, tend to prefer cooperative environments.

Cooperative learning is very essential for Central Americans. Cooperation and collectivity are always regarded as very essential values, while in this country what is valued is individualism and competition. (Carlos Cordova, San Francisco University, San Francisco, California) (24, p. 19)

Because of their belief that it is bad manners to try to excel over others, some Hispanic students may not volunteer answers or they may even pretend not to know the correct answer when called on. (22, p. 358)

There is evidence that Hawaiians are seldom concerned with the pursuit of success for the purely personal satisfaction involved. . . . Hawaiians apparently derive little personal pleasure from competing successfully against others and, in fact, avoid individual competition. . . . As an illustration, many children in our school refused to accept material rewards (e.g., cokes or candy) for high grades or successful competition unless the rewards could be shared with their friends. (25, pp. 55–56)

Native American parents desire their children to be successful, just as any other parents, but in a manner that is consistent with the cooperative and non-competitive tribal, community, and family values and aspirations. (17, p. 46)

Would comparing students to their peers be an effective or ineffective motivational device? In some cases, particularly with students who have been brought up in individualistic cultures, such comparisons can be highly motivating. However, students who have learned that such comparisons are bad may do whatever necessary to avoid appearing to be competitive with other individuals. After a friend has given the wrong answer, how will students who have been brought up to function cooperatively rather than competitively respond when they are called on to give the correct answer? Although it is difficult for many European American teachers to believe, many non–European American students, especially Hispanic Americans and Native Americans, pretend that they do not know the answer to a question or a problem if one of their peers has not given the right answer.

Calling upon a boy or girl to correct an answer or to supply information in response to a question missed by someone else, creates a problem situation for, in the Latino code of ethics, it is not considered proper for any individual to secure attention at the expense of another person (showing up his ignorance, for instance). (19, p 78)

If a question is asked and one child cannot answer it, no one else will because that means they would have placed themselves in a superior position over their peer. [American Indian student] (23, p. 135)

Perception of Assessors

What is the history of the relationship between the students' ethnic or socioeconomic groups and the group the assessors represent? Have the students personally experienced prejudice, oppression, rejection, or abuse by members of the assessors' ethnic or socioeconomic group? Have they been brought up to anticipate such treatment? How will students perceive and relate to assessors who are not members of their ethnic, socioeconomic, or regional group and whom they do not know? Will students perform poorly during assessment sessions because they are suspicious of their assessors and not because of a lack of potential or achievement? Will they feel more relaxed and perform better if they are familiar with the assessor?

Research (which needs to be updated) suggests that Hispanic American students perform better with Hispanic American examiners (27, 30). As the following quotation reveals, many African American students are brought up to be suspicious of the motives and intentions of European Americans.

Black children are taught early to be suspicious of whites. . . . Thus Blacks grow up believing that whites cannot be trusted. Whether this is true or not is hardly the question, for we are dealing here with **perceptual** *realities of Blacks. . . . The effect of such an attitude on any testing situation in which the instrument is administered by a white is obvious. . . . From an intercultural point of view the testing situation is even more complicated. The situation itself, in all probability, is defined as being* cold *in the negative sense of that Black term. Black Americans looking at Euro-American interactional style often brand whites as cold and aloof. This feeling about whites will then be intensified if the situation is kept under the control of the tester. Not only does this environment ignore the means by which significant information is generally passed on among blacks . . . but it eliminates the possibility of establishing the kind of relationship that makes anything but hostile responses seem appropriate to the testee. In this sense it is not the questions per se which cause Black children difficulty, it is the testing environment in general and especially the techniques that are used to ask the questions. (28, pp. 338–339)*

Research about whether these attitudes actually affect how African American students react to the ethnic background of assessors has yielded inconsistent results. Studies of African American students that do not consider student characteristics such as age, mistrust of European Americans, socioeconomic background, or other situational factors (such as the level of difficulty of the assessment procedure and the role of the assessor) tend to find that assessors' ethnic background does not affect the results of assessment procedures. However, results that consider these factors have indicated the opposite. For example, pre-school African American students perform better with African American assessors (31). African American students who mistrust European Americans also perform better with African American assessors, but ethnic background has no effect on those who do not mistrust European Americans (32). Although assessors' ethnic background does not affect the results of assessments of middle-class African American students, research that was done in the 1970s and early 1980s indicates that African Americans students from low income backgrounds perform better with African American assessors. They score higher on standardized tests when given social reinforcement by African American assessors and give them longer and elaborate responses (26, 33).

The reasons for these age and socioeconomic effects have not been explored. Some researchers have suggested that because young children are likely to be unfamiliar with European Americans and have less interaction with them as individuals, they are less likely to trust them. They also propose that students from low-income backgrounds are better able to overcome their discomfort with an unfamiliar and/or threatening assessment procedure when their assessors are familiar. Although most assessors are unfamiliar to students, the administrative procedures for most standardized tests discourage assessor familiarity or friendliness. They also provide little or no opportunity for assessors to engage students in activities that will help them to gain their trust.

There is also evidence that some students from some cultures may perform better with same-gender rather than different-gender assessors. In some cultures students try harder with male assessors because in their culture males are more highly regarded and respected than females (29).

Communication Style

Students' communication styles can also influence the results of their assessments. As was noted in Chapter 6, assessors who prefer direct expression may mistakenly think that African American and Hispanic American students who use a more poetic and analogous speech pattern are "beating around the bush," cannot think straight, or have communication problems (3, 22).

Also as noted previously, some students (e.g, Hispanic Americans and Japanese Americans) expect others to be sensitive enough to their feelings and problems that it is unnecessary for them to be open and direct about their needs. If they have to do so, they may experience a loss of self-respect and think that others have also lost respect for them as well (3, 34, 36).

> *Because Hispanics tend to feel that it reflects negatively on their self-worth to admit that they do not know something or cannot do something, Hispanic students who are less accustomed to asking questions and expressing doubts and confusions may not admit that they do not understand directions or items included in assessment procedures. (3, p. 176)*

Therefore, assessors should not assume that students who do not ask for help in understanding directions and so on are really ready to perform the required assessment task.

Children are brought up to be more or less loquacious with adults. For example, many Native American, Asian and Pacific American, and Hispanic American students are expected to talk less and listen more when they converse with adults in comparison to European American students (3, 18, 35). Thus, they may respond in as few words as possible during assessment procedures and be penalized for not saying enough or providing enough details.

Learning Style

Dependent Versus Independent Learners
No children are brought up to be completely dependent on or independent of adults. However, some youngsters are trained to accomplish things on their own, others are brought up to be more dependent on the aid, support, opinions, and feedback of their parents and other significant adults. It is important to know whether students are prepared to be relatively self-reliant and independent during the assessment process or require a great deal of guidance and feedback to perform at their optimum level. Most standardized assessment procedures do not permit assessors to provide dependent learners with the supportive environment they require to demonstrate their accomplishments.

Reflective/Analytical Versus Spontaneous/Intuitive
No one is completely reflective/analytical or spontaneous/intuitive, but there are cultural differences among people along this continuum. Therefore, it is important to know whether children's cultures stress analyzing and reflecting on questions and problems and being sure to know the answer or solution before saying anything, or emphasize responding intuitively and spontaneously in terms of what occurs to them immediately. Shade describes the difference as follows:

> Some people are rather anxious to insure that they gather all the information possible before being asked to respond and they have a need to be accurate. These individuals are considered to be reflective *while those individuals who respond immediately to what is presented without regard to the fact they may be erroneous are labeled as* impulsive *learners. (40, p. 17)*

How long does it take for students to prepare their answers when called on in class or asked to respond to a question during the assessment process? Native American students tend to look at all sides of an issue, examine their possible implications, and make sure they know the answer before they are ready to express their opinion. Assessors who do not allow students sufficient time to prepare their answers before calling on someone else or moving on to the next item may mistakenly believe that the students do not know something, are slow learners, and so on (41).

Risk Taking

How sure do students have to be that they know the answer, can complete a task, or have a correct opinion before they will risk a response during assessment? How likely are they to choose an answer they are not completely sure of on a multiple choice item that deducts for incorrect answers?

> *A Japanese youth . . . should remain silent rather than exhibiting a faulty understanding or command of a skill. To put forth a mistaken answer or an unperfected skill is a personal disgrace and an insult to the teacher and the discipline. (34, p. 19)*

> *A reluctance to try too soon and the accompanying fear of being "shamed" if one does not succeed may account for the seemingly passive uninterested and unresponsive attitude of Indian students. (39, p. 28)*

> *The Hispanic culture discourages guessing (hablando sin saber). Thus, Hispanic students may be penalized on assessment procedures which require students to respond when they are uncertain of the correct answer. (3, p. 177)*

Global Perception Versus Analysis of Details

Some students, such as African Americans and Hispanic Americans, tend to be global learners; others, including many middle-class European Americans, typically are more analytical. Global learners perceive things in a holistic manner. They perceive the whole of an event, idea, or image and the relationships between its parts simultaneously. They see everything as a part of the whole and use few discrete categories to notice differences among the parts. Analytic learners can easily divide the whole into subcategories based on differences. Therefore, students' performance on achievement and other types of assessment procedures may depend, in part, on whether the tasks they are required to perform fit their particular global or analytic learning style.

Stimulation and Variety

Students differ in terms of their tolerance for and willingness to continue to perform assessment tasks that are boring, monotonous, tedious and repetitious. Research indicates that the performance of African American students who come from homes that are highly stimulating increases when the format of an assessment procedure includes more task variation, but the performance of African American and European American students from homes that are not highly stimulating does not improve with increased variability (38; also see "High Versus Low Stimulation" in Chapter 10.) Boykin explains this on the basis of the home environment to which many African Americans are accustomed.

> *The home and immediate ecological environments of a preponderance of Black children afford levels of physical stimulation that are high in both intensity and variability. . . . One consequence of growing up in such environments may be a heightened responsiveness to stimulus change. . . . It would seem reasonable,*

moreover, that in a problem solving context, Black children would find tasks pre-sented in a relatively monotonous fashion even more intolerable than their coun-terparts from more placid settings. Thus, it would seem that increased variation should have a greater positive effect on the task performance of Black children. (38, pp. 470–471)

Activity Level

Students' willingness to sit still for long periods of time is greatly influenced by their ethnic and socioeconomic backgrounds (37). Because some students may have difficulty sitting quietly and completing sedentary assessment activities for long periods of time, their performance may indicate their difficulty in adjusting to the requirements of the assessment situation, not what they have achieved or learned or what they could accomplish if they were assessed in a more culturally appropriate manner.

Pace

People from different cultures work and play at different paces. Some students attempt to accomplish as much as possible within a given period of time; others prefer a relaxed, steady pace. Slower-working students who correctly answer all the items that they have time to complete on standardized tests may receive a lower score than students who rush through the test and miss items that those working at a slower pace answer correctly. It is important, therefore, to determine whether students can demonstrate what they know and have achieved in school on timed evaluations or merely appear to have accomplished less than they have because they are unable to complete the evaluation procedure.

Some students who are accustomed to working at a slower pace—African Americans, Brazilian Americans, Filipino Americans, Hawaiian Americans, and Samoan Americans, among others—may make more errors when required to work as fast as they can. Students accustomed to a faster pace—for example, Japanese Americans and Chinese Americans—continue to perform as well when they are told to work as fast as they can (42–44). For all of these reasons, it is essential to use untimed procedures when assessing students who are not accustomed to rushing through things.

Response Style

Cultures differ in the degree to which they encourage intense or subdued responses to life. For example, in comparison to European American students, African American students are more likely to respond intensely to things in general and to select extreme responses on scales that ask if they strongly agree or just agree, or if they strongly disagree or just disagree (45, 46). Therefore, assessors should consider students' response style when they interpret their responses to items on assessment procedures.

Assessment Materials and Procedures

The materials and procedures that assessors use are another significant source of bias. The primary sources of such bias are technical bias, content bias, format bias, and linguistic bias.

Technical Bias

Assessment procedures must be reliable and valid. If they are not, then decisions based on the data they provide will be discriminatory. For an assessment procedure to be useful the score/results that are obtained should be correct. For example, students who have behavior problems should appear that way to different observers, and they should appear to have problems regardless of the particular time they are observed or evaluated or the particular situation in which they are evaluated. If this is not true, then judgments about students might depend on the persons who observe them, the time at which they are observed, or the situation in which they are observed. Procedures are reliable when they produce consistent results regardless of the observer, the time, or the situation.

Procedures that are reliable for some students may be unreliable when used with other students. Because the reliability of most procedures is determined by studying their use with predominantly European American students, many procedures may be unreliable when used with non-European students. For example, observers who are biased against certain groups such as African American students or who do not know about the cultural determinants of their behavior may perceive that behavior differently than observers who are not prejudiced against these students or knowledgeable about their culture.

Procedures that are valid measure what they claim to measure and accomplish what they are designed to achieve. For example, intelligence tests or tests of learning potential are supposed to measure students' ability to learn and to predict how much students will learn in certain situations when they are given certain kinds and amounts of assistance. If they do not measure a student's capacity to learn and predict accurately how students will function in specific learning situations, they are invalid, useless, and even harmful.

For example, students' current knowledge about a particular item (such as how far is it from one place to another or the height of the average American adult male) or their ability to perform a particular task (such as forming a design from blocks) can indicate their learning potential or help assessors to predict how they will learn in the future, but only under certain conditions. The students must have been exposed to the information or task and have had sufficient practice to learn it; they must be motivated to demonstrate their knowledge or ability to assessors; and they have to be permitted to do so in a way that fits their performance style. Non–European American, poor, and limited English proficient students are not always exposed to the same materials, tasks, environments and so on as European American, middle-class, and English proficient students. They may not be as motivated to demonstrate their ability and knowledge during the assessment procedure, and they have different learning and communication styles. Therefore, procedures that are valid with European American middle-class students may be invalid when used with non–European American and poor students.

Content Bias

Content bias may occur because different teachers, schools, and school districts include different content in the courses they offer at each grade level and because students bring different experiences to the assessment situation for contextual and cultural reasons.

Because of differences in the contents of the curriculum to which students are exposed, students' scores on standardized achievement tests may depend on the match between what the procedure measures and what they have been taught (47, 50, 52). After determining that third- and fourth-grade students obtained different scores on each of four standardized reading achievement tests, Good and Salvia concluded that one cannot always determine whether "a student's reading score reflects deficient reading skills or the selection of a test with poor content validity for the pupil's curriculum" (52, p. 56).

Inner city schools, rural schools, and suburban schools include very different skills in their curriculum. Migrant students who move from school to school may miss a considerable amount of course content. For these reasons, assessment procedures may evaluate students on what they should have been taught, not on what they were actually taught (47).

Some educators believe curriculum-based assessment is an effective way to avoid such content bias. Curriculum-based assessment is an approach that aims to assess students in terms of the curriculum that they have actually been exposed to in class. This avoids the bias that results in assessing students on knowledge and skills that they have not studied or practiced and including items that depend on family and community values. The advantages and disadvantages of this approach are discussed later in this chapter.

Some educators claim that the contents of many assessment materials are biased against non–European American and poor students because the context of their lives and their cultural backgrounds expose them to very different experiences than those of middle-class American students. "A body of knowledge based on the experiences of a white middle class community cannot help but create a disadvantage for members of communities which differ from the mainstream" (50, p. 178).

These educators suggest that questions such as how far is it from one place to another are only relevant if students are familiar with the places, asking why it is better to pay bills by check rather than cash is not relevant to children whose parents cannot afford a checking account, and whether it is better to build houses from bricks rather than wood depends on the geographic region in which students grow up.

Measuring independence or motor control by determining if children can drink out of a cup or ride a tricycle or throw a ball overhand can lead to incorrect conclusions if they still drink from a bottle, play soccer rather than baseball, are too poor to own a tricycle, or live in an area where the traffic makes it is too dangerous for children to ride a tricycle. Evaluating students' short-term memory by having them repeat a series of digits backward or forward can provide accurate information for students who have had an opportunity to practice remembering numbers in a series. However, some students come from places where they and their friends have telephone numbers and street addresses, others come from rural areas in the United States or elsewhere where there is little reason to remember numbers.

Some items are biased because they involve family and community values. The answers to such items as what you should do if a smaller child hits you, why it is better to give money to a charitable organization than to a street beggar, and what you should do if you lose something that belongs to your friend depend on the values and experiences to which students have been exposed.

Other educators and psychologists question whether such items are really biased (49, 55). They claim that one cannot determine if an item or content is biased merely by examining it, because that is too subjective; they maintain that one has to actually determine statistically whether an item is more difficult for one group than another; and they point out that some items that were judged to be biased have turned out to be no more difficult for the group that they are supposed to be biased against than for any other group. Presently, there is very little research to support this point of view.

Educators who believe that there is a great deal of content bias in assessment procedures have suggested that one way to reduce such bias is to eliminate any items that are more difficult for some groups than for others (51, 55, 59). They complain that although test publishers eliminate items that are more difficult for one gender or the other in order to eliminate gender bias, they do not do the same thing for items that are more difficult for certain ethnic, socioeconomic, or regional groups.

Other educators and psychologists feel that the differences in the scores that various groups receive on these items represent real differences in ability or achievement between groups (54). They advise test publishers to continue to include such items in their assessment materials.

In the 1970s and early 1980s educators and psychologists developed a number of culture-specific assessment instruments, primarily for African Americans, that included content that was more relevant to the students' experiences, pictures of African Americans in more culturally relevant situations, and so on. The majority of these instruments were designed to evaluate African Americans' personality characteristics, their priorities in life, the extent to which they are aware of and identify with their African heritage, their knowledge of the oppressive nature and effects of racism, their willingness to resist anti–African American pressures and threats, their attitudes toward African American issues, their mistrust of European Americans, and their identification with African American values, customs, and institutions (48, 53, 56–58, 60).

Research indicates that persons assessed with these instruments provide more data and data that is more valid. The instruments can be used to obtain information about certain aspects of students' personalities and their attitudes about European American teachers and European American values. However, they provide only a limited amount of the information needed to evaluate African American students functioning in school.

A number of culture-specific instruments have also been developed for use with Hispanic American students. Most of these instruments are designed to be administered in Spanish to limited English proficient students who have not assimilated to the mainstream European American culture (see the section on linguistic bias). Few of them are designed for use with English proficient Hispanic American students.

There are very few culture-specific assessment instruments available for other groups. This may indicate that it is not profitable to develop and market culture-specific procedures for small numbers of students. Thus, for the present, culture-specific instruments are not a viable option for assessors who wish to avoid content bias.

Format Bias

The format of an assessment procedure refers to how tasks, questions, and so on, are posed to students and how students are required to respond to them. Format characteristics such as whether students are asked to recognize the correct answer or solution to a problem or to produce it themselves; whether they respond orally, in writing, or by performing a task; whether there are time limits; whether items get progressively more difficult; and what materials the students work with—all can affect students' performance. When there is a poor match between how students function and the format of an assessment procedure, students may not be able to show what they know and can do. Space permits a discussion of only a few examples of format problems.

Students who are immigrants or who have attended atypical schools on reservations may have difficulty adjusting to the unfamiliar format of many standardized tests. For example, some assessment procedures require students to fail five, six, or even seven similar items before they can go on to the next group of items. This can be devastating to students who respond poorly to such experiences and to students who are not accustomed to taking tests in which they fail many items and still do well. Assessment materials that can be used with students who function at many different levels often contain both very easy and very difficult problems on the same page. This can be very frightening and demoralizing to students who see many problems or items that are too difficult for them and do not understand that the difficult ones are for students who are older or in a higher grade.

As was noted earlier, some students, particularly African Americans, Hispanic Americans, and Native Americans, cannot always show what they can do on timed procedures. Stringent time limits galvanize some students to work efficiently and perform at their optimal level, but those who are anxious or who work at a slower pace perform less adequately under time pressures (4).

> *Achievement tests with stringent time limits do not just measure what skills children have acquired or what they know but in addition whether or not they can demonstrate this knowledge quickly and under time pressure and testing stress. (4, p. 16)*

Providing these students with the time they need to complete an assessment at the pace at which they are accustomed to work yields more accurate information about what they know and can do (61).

Cultural factors may make it difficult for some students to engage in certain required activities during the assessment process. For example, on assessment of fine motor coordination, Hmong American children would not demonstrate that they could use pincers to pick up an object because the raisins they were required to pick up resembled Hmong medicines that they were warned to avoid (62).

Finally, whether students are required to respond orally or in writing, in a multiple choice or short essay format, verbally or kinesthetically, and so on, during the assessment process can determine if they are able to demonstrate their true capability and achievement. To deal with this problem, Gardner suggests that

> *Achievement tests should be designed so that students have some room for flexibility. For example a cluster of three or four items that examine a particular skill from different viewpoints and tests it in different ways could be set. . . . [so that] a pupil who can answer any one of them correctly will have demonstrated his/her mastery of that skill and should receive full credit for it—even if he/she had erred on some of the other items in that cluster. (43, p. 234)*

Linguistic Bias

Assessments conducted in a language or dialect in which students are not proficient or in only one language when students require two languages to function adequately and explain themselves fully do not provide a true picture of what students know or can do.

Limited English Proficiency

At first glance, one might think that LEP students should be assessed in their native languages. However, the choice of which language or languages should be used to assess students is a much more complicated issue.

Students who have no proficiency in English clearly need to be assessed in their native language. Those who are truly proficient in English can be assessed completely in English. However, many other students need to be assessed in two languages to demonstrate what they know and can do.

Many limited English proficient students have two vocabularies—a home vocabulary and a school vocabulary. Students in bilingual programs learn a great deal of the content of the curriculum in their native language. Students in English as a second language programs or in regular English language classes learn much of the material in English. Thus, until students are completely proficient in English, those in bilingual programs may have to use their native language to demonstrate their mastery of school-related material, and those in English as a second language or English submergence programs will be unable to demonstrate their school-related achievement unless it is assessed in English. Regardless of the program students are in, their English vocabulary is likely to be limited to what they are learning in school for quite some time. As a result, students are likely to have to use their native languages to express most of what they have learned at home and in their community. These differences must be taken into account when decisions are made regarding the language or languages in which students should be as to assessed in general. Because students need to be assessed in the language in which they will function best on each particular task, skill, or knowledge area, individual differences in native language and English language proficiency must be considered when decisions are made about the language or languages in which each aspect of the assessment should be conducted. A general principle to follow is to make sure students are assessed in both English and their native languages, because research indicates that limited English proficient students usually score higher when assessed in both languages rather than in either their native language or English alone (61, 63).

The goal of providing students with linguistically appropriate assessment services in the more than one hundred languages spoken by limited English proficient students in the United States has proved difficult to achieve for two reasons. Very few of the educators and psychologists who are responsible for assessing students are bilingual. This is particularly true for languages other than Spanish, and, except for Spanish language materials, there is very little assessment material in the many languages spoken by the millions of limited English proficient students in the public schools. The two approaches that have been used to overcome these difficulties are to translate assessment materials into other languages and to use interpreters during the assessment process. Both of these approaches are problematic.

Translating materials into students' native languages can improve the performance of limited English proficient students (61, 64). However, a number of problems must be avoided before these benefits can be achieved.

Using material translated into students' native languages when their preferred language for the task or problem is English because they have learned it in English will not benefit students.

Poorly translated materials will not improve the validity of an assessment. Back translations can eliminate this problem. In a back translation the material that has been translated from English is translated back into English in order to detect any distortion in meaning that resulted from original translation. If the meanings of the back translation and the original are the same, then the translation is probably correct. If they are different, there is good chance that the meaning was changed when the material was translated from English. It is also important to be sure that students speak the dialect of the translation to avoid linguistic bias.

Translating material will not necessarily eliminate its content bias. Therefore, it is often necessary to adapt the content as well the language of the material to the cultural, contextual, and linguistic characteristics of the students with whom they are to be used. Actual examples of content change in translations include changing the question "How are a peach and a plum alike?" to "How are an orange and a banana alike?"; replacing a marble game with a card game; and modifying "How far is it from New York to Chicago" to "How far is it from New York to Puerto Rico."

Sometimes it is also necessary to accept alternative correct answers to some items. For example, to middle-class European American children, what is absurd about a picture of man carrying an umbrella upside down is that the umbrella is in a position in which it will not protect him from rain. However, to Puerto Rican American children the absurdity is that a *man* is carrying an umbrella in any position because males do not carry umbrellas. On a vocabulary test a translated word may have more than one meaning. For example, translating "courage" into "*valor*" becomes problematic because "*valor*" means "value" as well as "bravery" in Spanish.

Translating material often changes the level of difficulty of items. "Dog," a very easy word to read or spell in English translates to "*perro*" in Spanish, a more difficult word because of the double r. Translating "building" to "*edificio*" makes the item easier.

Translating materials does not make the norms of a standardized assessment procedure any more appropriate for students who are not well-represented in the norm sample, nor does it eliminate the format bias of procedures that provide students with only limited amounts of time, require them to make many errors before they are allowed to go on to the next group of problems, and so on.

> *It was discovered that some Vietnamese children, when asked to pick up the blue block, would instead pick up the green block. The Vietnamese language classifies colors into four families: green, red, yellow, and purple. Blue is in the green family, so that words for green and blue are similar (Xahn). To distinguish it is necessary to say "Xahn lo" (blue like the sky) or "Xahn la cay" (green like the leaves) to ensure that the child correctly differentiates between green and blue. (62, p. 482)*

Assessors who cannot evaluate limited English proficient students and interview their parents in their native language require the assistance of interpreters. As the following quote indicates, when properly used interpreters can be very helpful.

> *I strongly believe in the use of language and cultural mediators or interpreters, as I have seen dramatic differences in the behaviors of both children and adults. We find a significant difference in how quickly the family develops trust and*

responds, how much information they volunteer, and how well they establish a relationship. (68, p. 9)

The use of untrained or poorly prepared interpreters, however, can create many problems (65). Untrained interpreters may identify with the student and want the student to do well. This may lead interpreters to prompt the right answer from the student or modify students' answers so that they are closer to the acceptable response. Interpreters who are not equally fluent in both languages may translate incorrectly to the student or assessor. Interpreters who are fluent in the student's languages but not knowledgeable about their cultural background may translate correctly but conduct the assessment in a culturally inappropriate manner or fail to notice content and format bias. If they are from a different socio-economic, religious, racial, or ethnic background than the students, the interpreters may be prejudiced against them.

To avoid or at least minimize these potential problems, interpreters should be trained in the principles of assessment, human development, and so on. They should be equally competent in both languages, equally familiar with mainstream culture and the students' culture, and, if possible, familiar with the communities in which students live and the subgroups to which they belong. The references at the end of the chapter contain much useful information on the training and use of interpreters in the assessment of culturally and linguistically different students (66–69).

Dialect

Although in the 1970s a few studies found that nonstandard dialect speakers are not penalized when they are assessed in standard English (70–73), the vast majority of research at the time and virtually all that has been carried out since then indicates that nonstandard dialect–speaking students who are poor, African American, Native American, Hispanic American, or from Appalachian areas perform poorly when they are assessed in standard English (74–77, 79, 80, 82–85, 87–91, 94–97). There is also considerable evidence that these biased results can lead educators to underestimate students' academic achievement and language ability. (78, 80, 83, 84).

The following are some of the causes of dialect bias during the assessment process.

- Educators and others discriminate against nonstandard English dialects (see Chapter 6).
- Questions on assessment procedures are often asked using vocabulary that is not familiar to students—i.e., "behind the sofa" rather than "in back of the couch," "beginning to climb" instead of "starting to climb" (97). As a result, students appear to lack information and skills that they actually possess and would be able to demonstrate if they understood the question or directions.
- Some dialect speakers may read material written in their own dialect better than material in standard English (93).

- Students tend to remember better material that is in their dialect (74, 83).
- Students are better able to discriminate between sounds that are present in their own dialect (77, 81, 91).
- Students may misunderstand items and directions because they are given in a different dialect. As an example, European American students who are asked to find which of four pictures shows "delight" may have little difficulty identifying the picture of a girl happily eating an ice cream cone. However, African American students who do not speak standard English may hear "de" (the) "light" and select the picture of a boy reading who needs a light (86).
- What may appear to be articulation problems and other types of speech disorders can be omissions and substitutions that conform to speech patterns present in a student's dialect (82, 95).

Suggestions for avoiding bias during the assessment of nonstandard English speakers include the following (80, 84, 87, 88, 92, 94, 95):

- Become knowledgeable about the characteristics of the dialects spoken by the nonstandard English–speakers. There are many descriptions of the major differences between standard English and the various nonstandard English dialects that can help you to avoid mistaking dialect differences for possible speech disorders (76, 98, 99).
- Examine your attitudes about nonstandard dialects for possible bias.
- Avoid stereotyping all members of a group as nonstandard speakers. Determine whether each individual student is a standard or nonstandard dialect speaker. Keep in mind that working-class and younger students are more likely to use nonstandard dialects.
- Use assessment procedures only with students who use the dialect for whom the test has been standardized.
- Do not consider differences in oral reading due to dialect differences such as mispronunciations or adding or omitting endings that indicate plurals, tense, and the like, as reading errors.
- Accept answers that conform to a student's dialect as correct even though they may not be acceptable according to the manual.
- Make sure students understand the directions and the items included in any assessment procedure. Be prepared to use alternate instructions in both dialects and to express the contents in both dialects.

Gender Bias

The contents and language of an assessment procedure can also be biased against one gender or the other. Although the effect is not very large, each gender is more likely to answer correctly test items that deal with objects and topics that interest them and those that use same-gender pronouns (male students do somewhat better when pronouns are he, him, and his, and females score higher when pronouns refer to she, her, and hers). Studies conducted in the 1970s and early 1980s indicate that test items tend to include more male pronouns and more material that fits stereotypical male interests. If this situation has not been corrected in recent years, female students may still be placed at a disadvantage when they are assessed with these materials (100–106).

Formal, Standardized, Norm-Referenced Assessment Versus Informal, Nonstandardized, Criterion-Referenced Assessment

Assessment procedures can be divided into two categories: formal, standardized, norm-referenced procedures, and informal, nonstandardized, criterion-referenced procedures. Assessors use the terms somewhat differently and do not always agree about which are which. In general, formal assessment procedures are those that deviate from regular classroom practices. They are usually designed to determine how students are doing in relation to criteria that are more universal and less applicable or geared to the particular students' situations. In order to make such comparisons, formal procedures are administered and scored in a standardized way. The interpretation of the scores is typically accomplished by comparing an individual's score to norms obtained from a sample of students that are believed to represent the population of students with whom the procedure will be used. Standardized achievement tests are good examples of these procedures.

Informal procedures are those that can easily be incorporated into the classroom without interfering with daily activities. Informal procedures typically involve evaluating what students do, how they function, and what they have learned in relation to the curriculum they are exposed to or the goals and standards of their particular teacher or school. This can be done in an unstructured manner by observing how students function and evaluating their work or in a structured way by using observation checklists and scales and lists of specific evaluative criteria.

Unlike norm-referenced assessment approaches, in which individual students are compared to a norm sample of students, criterion-referenced assessment is designed to compare an individual student to a set of criteria or performance standards such as the number of words spelled correctly or the skills needed to perform a specific task. Criterion-referenced assessment procedures describe students' achievement, knowledge, behavior, and so on, rather than compare students to each other (107, 108).

In norm-referenced testing, learning a particular skill is important only to the extent that differential learning allows the examiner to rank individuals in order, from those who have learned many skills to those who have learned few. The emphasis is on the relative standing of children rather than on absolute mastery of content. On the other hand, criterion-referenced testing interprets achieve-

ment by describing in behavioral terms the child's performance regarding a particular instructional objective. (107, p. 222)

Typically, criterion referenced assessment materials are constructed by individual teachers, departments, or school districts to compare their students to some criteria that they have developed. However, criterion-referenced materials are also available from commercial publishers.

The results of a formal procedure might indicate that the student is functioning at the fourth grade in vocabulary (because her scores on the test were the same as the average of fourth graders in the norm sample) or that she is in the top 10% of fourth graders (because her scores on the vocabulary test were higher than 90% of the fourth graders in the norm sample). The results of an informal nonstandardized procedure might indicate that a student has learned 85% of the vocabulary words that a teacher assigned the class.

Experts disagree about which of the two assessment approaches is most and least subject to the kinds of bias described earlier. The advantages and disadvantages of using each approach with limited English proficient, non–European American, and poor students are discussed next.

Formal, Standardized, Norm-Referenced Assessment

Educators and other concerned persons have been criticizing the standardized tests used in schools with poor and non–European American students since the early 1920s (109–112). However, criticisms of standardized assessment approaches did not appear regularly or receive a great deal of attention from educators and psychologists until 1968, when the Association of Black Psychologists, a subgroup of the American Psychological Association, called for a moratorium on the standardized testing of African American students. The association criticized achievement, intelligence, aptitude, and performance tests because they were being used to

1. *Label black people as uneducable*
2. *Place black children in special education*
3. *Perpetuate inferior education*
4. *Assign black children to lower educational tracks*
5. *Deny black children higher educational opportunities*
6. *Destroy positive intellectual growth and development of black people (116, pp. 17–18)*

Williams, an officer and spokesperson for the association claimed that

1. *Children who are misclassified and labeled as "different" may be permanently stigmatized and may experience rejection by those in their immediate environment.*
2. *They may be assigned to inferior educational programs or deprived of their freedom through commitment to an institution.*

3. *They may be excluded from opportunities which are vital for the full development of their emotional and physical existences.*

4. *They may be committed to institutions, which define and confirm them as delinquent, retarded or emotionally disturbed. Thus, the child will manifest behaviors which are appropriate to his label. They become more inclined to crime, more disturbed than they would be under more normal growth conditions and less bright than they could be. (117, pp. 3–4, 8–9)*

Other criticisms of standardized assessment have included the following (113–115):

- They do not accurately/validly describe how students function in the present nor predict how students will function in the future.
- They ask "Do you know what I know?" rather than "What is it that you know?" (114, p. 29)
- The data collected with standardized instruments are typically collected in nonclassroom situations under unusual circumstances by unfamiliar assessors and therefore do not reflect how students function in real-life classrooms with real-life teachers.
- Percentile ranking, grade-level placements, and other norms provided by standardized tests are not realistic because national norms are not necessarily true for a given school district, school, or class. The contents of courses taught at the seventh-grade level in a predominantly middle-class suburban school may be very different from the course contents in a school serving predominantly poor urban students. Thus, students who score at the seventh-grade level on nationally normed reading tests may actually be functioning at a much lower level than the typical seventh-grade student in a middle-class neighborhood suburban school and at a much higher level than the typical seventh-grade student in some other school districts.
- Standardized assessment procedures are not easily adapted to students' contextual, cultural, and linguistic characteristics.
- They measure different attributes with different groups of students. When used with limited English proficient, non–European American, and poor students these procedures measure what students have been exposed to, how fast they can work without making careless mistakes, how motivated they are to succeed and do their best, how well they can adapt to the particular format of the procedure, how they respond to pressure, and so on, not their achievement, learning potential, or whatever else the procedures may measure when used with European American middle-class students who are English proficient and speak standard English.
- They require all students to fit a preconceived mold.

Despite the lip-service we pay to the myriad ways in which individuals differ, and claim to celebrate this variety, our practices speak otherwise. In fact it is performance on these tests—with their narrow and rigid definition both of when children should be able to perform particular skills and how they should be able to exhibit their knowledge—that determines whether we see children as "okay" or not. In the process we damage all children—we devalue the variety of strength they bring with them to school. All differences become handicaps. (115, p. 47)

The Council of the American Psychological Association disagreed with the Black Psychological Association's call for a moratorium on standardized testing. They maintained that

Good psychological decisions require good evidence, and some of the most useful and reliable evidence comes from well-designed and properly interpreted standardized tests. . . . Yet for a variety of reasons, some valid and some not, testing has been the constant target of attack, joined in often by political figures or by the popular media. Testing continues to play an informative role in psychological decisions, for example in counseling practice and educational guidance, yet the science and profession of psychology are damaged by lopsided attacks, which often go without correction, comment or rebuttal. . . .

Now, therefore, the Council of the American Psychological Association asserts the following:

1. *Standardized testing, competently administered and evaluated, is a valuable tool in individual, educational, and personnel decision-making.*
2. *Abuses of testing, through unwarranted labeling or interpretation, are to be avoided as are abuses of any valuable tool. (119)*

Arguments in support of the use of standardized assessment procedures have included the following (118–122):

- Standardized assessment procedures provide reliable and valid data that describe what students know and can do and predict how much they will be able to learn and what they will be able to accomplish.
- Standardized assessment procedures are not biased.

A considerable body of literature fails to substantiate cultural bias against native-born American ethnic minorities with regard to the use of well-constructed, adequately standardized intelligence and aptitude tests. (121, p. 255)

- Standardized tests predict how students will perform in biased and discriminatory schools.

Perhaps the inequities lie in the traditional education rather than merely in the tests. Intelligence tests are satisfactory predictors of success in traditional education. That the educational system fails to adjust to a culturally pluralistic society is not the fault of tests. Schools seem to prepare students to function in the mainstream, majority culture. If the nature of schools changed radically, mental tests might lose their high predictive validity and no longer be useful. (120, p. 78)

- The problem is not standardized tests, but their misuse.
- The elimination of objective standardized approaches to assessment will lead to more subjective, less reliable, and less valid assessment procedures, and to the very bias that objective standardized instruments are designed to avoid.
- Because students eventually are going to have to function in the mainstream, their performance should be assessed in terms of mainstream content, format, and norms.
- Objective and standardized measures are necessary to compare the achievement of different groups in order to identify inequities and problem areas that need to be corrected.

Test results provide a way for the public to monitor educational standards over time. Test results also help teachers and school officials to indentify weaknesses in instruction and curriculum. Tests provide the data that enable parents and others to keep the pressure on communities, schools, and educators to "close the gap" between the performance of black students and that of whites—pressure that is finally bringing results. (118 p. 624)

Pluralistic Norms

In the 1970s a number of researchers attempted to improve the validity of norm-referenced tests by providing different norms for different groups of students. In theory, the use of pluralistic norms for different groups allowed assessors to compare students to others like them from a similar background, with the same motivation to do well, and the same exposure to the tasks and information.

This approach was criticized on a number of grounds (49, 123–126).

- Pluralistic norms do not compare students to others who are like them because students from similar ethnic or socioeconomic backgrounds are actually very different. For example, they are not all equally motivated to succeed either in school or when they are assessed, and their exposure at home to school-related information and the support they receive from their parents may be very different.
- The original national norms reflect the reality at the moment. Thus, if students are compared to a small select group using pluralistic norms, then the results cannot predict how they will function in mainstream America when they have to compete with many others who do not share the same socioeconomic, ethnic, or regional background.

If the question is how a particular Chinese-American fifth-grade boy compares in reading to other fifth-grade Chinese-American boys, then culturally appropriate norms would be used. On the other hand, if the question is how this same boy compares with other fifth-grade boys in general, then much broader norms naturally must be consulted. (125, p. 207)

- Lowering standards by using pluralistic norms will lead to the selection of students for programs such as gifted and talented who may not succeed.

If the goal of achieving a desegregated society is still seen as worth pursuing (a value judgement), then the minority child should be compared against a national reference group, for this is the group with which the minority child must compete. When one is looking for a physician to treat him, he does not add 10 points to the physician's competency score to offset limitations stemming from sociocultural background; instead, one looks for the most competent physician, regardless of racial or ethnic background. (49, p. 62)

- Pluralistic norms encourage educators, psychologists, and society in general to accept stereotypical ideas that all in a group or subgroup are alike. Because pluralistic norms are usually lower for most non–European American group, they encourage educators, psychologists, and others to believe these groups of students are less capable and to expect less from them, and this can result in self-fulfilling prophesies.

Studies done in the late 1970s and early 1980s indicated that assessors' decisions based on pluralistic norms were no more valid than those based on traditional national norms when students' schools did not use multicultural approaches. Estimates of students' learning potential that were based on pluralistic norms yielded less-valid predictions of their achievement in schools that were designed for the dominant European American middle-class culture than their original IQ scores (123, 126).

SELF-QUIZ: Content, Format, and Norms

What is your opinion about modifying the content, format, and norms of assessment procedures? Do you think that adapting them to students' cultural, contextual, and geographical backgrounds makes them less biased and more useful? Or do you believe that all students should be assessed on the same contents, in the same way, and compared to norms based on a national sample? State the reasons for your opinion.

Informal, Nonstandardized, Criterion-Referenced Assessment

Educators have always used informal approaches to assess students. The typical weekly spelling, math, and social studies tests are examples of informal approaches to assessing students' academic progress. Determining if a student who is a refugee has emotional problems or is merely conforming to a cultural pattern by comparing his behavior to that of other students who have a similar contextual, ethnic, and socioeconomic background is an example of informal assessment of students' behavior (126, 127). Asking parents to compare a student's behavior at home and in the community with those of her siblings, cousins, or other neighborhood children is an example of a culturally appropriate informal way of evaluating students' out of school achievement (128). The references at the end of the chapter include practical suggestions for educators who wish to develop their own criterion-referenced procedures (108, 126, 127).

Informal, nonstandardized, criterion-referenced assessments can have many advantages over formal, standardized, norm-referenced assessment.

- The information they provide has a more direct relationship to the decisions teachers have to make about instructing and managing students (e.g., what their strengths and weaknesses are, what skills they have and have not acquired, and where to begin with particular students).
- The criteria students are measured against are those deemed important by the assessor rather than the standardized test developers.
- They evaluate students in terms of activities, skills, and subject matter that they have actually been taught and practiced.
- They can be used to determine if students have accomplished the goals set by the teacher, department, or school district.

However, some educators and psychologists have serious questions about informal, nonstandardized, criterion-referenced assessment approaches. The following are typical of their concerns.

- Because educators are not as knowledgeable about principles of assessment as professional test developers, the criterion-referenced procedures they prepare may not be as reliable or valid.
- Many teachers have biased expectations for certain groups of students and evaluate them in a discriminatory manner. Standardized assessment can help avoid such discrimination; allowing biased teachers to develop their own assessment procedures would increase discriminatory assessment, not prevent it.
- Criterion-referenced assessment does not facilitate comparisons between schools and programs that employ different criteria to measure students' progress. Thus, it would be exceedingly difficult to determine if some pro grams and schools are succeeding more than others.
- Comparing students to a limited, particular set of criteria does not indicate how they are functioning in comparison to other students in general or enable educators to predict how students will function in society, where criteria may be very different.

In recent years, proponents of nonstandardized, informal assessment have developed a number of new, well-thought-out and organized, informal, nonstandardized approaches that they believe to be superior to standardized assessment. Three approaches that are particularly popular are portfolio assessment, curriculum-based assessment, and test-teach-test approaches.

Portfolio Assessment
Portfolio assessment, also called assessment in context, situational testing, and authentic assessment, is a particular form of criterion-referenced assessment that emphasizes assessing what students actually do or perform. Portfolio assessment has been defined as "a purposeful, chronological collection of student work,

designed to reflect student development in one or more areas over time and student outcomes at one or more designated points in time" (129, p. 256).

Portfolios contain evidence of students' work that tells the story of their accomplishment and process of achieving it. The material in a portfolio can be constructed, created, or described by students, audiotaped, written, videotaped, or photographed. Portfolios can contain only students' final, completed work or their work at different stages over time, showing how their work improved. Portfolios may include a number of totally different tasks or the same task performed many times over the course of weeks, months, a semester, or a year.

> *The portfolio collection should not be restricted simply to the student's best work. It should also include drafts, outlines, and early attempts; these are equally important to the task of demonstrating what the student has learned and the specific skills and concepts mastered. (132, pp. 12–13)*

Portfolios may also contain students' grades, test scores, honors, and testimonies from others, teachers' observation and evaluation of students' performance, interview protocols, student self-reports, and so on.

Proponents of portfolio assessment believe it offers educators all of the advantages of criterion-referenced assessment noted earlier. In addition they claim that

- Portfolio assessment evaluates students in terms of the real-life authentic tasks in the situations in which students are actually functioning.
- It provides much more detailed and comprehensive data than an answer on a multiple choice item.
- It provides information about how students learn.

Portfolio assessment "reaches well beyond the 'snapshot' examination that captures only the student's knowledge and capabilities at a specific moment" (132, p. 3).

- It enables students' to use their preferred learning and communication styles and linguistic ability in English and their native language in order to demonstrate their accomplishments.
- It encourages students to take responsibility for their own learning.
- It assists teachers to establish assessment target standards (goals and priorities)—measurable objective standards against which students' progress is evaluated.

The concerns that have been expressed about criterion-referenced assessment in general also apply to portfolio assessment. Two concerns should be emphasized:

- It is important that assessors use objectives/standards/goals against which students' performance can be measured in order to avoid subjectivity.

- Since teachers' evaluations of poor and non–European American students can be prejudiced, the use of subjective portfolio assessment may lead to even more bias than results from objective standardized procedures.

Research indicates that educators can be trained to evaluate portfolios in a reliable manner (131). Anecdotal evidence suggests that portfolio assessment can produce useful assessment information about European American, non–European American, and limited English proficient students (130). However, there is little research evidence that decisions based on students' portfolios are more valid than those based on standardized, norm-referenced assessment procedures. Therefore, French's conclusion about the validity of portfolio assessment with limited English proficient students probably applies equally well to all students.

There appears to be great potential in the use of portfolio with LEP students. However, the value is yet to be determined. Experimentation, perhaps as much as ten years of it, will be needed. Thankfully, that experiment is underway. (129, p. 271)

Curriculum-Based Assessment

Curriculum-based assessment is a relatively new and not very widely used approach that evaluates students in terms of the curriculum to which they have and are being exposed (133–139). To use a curriculum-based evaluation approach, a school district or a similar entity establishes the contents and objectives of a particular curriculum (such as fifth-grade math, third-grade spelling, American History 2, or Spanish 3) and develops a series of probes—assessments that teachers and others can employ to determine how well students have achieved each of these objectives. Examples of typical probes include the number of words students read correctly in a reader or word list and the number of words spelled correctly from a spelling list in one or two minutes.

These probes can be used to compare students' achievement of the objectives of the curriculum to their peers' achievement on the same curriculum. By evaluating a student's achievement in many areas of the curriculum (i.e., reading, spelling, written language, and math computation), educators can obtain an estimate of the student's overall ability. The educators can then compare this estimate to students' achievement in a particular subject area to determine whether it is significantly below their general potential. Curriculum-based assessment can also be used to monitor students' progress in the curriculum and to determine whether students have achieved a particular goal.

Curriculum-based assessment offers some advantages over standardized tests.

- It avoids the problem of assessing students on tasks, skills, and knowledge that they have not been taught.
- It does not compare students to norms based on a national sample of students, many of whom attend schools that do not resemble theirs and live in other parts of the country.

- Since it can be administered informally as part of the regular classroom activities, it may make students less anxious and thereby provide a more accurate measure of their achievement.
- It can be used repeatedly with students, whereas standardized tests have to be administered sparingly because they usually do not come in many alternate forms.
- It is more sensitive to short-term improvement in student achievement and provides information that can be used to make day-to-day instructional decisions.

Curriculum-based assessment also has some disadvantages and limitations.

- It requires a standardized schoolwide or school district–wide curriculum.
- It focuses primarily on achievement of basic academic skills and objectives in reading, spelling, written language, and math computation.
- It can be very expensive to develop.
- Whereas standardized test publishers almost always provide information about their tests' reliability and validity, school systems that develop curriculum-based assessment procedures have to do this for themselves. In the absence of such information, educators cannot be confident that the assessment procedures accurately and reliably measure what they are supposed to measure.
- It does not provide information about the causes of students' lack of progress toward the attainment of curriculum objectives.
- The format is often too inflexible to be adapted to the needs of students from diverse socioeconomic, contextual, and cultural backgrounds.
- Few school districts have used this approach to evaluate limited English proficient students.
- Although students are typically compared to other students in their districts, some groups may be so small (e.g., migrant students and non–European American students) that they may actually be compared to students very unlike themselves. This can be reduced by selecting class, schoolwide or school district–wide norms, if they are available, depending on which would be more representative of students' backgrounds.
- If students are functioning below their potential in most areas of the academic curriculum, estimations based on their average level of achievement may underestimate their potential.
- The use of local norms may encourage low expectations for students if able students' goals are based on the average or typical scores of their peers or if the local norms are below the national average.

Given these advantages and limitations, curriculum-based assessment approaches appear to be a promising method of obtaining information about students. However, for the present at least, because the information it provides is limited to academic achievement, especially in basic skills areas and it does not necessarily provide information that is free from contextual, cultural linguistic, and gender bias, its current usefulness with poor, non–European American, and limited English proficient students has not yet lived up to its promise.

Test-Teach-Test

The test-teach-test approach, also called assisted assessment, reciprocal teaching, and dynamic assessment is an assessment method that is designed to evaluate students' learning potential by studying how they actually learn (140–143). As its name implies, the test-teach-test approach includes three steps. First, students' achievement or functioning is assessed. Then assessors attempt to remediate or improve the students' functioning or achievement. Finally, students are reevaluated in order to determine the extent of improvement that can be expected as well as how much and what kinds of additional help are required for a given amount/degree of improvement.

Traditional approaches are based on the assumption that students' learning potentials are reflected in what they have learned. These approaches measure what students know and can do and attribute more learning potential to students who know more of the information and can do more of the tasks included in the assessment procedure. The test-teach-test method, however, provides a direct measure of the extent to which students can learn if given additional help. It also reveals how much and what kinds of additional help students require to reach a specific goal or standard. It focuses on the trainability or educability of students' cognitive processes (learning ability).

Advantages claimed for the test-teach-test approach include the following (2, 140–143):

- It is a more valid measure of their learning potential than traditional measures of IQ because it studies students' learning.
- Since it evaluates new, not old, learning, unlike traditional approaches, it does not require assuming that all students have been equally exposed to the information and have had equal opportunity to practice the tasks on which they are being assessed.
- It provides information about students' strengths and weaknesses and responds to their weaknesses by providing the feedback, practice, and support students may need to learn.
- It is a normal component of classroom activities rather than a test and therefore is less threatening and anxiety provoking.
- It provides the initial guidance and modeling that students may require to learn.
- It teaches students the learning strategies they need to succeed and when and how to use them.

A number of concerns have been raised about the test-teach-test approach. Two are especially important:

- There is insufficient data to determine the validity and reliability of the data the approach produces.
- The method can produce biased data if assessors are not sufficiently knowledgeable about students to adapt the instructional techniques they use in the teaching phase of the approach to students' cultural, contextual, gender, and linguistic characteristics. When assessors use inappropriate instructional techniques they may incorrectly attribute the students' limited improvement to their "limited learning potential" rather than to the assessors' inappropriate teaching techniques.

Interpretation of Data

Assessors' interpretation of the data they collect by means of formal, standardized, norm-referenced assessment; informal, nonstandardized, criterion-referenced assessment; and test-teach-test assessment can be problematic. Standardized procedures make it difficult for assessors to determine why students obtain the scores they do. Unless they examine student's answers carefully and/or interview them, they cannot tell from students' scores alone if students were familiar with the procedure, if they lacked sufficient time to complete the procedure, whether they did not ask questions when they did not understand the directions, whether they would not guess when guessing was to their advantage, whether they were not motivated to perform their best, and so on.

Informal, nonstandardized, criterion-referenced assessment and test-teach-test assessment are also subject to assessor bias. As was noted earlier, many assessors are biased against non–European American and poor students. Those who are are not prejudiced may mistakenly interpret what they observe from their own cultural, contextual, and gender point of view. As Hilliard pointed out many years ago,

> A given style user will take the behavior of another style user and will not experience it as that behavior actually is, but will reinterpret that experience in terms of her own experiential views or her own experiential framework, thus frequently losing the essence of the experience of the person being observed. In some cases the assessor can comprehend the experiences of another style user only by actually "changing" that person's experience. (114, p. 44)

To avoid such bias, assessment results should be reported along with a description of the context in which they were obtained and any limitations due to the assessors' lack of knowledge or experience (144). This should include such contextual factors as students' familiarity with the material and format of the procedure, whether they were anxious or tense while they were being assessed, their motivation to perform well, whether they completed all parts and items of the procedure or were limited by time constraints, their reaction to the assessor, possible linguistic problems, and so on. Assessor limitations might include lack of fluency in the language spoken by students, inability to interpret the results obtained in terms of students' experiences, possible assessor bias, and so on.

Summary

Assessment procedures have not been very effective when used with non–European American, limited English proficient, and poor students. In recent years, considerable progress has been made toward the goal of nonbiased assessment. Assessors are becoming more sensitive to how students' contextual, cultural, linguistic, and gender characteristics can affect the assessment process. New, promising approaches to assessment—such as curriculum-based assessment, portfolio assessment, and test-teach-test—appear to offer the possibility of less biased data, although their validity has not yet been established.

There is still much need for improvement. The major sources of bias in the assessment process continue to include failure to adapt procedures to the contextual, cultural, linguistic, and gender differences among students; assessors' discriminatory practices against and lack of information about non–European American and poor students; inadequacies in assessment materials and procedures; and mistakes in the interpretation of the information obtained.

Activities

1. Describe yourself in terms of the student characteristics discussed in this chapter. Then ask a few of your peers whose backgrounds are unlike yours to do the same. Do you observe many similarities or differences among individuals from different backgrounds?

2. Most professors use one assessment approach with all students regardless of their background. A few professors offer students a choice between oral and written exams or between multiple choice and essay formats. Some professors provide students with as much time as they need to complete their exams; others typically require some of their students to rush through their exams or hand in incomplete work. Some professors are flexible about deadlines for completing work such as papers; others lower students' grades if their work is late or even refuse to accept it. A few professors use portfolio assessment, videotapes, and other innovative approaches to assess students. How have your professors evaluated you over the years? Which of them have used a multicultural approach to assess students? Which of them have employed the same approach with all students? Is there one particular format that you prefer? How often have your professors used it?

3. How would you like your achievement to be evaluated in the course in which you are using this text? Compare your preference to those of other students in the course. Are you basically in agreement or do many of you have different preferences?

References

Test anxiety is the focus of the following references.

1. Clawson, T. W., Firment, C. K., & Trower, T. L. (1981). Test anxiety: Another origin for racial bias in standardized testing. *Measurement and Evaluation in Guidance, 13*(4), 210–215.
2. Dao, M. (1991). Designing assessment procedures for educationally at-risk Southeast Asian–American students. *Journal of Learning Disabilities, 24*(10), 594–601.
3. Grossman, H. (1984). *Educating Hispanic Students: Cultural Implications for Instruction, Classroom Management, Counseling, and Assessment.* Springfield, IL: Charles C Thomas.
4. Hill, K. T. (1980). *Eliminating Motivational Causes of Test Bias. Final Report, October 1, 1976, through March 31, 1980.* ERIC ED 196–936.
5. Nguyen, K. T. (1984). *Assessing and Counseling Vietnamese Exceptional Students: Some Cultural Factors to Be Considered.* Santa Clara, CA: Santa Clara County Office of Education.
6. Payne, B. D. (1984). The relationship of test anxiety and answer-changing behavior: An analysis by race and sex. *Measurement and Evaluation in Guidance, 16*(4), 205–211.

The following references discuss students' familiarity with assessment procedures and the effects of training in test-wiseness on students' subsequent performance.

7. Bangert-Drowns, R. L., Kulik, R. L., & Kulik, C. C. (1983). Effects of coaching programs on achievement test scores. *Review of Educational Research, 53,* 571–585.
8. Benson, J., Urman, H., & Hocevar, D. (1986). Effects of test-wiseness training and ethnicity on achievement of third- and fifth-grade students. *Measurement and Evaluation in Counseling and Development, 18*(4), 154–162.

9. Brescia, W., & Fortune, J. C. (1988). *Standardized Testing of American Indian Students.* Las Cruces, NM: New Mexico State University. ERIC/CRESS.
10. Bridgeman, B., & Buttram, J. (1975). Race differences on nonverbal analogy test performance as a function of verbal strategy training. *Journal of Educational Psychology, 67*(4), 586–590.
11. Haladyna, T. M., Nolen, S. B., & Hass, N. S. (1991). Raising standard achievement scores and the origins of test score pollution. *Educational Researcher, 20*(5), 2–7.
12. Kalechstein, P., Kalechstein, M., & Doctre, R. (1981). The effects of instruction on test-taking skills in second-grade black children. *Measurement and Evaluation in Guidance, 13*(4), 198–202.
13. McPhail, I. P. (1985). Instructional strategies for teaching test-wiseness. In C. Brooks (Ed.), *Tapping Potential: English Language Arts for the Black Learner.* Urbana IL: National Council of Teachers of English.
14. Samson, G. E. (1985). Effects of training in test-taking skills on achievement test performance: A quantitative synthesis. *Journal of Educational Research, 78*(5), 266.
15. Sarnacki, R. E. (1979). An examination of test-wiseness in the cognitive test domain. *Review of Educational Research, 49,* 252–279.
16. Schubert, J., & Cropley, A. (1972). Verbal regulation of behavior and IQ in Canadian Indian and white children. *Developmental Psychology, 7,* 295–301.

The relationship between students' motivation and their functioning during assessment procedures is discussed in these references.

17. Burgess, B. J. (1978). Native American learning styles. In L. Morris, G. Sather, & S. Scull (Eds.), *Extracting Learning Styles from Social/ Cultural Diversity: A Study of Five American*

Minorities. Norman, OK: Southwest Teacher Corps Network.

18. Chamberlain, K. P., & Medinos-Landurand, P. (1991). Practical considerations for the assessment of LEP students with special needs. In E. V. Hamayan & J. S. Damico (Eds.), *Limiting Bias in the Assessment of Bilingual Students*. Austin, TX: PRO-ED.

19. Condon, E. C., Peters, J. Y., & Sueiro-Ross, C. (1979). *Special Education and the Hispanic Child: Cultural Perspectives*. Philadelphia: Temple University, Teacher Corps Mid-Atlantic Network.

20. Deyhle D. (1987). Learning failure: Tests as gatekeepers and the culturally different child. In H. E. Trueba (Ed.), *Success or Failure?* Rawley, MA: Newbury House.

21. Goldstein, B.L. (1988). In search of survival: The education and integration of Hmong refugee girls. *Journal of Ethnic Studies, 16*(2), 1–27.

22. Grossman, H. (1990). *Trouble Free Teaching: Solutions to Behavior Problems in the Classroom.* Mountain View, CA: Mayfield.

23. Lyons, G. (1979). A high school on an Indian reservation: A question of survival, developing goals, and giving leadership. *British Educational Administration Society, 7*, 130–138.

24. National Coalition of Advocates for Students. (1988). *New Voices: Immigrant Students in U.S. Public Schools*. Boston: Author.

25. Slogett, B. B. (1971). Use of group activities and team rewards to increase individual classroom productivity. *Teaching Exceptional Children, 3*(2), 54–66.

The effects of assessor characteristics on the outcome of assessment procedures is discussed in the following references.

26. Gantt, W. N., Wilson, R. M., & Dayton, C. M. (1974–1975). An initial investigation of the relationship between syntactical divergency and the listening comprehension of black children. *Reading Research Quarterly, 10*(2), 193–211.

27. Garcia, A. B., & Zimmerman, B. J. (1972). The effect of examiner ethnicity and language on the performance of bilingual Mexican-American first graders. *Journal of Social Psychology, 87*, 3–11.

28. Gay, G., & Abrahams, R. D. (1973). Does the pot melt, boil, or brew? Black children and white assessment procedures. *Journal of School Psychology, 11*(4), 330–340.

29. Gollnick, D., & Chinn, P. (1988). *Multicultural Education in a Pluralistic Society*. St. Louis: Mosby.

30. Mishra, S. P. (1980). The influence of examiners' ethnic attributes on intelligence test scores. *Psychology in the Schools, 17*(1), 117–121.

31. Ratusnik, D. L., & Koenigsknecht, R. A. (1977). Biracial testing: The question of clinicians' influence on children's test performance. *Language, Speech, and Hearing Services in Schools, 8*(3/4), 5–14.

32. Terrell, F., & Terrell, S. L. (1983). The relationship between race of examiner, cultural mistrust, and the intelligence test performance of black children. *Psychology in the Schools, 20*, 367–369.

33. Terrell, F., Terrell, J. L., & Taylor, J. (1981). Effects of type of reinforcement on the intelligence test performance of retarded black children. *Psychology in the Schools, 18*, 225–227.

These references deal with the relationship between communication style and assessment results.

34. California State Department of Education. (1987). *Handbook for Teaching Japanese-Speaking Students*. Sacramento, CA: Author.

35. Crago, M. (1988). *Cultural Context in Communicative Interaction of Inuit Children*. Unpublished doctoral dissertation. Montreal: McGill University.

36. National Council of La Raza. (1986). *Beyond Ellis Island: Hispanics—Immigrants and Americans*. Washington, DC. Author.

The influence of students' learning style on their functioning during the assessment process is the focus of the following references.

37. Almanza, H. P., & Mosley, W. J. (1980). Cultural adaptations and modifications for culturally diverse handicapped children. *Exceptional Children, 46*(8), 608–614.

38. Boykin, A. W. (1982). Task variability and the performance of black and white school children. *Journal of Black Studies, 12*(4), 469–485.

39. Longstreet, E. (1978). *Aspects of Ethnicity*. New York: Teachers College Press.

40. Shade, B. J. (1979). *Racial Preference in Psychological Differentiation: An Alternative Explanation for Group Differences*. ERIC ED 179–672.

41. Tharp, G. (1989). Psychocultural variables and constants: Effects on teaching and learn-

ing in schools. *American Psychologist, 44*(2), 349–359.

How the pace at which students work and play can affect the results of assessments is the focus of the following references.

42. Ayabe, H. I. (1978). Ethnic-culture, reflection impulsivity and locus of control. *Educational Perspectives, 17*(4), 10–12.

43. Gardner, W. E. (1977). A model for creating a more hospitable achievement test environment for black elementary students. *Negro Educational Review, 28*(3/4), 229–236.

44. Levine, R. V., West, L. J., & Reis, H. T. (1980). Perceptions of time and punctuality in the United States and Brazil. *Journal of Personality and Social Psychology, 38*(4), 541–550.

African American students' tendency to select extreme responses on Likert Scales is documented in these references.

45. Bachman, J. G., & O'Malley, P. M. (1984). Yea-saying, nay-saying and going to extremes: Are black-white differences in survey results due to response styles? *Public Opinion Quarterly, 48*, 409–427.

46. Bachman, J. G., & O'Malley, P. M. (1984). Black-white differences in self-esteem: Are they affected by response styles? *American Journal of Sociology, 90*(3), 624–639.

Content bias in assessment procedures is the focus of the next articles.

47. Bagby, S. A. (1981). *Educational Testing for Migrant Students.* Las Cruces, NM: ERIC Clearinghouse on Rural Education and Small Schools.

48. Baldwin, J. A., & Bell, Y. R. (1985). The African Self-Consciousness Scale: An Africentric personality questionnaire. *Western Journal of Black Studies, 9*(2), 61–68.

49. Clarizio, H. F. (1982). Intellectual assessment of Hispanic children. *Psychology in the Schools, 19*(6), 61–71.

50. Conroy, A. A. (1992). The testing of minority language students. *Journal of Educational Issues of Language Minority Students, 2*, 175–186.

51. Fagen, J. (1987). Golden Rule revisited: Introduction. *Educational Measurement: Issues and Practice, 6*(2), 5–8.

52. Good, R. H., III, & Salvia, J. (1988). Curriculum bias in published norm-referenced read-

ing tests: Demonstrable effects. *School Psychology Review, 17*(1), 51–60.

53. Hawley, L. , & Williams, R. L. (1981). Feeling-tone and card preference of black college students for the TCB and TAT. *Journal of Non-White Concerns, 10*(1), 45–48.

54. Jaeger, M. M. (1987). NCME opposition to proposed Golden Rule legislation. *Educational Measurement: Issues and Practice, 6*(2), 21–22.

55. Rooney, J. P. (1987). Golden Rule on "Golden Rule." *Educational Measurement: Issues and Practice, 6*(2), 9–12.

56. Terrell, F., & Taylor, J. (1978). The development of an inventory to measure certain aspects of black nationalist ideology. *Psychology, A Quarterly Journal of Human Behavior, 15*, 31–33.

57. Terrell, F., & Terrell, S. (1981). An inventory to measure cultural mistrust among blacks. *Western Journal of Black Studies, 5*(3), 180–185.

58. Weaver, V. (1981). Racial attribution, story length, and feeling-tone of young black males to TCB and TAT. *Journal of Non-White Concerns, 10*(1), 31–43.

59. Weiss, J. (1987). The Golden Rule bias reduction principle: A practical reform. *Educational Measurement: Issues and Practice, 6*(2), 23–25.

60. Williams, R. L., & Johnson, R. C. (1981). Progress in developing Afrocentric measuring instruments. *Journal of Non-White Concerns, 10*(1), 3–18.

Format bias is the focus of these references.

61. Llabre, M. M. (1988). *Test-Related Factors Affecting Test Performance of Hispanics.* Paper presented at the annual conference of the American Education Research Association, New Orleans.

62. Miller, V., Onotera, R. T., & Deinard, A. S. (1984). Denver Developmental Screening Test: Cultural variations in Southeast Asian children. *Journal of Pediatrics, 104*(3), 481–482.

The effects of linguistic bias is the focus of these references.

63. Bergan, J. R., & Marra, E. B. (1979). Variations in IQ testing and instruction and the letter learning and achievement of Anglo and bilingual Mexican-American children. *Journal of Educational Psychology, 71*(6), 819–826.

64. Levandowski, B. (1975). The difference in intelligence test scores of bilingual students on an English version of the intelligence test

as compared to a Spanish version of the test. *Illinois School Research, 11*(3), 47–51.

The following references deal with effective use of interpreters during the assessment process.

65. Del Green Associates. (1983). *A Review of Research Affecting Educational Programming for Bilingual Handicapped Students*. Final Report. ERIC ED 267–555.

66. Figueroa, R. A. (1989). Using interpreters in assessments. *Communique, 17*(7), 19.

67. Langdon, H. W. (1988). *Interpreters/Translators in the School Setting Module*. Sacramento: California State Department of Education.

68. Metz, I. B. (1991). Comments. In M. Anderson & P. F. Goldberg (Eds.), *Cultural Competence in Screening and Assessment: Implications for Services to Young Children with Special Needs Ages Birth Through Five*. Minneapolis: PACER Center.

69. National Clearinghouse for Bilingual Education. *Meet the Needs of Handicapped Language Minority Students and Their Families*. Washington, DC: National Clearinghouse for Bilingual Education.

The following researchers have not found bias when nonstandard dialect speakers are assessed in standard English.

70. Desberg, P., Marsh, G., Schneider, L. A., & Duncan-Rose, C. (1979). The effects of social dialect on auditory sound blending and word recognition. *Contemporary Educational Psychology, 4,* 14–144.

71. Frentz, T. S. (1971). Children's comprehension of standard and Negro nonstandard English sentences. *Speech Monographs, 38,* 10–16.

72. Hockman, C. H. (1973). Black dialect reading tests in the urban schools. *Reading Teacher, 26,* 581–583.

73. Nolen, P. (1972). Reading of non-standard dialect materials, a study at grades two and four. *Child Development, 43,* 1092–1097.

The references listed here describe bias resulting from assessing nonstandard dialect speakers with standard English procedures and how to avoid it.

74. Baratz, J. (1969). *Language and Cognitive Assessment of Negro Children: Assumptions and Research Needs*. Paper presented at the annual meeting of the American Speech and Hearing Association, Washington, DC.

75. Benmaman, V., & Schenck, S. J. (1986). *Language Variability: An Analysis of Language Variability and Its Influence upon Special Education Assessment*. ERIC ED 296–532.

76. Bliss, L. S., & Allen, D. V. (1981). Black English responses on selected language tests. *Journal of Communication Disorders, 14,* 225–233.

77. Bryen, D. N. (1976). Speech-sound discrimination ability on linguistically unbiased tests. *Exceptional Children, 42*(4), 195–201.

78. Burke, S. M., Pflaum, S. W., & Knafle, J. D. (1982). The influence of Black English on diagnosis of reading in learning disabled and normal readers. *Journal of Learning Disabilities, 15*(1), 19–22.

79. Byrd, M. L. , & Williams, H. S. (1981). *Language Attitudes and Black Dialect: An Assessment. (1) Language Attitudes in the Classroom. (2) A Reliable Measure of Language Attitude*. ERIC ED 213–062.

80. Cartledge, G., Stupay, D., & Kaczala, C. (1984). *Formal Language Assessment of Handicapped and Nonhandicapped Black Children*. ERIC ED 250–348.

81. Evans, J. S. (1972). Word-pair discrimination and imitation abilities of preschool Spanish-speaking children. *Journal of Learning Disabilities, 7*(9), 49–56.

82. Fisher, D., & Jablon, A. (1984). An observation of the phonology of black English speaking children. In Queens College Department of Communication Arts and Sciences. *Working Papers in Speech-Language Pathology and Audiology*. Flushing, Queens: City University of New York.

83. Harber, J. R. (1980). Issues in the assessment of language and reading disorders in learning disabled children. *Learning Disability Quarterly, 3*(4), 20–28.

84. Hemingway, B. L., Montague J. C., Jr., & Bradley, R. H. (1981). Preliminary data on revision of a sentence repetition test for language screening with black first grade children. *Language, Speech, and Hearing Services in Schools, 12,* 145–152.

85. Jensen, L. J. (1976). Dialect. In P. A. Allen (Ed.), *Findings of Research in Miscue Analyses: Classroom Implications*. Urbana, IL: National Council of Teachers of English.

86. Mackler, B., & Holman, D. (1976). Assessing, packaging, and delivery: Tests, testing, and race. *Young Children, 31*(5), 351–364.

87. Musselwhite, C. R. (1983). Pluralistic assessment in speech-language pathology: Use of dual norms in the placement process. *Language, Speech, and Hearing Services in Schools, 14*, 29–37.

88. Norris, M. K., Juarez, M. J., & Perkins, M. N. (1989). Adaptation of a screening test for bilingual and bidialectal populations. *Language, Speech, and Hearing Services in Schools, 20*(4), 381–390.

89. Ramstad, V. V., & Potter, R. E. (1974). Differences in vocabulary and syntax usage between Nez Perce Indian and white kindergarten children. *Journal of Learning Disabilities, 7*(8), 35–41.

90. Rivers, L. W. (1978). The influence of auditory-, visual-, and language-discrimination skills on the standardized test performance of Black children. *Journal of NonWhite Concerns, 6*(3), 134–140.

91. Ross, H. W. (1979). Wepman Test of Auditory Discrimination: What does it discriminate? *Journal of School Psychology, 17*(1), 47–54.

92. Seymour, H. N., & Seymour, C. M. (1977). A therapeutic model for communicative disorders among children who speak Black English vernacular. *Journal of Speech and Hearing Disorders, 42*, 238–246.

93. Thurmond, V. B. (1977). The effect of Black English on the reading test performance of high school students. *Journal of Educational Research, 70*(3), 160–163.

94. Vaughn-Cooke, F. B. (1980). Evaluation the language of black English speakers: Implications of the Ann Arbor decision. In M. F. Whileman (Ed.), *Reactions to Ann Arbor: Vernacular Black English and Education.* Arlington VA: Center for Applied Linguistics.

95. Wartella, A. B., & Williams, D. (1982). *Speech and Language Assessment of Black and Bilingual Children.* ERIC ED 218–914.

96. Weiner, F. D., Lewnay, L., & Erway, E. (1983). Measuring language competence of Black American English. *Journal of Speech and Hearing Disorders, 48*, 76–84.

97. Williams R. L., & Rivers, L. W. (1972). *The Use of Standard Versus Non-Standard English in the Administration of Group Tests to Black Children.* Paper presented at the annual meeting of the American Psychological Association, Honolulu.

The following references provide descriptions of expected differences that may occur in responses on some standardized tests given to speakers of nonstandard dialects.

98. Deyhle, D. (1985). Testing among Navajo and Anglo students: Another consideration of cultural bias. *Journal of Educational Equity and Leadership, 5*, 119–131.

99. Hunt, B. C. (1974–1975). Black dialect and third and fourth graders' performance on the Gray Oral Reading Test. *Reading Research Quarterly, 10*, 103–123.

The following references discuss gender bias in test items.

100. Brown, F. G. (1980). Sex bias in achievement test items: Do they have any effect on performance? *Teaching of Psychology, 7*(1), 24–26.

101. Doolittle, A. E. (1986). *Gender-Based Differential Item Performance in Mathematics Achievement Items.* ERIC ED 270–464.

102. Dwyer, C. A. (1979). The role of tests in producing sex-related differences. In M. A. Witting & A. C. Peterson (Eds.), *Sex-Related Differences in Cognitive Functioning: Developmental Issues.* New York: Academic Press.

103. Ekstrom, R. B., Lockheed, M. E., & Donlon, T. F. (1979). Sex differences and sex bias in test content. *Educational Horizons, 58*(1), 47–52.

104. Faggen-Steckler, J., McCarthy, K. A., & Tittle, C. K. (1974). A quantitative method for measuring sex "bias" in standardized tests. *Journal of Educational Measurement, 11*, 151–161.

105. Plake, B. S., Hoover, H. D., & Loyd, B. H. (1980). An investigation of the Iowa Test of Basic Skills for sex bias: A developmental look. *Psychology in the Schools, 17*(1), 47–52.

106. Tittle, C. K. (1974). Sex bias in educational measurement: Fact of fiction? *Measurement and Evaluation in Guidance, 6*, 219–226.

The differences between formal, standardized, norm-referenced assessment and informal, non-standardized, criterion-referenced assessment are discussed in these references.

107. Olion, L., & Gillis-Olion, M. (1984). Assessing culturally diverse exceptional children. *Early Childhood Development and Care, 15*, 203–232.

108. Plata, M. (1982). *Assessment, Placement, and Programming of Bilingual Exceptional Pupils: A Practical Approach.* Reston, VA: ERIC Clearinghouse on Handicapped and Gifted Children.

Examples of early criticism of standardized tests are found in the following references.

109. Bond, H. M. (1924). What the army "intelligence" tests measured. *Opportunity, 2,* 197–202.
110. Colvin, S. S., & Allen, R. D. (1923). Mental tests and linguistic ability. *Journal of Educational Psychology, 14*(1), 1–20.
111. Frazier, E. F. (1928). The mind of the American Negro. *Opportunity, 6,* 263–266.
112. Thompson, C. H. (1928). The educational achievement of Negro Children. *Annals of the American Academy of Political and Social Sciences, 140,* 193–205.

The disadvantages and limitations of standardized assessment procedures are discussed in the following references.

113. Executive Committee of the Council for Children with Behavior Disorders. (1989). Best assessment practices for students with behavioral disorders: Accommodation to cultural diversity and individual differences. *Behavior Disorders, 14*(4), 263–278.
114. Hilliard, A. G., III. (1976). *Alternatives to IQ Testing: An Approach to the Indentification of Gifted "Minority" Children.* ERIC ED 148–038.
115. Howe, H., & Edelman, M. (1985). *Barriers to Excellence: Our Children at Risk.* Boston: National Coalition of Advocates for Students.
116. Williams, R. L. (1974). A history of the Association of Black Psychologists: Early formation and development. *Journal of Black Psychology, 1*(1), 9–24.
117. Williams, R. L. (Guest Editor). (1975). *Testing of the Afro-American. Journal of Afro-American Issues, 3.* In R. L. Williams & H. Mitchell, (Eds.), *Whatever Happened to ABPSI's Moratorium on Testing: A 1968–1977 Reminder.* St. Louis: Washington University.

The point of view of authors and groups who favor the continued use of standardized assessment procedures is included in the following references.

118. Anrig, G. R. (1985). Educational standards, testing, and equity. *Phi Delta Kappan, 66*(9), 623–625.
119. Council of the American Psychological Association. (1976). Resolution on Standardized Testing. Washington, DC. In R. L. Williams & H. Mitchell (Eds.), *Whatever Happened to*

ABPSI's Moratorium on Testing: A 1968–1977 Reminder. St. Louis: Washington University.
120. Muir, S. P. (1984). IQ tests: Should they be used? *Social Education, 84,* 72–78.
121. Reynolds, C. R. (1983). Test bias: In god we trust; all others must have data. *Journal of Special Education, 17*(3), 241–260.
122. Reschly, D. J. (1981). Psychological testing and educational classification and placement. *American Psychologist, 36*(10), 1094–1102.

The following reference discusses the validity of pluralistic norms.

123. Oakland, T. (1983). Concurrent and predictive validity estimates for the WISC-R IQs and ELPs by racial-ethnic and SES groups. *School Psychology Review, 12*(1), 57–61.
124. Richardson, J. C. (1989). Pro IQ testing: We're not the bad guys. *Diagnostique, 14*(2), 136–146.
125. Tolor, A. (1978). Assessment myths and current fads: A rejoinder to a position paper on nonbiased assessment. *Psychology in the Schools, 15*(2), 205–209.
126. Wilen, D. K., & Sweeting, C. M. (1986). Assessment of limited English proficient Hispanic students. *School Psychology Review, 15*(1), 59–75.

References that describe informal assessment approaches are listed next.

127. Alessi, G. J., & Kaye, J. H. (1983). *Behavior Assessment for School Psychologists.* Kent, OH: National Association of School Psychologists.
128. Pelligrini, S., & Grossman, H. (1985). *Bilingual Home Inventory.* Sacramento: California State Department of Education, Office of Special Education.

Portfolio assessment is the focus of the following references.

129. French, R. L. (1992). Portfolio assessment and LEP students. In *Proceedings of the Second National Research Symposium on Limited English Proficient Student Issues: Focus on Evaluation and Measurement,* Vol. I. Washington, DC: U.S. Department of Education, Office of Bilingual Education and Minority Languages Affairs.
130. Heath, D. (1993). Using portfolio assessment with secondary LEP students yields cross-cultural advantages for all. *BEOutreach, 4*(1), 27.
131. Resnick, L. B., & Resnick, D. P. (1989). *Assessing the Thinking Curriculum: New Tools for*

Educational Reform. Unpublished manuscript. Pittsburgh: Learning Research and Development Center, University of Pittsburgh and Carnegie-Mellon University.

132. Walters, J. (1992). Application of multiple intelligence research in alternative assessment. In *Proceedings of the Second National Research Symposium on Limited English Proficient Student Issues: Focus on Evaluation and Measurement*, Vol. I. Washington, DC: U.S. Department of Education, Office of Bilingual Education and Minority Languages Affairs.

These references deal with curriculum-based assessment.

133. Howell, K. W., Fox, S. L., & Morehead, M. K. (1993). *Curriculum-Based Evaluation: Teaching and Decision Making*, (2nd. ed.). Pacific Grove, CA: Brooks/Cole.
134. Marston, D. (1988). Measuring academic progress on IEP's: A comparison of graphic approaches. *Exceptional Children, 55*(1), 38–44.
135. Marston, D., & Magnusson, D. (1988). Curriculum-based measurement: District level implementation. In J. Graden, J. Zins, & M. Curtis (Eds.), *Alternative Educational Delivery Systems: Enhancing Instructional Options for All Students.* Washington, DC: National Association of School Psychologists.
136. Ponti, C. R., Zins, J. E., & Graden, J. L. (1988). Implementing a consultation-based service delivery system to decrease referrals for special education: A case study of organizational considerations. *School Psychology Review, 17*(1), 89–100.
137. Shinn, M. R. (1988). Development of curriculum-based local norms for use in special education decision-making. *School Psychology Review, 17*(1), 61–80.
138. Shinn, M. R., & Hubbard, D. D. (1992). Curriculum-based measurement and problem-solving assessment: Basic procedures and outcomes. *Focus on Exceptional Children, 24*(5), 1–20.
139. Tindal, G. A., & Marston, D. B. (1990). *Classroom-Based Assessment.* Columbus, OH: Merrill.

The test-teach-test approach is the topic of the references that follow.

140. Brown, A. L., Campione, J. C., Webber, L. S., & McGilly, K. (1992). Interactive learning environments: A new look at assessment and instruction. In B. R. Gifford & M. C. O'Connor (Eds.), *Changing Assessments: Alternative Views of Aptitude, Achievement, and Instruction.* Boston: Kluwer Academic Publishers.
141. Brown, A. L., & Campione, J. C. (1987). Linking dynamic assessment with school achievement. In C. S. Lidz (Ed.), *Dynamic Assessment.* New York: Guilford Press.
142. Campione, J. C. (1989). Assisted assessment: A taxonomy of approaches and an outline of strengths and weaknesses. *Journal of Learning Disabilities, 22,* 151–165.
143. Feuerstein, R. (1979). *The Dynamic Assessment of Retarded Performers: The Learning Potential Assessment Device, Theory, Instruments, and Techniques.* Baltimore: University Park Press.

Interpretation bias is discussed in this reference.

144. Davis, J. D. (1986). *Proposals for Improving the NAEP Mathematics Assessment of Black Youth.* ERIC ED 279–674.

Chapter 10

Instruction in a Diverse Society

The goal of this chapter is to improve educators' ability to adapt their instructional methods to the ethnic, socioeconomic, and gender diversities among students. The chapter describes how students' relationship, cognitive, and motivational styles; time orientations; interests; degree of self-confidence; and comfort levels with certain educational activities differ. It also suggests how educators can accommodate their instructional techniques to these differences.

Relationship Style

How students have learned to relate to adults and their peers affects how they learn in school.

Participatory Versus Passive Learning

Some children are brought up to be active participants in the learning process. They are expected to ask questions of adults, discuss ideas, and so on. These students perceive educators as guides who lead and stimulate students' active learning. Other children are expected to be less active and more passive recipients of instruction and information. They tend to perceive teachers as fountains of information and students as passive learners. Active participatory learning has proven to be more effective than passive learning with most students, but all students are not equally prepared to function in such an environment. African American students prefer and learn more effectively in an interactive, participatory learning environment (1, 3). However, many Hispanic American, Asian American, and Pacific American students are expected to be passive learners. The following quotations describe the passive learning styles of Hispanic Americans and Southeast Asian Americans.

The Hispanic culture requires good students to be passive learners—to sit quietly at their desks, pay attention, learn what they are taught and speak only when they are called upon. Anglo educational methods often require students to be active students—to show initiative and leadership, to volunteer questions and answers, and to question the opinion of others. (2, p. 188)

Since they have been taught to learn by listening, watching (observing), and imitating, these students may have a difficult time adjusting to learning by active doing and discovering. . . . There is a lesser emphasis, as compared to the American school system, on critical thinking and judgmental questions. If a teacher were to ask a question on the relationship between two concepts, one might see Indochinese students searching through their notes or books for the answers, or they may display reluctance or discomfort. (4, p. 42)

In recent years, educators have begun stressing the value of active participatory learning. However, students who are not comfortable with this approach may require a great deal of direct instruction and supervision during self-directed activities until they become comfortable with a more active role. Meanwhile, some students may not fulfill their academic potential and their behavior may be incorrectly attributed to insecurity, shyness, or excessive passivity. The following quote describes how this applies to some Asian and Pacific American students.

The child does not volunteer to answer. He just sits and waits for his teacher to call upon him. So in the eyes of the American teacher, Asian children, as compared to American students, are dull, passive, unresponsive, and lack initiative. Most of the time, Asian children are ignored because of their absolute silence in class. (5, p. 11)

Aloof, Distant Versus Involved Personal Relations

Cultures differ in terms of the degree of personal involvement teachers are supposed to have with their students. In some cultures, educators' interest in and involvement with students are expected to be restricted to their functioning in school. In other cultures, educators are expected to be interested and involved with them as persons who are also students. In comparison to males, females prefer closer personal relationships with their teachers. As the following quotes indicate, Hispanic American and Native American students, among others, may learn more when their teachers show more interest in their out of school life.

While I was in school in Mexico I felt as if my teachers, the nuns, were my friends as well as my teachers. They asked about my family and my personal life. When I came here the teachers seemed very cold and aloof. It was very hard for me to adjust to the differences. (2, p. 46)

Village students tend to expect highly personalized, emotionally intense relationships. . . . with their teachers. . . . Village students consider it legitimate to expect a teacher to "care about" them as total persons, not as learners of a particular subject matter. (6, p. 312)

Dependent Versus Independent Learning

There are significant ethnic and gender differences in the extent to which students are trained to accomplish things on their own and to arrive at their own independent opinions and decisions, or are brought up to be dependent on the aid, support, opinions, and feedback of their parents and other adults. Compared to European American students, many, but not all, non–European American students, especially Hispanic Americans, Native Americans, Filipino Americans, and Southeast Asian Americans tend to be more interested in obtaining their teachers' direction and feedback (2, 9,12, 16).

> *Filipino children may be passive and may not show initiative, creativity, or independence. They may be reluctant, afraid, or slow to make decisions in the classroom. . . . To Filipino children, family approval is very important, and they usually rely on their parents to make decisions for them. (9, p. 34)*

In most cultures, females, especially young ones, are more adult-oriented than males. Females achieve more when adults are present than when they are absent (10). There is suggestive evidence that when they are young, their self-esteem is more dependent on feedback from others; males' self-esteem, however, may be more dependent on their ability to master their environment (8). European American females are also more likely to use learned helplessness when they are older as a way of influencing others (14). This is not true of African American females.

The genders are not equally susceptible to the influence of other people (7, 11, 13, 15, 17). Although some research indicates the contrary (15), girls are more likely than boys to modify their opinions and attitudes to conform to others and to copy what others model; boys tend to maintain their ideas and opinions despite what others may think or feel.

The reason why many females seek their teacher's feedback, learn more in their presence, and are more willing to modify their opinions to conform to those of others whereas males function independently is unclear. Some educators argue that females learn better in interpersonal situations whereas males learn better in impersonal ones; they believe females' learning is enhanced when they and their teachers are equally involved in the process of examining their experiences together; and they tend to evaluate the female style more favorably than the male style. Other educators attribute the difference to what they believe is female students' inability to function independently and feel that females need to develop independent learning skills.

Both learning styles have advantages and disadvantages. Some situations call for the ability to work independently and to maintain one's own opinions and attitudes in the face of opposition. Other situations require students to be able to work well with others and to modify their ideas and opinions when others have more experience, knowledge, and training. Students who cannot distinguish between these two situations and those who are too inflexible to adjust to others' opinions as the situation demands are at a distinct disadvantage. Thus, the most helpful approach educators can use may be to help all students learn to function in a bicultural manner.

Peer- Versus Adult-Oriented

In some cultures children look primarily to adults for guidance, support, and direction; children in other cultures, for example Hawaiian Americans, tend to learn from and are guided by other children and youth. Thus, research suggests that Hawaiian American students prefer to work with their peers in study groups rather than have teachers lecture to them and they learn more effectively in peer groups (18, 19).

Females are more adult-oriented; they seek the help, support and feedback of their teachers. Males are more responsive to feedback from their peers (20–23, 25). However, males who lack self-confidence in their abilities also require teacher feedback to perform well (24).

Educators would do well to consider these differences when they select students for such instructional activities as peer tutoring and decide how much teacher supervision to provide them.

Individualistic Versus Group-Oriented

Although no culture expects children to be completely individualistic or group-oriented, there are important cultural differences in the degree to which these relationship styles are emphasized. In some cultures, children are brought up to be relatively individualistic. Such children prefer to work alone. When they are assigned to groups, in comparison to more group-oriented students, they are likely to continue to work independently, neither soliciting nor offering assistance. Native American children are an example (18, 26). Although they may not be competitive with their peers, students who prefer to work alone may require considerable assistance before they can function well in cooperative learning environments.

Cognitive Style

All students do not perceive things the same way or use the same problem-solving techniques. The following are some of the most important cognitive style differences among students.

Reflective/Analytical Versus Impulsive/Spontaneous/Intuitive

Students differ in terms of how long they think about things before arriving at conclusions. Some children are brought up to analyze and reflect on questions and problems and to be sure they know the answer or solution before saying anything. Others respond more intuitively and spontaneously to the problems presented to them in terms of what occurs to them immediately.

Some people are rather anxious to insure that they gather all the information possible before being asked to respond and they have a need to be accurate. These individuals are considered to be reflective *while those individuals who respond immediately to what is presented without regard to the fact they may be erroneous are labeled as* impulsive *learners. (30, p. 17)*

Temperamental, ethnic, and gender factors help to determine which of these cognitive styles students use (29). Native Americans are an example of students who tend to look at all sides of an issue, examine their possible implications, and make sure they know the answer before they are ready to express their opinion (18).

Research conducted in the 1970s indicated that in comparison to males, females are better able to delay judgment until they have the information they need to begin a task. They are also able to wait for a more desirable reward or outcome rather than settle immediately for something less desirable (27, 28). More research is needed to determine whether this is still the case.

Students who are more reflective usually have an advantage over their more spontaneous peers. As a result, some educators who believe that all students should be reflective/analytical learners use techniques that have been recommended to modify the learning style of students with culturally determined impulsive, spontaneous, intuitive learning characteristics. This remains controversial.

In addition, some educators do not allow reflective students sufficient time to prepare their answer (wait time) before calling on someone else. This impedes students' learning and may lead teachers to conclude that they are unprepared or slow learners.

Global Perception Versus Analysis of Details

As noted in the previous chapter, global learners perceive things in a holistic manner. They perceive the whole of an event, idea, or image and the relationships between its parts simultaneously. They see everything as a part of the whole and use few discrete categories to notice differences among the parts. Analytic learners can easily divide the whole into subcategories based on differences. Global learners tend to do better in whole language approaches and sight vocabulary. Because analytic learners process individual parts sequentially and gradually build up to an understanding of the whole, a phonetic approach in which the parts of words are analyzed to obtain the meaning of the whole word is more to their liking. In comparison to European American students, African American, Asian and Pacific American, Hispanic American, and Native American students have a more global perceptual style (31–35).

The Native American sees little or no differentiation between religion and daily life, has little trouble with the anthropomorphism of inanimate objects, practices holistic medicine. . . . The Anglo, on the other hand, sees medicine as separate from nutrition and reading as separate from science or social studies or math. . . . The Anglo compartmentalizes by subject rather than seeing them all as a part of the relation to the person. (35, p. 24)

Afro-American people tend to prefer to respond to and with "gestalts" rather than to or with atomistic things. Enough particulars are tolerated to get a general sense of things. There is an impatience with unnecessary specifics. Sometimes it seems that the predominant pattern for mainstream America is the preoccupation with particulars along with a concomitant loss of a sense of the whole. (32, p. 38)

Unfortunately for global learners, the teaching style of many European American educators does not match their learning style.

Many a new topic in school is approached in an analytic, sequential manner. The topic is introduced a little bit at a time, in a carefully sequenced manner. Often the overall picture (global view) of a topic is not presented until the end of a teaching sequence. For many Native Indian children (and others) this approach would be much more effective if the overall purpose and the overall structure were described before the analytic sequence was begun. The term "advance organizers" has been used by some educators to describe this approach." (33, p. 26)

There is the belief that anything can be divided and subdivided into minute pieces and that these pieces add up to a whole. Therefore dancing and music can be taught by the numbers. Even art is sometimes taught this way. This is why some people never learn to dance. They are too busy counting and analyzing. (32, p. 38)

Aural, Visual, and Verbal Learners

Although all children without visual or auditory impairments learn both visually and aurally, there are significant culturally influenced differences among students. It is important to know whether students' cultures prepare people to be primarily aural or visual learners, or both, because this would influence whether particular students would learn more efficiently if material were presented orally or visually.

Do people learn visually by observing what transpires in their worlds or by reading about things? Are students better at remembering what they have seen or what they have read? Because of their life-styles, Native American students tend to be visual learners (33, 37, 39).

They scrutinize the face of adults; they recognize at great distances their family's livestock. They are alert to danger signs of changing weather or the approach of predatory animals. (37, p. 333)

Native Indian students frequently and effectively use coding with imagery to remember and understand words and concepts. That is, they use mental images to remember or understand, rather than using word association. This suggests that use of metaphors, images or symbols is more effective than dictionary-style definitions or synonyms in helping many Native Indian students learn difficult concepts. (33, p. 26)

On the other hand, many students, including African Americans, Hispanic Americans, Haitian Americans and Hmong Americans, tend to be aural learners (2, 29, 36, 38).

> *Haitians usually have a highly developed auditory ability as evidenced by the oral traditions and rote learning methods. When presented with flow charts and diagrams they may require additional assistance in attaching meaning to the visual presentation. (36, p. 33)*

The Hmong do not have a written language; therefore they have highly developed aural skills. "The Hmong are used to hearing long songs one or two times and then repeating them. Use of repetitive patterns and rhymes assists memorization" (38, p. 33).

Thus, it is extremely important to adapt instructional techniques to students' preferences for aural, visual, or verbal cognitive styles. At the very least, educators should employ a multisensory approach when they instruct a group of diverse learners.

Kinesthetic/Active/Energetic Learning Versus Calm, Inactive Verbal Learning

Students' ability to sit still for long periods of time is greatly influenced by their cultural background. Knowing whether youngsters are expected to sit in a quiet and controlled manner in most situations or are allowed to be active and noisy enables educators to use instructional techniques that both permit students a level of activity that approximates what they are accustomed to and provide them with ways to discharge their energy.

In general, in comparison to European Americans, African American students are more active and less able to adjust to the sedentary learning environments of American schools.

> *In many American schools and especially in inner city schools, children are expected to talk or to move about only when directed to do so by teachers. . . . Those children who talk and move about with or without teacher directions do not meet normative standards and expectations. . . . Euro-American children possess the movement repertoire that will satisfy the normative standards and expectations governing child behavior in elementary classrooms while the richer movement repertoire of Black children does not satisfy those normative standards. (40, p. 610)*

In comparison to females, males prefer learning that involves active manipulation to more sedentary learning environments (42). Because of these ethnic and gender differences, educators should know which of their students learn best by doing, manipulating, touching, and experiencing, and which prefer more sedentary approaches such as lectures, reading, written and oral explanations, and discussions of ideas.

Students also differ in terms of whether they function better in highly stimulating or more calm learning environments. African American and Hispanic American students are used to more stimulation than students typically experience in school. That may be why African American and Hispanic American students perform better and achieve more when the curriculum includes many different materials, makes frequent use of nonverbal instructional forms such as visual media or manipulative games, and allows more student autonomy than in classrooms that are teacher controlled, use a great deal of verbal learning, and involve limited use of different materials (44).

Numerous authors have suggested adapting the instruction techniques to African American and Hispanic American students' interest in music, singing, movement, and variety (41, 43). The following quote is an example of such suggestions.

> *Many African American children are exposed to high-energy, fast-paced home environments, where there is simultaneous variable stimulation (e.g., televisions and music playing simultaneously and people talking and moving in and about the home freely). Hence, low-energy, monolithic environments (as seen in many traditional school environments) are less stimulating. . . . Variety in instruction provides the spirit and enthusiasm for learning. When instructional strategies facilitate stimulus variety, using combinations of oral, print, and visual media, African-American students perform better. Instructional activities should include music, singing, and movement. (43, pp. 118–119)*

Nonverbal Cues

Students' sensitivity to nonverbal cues is influenced by their ethnic background and gender. As noted previously, African Americans, Asian and Pacific Americans, and Hispanic Americans tend to be more aware of and tuned into subtle nonverbal cues than European Americans. Females are also more sensitive than males to nonverbal cues (45, 46). Since people sometimes say things they do not mean and mean things they do not say, students who are sensitive to educators' nonverbal communication as well as their verbal communication may learn and understand more because they perceive more.

Trial and Error Versus "Watch Then Do"

In some cultures people tend to learn by trial and error. They observe, read about, or are told how something is done. Then they practice it under the supervision of a more knowledgeable and skilled individual. Learners are expected to make mistakes, because "practice makes perfect." In other cultures, individuals are expected to continue to watch how something is done as many times and for as long as necessary until they feel they can do it. Only when they are sure they can succeed do they demonstrate their ability to others.

Students who grow up in trial and error cultures can usually take in stride the mistakes they make in public when they volunteer answers or are called on.

Those who are accustomed to a "watch then do" approach have greater difficulty exposing themselves in public while they are learning from their mistakes. This is particularly true of Native American students (35, 47, 48).

> *Native Americans spend much more time watching and listening and less time talking than do Anglos. If they are interested in something they watch how it is done, they inspect the product, they watch the process, they may ask a quiet question or two. Then they may try it for themselves, often out of the public eye. They are their own evaluator to determine whether their effort was successful or needs improvement. When they feel comfortable, they will show what they have done to someone else, usually someone they trust. (35, p. 26)*
>
> *A reluctance to try too soon and the accompanying fear of being "shamed" if one does not succeed may account for the seemingly passive uninterested and unresponsive attitude of Indian students. (47, p. 28)*

Students who are uncomfortable with trial and error learning and exposing their errors to others may need educators to supervise them less and not pressure them to try things before they are ready to do so.

Argumentative/Forensic Instruction Versus Direct Instruction

Although all cultures use many different teaching techniques with children, only in some cultures do adults teach children by raising leading questions about their beliefs in order to guide them to a more correct or accurate understanding of things. In other cultures, children are accustomed to being told what is correct and unaccustomed to having their beliefs questioned critically.

> *Anglo education emphasizes verbal inquisitiveness, an argumentative discourse that is termed "forensics." In the Anglo-dominated school system, the child is encouraged, even pressured, both to ask and analyze questions . . . . There is consequently a built-in clash between the ethnic (Raza) home tradition and the Anglo school tradition of constant and formal questioning. The WASP "inquisition" would be highly hostile to the Mexican-American attitude of tolerance. (49, p. 64)*

As a result, educators may have to consider students' cognitive styles when deciding whether and how often to use instructional approaches that involve class discussions, debates, analysis of controversial topics, and the examination of students' opinions and beliefs.

Learning from Examples, Stories, and Morals Versus Direct Instruction

In some cultures (for example, Native American cultures), in addition to being told things directly, children are led to an understanding of life through the legends they learn, the morals of the stories they are told, and the examples they are shown. For them, direct instruction can be effectively supplemented by these more seemingly time-consuming instructional strategies.

Motivational Style

In some respects all students are similarly motivated. They would rather succeed than fail and learn to read than remain illiterate. However, because their cultural backgrounds help shape their perceptions about the value and role of education, they also have different motives.

Motivation to Succeed in School

Although students' desire to succeed in school is often influenced by a number of interrelated motivations, typically one or two reasons are paramount. Some students may desire to succeed academically, to go to college, to earn a lot of money, and to be successful materialistically; some strive to succeed in order to receive honor and prestige; and others may believe it is important to learn for its own sake.

Students' motivation to succeed in school is affected by ethnic, socioeconomic, and gender factors. As was noted in Chapter 3, some older African American and Hispanic American students, especially poor males, are motivated to avoid success in school or have lost their motivation to try to succeed (50–55). Many non-European and poor students are alienated, distrustful, angry, and disillusioned about the schools they attend and the teachers that instruct them because of the prejudice and discrimination they encounter. They believe that even if they do well in school, they will not obtain the same benefits that European American upper-class males receive from succeeding in school, particularly in the vocational area, and some of them are pressured by their peers not to conform or to do well in school because to do so is to act white.

For these reasons numerous African American and Hispanic American students, especially males, purposefully avoid academic success by cutting school and not studying. Many students who do achieve up to their potential hide their true motives by becoming disciplinary problems, acting the class clown, or keeping their efforts and accomplishments from their peers.

Although the evidence is somewhat inconsistent, it appears that many European American and Hispanic American females, particularly those from less affluent and poor backgrounds, have mixed feelings about and are uncomfortable with success in courses or occupations traditionally thought of as being in the male domain (57–61, 63). This applies to a lesser degree to African American females.

Research indicates that there are at least three reasons for this (56, 57, 61, 63). Some females are concerned that they may seem less feminine and be less popular with males if they outperform them in these areas. A second reason why some females are uncomfortable with success is that success provokes a conflict between their desires to achieve and their more traditional perception of the ideal female as less oriented to achievement and individualism than to collaboration and egalitarianism. In this vein, Tannen explains that

> *Appearing better than others is a violation of the girls' egalitarian ethic: People are supposed to stress their connection and similarity. . . . It is no wonder that girls fear rejection by their peers if they appear too successful and boys don't. Boys from the earliest age learn that they can get what they want—higher status—by displaying superiority. Girls learn that displaying superiority will not get them what they want—affiliation with their peers. For this they have to appear the same as, not better than their friends. (63, pp. 217–218)*

A third reason is the belief held by many non-European Americans including Hispanic Americans and Asian and Pacific Americans that a female's place is in the home (2, 38). For example, Lewis and colleagues explain that "There is also a suspicion among the Hmong regarding girls who are educated beyond the three or four years required for basic literacy and math skills. . . . The fear is that they will become like western women" (38, p. 32). There is also suggestive evidence that some males may be uncomfortable with success if they perceive success in school as a feminine characteristic (62).

Because of these gender, socioeconomic, and ethnic differences, educators should not assume that all of their students are equally motivated to succeed in school. They should be knowledgeable about each student's motivation and then decide how to handle each individual case. Although this may be a difficult task for secondary-level teachers who have many classes, this goal is more feasible for elementary-level teachers.

Learning on Demand Versus Learning What Is Relevant or Interesting

Are students prepared to spend equal time and energy learning whatever material is presented to them by teachers regardless of what they think and feel about the material? Or will their reactions to material depend on whether or not it interests them? All cultures require all children to learn many things whether they want to or not. However, some students, have been brought up in cultures in which they have considerable leeway to learn what is useful and interesting to them rather than what some others have decided they should learn. Other students are better prepared to study whatever teachers present to them. For example, Cortes believes that Hispanic American students whose parents are not well-educated are less willing to learn things that do not interest them.

> *Relevance is particularly important for students who do not come from families with high educational attainment. For students from families with examples of significant school achievement, education has built in relevance. They have role models . . . they are raised with the concept of a career. . . . Such a student is more likely to accept and play the educational game. (64, pp. 34–35)*

Other authors agree that Hispanic American students are less able to learn on demand.

> *Anecdotal evidence suggests that efficiency, automation and technology tend to be highly prized among Anglos, whereas humanistic concerns and open accep-tance of affective temperament take precedence among Chicanos. Given such variations in cultural concerns, it is not surprising that the tendency to learn liked materials more readily than disliked materials is more intensified among Chicanos than Anglos. (65, pp. 114–115)*
>
> *To the extent that response to demand could be called a learning style, the Hispanic population tends to demonstrate that tendency much less frequently than a middle-class, white group that is socialized almost from early childhood to produce on demand as is expected in school. (67, p. 19)*

Native American students have been described in the following way:

> *They prefer to learn information that is personally interesting to them; therefore, interest is a key factor in their learning. When these students are not interested in a subject, they do not control their attention and orient themselves to learning an uninteresting task. Rather, they allocate their attention to other ideas that are more personally interesting, thus appearing detached from the learning situa-tion. (68, p. 69)*

Some educators believe that students should attend to whatever their teach-ers present to them because their teachers know best. Other educators think that students should not be so compliant if what they are expected to learn is busy work that has no apparent relationship to their interests and goals or is not at their level. These educators tend to believe that teachers should not be quick to capitalize on students' willingness to learn whatever they are given. Instead they should use the feedback from their students to improve their instructional prac-tices.

Some students who are not ready to learn on demand may be willing to attend to material that does not interest them if teachers personally appeal to them to do so. For example, Kleinfeld reports that Native American students may be motivated to learn in order to please others and to avoid offending or hurting them. "Appealing to interpersonal values rather than purely academic values in a learning situation often motivates village students" (66, pp. 18–19).

Kleinfeld also points out that whereas Native American educators are com-fortable appealing to such motives, European American teachers who believe that students should be motivated to learn for intrinsic reasons may be reluctant to make the kinds of personal appeals that are necessary to motivate students. A Native American teacher responded to a Native American student as follows: "He just wouldn't attend speech class. Then I told him he was hurting the teacher's feelings because she thought he didn't like her. At that point he said he would go" (66, pp. 18–19). On the other hand a European American teacher reported, "He said he would study if I wanted him to. But I felt I should tell him that he should study it for himself not me" (66, pp. 18–19). Asian and Pacific American students may also respond to personal appeals: "Asian children are often found to be motivated extrinsically by their parents and relatives. They study hard because they want to please their parents and impress their relatives" (69, p. 84).

It is important to enhance the intrinsic motivation of students, especially if they have become discouraged because of the frustrations they experience in school. However, with some students it may be effective to temporarily use personal appeals to encourage students to engage in school work that will provide them with the successful experiences necessary to increase their intrinsic motivation.

Object- Versus People-Oriented Learners

All children in all cultures must learn many abstract concepts. However, some cultures deemphasize abstract learning and are more people-oriented. As a result, some students are interested in solving math problems about people rather than those that involve only numerical computations and studying human geography (how people live) rather than physical geography (rivers, topography, and so on), whereas other students may prefer more abstract, object-oriented curricular contents. In comparison to European Americans, Hispanic Americans, African Americans, and Native Americans are more people-oriented (2, 70, 71).

> In comparison to the Anglo culture, the Hispanic culture emphasizes people over ideas. . . . As a result some Hispanic students may relate better to a person-centered rather than thing- or idea-centered curriculum. (2, pp. 42–43)

> Research has suggested that white children are very object-oriented. That is, they have numerous opportunities to manipulate objects and discover properties and relationships. Consequently, this society's educational system is very object-oriented. Classrooms are filled with educational hardware and technology. . . . Research with black children, in contrast, has found them to be very people-oriented. Most black children grow up in large families where they have a great deal of human interaction. . . . When this cultural trait is acknowledged, the result will be more human interaction in the learning process. (71, pp. 19–20)

Cooperative, Competitive, and Individualistic Learners

Cultures differ in the degree to which they stress cooperation, competition, and individualism. Therefore, it is important to know whether particular students respond better to competitive, individualistic, or cooperative motivating techniques and learning environments. Nowadays educators are encouraged to use cooperative learning and peer tutoring with students, but some students are less receptive than others to these approaches.

There are many significant ethnic, socioeconomic, and gender differences in students' preferences for competitive or cooperative learning environments. As was noted in the previous chapter, some students, including African Americans, Asian and Pacific Americans, Filipino Americans, Hawaiian Americans, and Hispanic Americans, tend to be brought up to be cooperative, whereas other cultures typically encourage students to be more competitive and/or individualistic.

European American gifted, average, and low-ability females, particularly those from poor backgrounds, usually prefer cooperative learning environments and may learn better in certain kinds of cooperative situations. In group settings they are more oriented toward group rather than individualistic goals. European American males tend to respond better to competitive and individualistic situations whether they are high or low achievers. (21, 72–77, 79, 81, 82, 84, 85, 88, 89). These gender stereotypes do not apply to the same degree to Native American and Hispanic American males, who grow up in much less competitive environments (80, 83, 86, 87).

Ethnic groups also have different approaches to cooperation. In the European American culture, for example, when people are working cooperatively everyone is supposed to do her or his share. To carry one's load is a guiding principle. Because this is not true of all cultures, the difference can create problems for teachers. Jaramillo points out that a European American teacher

> *is likely to be personally irked if he finds that some child isn't doing his share when engaged in a group task. Latin cultures typically do not put such requirements on individuals when they are working as part of a group. A group member who does not happen to be working will not be offensive. Those members of the group who best qualify or are most interested in performing the task will probably take it upon themselves to do the bulk of the labor. It is generally understood that each individual has special talents, and he will contribute when these talents are called for. (78, p. 9)*

Some students are taught to be self reliant—to be individualistic and to rely only on themselves to accomplish their goals and deal with the challenges, difficulties, and problems they face. Other students are brought up to expect and count on the help and the cooperation of others and to reciprocate in kind. Individualistic students who prefer to work on their own may have difficulty adjusting to working in groups or committees, even though they are noncompetitive.

These ethnic and gender differences have important educational implications. Since some students learn more efficiently in cooperative learning environments whereas others learn more in competitive or individualistic settings, their achievement depends in part on whether their teacher's instructional style matches their own cooperative, competitive, or individualistic learning style. Educators should consider these ethnic differences when they select learning environments and reward systems for students.

Students who learn better in competitive or individualistic situations tend to have an advantage because these environments predominate (90). However, the positive results of cooperative learning on many students' achievement, attitudes, and interpersonal relationships has been demonstrated repeatedly (91–101). Typically, interethnic relationships improve and students learn more, get along better with their peers, and feel better about themselves, their peers, and school when they learn in cooperative environments.

However, research also indicates, that these results characterize only some, not all students. In general, females, African Americans, Hispanic Americans, and students who have a cooperative learning style tend to experience the greatest academic gains from cooperative learning (21, 102, 103). Students who prefer competitive learning environments do better under competitive situations. (104).

Research suggests that female students tend to achieve more in single-sex cooperative learning situations than in mixed-sex cooperative groups (105, 106). There are many possible reasons for this. Moody and Gifford believe one of the reasons for this is that females participate and lead less in mixed-gender groups. They suggest that

> *Females are forced to take leadership and responsibility in laboratory groups when working with only other females. . . . If increased female leadership and participation is desired, then grouping by gender can accomplish this objective. (106, p. 16, 17)*

Another reason why females are often the losers in mixed-sex groups is because although they tend to be the providers of assistance they are rejected by males when they ask for assistance. In addition, as was noted earlier, in mixed-sex cooperative groups females often revert to a pattern of not interacting with male students, allowing males to dominate them and viewing themselves as less helpful, less important, and less visible (107, 109, 112, 113, 114, 116, 118), and there is some evidence that they may behave more competitively than they otherwise do (115). Males may actually learn more and perform better than females in cooperative mixed-sex groups because they often ignore females, contribute most of the ideas, do most of the talking, and typically function as the group leaders (108, 109, 110, 117).

Peterson and Fennema point out other problems that can result in mixed-sex cooperative groups (111). They suggest that although girls' achievement may improve in cooperative learning groups, such groups may make girls even less independent, and that could further impair their already inadequate high-level thinking skills in courses such as mathematics. They are also concerned that cooperative activities may impede the higher-level mathematics achievement of independent, competitive boys.

In mixed groups, girls tend to be equally responsive to requests from and reinforcement by either sex. However, boys are responsive primarily to other males (119–122). Females are also less likely than males to participate in group discussions and to assume leadership positions (123–126).

Females can benefit from mixed-gender cooperative groups. They are more likely to do so when they have been given advanced training, so they can function as experts/leaders of the group, and they have had prior experience with the group task, so they are familiar with what is to be learned, and when educators prepare students to function in a more egalitarian manner.

The experiences of some African American students in mixed-ethnic cooperative groups may be similar to the negative experiences of many females (112, 127). Piel and Conwell claim that

> *White children and black children may not be getting the same experience from a cooperative learning experience. . . . If white children assume leadership roles and black children assume more subservient roles then the purpose for cooperative groups seems to be somewhat diminished. (112, p. 14)*

There is also some evidence that some African American students perform best when they cooperate with other African Americans and compete with European Americans (128).

Finally, there is suggestive evidence that whether or not students benefit from cooperative learning depends in part on their self-concepts (129). When students with high and low self-concepts work together, those with high self-concepts are less likely to function cooperatively, thereby thwarting the goals of the cooperative learning experiences.

Thus, educators should not assume that cooperative learning experiences will automatically benefit all students. Students, especially those who are likely to dominate others and those who tend to allow others to assume dominant positions, must be prepared for cooperative learning in order for all of the members of the group to reap the benefits associated with this approach.

Experts suggest that the following components are required for an effective cooperative learning experience. These steps should be considered as a list of characteristics of effective cooperative learning approaches rather than as steps to follow exactly as listed.

- Familiarize yourself with the variety of cooperative learning techniques available to teachers. The references in the bibliography are a good source of information.
- Inform students of the cooperative procedures they should follow and teach them how to follow them.
- Prepare all students, especially those that are accustomed to accepting subservient positions, to assume the expert/leadership role.
- Sensitize all students, especially male students and others who are prone to use group situations to dominate others, to the importance of allowing all students to take on all the roles available to group members.
- Determine your students' learning styles. Those who have a cooperative learning style may be ready to profit from such experiences. However, you may need to prepare those who tend to do better in competitive or independent learning situations to function better in more cooperative settings before they can profit from them.
- Monitor the groups closely to discourage the kinds of problems discussed earlier and intervene as quickly as possible when problems arise.

SELF-QUIZ: Selecting Students for Cooperative Learning Experiences

With which students do you think cooperative learning should be used? Do you think that cooperative learning should be used primarily with those who appear to favor this type of learning or with all students? Would you assign students to cooperative learning groups? If so, what criteria would you use to determine which students to assign to such groups? Would you allow students to choose their own learning environments?

Risk Taking

Will students choose tasks that are challenging and novel if these also involve risk of failure or rejection, or will they stick to those that are familiar? Will they be adventurous or play it safe? How sure do students have to be that they know the answer or that their opinion is correct before they will risk responding to their teacher's question?

With many exceptions, girls tend to react less positively than boys to difficult and challenging situations. They often are less persistent when faced with difficult tasks in school and are less likely to take risks (130–132), and they tend to expect to do less well and perform less adequately than boys following failure or the threat of failure (133, 134). European American students appear more willing to take risks than Asian and Pacific American students (135, 136).

These cultural inhibitions may make it difficult for some Asian and Pacific American students, other groups of non–European American students with similar inhibitions, and females to take risks or bounce back from failure. These cultural inhibitions may also make it difficult for some gifted and talented students from these backgrounds to capitalize on their gifts and talents in creative ways.

Time Orientation

Because time is a primary concern in the United States, it is easy to assume that all cultures have similar attitudes about time. However, this is not the case.

Present Versus Future Orientation

There are significant differences in the extent to which people sacrifice present satisfactions for future goals. Although all ethnic groups are concerned about and prepare for the future, some are more present- than future-oriented.

> *The time many Mexican Americans value most is the present. Finishing a conversation with an old friend may be more important than keeping an appointment with a doctor. Making plans for the future may be less important than living to the fullest at the moment in hand. Many Mexican Americans perceive the time-serving ways of the Anglo as a misappropriation of the present. . . . The entire system of American education revolves about a ritualistic adherence to the*

ticking of the clock. What is the Mexican American child's reaction to the rigid schedules and the incessant pressures to plan for the future? How does he view a reward system that is programmed to respond to him at six week intervals? (142, p. 641)

Pacific peoples have learned to focus on meeting present needs and expecting little change. Americans value change, are future oriented, and expect that objectives will be achieved as a result of hard work. (139, p. 264)

Other ethnic groups, such as European Americans and some Asian Americans, are more future-oriented. Because individuals differ in these respects, it is important to know whether students can work toward the accomplishment of long-term goals and rewards or are more responsive to short-term goals, immediate satisfaction, and immediate reinforcement. It is also important to ask whether students who have a tedious, boring, or irksome job to do will start it immediately, postpone it to a more convenient time, or wait until it's almost too late to complete it.

Punctuality

Do people keep to rigid schedules, or are beginning and ending times flexible? Is time measured exactly or approximately? When students arrive late to class or a meeting are they unmotivated or merely operating in a different time frame? How do people perceive lateness? In some cultures, when a person is late it reflects primarily on the late person, who is seen as irresponsible. In others, lateness is perceived as a statement about the late person's disrespectful attitude toward those who have been kept waiting.

Are students accustomed to starting tasks when they are supposed to, and completing them within a specified time period? If they are not, they will have problems functioning in American schools. African Americans, Hispanic Americans, and Native Americans, among others, have a much more flexible attitude about time and punctuality (141, 144).

On the whole, Anglo Americans perceive time as a precious commodity to be conserved and budgeted carefully. . . . Hispanic societies, on the other hand, tend to treat time in a casual manner, accommodating its passage to their needs, rather than letting themselves be controlled by it. . . . In school, all activities are segmented into a strict time schedule which orchestrates the entire class to perform the same tasks in exact unison. For the Hispanic student, this imposition of a rigid chronological regimentation brings unfamiliar confusion and confinement for, at home, he has always been master of his "time" and been allowed to exercise his individuality within the casual rhythm of family life. (140, p. 67)

Three Eskimo high school seniors given scholarships to a Washington university flunked out after their first semester. High school counselors who came to investigate the failure of such promising students found them cowering in their dormitory rooms and discovered they had been terrified by the ringing of bells and classes ending in such a flurry of activity and of the rush of students to other classes to be on time. No one in their village had owned a watch or clock; thus they were unprepared for the university situation. (137, p. 5)

Pace

As was noted in the previous chapter, students who are accustomed to working at a slower pace make more errors when instructed to work as fast as they can. Students accustomed to a faster pace continue to perform as well when they are told to work as fast as they can (138, 143).

Condon and colleagues point out that Hispanic American students have difficulty keeping to the fast pace set by many European American teachers.

The entire curriculum of the school is crowded into a tight schedule which features endless sequences of fast-moving and closely-timed activities, such as quizzes, tests and spelling bees. The emphasis placed on a "clock-watch" performance of assigned tasks becomes a haunting nightmare for any learner functioning at a slower tempo, as is the case for Hispanic children who have been brought up in a relaxed home atmosphere where minutes (sometimes hours or days) are not seen as critical factors. (140, p. 68)

Educators who reward students for the amount of work they accomplish—how many problems or pages they have done—rather than the quality of their work may unwittingly cause some of them to make mistakes. They may also give students the message that it is more important to complete something fast than to do it correctly.

Self-Confidence

Students' self-confidence about school success depend on their beliefs in their ability to learn and their ability to control their own lives (their locus of control). Males and females tend to differ in both of these respects. Ethnic and socioeconomic differences appear to be primarily in the area of students' beliefs about their abilities to control their lives.

Ability to Learn

Gender differences in students' self-confidence about school has been the subject of considerable research. Although it is not true of African Americans, in most ethnic groups females tend to be less self-confident than males about school, especially in situations that are in the "male domain" such as mathematics and science courses, in competitive situations, and when they lack objective information about how well they have done or can do in situations that involve mastery of tasks in the male domain (145–152). Females are not less self-confident than males in courses such as reading that are not perceived to be in the male domain and in situations that involve their perceived ability to develop friendly relationships with others, to be popular, to resolve conflicts with others, to break bad habits, to gain self-insight, and so on. There is little evidence that there also are gender differences in students' overall self-concepts and self-esteem (21).

As was noted in Chapter 3, students from different ethnic and socioeconomic backgrounds start school equally confident about their ability to learn. Unfortunately, after spending a number of years in school, many, but far from all, poor, African American, Hispanic American, and Native American students lose much of their self-confidence about school.

Locus of Control

Students differ in the extent to which they believe they are in control of and responsible for what happens to them in their lives in general and in school in particular. There is no consistent evidence that males and females differ in the extent to which they believe that they are in control of and responsible for what happens to them outside of school. The results of studies that have examined how students explain their school-related experiences as contrasted to experiences in their lives in general paint a different picture. Although a few researchers have found no gender differences, most studies indicate that males and females attribute their academic successes and failures to different factors. Researchers who have compared males' and females' beliefs about whether they or external factors have greater influence over their general school performance have found that in comparison to males, females, especially those with from poor backgrounds, are more likely to attribute their general academic performance to internal factors (153, 157, 165). In courses such as math and science that are thought to be in the male domain, females tend to attribute their poor performance to internal factors such as lack of ability and their success to external factors such as luck rather than effort or ability (154–156, 158, 160, 162, 163, 166). Males' attributions are different. They are more likely to attribute their failures to external factors and their success to internal factors across courses and subjects (159, 161–164).

There are significant ethnic differences in students' locus of control (140, 167–170). European American students are most likely to believe that they rather than external factors control what happens to them. Japanese and Chinese Americans follow close behind. Hispanic American students tend to have a more external locus of control (168). The following quotation compares the optimistic European American view embodied in the expression "If at first you don't succeed, try, try again." to the fatalism of Hispanic Americans, who do not have the same confidence in their ability to shape their lives.

> *This optimistic outlook on life is not shared by most Spanish speakers who have learned that one should not expect too much of life, and that it is best to dismiss the future with a fatalistic shrug of the shoulders—que sera, sera (what will be will be). (140, p. 63)*

As was noted in Chapter 3, African Americans and Native Americans do not assume that they can control many aspects of their lives because they are aware of their lack of power in an environment characterized by pervasive prejudice against them. Because of this, they are less optimistic that they can assure themselves a good life by their own efforts (167, 169).

> *White folks think that because they have a good day today every day has to be good. They can't take bad times. Black folks know better. They're happy for any good days that come their way because they know they can't have them all the time. (167)*

In general, research conducted primarily in the 1960s indicated that students with an internal locus of control tended to achieve more in school than those whose locus of control was external, because they tried harder to succeed and to improve when they did poorly (171–174). However, whether this principle applies to poor, African American, Native American, and Hispanic American students has been a matter of controversy. Some educators argue that because many of these students grow up in a racist and prejudiced environment, it may be self-destructive for them to believe that they are completely in control of their lives in spite of the racism and prejudice that surrounds them. Students who correctly understand when external factors beyond their control are to blame for their failures may strive to change them, but students who incorrectly blame themselves or hold themselves responsible for failure caused by unfairness, prejudice, and economic injustice may give up.

Sometimes students who are often the victims of prejudice and discrimination incorrectly blame these factors for problems they themselves cause. This can shield them from the self-criticism that is necessary for self-improvement. Thus, although it is important for students not to blame themselves for the problems others cause them, it is also important for them not to blame others for problems they cause themselves.

To date, there is insufficient research to determine the relationship between locus of control and school achievement for students who belong to groups that experience prejudice and discrimination.

Students who can attempt to accomplish things that involve the possibility of failure and can bounce back from the unavoidable failures that all students experience from time to time will do better over time than those who avoid possible failure and who are too discouraged by failure to try again. Students who avoid difficult and challenging situations deny themselves growth opportunities, and students who incorrectly attribute their poor performance to their imagined lack of ability are less likely to attempt to succeed the next time they face a similar challenge.

Self-Confidence Enhancement

Research indicates that dedicated teachers can improve their students' self-concepts and self-esteem when they make the effort to do so (175–181). The first step is to identify students who lack self-confidence. This can be done informally by observing students at work, at play, and during their interactions with others. You can also talk with them about what they think of themselves. Several validated formal assessment instruments are available for this purpose. The Piers-Harris Children's Self-Concept Scale (186) and the Self-Observation Scales (184) provide information about students' overall perceptions of themselves. Other instruments—such as the Perceived Competency Scale for Children (183), the Nowicki Strickland Locus of Control Scale for Children (185), and the Coopersmith Self-Esteem Inventory (182)—have a more narrow focus. Some of these instruments may be dated because they were developed in the late 1960s and early 1970s. In addition, as was noted in the previous chapter, they may not be culturally appropriate for some students. You may find a culture-specific instrument to be more valid for your purposes, especially if you are working with African American students.

Many suggestions have been offered to enhance students' self-confidence in their ability to learn and control their lives. The following techniques can be used to improve students' confidence in their ability to learn (21, 175–181).

- Good instructional techniques individualized to students, strengths and weaknesses are probably the most effective way to enhance students' self-confidence. Selecting work at their ability levels, organizing their assignments to ensure success, and providing support and information when they need it can help many students with poor self-concepts succeed despite their beliefs that they can't.
- You may be able to counteract students' pessimistic self-perceptions by helping them see the strengths and skills they bring to each task, by expressing your personal belief that they can succeed, and by explaining how their past experiences can be poor predictors of the present if they practice, study, and concentrate more and learn from their mistakes. Students can learn vicariously by reading books and seeing films about others who have had experiences like theirs. Exposing students who don't believe that they can succeed to stories of real-life people who have actually done so can be inspirational.
- If students see their accomplishments as inadequate because they judge themselves by culturally inappropriate standards, help them to be more accepting of themselves and their cultural styles
- Provide students with opportunities to succeed in areas where they feel adequate so that their positive feelings in one area will generalize to other areas.
- Encourage students to make positive rather than negative statements about themselves and reinforce them when they do so.

These approaches can help students believe that they have the power to achieve what they set out to accomplish.

- Demonstrate your trust and faith that they can be self-managing and self-motivating enough to attain the goals they determine for themselves with a minimum of external guidance.

- In keeping with their maturity level, allow students to choose among alternative learning activities, centers, manipulatives, and instructional materials and permit them to generate or develop some of the alternatives themselves within limits you set. This will enhance their perceptions that they, and not others, are responsible for what they do in class. This also gives them another opportunity to experience your faith in them.
- Provide dependent students with assistance only when they request it, and gradually wean them from needing your assistance.
- Ask students what they think about their own work rather than expressing your opinion. This demonstrates your faith that they can evaluate themselves
- Teach students who seek extrinsic rewards to reward themselves.

As has been noted throughout this text, students from certain ethnic groups are more likely to suffer experiences that attack their self-confidence. Thus, many, but certainly not all, of the students in these ethnic groups can profit from instructional techniques that are designed to counteract these harmful experiences. The following self-confidence–enhancing suggestions are representative of the techniques educators can use (187–193).

Pepper lists the following aspects that should be included in a self-concept enhancement program for Native American students.

> *Teach the true history of the American Indian and the value of Indian culture to all children. . . . Value and accept the Indian child as he is. . . . Use words that build the Indian child's self-esteem and feelings of adequacy. . . . Show faith in the Indian child so he can believe in himself. . . . Plan for experiences that are guaranteed to give success. (192, pp. 143–144)*

The following seven-step process has been shown to be effective with African American students (188).

- Students discuss people's dreams and aspirations and what might become of them.
- Students analyze their ability to make decisions and their power at home in their community and at school.
- Students identify their personal desires and dreams and the kind of person they would like to become.
- Students set a short-term goal.
- Students prepare a plan of action to meet the goal and identify the individuals and material resources available to them.
- Students' progress toward the achievement of the goal is monitored periodically.
- At the end of the period, students analyze their actions to understand why their goals were or were not met.

The many multicultural activities described in Chapter 4 can improve students' faith in their ability to learn and control their lives. As Wood points out, studying the history and contributions of non–European Americans increases students' self-confidence.

> *When students become aware of the worth of their own histories, they can come to value their own perceptions and insights. They will not have to rely upon the history of the dominant culture to validate their experiences and truths. Rather they can look to themselves as useful members of a cultural tradition that empowers them to speak with their own voices. This has indeed been the experience of minorities in this country as they have strived to recover a sense of their own worth within an understanding of their value to the culture at large. Teachers need to incorporate such a historical perspective within the curriculum for all children, so that this sense of self-worth will permeate their social actions. (193, p. 235)*

Interests

As was noted previously, some educators believe that schools cater to the interests of European Americans and offer non–European American students an irrelevant curriculum that contributes to their school-related problems. African American educators are particularly critical of the "Eurocentric" curriculum of American schools. To correct this, they suggest that teachers should include in the daily curriculum ethnocentric materials and content that deal with topics and themes that are relevant to other ethnic groups.

> *Most African-American children sit in classrooms, yet are outside the information being discussed. The white child sits in the middle of the information, whether it is literature, history, politics or art. The task of the Afrocentric curriculum is finding patterns in African-American history and culture that help the teacher place the child in the middle of the intellectual experience. This is not an idea to replace all things European, but to expand the dialogue to include African-American information. (194, p. 46)*

Other educators disagree. For example, former Secretary of Education William Bennet stated, "I think it will further alienate the poor who are already tenuously connected to American culture. . . . It's a mistake to think that these kids are going to get any more interested in schools by studying more about Africa" (195, p. 45).

Research is not very supportive of the latter position. Although children and youth share many interests in common, ethnic and gender groups do have somewhat different interests. For example, a study of the reading interests of African American and European American sixth-grade students found that the two books most preferred by African American students were the books least preferred by European American students. (200).

Chapter 4 and the references at the end of this chapter include many suggestions for making the curriculum more relevant to all students, not just European American males (194–201).

Acceptable and Unacceptable Learning Activities

Students differ not only in how they prefer to learn, but also in what they prefer to learn. For example, because of their religious or moral upbringing some students are unable to participate in various school activities. Jehovah's Witnesses do not allow their children to participate in holiday celebrations. Some Christian groups do not want their children to participate in discussions of morality. Hispanic females may be uncomfortable about participating in physical education activities that require them to wear shorts, and "Indian students may not feel comfortable participating in some activities required in biology and other science classes. Destruction of life for the sole purpose of examining an organism may not be tolerable" (202, p. 44).

Field-Sensitive and Field-Independent Learning and Behavior Characteristics

There is considerable evidence that some of the learning characteristics described earlier are interrelated. Researchers have identified two groups of learning characteristics, which have been labelled field-sensitive and field-independent. Research conducted in the 1970s indicates that some ethnic groups tend to be primarily field-sensitive (e.g., African Americans and Hispanic Americans) whereas others are predominantly field-independent (e.g., European Americans). Within most ethnic groups, females tend to be more field-sensitive than males.

No group or individual is completely field-independent or field-sensitive. An individual or an ethnic group may function in a predominantly field-sensitive or field-independent way, but aspects of the opposite styles also exist in their personalities. Some examples of characteristics that tend to belong to either the field-sensitive or field-independent personality type are (29)

- *Whether people rely more on internal clues such as their own feelings, ideas, values, and experiences to understand the world around them (field-independent) or on information from their surroundings (field-sensitive)*
- *Whether they prefer solitary activities, personal time, and more distant, aloof relationships (field-independent) or are sociable, gregarious, and interested in helping people (field-sensitive)*
- *Whether they work better individually (field-independent) or in groups (field-sensitive)*
- *Whether they are relatively indifferent to the feelings, ideas, opinions, attitudes, and so on, of others when they decide what to do or how to do it (field-independent) or are sensitive to and responsive to what others feel and think and consider how their actions may affect others (field-sensitive)*
- *Whether they prefer to maintain considerable physical distance when they talk with others (field-independent) or to be in close proximity to them (field-sensitive)*
- *Whether they are indifferent to praise and criticism from others (field-independent) or react intensely to being praised and criticized (field-sensitive)*

- *Whether they function better in competitive situations (field-independent) or under cooperative conditions (field-sensitive)*
- *Whether they prefer to work independently (field-independent) or seek feedback, guidance, and approval from others (field-sensitive)*
- *Whether they prefer abstract, theoretical tasks such as math computational problems (field-independent) or tasks that involve human issues and concerns such as math word problems (field-sensitive)*
- *Whether they respond better to impersonal rewards such as money, toys, candy, time off, and so on (field-independent) or personal rewards such as praise, smiles, pats on the back, and the like (field-sensitive)*

Avoiding Misleading Stereotypes

As noted in the preface and throughout this text, the learning characteristics discussed in this chapter do not apply to all members of a given ethnic or gender group. Whether people conform to a particular ethnic or gender stereotype depends on many different factors. Two of these factors, their socioeconomic background and their acculturation, are discussed next.

Socioeconomic Effects

In the United States, middle-class students are less likely to conform to traditional gender stereotypes. As a result of research that was conducted primarily in the 1970s, we now realize that ethnic stereotypes also do not apply equally to all socioeconomic classes (203–211). In the United States, ethnic differences between African Americans or Hispanic Americans and European Americans are greatest among poor individuals and smallest among middle- and upper-class individuals. This may be because members of these groups may have to reject their ethnic background and assimilate to the European American middle-class culture in order to succeed in a European American middle-class–dominated society. There is also suggestive evidence that socioeconomic class does not play as important a role among some other ethnic groups—for instance, Jewish Americans, Chinese Americans, and Japanese Americans. The cause of this may possibly be that it is less necessary for them to deny their cultural heritages in order to enter the middle class.

It is often difficult to determine whether ethnicity or socioeconomic class is more influential in a particular situation. Thus, Havighurst asks,

> *A given person is a middle-class black, or a working-class black. Is he more accurately described by his social class or by his ethnicity? Another person is an upper-working-class Pole or an upper-middle-class Pole. Which takes precedence for him, his ethnicity or his social class? (206, pp. 56–57)*

Because ethnic and socioeconomic factors interact to influence ethnic and gender traits, numerous educators attribute some of the learning characteristics of many non–European American students described in this text to socioeconomic, not ethnic, factors. They claim that in the United States there is a vast difference between the child-rearing practices, learning styles, behavior styles, standard of living, experiences, access to the many advantages offered to most citizens, and so on, of the poor and of the middle and upper classes. They believe that because African American, Native American, and Hispanic American students are more likely than European American students to come from poor backgrounds, many of the differences some people attribute to ethnicity are actually the result of contextual factors associated with socioeconomic class.

Unfortunately, few researchers have studied socioeconomic differences within the many ethnic groups in the United States. Given the lack of research in this area, it is presently impossible to state with any degree of accuracy which, if any, of the learning characteristics attributed in this chapter to an ethnic group in general or to a particular gender within that ethnic group are actually restricted to a particular socioeconomic class within that group. Perhaps the most reasonable conclusion at this time is that educators should not assume that any particular learning trait is equally characteristic of all socioeconomic classes within a particular ethnic group.

Acculturation Effects

Poor and non–European American students have at least four options for resolving the cultural conflicts they experience when their learning and behavior characteristics do not meet the expectations of the middle-class European American–oriented schools (212, 213). They can maintain the values, beliefs, and practices of their cultural heritage and reject the mainstream culture (traditional/cultural resistance). They can reject their heritage culture and adopt the mainstream culture (assimilation/cultural shift). They can identify with and accept both cultural systems and select which one is more appropriate for a given situation (bicultural/cultural incorporation). They can combine and alter both their original cultural norms and the alternate ones to create a new unique set of norms (cultural transmutation).

Many non–European American students have maintained most aspects of their culture including their learning and behavior characteristics, which are different then those expected by school personnel. The learning and behavior characteristics of others who have lost or given up a great deal of their traditional culture parallel those of European American middle-class students. Some are bicultural, and some are functioning in a way that represents, at least to some degree, cultural transmutation.

The pace at which individuals assimilate to a different culture, the type of acculturation they choose, and the areas in which they manifest these different types of acculturation depend on many factors. Some of these factors are their age at immigration, their gender, their level of education, whether they are immigrants or refugees, the number of generations their family has been living in the other culture, their previous intercultural experience, the length of time they have been exposed to the other culture, the degree to which they interact with members of the other culture, their ability to speak the language of the other culture, the amount of compatibility between the two cultures, their attitudes about the other culture, the relationship between members of the original and the other cultures, the amount of support they have within their original cultural group, the ethnic make up of their neighborhood, and the types and degree of pressure and encouragement they experience to maintain their original culture or to assimilate (213, 215, 217–220, 224, 227, 229, 231).

Assessing Learning Characteristics and Acculturation

For the many reasons just cited, one cannot understand students' learning characteristics on the basis of their names, ethnic backgrounds, or skin shade. It is necessary to understand each student as a unique individual, rather than stereotypically. To do so, educators can assess the learning styles of all students, regardless of their gender and ethnic background, and the degree and type of acculturation of non-European and poor students.

Learning Characteristics

Students' learning characteristics can be evaluated informally. The various characteristics discussed in this chapter can serve as checklists or guides for observing how they learn. Educators can also choose from a wide selection of formal assessment procedures for evaluating students' learning characteristics (233–237). Some are designed for students in general (e.g., the Learning Style Inventory [234, 237]); others are aimed at non–European American students in particular (e.g., the Ramirez and Castaneda Behavior Rating Scales [212]).

The regular and primary versions of the Learning Style Inventory involve students in the assessment process by having them state whether or not various statements apply to them. Following are some sample items from the instrument.

> The things I remember best are the things I hear.
> Noise usually keeps me from concentrating.
> I like to be given choices of how I can do things.
> I like to be told exactly what to do.

The Ramirez and Castenada Behavior Rating Scale is designed to evaluate whether students are field-sensitive or field-independent learners. Although the instrument was designed for use with Hispanic American students, it can be useful to evaluate students from other ethnic groups. It is also a useful tool to examine some gender stereotypes, because many, but certainly not all, females prefer a field-sensitive learning style, whereas males tend to be more field-independent.

The scale also has items to evaluate whether teachers employ field-sensitive or field-independent instructional styles. By using both the teaching style and learning characteristics sections of this instrument, teachers can determine

The Ramirez and Castenada Behavior Rating Scale

Field-Sensitive	Field-Independent
Student	
Likes to work with others to achieve a common goal	Prefers to work independently
Seeks guidance and demonstration from teacher	Likes to try new tasks without teacher's help
Is sensitive to feelings and opinions of others	Is task oriented; is inattentive to social environments when working
Teacher	
Encourages cooperation and development of group feeling; encourages class to think and work as a unit	Encourages competition between individual students
Humanizes curriculum; attributes human characteristics to concepts and principles	Relies on graphs, charts, and formulas
Is sensitive to children who are having difficulty and need help	Encourages independent student achievement; emphasizes individual effort

whether their teaching style matches a particular student's learning characteristics and so accommodate their teaching to her or his needs. The table shows examples of items in the students' and teachers' versions.

Acculturation

As was noted in the previous chapter, it takes immigrant students who have spent the first four, five, or more years of their lives somewhere else a number of years to assimilate to a significant degree to the way things are done in the United States, even if they and their parents want to learn the new ways as quickly as possible. Thus, if immigrant students have not been here at least for a few years, you can assume that their classroom functioning will be affected by many of the cultural factors the students or their parents brought with them. The same principle would apply to many other students who have to adjust to unfamiliar school environments, including Native American students, rural students, and students who attend schools that serve children and youth from a different socioeconomic class.

Students' cumulative folders should include the information you need to determine how long they have been in this country, whether they attended school prior to coming here, and if so, the kind of school experiences they had. You can also obtain some information about Native American or rural students from their cumulative folder. However, you may have to rely on the students themselves, their parents, and sometimes agencies that are working with the students for most of the information you need.

Additional information can be obtained in the following ways.

1. *Observe the students' behavior.* Answer the following questions about students' behavior.

1. Do students socialize only with students from their same ethnic or social backgrounds, only with European American students, or with all types of students?
2. What language do bilingual students prefer to use when they are not in class (at lunch, recess, after school): English only, their native language, or a mixture of both?
3. Do students dress like typical European American students or in ways that identify them as members of a different group?
4. What do the statements students make about the European American culture and the culture of their homes reflect about their cultural identity? Do they express pride in their ethnic or racial background or reject it? Do they comment positively or negatively about the European American culture?
5. Do students' reactions to national and ethnic holidays indicate a bicultural identity or a preference for one type of holiday over the other?

2. *Consult with colleagues.* Ask colleagues (other teachers, paraprofessionals, and so on) who are knowledgeable about students' cultures to observe them and tell you whether they think their actions indicate they are traditional, assimilated, or bicultural.

3. *Interview the student.* Ask students if any of the classroom procedures, routines, rules, or social patterns are difficult for them to follow or conflict with how they are used to doing things at home. Inquire about whether they ever feel pressured in school to behave in ways that make them uncomfortable because they behave differently at home or in their neighborhoods. Determine whether students listen to and watch music, radio, movies, and television programs in their native language, English, or both languages. Listen to how students describe themselves. Do they say that they are Mexican, Vietnamese, Russian and so on; Mexican American, Vietnamese American, Russian American, and so on; or just American?

There are numerous formal assessment instruments for evaluating students' acculturation (214, 216, 217, 222–226, 228, 230). These instruments study the extent to which students are involved in their original and the European American cultures by requiring them to respond to a series of questions about their friendships both in and out of school, the activities they engage in, their recreational habits, the language or languages they speak, their attitudes and values, how they identify themselves, and so on. Typical items include: "What is the ethnic origin of your friends—exclusively Hispanic, Vietnamese, Chinese Americans; mostly Hispanic, Vietnamese, Chinese Americans; both Hispanic, Vietnamese, Chinese Americans and European Americans; mostly European Americans; exclusively European American? How do you call yourself—Hispanic, Vietnamese, Chinese;

SELF-QUIZ: Informal Assessment

1. Compare the following three Korean American teenagers in terms of their level of acculturation to the United States along the traditional, bicultural, assimilated continuum.
2. Would you use different instructional strategies with each student because of their different types of acculturation? If so, how would you teach them differently?

Jae came to the United States when he was going on 10 years old. He has been here for five years. He speaks both Korean and English with friends and also at home. He reads English and Korean newspapers and magazines, watches Korean and English TV, eats European American and Korean food, and admires both Americans and Koreans. He belongs to some American groups but goes to a Korean church. His friends speak many languages, but most of them are English speaking. His closest friend is a Vietnamese American immigrant.

Jae does not want to lose his ability to speak Korean. He deplores the fact that there are no Korean books for his age group to read. Responding to a question about how he identifies himself, he stated,

I'm Korean. . . because I'm from Korea. . . . My brains, you know are washed up by Korean culture. Then I speak Korean. Even though I work with American Kids, I still don't forget I'm Korean and I look forward to getting along more with Korean people. And when I get a job, I'll look Korean even though I'll have citizenship because I don't have white skin. They'll still be prejudiced a little bit that I'm Oriental. They're not going to look at me as American. . . . So I'm Korean. (232, p. 13)

Mi Cha has been in the United States for seven years, since she was 9. She considers herself Korean American. Her friends speak English and Korean, but she spends most of her time with a group of Korean teenagers who belong to a Korean church. She describes herself in the following way.

I can't really speak good English. I can speak fluently in Korean but I don't know about deep words, you know. So I'm in the middle. Half English and half Korean. I know I'm Korean. I'm more into Korea than America. That's why I hang around a lot with Korean people who are older than me. They teach me a lot in Korean and I really learn a lot of Korean there. I will probably live my whole life here, probably learn American as I grow. But if you don't join Korean people you don't learn.

I would marry a Korean guy. . . . I think we could get along better. . . . American people think differently than Korean people. . . . I'm not going to be over men. It's better if they're over me. But they'll not rule me where I have to do every little thing like that. . . I want an equal chance but I could serve him. It will be easier for me. (232, p. 13)

Danny has been in the United States for 11 or 12 years, since he was 5 or 6 years old. Danny does not remember anything about Korea. He does not know much about Korea and would like to learn more. However, he does not appear to be too interested in visiting his native land. He speaks both languages fluently, but he prefers to speak English because he is embarrassed by the mistakes he makes in Korean. He cannot read Korean. He would like to learn, but does not have the time. Although he identifies himself as Korean American, he feels more American than Korean.

He dates both Korean and European American girls. His best friend is European American. He only knows a few Korean friends, and they all speak English. He says that the new Korean kids in school have their own friends. He would like to help them, but he is too busy with football practice and other things.

His mother cooks Korean food at home. Although he claims to like Korean foods, he does not eat much spicy Korean food any more.

(Adapted from (232), with permission.)

Hispanic, Vietnamese, Chinese American; American? What kind of music do you prefer to listen to—Hispanic, Vietnamese, Chinese, American?"

Some instruments also include questions about students' parents such as their citizenship, the languages they speak, the kind of jobs they work at, the amount of education they have completed, and the number of children they have had, because assimilated and nonassimilated families tend to differ along these lines. One instrument is based on a series of questions designed to determine whether the persons being assessed consider themselves to be "insiders" or "outsiders" in relation to the dominant culture (222).

The students' answers are then compared to a sample group of students from similar backgrounds, enabling educators to determine the extent to which students have remained traditional, assimilated, or become bicultural, whether they identify with one or both cultures, and whether they are growing up in an assimilated or a traditional home.

Until recently, most experts viewed acculturation as a process of change along a continuum from unassimilated to highly assimilated (215–217, 221, 223, 225, 227, 228, 230). Therefore, most instruments indicate students' overall level or type of acculturation along this continuum—the extent to which they are traditional, assimilated, or bicultural. Because these instruments yield a score that indicates students' general level of acculturation, they can easily be misinterpreted. We now realize that students and others do not assimilate at the same pace in all areas of their lives. Thus, an overall score can underestimate the extent of their assimilation in one area and overestimate their adaptation in another. As Mendoza and Martinez state,

> Some cultural traits tend to be assimilated more rapidly than others. Language usage, dress customs, and technological necessities, for instance, are generally incorporated much faster than abstract or less tangible qualities that involve values, sentiments, esthetic preferences, or attitudes on various socialization practices. (224, p. 73)

Despite the limitation of the instruments currently available, the information they provide can serve as a starting point for continued examination of how students deal with cultural incompatibilities. Most of these instruments currently available assess Hispanic Americans. However, they can be adapted, and translated if necessary, for use with other ethnic and language groups.

These formal and informal procedures will provide you with a place to begin; they will give you a general understanding of the degree to which students are acculturated; and they will help alert you to the possible existence of cultural differences. However, they do not provide the information needed to determine whether students are characterized by a particular cultural trait—information that is necessary to enable you to consider individual students' cultural characteristics when you choose educational approaches to use with them. To do this requires more detailed information about the way individual students function in school.

Summary

There are significant gender and ethnic differences in students' relationship, cognitive, and motivational styles; time orientations; interests; degree of self-confidence; and comfort level with certain educational activities. When educators adapt their instructional approaches to these learning characteristics, students learn more efficiently.

These learning characteristics do not apply to all members of a given ethnic or gender group. Students' socioeconomic background and level of acculturation help to determine whether particular students will conform to a particular ethnic or gender stereotype. In order to understand each student as a unique individual, educators can assess their learning characteristics and the degree and type of their acculturation to European American middle-class–oriented schools.

Activities

1. Ask some students from different cultural backgrounds in the courses you are taking or some friends to describe their learning style preferences. You can interview them informally or prepare an informal questionnaire. Do you notice any of the cultural differences reported in this chapter?

2. Using the list of learning characteristics included in this chapter as a guide, prepare descriptions of the traits that you believe are characteristic of male and female students. Then ask a few of your friends or fellow students to review your list and tell you which traits they do and do not accept as being characteristic of their group.

3. Interview some individuals from an ethnic group that interests you and prepare a description of the educationally relevant cultural characteristics of the group as they perceive them.

4. Use the Ramirez and Castaneda Behavior Rating Scale to compare the learning characteristics of some of your male and female professors. Do you observe any of the gender differences reported in the literature?

References

The following references discuss participatory and passive learning.

1. Gersten, R., & Keating, T. (1987). Long-term benefits from direct instruction. *Educational Leadership, 44,* 28–31.
2. Grossman, H. (1984). *Educating Hispanic Students: Cultural Implications for Instruction, Classroom Management, Counseling, and Assessment.* Springfield, IL: Charles C Thomas.
3. Grossman, H. (1994). *Special Education in a Diverse Society.* Needham, MA: Allyn and Bacon.
4. Kang-Ning, C. (1981). Education for Chinese and Indochinese. *Theory into Practice, 20*(1), 35–44.
5. Wong, M. K. (1978). Traditional Chinese culture and behavior patterns of Chinese students in American classrooms. In *Second*

Annual Forum on Transcultural Adaptation (Proceedings): Asian Students in American Classrooms. Chicago: Illinois Office of Education.

Ethnic differences in whether students prefer aloof and distant or involved and personal relations with teachers are included in this reference.

6. Kleinfeld, J. (1975). Effective Teachers of Indian and Eskimo High School Students. *School Review, 83*(2), 301–344.

Ethnic and gender variability in students' preferences for dependent or independent learning is the focus of these references.

7. Becker, B. J. (1986). Influence again: An examination of reviews and studies of gender differences in social influence. In J. S. Hyde & M. C. Linn (Eds.), *The Psychology of Gender.* Baltimore: The Johns Hopkins University Press.
8. Brutsaert, H. (1990). Changing sources of self-esteem among girls and boys in secondary school. *Urban Education, 24*(40), 432–439.
9. California State Department of Education. (1986). *Handbook for Teaching Pilipino-Speaking Students.* Sacramento: Author.
10. Caplan, P. (1979). Beyond the box score: A boundary condition for sex differences in aggression and achievement striving. In B. Maher (Ed.), *Progress in Experimental Personality Research,* Vol. 9. New York: Academic Press.
11. Cooper, H. M. (1979). Statistically combining independent studies: A meta-analysis of sex differences in conformity research. *Journal of Personality and Social Psychology, 37,* 131–146.
12. Dao, M. (1987). *From Vietnamese to Vietnamese American.* San Jose: San Jose State University.
13. Eagly, A. H., & Carli, L. L. (1981). Sex of researchers and sex-typed communications as determinants of sex differences in influenceability: A meta-analysis of social influence studies. *Psychological Bulletin, 90,* 1–20.
14. Parsons, J. E. (1982). Sex differences in attributions and learned helplessness. *Sex Roles, 8*(4), 421–432.
15. Van Hecke, M., Tracy, R. J., Cotter, S., & Ribordy, S. C. (1984). Approval versus achievement motives in seventh-grade girls. *Sex Roles, 11*(1), 33–41.
16. Wauters, J. L., Bruce, K. M., Black, D. R., & Hocker, P. N. (1989). Learning styles: A study of Alaskan Native and non-Native students.

Journal of American Indian Education, Special Issue, August, 53–62.
17. Wulatin, M. L., & Tracy, R. J. (1977). *Sex Differences in Children's Responses to Achievement and Approval.* Paper presented at the meeting of the Midwestern Psychological Association, Chicago.

Factors that influence whether students are peer oriented or adult oriented are discussed in the following references.

18. Tharp, R. G. (1989). Psychocultural variables and constants: Effects on teaching and learning in schools. *American Psychologist, 44*(2), 349–359.
19. Tharp, R. G., & Gallimore, R. (1988). *Rousing Minds to Life: Teaching, Learning and Schooling in Social Context.* Cambridge, England: Cambridge University Press.

Gender differences in seeking teacher help, support, and feedback are the focus of the following reference.

20. Eiszler, C. F. (1982). *Perceptual Preference as an Aspect of Adolescent Learning Styles.* ERIC ED 224–769.
21. Grossman, H., & Grossman, S. (1994). *Gender Issues in Education.* Needham, MA: Allyn and Bacon.
22. Henry, S. E., Medway, F. J., & Scarbro, H. A. (1979). Sex and locus of control as determinants of children's responses to peer versus adult praise. *Journal of Educational Psychology, 71*(5), 604–612.
23. Nelson-LeGall, S., & Glor-Scheib, S. (1983). *Help-Seeking in Elementary Classrooms: An Observational Study.* ERIC ED 230–286.
24. Stewart, M. J., & Corbin, C. B. (1988). Feedback dependence among low confidence preadolescent boys and girls. *Research Quarterly for Exercise and Sport, 59*(2), 160–164.
25. Sullivan, H. J. (1986). Factors that influence continuing motivation. *Journal of Educational Research, 80*(2), 86–92.

This reference explores student differences in individualistic or group orientation.

26. Barnhardt, C. (1982). Tuning-in: Athabaskan teachers and Athabaskan students. In R. Barnhardt (Ed.), *Cross-Cultural Issues in Alaskan Education,* Vol. 2. ERIC ED 232–814.

Factors that contribute to differences among students in terms of reflective/analytical versus impulsive/spontaneous/intuitive cognitive styles are discussed in these references.

27. Farkas, G., Grobe, R. P., Sheenan, D., & Shuan, Y. (1990). Cultural resources and school success: Gender, ethnicity, and poverty groups within an urban school district. *American Sociological Review, 55,* 127–142.
28. Forslund, M. A., & Hull, R. E. (1974). Teacher sex and achievement among elementary school pupils. *Education, 95,* 87–89.
29. Grossman, H. (1990). *Trouble Free Teaching: Solutions to Behavior Problems in the Classroom.* Mountain View, CA: Mayfield.
30. Shade, B. J. (1979). *Racial Preference in Psychological Differentiation: An Alternative Explanation for Group Differences.* ERIC ED 179–672.

Ethnic contributions to students' preferences for global perception or analysis of details is the subject of the following references.

31. Chan, D. M. (1986). Curriculum development for limited English proficient exceptional Chinese children. *Rural Special Education Quarterly, 8*(1), 26–31.
32. Hilliard, A. (1976). *Alternatives to I. Q. Testing: An Approach to the Identification of Gifted Minority Children.* Sacramento: Final Report to the California State Department of Education.
33. More, A. J. (1987). Native Indian learning styles: A review for researchers and teachers. *Journal of American Indian Education, 27*(1), 17–29.
34. More, A. J. (1989). Native Indian learning styles: A review for researchers and teachers. *Journal of American Indian Education,* Special Issue, August, 15–28.
35. Rhodes, R. W. (1988). Holistic/teaching learning for Native American students. *Journal of American Indian Education, 27*(2), 21–29.

The effects of ethnic background on students' preferences for aural, visual, or verbal learning situations are discussed in these references.

36. Hallman, C. L., Etienne, M. R., & Fradd, S. (1982). *Haitian Value Orientations.* Monograph Number 2. ERIC ED 269–532.
37. John, B. (1972). Styles of learning—styles of teaching: Reflections of the education of Navajo children. In D. Cazden, V. John, & D. Hymes (Eds.), *Functions of Language in the Classroom.* New York: Teachers College Press.
38. Lewis, J., Vang, L., & Cheng, L. L. (1989). Identifying the language-learning difficul-
ties of Hmong students: Implications of context and culture. *Topics in Language Disorders, 9*(3), 21–37.
39. Swisher, K., & Deyhle, D. (1989). The styles of learning are different, but the teaching is just the same: Suggestions for teachers of American Indian youth. *Journal of American Indian Education,* Special Issue, August, 1–14.

Kinesthetic/active, energetic, stimulating learning environments and calm, inactive verbal learning environments are contrasted in the references below.

40. Almanza, H. P., & Mosley, W. J. (1980). Cultural adaptations and modifications for culturally diverse handicapped children. *Exceptional Children, 46*(8), 608–614.
41. Boykin, A. W. (1984). Reading achievement and the social-cultural frame of reference of Afro-American children. *Journal of Negro Education, 53*(4), 464–473.
42. Eiszler, C. F. (1982). *Perceptual Preference as an Aspect of Adolescent Learning Styles.* ERIC ED 224–769.
43. Franklin, M. E. (1992). Culturally sensitive instructional practices for African-American learners with disabilities. *Exceptional Children, 59*(2), 115–122.
44. Simpson, C. (1981). Classroom organization and the gap between minority and nonminority student performance levels. *Educational Research Quarterly, 6*(3), 43–53.

The following studies indicate that females are more sensitive to nonverbal cues.

45. Hall, J. C. (1978). Gender effects in decoding nonverbal cues. *Psychological Bulletin, 85,* 845–857.
46. Rosenthal, R., Hall, J. A., DiMatteo, M. R., Rogers, P. L., & Archer, D. C. (1979). *Sensitivity to Non-Verbal Communication.* Baltimore: The Johns Hopkins University Press.

These references are concerned with trial and error learning.

47. Longstreet, E. (1978). *Aspects of Ethnicity.* New York: Teachers College Press.
48. Rhodes, R. W. (1990). Measurement of Navajo and Hopi brain dominance and learning styles. *Journal of American Indian Education, 29*(2), 29–40.

Argumentative/forensic instruction versus direct instruction is the focus of the following reference.

49. Burger, H. G. (1972). Ethno-lematics: Evoking "shy" Spanish-American pupils by cross-cultural mediation. *Adolescence, 6*(25), 61–76.

Ethnic and gender variations in students' motivation to succeed in school is the focus of these references.

50. Comer, J. P. (1990). What makes the new generation tick? *Ebony, 45*(10), 34, 37, 38.
51. Ford, D. Y. (1991). *Self-Perceptions of Social, Psychological, and Cultural Determinants of Achievement Among Gifted Black Students: A Paradox of Underachievement.* Unpublished doctoral dissertation, Cleveland State University, Ohio.
52. Ford, D. Y. (1992). The American achievement ideology and achievement differentials among preadolescent gifted and nongifted African American males and females. *Journal of Negro Education, 61*(1), 45–64.
53. Fordham, S. (1988). Racelessness as a strategy in Black students' school success: Coping with the burden of "acting White." *Urban Review, 18,* 176–207.
54. MacLeod, J. (1987). *Ain't No Makin' It: Leveled Aspirations in a Low-Income Neighborhood.* Boulder, CO: Westview.
55. Ogbu, J. U. (1990). Minority education in comparative perspective. *Journal of Negro Education, 59,* 45–57.

References that deal with gender differences in motivation to avoid success are listed next.

56. Crovitz, E. (1980). A decade later. Black-white attitudes toward women's familial roles. *Psychology of Women Quarterly, 5*(2), 170–176.
57. Fleming, J. (1978). Fear of success, achievement related motives and behavior in Black college women. *Journal of Personality, 46,* 694–716.
58. George, V. D. (1981). *Occupational Aspirations of Talented Black Adolescent Females.* ERIC ED 206–976.
59. George, V. D. (1986). Talented adolescent women and the motivation to avoid success. *Journal of Multicultural Counseling and Development, 14*(3), 132–139.
60. McCorquodale, P. (1983). *Social Influences on the Participation of Mexican American Women in Science* (N.I.E. Final Report 6–79–011). Tucson: University of Arizona.

61. Roberts, L. R. (1986). *Gender Differences in Patterns of Achievement and Adjustment During Early Adolescence.* ERIC ED 288–134.
62. Stockard, J., Schmuck, P. A., Kemper, K., Williams, P., Edson, S. K., & Smith, M. A. (1980). *Sex Equity in Education.* New York: Academic Press.
63. Tannen, D. (1990). *You Just Don't Understand.* New York: William Morrow.

These references describe ethnic group differences in students' willingness to learn on demand.

64. Cortes, C. E. (1978). Chicano culture, experience and learning. In L. Morris, G. Sather, & S. Scull (Eds.), *Extracting Learning Styles from Social/Cultural Diversity: A Study of Five American Minorities.* Norman, OK: Southwest Teacher Corps Network.
65. Garza, R. T. (1978). Affective and associative qualities in the learning styles of Chicanos and Anglos. *Psychology in the Schools, 15*(1), 111–115.
66. Kleinfeld, J. (1975). *Effective Teachers of Indian and Eskimo Students.* Fairbanks: Institute of Social, Economic, and Government Research, University of Alaska.
67. Rabiannski-Carriuolo, N. (1989). Learning styles: An interview with Edmund W. Gordon. *Journal of Developmental Education, 13*(1), 18–20, 22.
68. Walker, B. J., Dodd, J., & Bigelow, R. (1989). Learning preferences of capable American Indians of two tribes. *Journal of American Indian Education, Special Issue,* August, 63–71.
69. Yao, E. L. (1987). Asian-immigrants students—Unique problems that hamper learning. *NASSP Bulletin, 71*(503), 82–88.

These references argue that Native American and African American students are less object-oriented and more people-oriented learners.

70. Burgess, B. J. (1978). Native American learning styles. In L. Morris, G. Sather, & S. Scull (Eds.), *Extracting Learning Styles from Social/Cultural Diversity: A Study of Five American Minorities.* Norman, OK: Southwest Teacher Corps Network.
71. Hale, J. (1978). Cultural influences on learning styles of Afro-American children. In L. Morris, G. Sather, & S. Scull (Eds.), *Extracting Learning Styles from Social/Cultural Diversity: A Study of Five American Minorities.* Norman, OK: Southwest Teacher Corps Network.

The references listed here focus on ethnic and gender differences in preferences for competitive, cooperative, and individualistic learning environments.

72. Allen, J. L., O'Mara, J., & Long, K. M. (1987). *The Effects of Communication Avoidance, Learning Styles and Gender upon Classroom Achievement.* ERIC ED 291–111.
73. Alvino, J. (1991). An investigation into the needs of gifted boys. *Roeper Review*, 13(4), 174–180.
74. Dalton, D. W., Hannafin, M. J., & Hooper, S. (1989). Effects of individual and cooperative computer assisted instruction on student performance and attitudes. *Educational Technology Research and Development*, 37(2), 15–34.
75. Englehard, G., Jr., & Monsas, J. A. (1989). Performance, gender and the cooperative attitudes of third, fifth, and seventh graders. *Journal of Research and Development in Education*, 22(2), 13–17.
76. Fennema, E. H., & Peterson, P. L. (1985). Autonomous learning behavior: A possible explanation of gender-related differences in mathematics. In L. C. Wilkinson & C. B. Marrett (Eds.), *Gender Influences in Classroom Interaction.* New York: Academic Press.
77. Harpole, S. H. (1987). *The Relationship of Gender and Learning Styles to Achievement and Laboratory Skills in Secondary School Chemistry Students.* ERIC ED 288–728.
78. Jaramillo, M. L. (1973). *Cautions When Working with the Culturally Different Child.* ERIC ED 115–622.
79. Kagan, S., & Madsen, M. C. (1972). Rivalry in Anglo-American and Mexican children of two ages. *Journal of Personality and Social Psychology*, 24, 214–220.
80. Kagan, S., Zahn, G. L., & Gealy, J. (1977). Competition and school achievement among Anglo-American and Mexican-American children. *Journal of Educational Psychology*, 69(4), 432–441.
81. Lewis, M. A., & Cooney, J. B. (1986). *Attributional and Performance Effects of Competitive and Individualistic Feedback in Computer Assisted Mathematics Instruction.* ERIC ED 271–287.
82. Lockheed, M. E., Harris, A. M., & Nemceff, W. P. (1983). Sex and social influence: Does sex function as a status characteristic in mixed-sex groups of children? *Journal of Educational Psychology*, 75, 877–888.
83. McClintock, C. (1974). Development of social motives in Anglo-American and Mexican children. *Journal of Personality and Social Psychology*, 29, 348–354.
84. Moely, B. E., Skarin, K., & Weil, S. (1979). Sex differences in competition-cooperation behavior of children at two age levels. *Sex Roles*, 5(31), 329–342.
85. Peterson, P., & Fennema, E. (1985). Effective teaching, student engagement in classroom activities, and sex-related differences in learning mathematics. *American Educational Research Journal*, 22(3), 309–334.
86. Strube, M. J. (1981). Meta-analysis and cross-cultural comparison: Sex differences in child competitiveness. *Journal of Cross-Cultural Psychology*, 12(1), 3–20.
87. Swisher, K. (1990). Cooperative learning and the education of American Indian/Alaskan Native students: A review of the literature and suggestions for implementation. *Journal of American Indian Education*, 29(2), 36–43.
88. Webb, N. M., & Kenderski, C. M. (1985). Gender differences in small-group interaction and achievement in high- and low-achieving classes. In L. C. Wilkinson & C. B. Marrett (Eds.), *Gender Influences in Classroom Interaction.* New York: Academic Press.
89. Wilkinson, L. C., Lindow, J., & Chiang, C. P. (1985). Sex differences and sex segregation in students' small-group communication. In L. C. Wilkinson & C. B. Marrett (Eds.), *Gender Influences in Classroom Interaction.* New York: Academic Press.

The following reference documents the fact that competitive learning environments predominate in American schools.

90. Johnson, D. W., & Johnson, R. T. (1987). *Learning Together and Alone: Cooperation, Competition and Individualization,* (2nd ed.). Englewood Cliffs, NJ: Prentice Hall.

These references document the positive effects of cooperative learning.

91. Aronson, E., Blaney, N., Sikes, J., & Snapp, M. (1978). *The Jigsaw Classroom.* Beverly Hills: Sage.
92. Asher, C. (1986). Cooperative learning in the urban classroom. *ERIC Digest, 30.*
93. DeVries, D. K., Edwards, K. J., & Slavin, R. (1978). Biracial learning teams and race relations in the classroom: Four field experiences using Teams-Games-Tournaments. *Journal of Educational Psychology*, 70, 356–362.

94. DeVries, D. K., & Slavin, R. E. (1978). Teams-Games-Tournaments: A research review. *Journal of Research and Development in Education*, *12*, 28–38.

95. Humphreys, B., Johnson, R. T., & Johnson, D. W. (1982). Effects of cooperative, competitive and individualistic learning on students' achievement in science class. *Journal of Research in Science Teaching*, *19*(5), 351–356.

96. Johnson, R. T., & Johnson, D. W. (1981). Effects of cooperative and individualistic learning experiences on interethnic interaction. *Journal of Educational Psychology*, *73*, 444–449.

97. Johnson, D. W., Johnson, R. T., Holubec, E. J., & Roy, P. (1984). *Circles of Learning*. Alexandria, VA: Association for Supervision and Curriculum Development.

98. Johnson, R. T., Johnson, D. W., Scott, L. E., & Ramolae, B. A. (1985). Effects of single-sex and mixed-sex cooperative interaction on science achievement and attitudes and cross-handicap and cross-sex relationships. *Journal of Research in Science Teaching*, *22*(3), 207–220.

99. Johnson, D. W., Maruyama, G., Johnson, R., Nelson, D., & Skon, L. (1981). Effects of cooperative, competitive, and individualistic goal structures on achievement: A meta analysis. *Psychological Bulletin*, *89*, 47–62.

100. Schofield, J. W. (1982). *Black and White in School: Trust, Tension, and Tolerance*. New York: Praeger.

101. Slavin, R. E., & Oickle, E. (1981). Effects of cooperative learning teams on student achievement and race relations: Treatment by race interactions. *Sociology of Education*, *54*, 174–180.

The selective benefits of cooperative learning are described in these references.

102. Calderon, M. E., Tinajero, J. V., & Hertz-Lazarowitz, R. (1992). Adapting cooperative integrated reading and composition to meet the needs of bilingual students. *Journal of Educational Issues of Language Minority Students*. Special Issue, *10*, 79–106.

103. Glassman, P. (1988). *A Study of Cooperative Learning in Mathematics, Writing and Reading as Implemented in Third, Fourth and Fifth Grade Classes: A Focus upon Achievement, Attitudes and Self-Esteem for Males, Females, Blacks, Hispanics and Anglos*. ERIC ED 292–926.

104. Knight, G. P., Nelson, W., Kagan, S., & Gumbiner, J. (1982). Cooperative-competitive social orientation and school achievement among Anglo-American and Mexican-American children. *Contemporary Educational Psychology*, *7*, 97–106.

The positive effects of single-sex cooperative groups on females is discussed in these references.

105. Kahle, J. B., & Lakes, M. K. (1983). The myth of equality in science classrooms. *Journal of Research in Science Teaching*, *20*, 131–140.

106. Moody, J. D., & Gifford, V. D. (1990). *The Effect of Grouping by Formal Reasoning Ability, Formal Reasoning Ability Levels, Group Size, and Gender on Achievement in Laboratory Chemistry*. ERIC ED 326–443.

Documentation of the effects of mixed-sex groups on students is found in the following references.

107. Chalesworth, W. R., & LaFrenier, P. (1983). Dominance, friendship utilization and resource utilization in preschool children's groups. *Ethology and Sociobiology*, *4*, 175–186.

108. DeVries, D. K., & Edwards, K. J. (1974). Student teams and learning games: Their effects on cross-race and cross-sex interaction. *Journal of Educational Psychology*, *66*(5), 741–749.

109. Lockheed, M. E., & Harris, A. M. (1984). Cross-sex collaborative learning in elementary classrooms. *American Educational Research Journal*, *21*(2), 275–294.

110. Lockheed, M. E., Harris, A. M., & Nemceff, W. P. (1983). Sex and social influence: Does sex function as a status characteristic in mixed-sex groups of children? *Journal of Educational Psychology*, *75*, 877–888.

111. Peterson, P., & Fennema, E. (1985). Effective teaching, student engagement in classroom activities, and sex-related differences in learning mathematics. *American Educational Research Journal*, *22*(3), 309–334.

112. Piel, J. A., & Conwell, C. R. (1989). *Differences in Perceptions Between Afro-American and Anglo-American Males and Females in Cooperative Learning Groups*. ERIC ED 307–348.

113. Powlishta, K. (1987). *The Social Context of Cross-Sex Interactions*. Paper presented at the biennial meetings of the Society for Research in Child Development, Baltimore.

114. Siann, G., & Macleod, H. (1986). Computers and children of primary school age: Issues and questions. *British Journal of Educationol Technology*, *17*, 133–144.

115. Skarin, K., & Moely, B. E. (1974). *Sex Differences in Competition-Cooperation Behavior of Eight-Year-Old Children.* ERIC ED 096–015.

116. Underwood, G., McCaffrey, M., & Underwood, J. (1990). Gender differences in a cooperative computer-based language task. *Educational Research, 32*(1), 44–49.

117. Webb, N. (1984). Microcomputer learning in small groups: Cognitive requirements and group processes. *Journal of Educational Psychology, 76*(6). 1076–1088.

118. Wilkinson, L. C., Lindow, J., & Chiang, C P. (1985). Sex differences and sex segregation in students' small-group communication. In L. C. Wilkinson & C. B. Marrett (Eds.), *Gender Influences in Classroom Interaction.* New York: Academic Press.

Gender differences in responsiveness to peers' requests and reinforcement is discussed in the following references.

119. Fagot, B. I. (1985). Beyond the reinforcement principle: Another step toward understanding sex roles. *Developmental Psychology, 21,* 1097–1104.

120. Lamb, M. E., Easterbrook, A. M., & Holden, G. W. (1980). Reinforcement and punishment among preschoolers: Characteristics, effects, and correlates. *Child Development, 51,* 1230–1236.

121. Serbin, L. A., Sprafkin, C., Elman, M., & Doyle, A. B. (1984). The early development of sex differentiated patterns of social influence. *Canadian Journal of Social Science, 14*(4), 350–363.

122. Wilkinson, L. C., & Marrett, C. B. (Eds.). (1985). *Gender Influence in Classroom Interaction.* New York: Academic Press.

Gender differences in leadership assumption and participation in mixed-sex groups are treated in the following references.

123. Lockheed, M. E. (1977). Cognitive style effects on sex status in student work groups. *Journal of Educational Psychology, 69,* 158–165.

124. Lockheed, M. E. (1985). Sex and social influence: A meta-analysis guided by theory. In J. Berger & M. Zeldich (Eds.), *Status, Attributions, and Rewards.* San Francisco: Jossey-Bass.

125. Lockheed, M. E., & Hall, K. P. (1976). Conceptualizing sex as a status characteristic: Application to leadership training strategies. *Journal of Social Issues, 32*(3), 111–124.

126. Webb, N. M., & Kinderski, C. M. (1985). Gender differences in small group interaction and achievement in high-and low-achieving classes. In C. Wilkinson & C. B. Marrett (Eds.), *Gender Influence in Classroom Interaction.* New York: Academic Press.

The experiences of different ethnic groups in cooperative learning groups is discussed in these references.

127. Conwell, C. R., Piel, J. A., & Cobb, K. B. (1988). *Students' Perceptions When Working in Cooperative Problem Solving Groups.* ERIC ED 313–455.

128. Fry, P. S., & Coe, K. J. (1980). Achievement performance of internally and externally oriented black and white high school students under conditions of competition and cooperation expectancies. *British Journal of Educational Psychology, 50,* 162–167.

This reference discusses the relationship between students' self-concepts and the outcome of cooperative learning activities.

129. DeVoe, M. W. (1977). Cooperation as a function of self-concept, sex and race. *Educational Research Quarterly, 2*(2), 3–8.

The focus of the references listed here is gender differences in risk taking and reactions to challenges and failure.

130. Ginsburg, H. J., & Miller, S. M. (1982). Sex differences in children's risk-taking behavior. *Child Development, 53*(2), 426–428.

131. Licht, B. G., Kistner, J. A., Ozkaragoz, T., Shapiro, S., & Clausen, L. (1985). Causal attributions of learning disabled children: Individual differences and their implications for persistence. *Journal of Educational Psychology, 77*(2), 208–216.

132. Licht, B. G., Linden, T. A., Brown, D. A., & Sexton, M. (1984). *Sex Differences in Achievement Orientation: An "A" Student Phenomenon.* ERIC ED 252–783.

133. Miller, A. (1986). Performance impairment after failure: Mechanisms and sex differences. *Journal of Educational Psychology, 78*(6), 486–491.

134. Reyes, L. H. (1984). Affective variables and mathematics education. *Elementary School Journal, 84*(5), 558–581.

These references discuss ethnic difference in risk taking.

135. Kishi, G., & Hanohano, M. (1992). *Hawaiian-American vs Caucasian-American Values.* Paper presented at the Council for Exceptional Children Topical Conference on Culturally and Linguistically Different Exceptional Children, Minnesota.

136. Kitano, M. K. (1986). Gifted and talented Asian children. *Rural Special Education Quarterly, 8*(1), 9–13.

These references deal with different ethnic concepts of time.

137. Allameh, J. (1986). *Learning Among Culturally Different Populations.* ERIC ED 273–137.

138. Ayabe, H. I. (1978). Ethnic culture, reflection impulsivity and locus of control. *Educational Perspectives, 17*(4), 10–12.

139. Brady, M. P., & Anderson, D. D. (1983). Some issues in the implementation of P.L. 94–142 in the Pacific Basin Territories. *Education, 103*(3), 259–269.

140. Condon, E. C., Peters, J. Y., & Sueiro-Ross, C. (1979). *Special Education and the Hispanic Child: Cultural Perspectives.* Philadelphia: Temple University, Teacher Corps Mid-Atlantic Network.

141. Dodd, J. M. (1992). *Preventing American Indian Children from Overidentification with Learning Disabilities: Cultural Considerations during the Prereferral Process.* Paper presented at the Council for Exceptional Children Topic Conference on Culturally and Linguistically Diverse Exceptional Children, Minneapolis.

142. Felder, D. (1970). The education of Mexican Americans: Fallacies of the monocultural approach. *Social Education, 34*(6), 639–642.

143. Levine, R. V., West, L. J., & Reis, H. T. (1980). Perceptions of time and punctuality in the United States and Brazil. *Journal of Personality and Social Psychology, 38*(4), 541–550.

144. Morgan, C. O., Guy, E., & Celini, H. (1986). The rehabilitation of disabled Native Americans. *Journal of Rehabilitation, 52,* 25–311.

Gender differences in students' confidence in their ability to succeed in school are the focus of the following references.

145. Eccles, J., Adler, T. F., & Meece, J. L. (1984). Sex differences in achievement: A test of alternate theories. *Journal of Personality and Social Psychology, 68,* 119–128.

146. Hyde, J., & Fennema, E. (1990). *Gender Differences in Mathematics Performance and Affect: Results of Two Meta-Analyses.* Paper presented

at the annual meeting of the American Educational Research Association, Boston.

147. Levine, G. (1990). *Arithmetic Development: Where are the Gender Differences?* Paper presented at the annual meeting of the American Educational Research Association, Boston.

148. Matyas, M. L. (1984). *Science Career Interests, Attitudes, Abilities, and Anxiety Among Secondary School Students: The Effects of Gender, Race/Ethnicity, and School Type/Location.* ERIC ED 251–309.

149. Meece, J. L., Parsons, J. E., Kaczala, C. M., Goff, B., & Futterman, R. (1982). Sex differences in math achievement: Toward a model of academic choice. *Psychological Bulletin, 91,* 324–348.

150. Richman, C. L., Clark, M. L., & Brown, K. P. (1984). General and specific self-esteem in late adolescent students: Race x gender x SES effects. *Adolescence, 20*(79), 555–566.

151. Stevenson, H. W., & Newman, R. S. (1986). Long-term prediction of achievement and attitudes in mathematics and reading. *Child Development, 57,* 646–659.

152. Travis, C. B., McKenzie, B. J., & Wiley, D. L. (1984). *Sex and Achievement Domain: Cognitive Patterns of Success and Failure.* ERIC ED 250–601.

The reference that follows deals with gender differences in students' perceptions of their ability to exert control over their lives and their attribution of the cause of their successes and failures in school.

153. Dyal, J. A. (1984). Cross-cultural research with the locus of control construct. In H. M. Lefcourt (Ed.), *Research with the Locus of Control Construct. Vol. 3: Extensions and Limitations.* New York: Academic Press.

154. Evans, E. D., & Engleberg, R. A. (1988). Student perceptions of school grading. *Journal of Research and Development in Education, 21*(2), 45–54.

155. Frey, K. S., & Ruble, D. N. (1987). What children say about classroom performance: Sex and grade differences in perceived competence. *Child Development, 58,* 1066–1078.

156. Lewis, M. A. (1989). *Consistency of Children's Causal Attributions Across Content Domains.* ERIC ED 306–488.

157. Lopez, C. L., & Harper, M. (1989). The relationship between learner control of CAI and locus of control among Hispanic students.

Educational Technology Research and Development, 37(4), 19–28.

158. McMahan, I. D. (1982). Expectancy of success on sex-linked tasks. *Sex Roles, 8,* 949–958.

159. Powers, S., & Wagner, M. J. (1983). *Achievement Locus of Control of Hispanic and Anglo High School Students.* ERIC ED 230–355.

160. Reyes, L. H., & Padilla, M. J. (1985). Science math and gender. *Science Teacher, 52*(6), 46–48.

161. Ryckman, D. B., & Peckman, P. D. (1986). Gender differences in attribution patterns in academic areas for learning disabled students. *Learning Disabilities Research, 1*(2), 83–89.

162. Ryckman, D. B., & Peckman, P. D. (1987a). Gender differences in attribution for success and failure. *Journal of Early Adolescence, 7,* 47–63.

163. Ryckman, D. B., & Peckman, P. D. (1987b). Gender differences in attribution for success and failure across subject areas. *Journal of Educational Research, 81,* 120–125.

164. Stipek, D. J. (1984). Sex differences in children's attributions for success and failure on math and spelling tasks. *Sex Roles, 11*(11/12), 969–981.

165. Turner, R. R. (1978). Locus of control, academic achievement, and follow through in Appalachia. *Contemporary Educational Psychology, 3,* 367–375.

166. Willig, A. C., Harnisch, D. L., Hill, K. T., & Maehr, M. L. (1983). Sociocultural and educational correlates of success-failure attributions and evaluation anxiety in the school setting for Black, Hispanic and Anglo children. *American Educational Research Journal, 20*(3), 385–410.

Ethnic differences in students' perceptions of their ability to exert control over their lives is the focus of these references.

167. Ashe, R. Personal communication.

168. Ayabe, H. I. (1977). *Measuring Locus of Control at the College Level.* Paper presented at the annual conference of the Hawaiian Psychological Association, Honolulu.

169. Shade, B. J. (1979). *Racial Preference in Psychological Differentiation: An Alternative Explanation for Group Differences.* ERIC ED 179–672.

170. Tashakkori, A., & Thompson, V. D. (1990). *Race Differences in Self-Perception and Locus of Control During Adolescence and Early Adulthood.* ERIC ED 327–806.

The relationship between locus of control and school achievement is discussed in these references.

171. Coleman, J. S., Campbell, E. Q., Hobson, C. J., McPartland, J., Mood, A. M., Weinfeld, F. D., & York, R. L. (1966). *Equality of Educational Opportunity.* Washington, DC: U.S. Government Printing Office.

172. Crandall, V., Katkovsky, W., & Crandall, V. (1965). Children's beliefs in their own control of reinforcement in intellectual and academic achievement situations. *Child Development, 36,* 91–109.

173. Epps, E. G. (1969). Negro academic motivation and performance: An overview. *Journal of Social Issues, 25*(3), 5–11.

174. Wilson, K. R., & Allen, W. R. (1987). Explaining the educational attainment of young black adults: Critical familial and extra-familial influences. *Journal of Negro Education, 56*(1), 64–76.

These references discuss the efficacy efforts to improve students' self-confidence.

175. Canfield, J., & Wells, H. C. (1976). *100 Ways to Enhance Self-Concept in the Classroom.* Englewood Cliffs, NJ: Prentice Hall.

176. De Charms, R. (1976). *Enhancing Motivation.* New York: Irvington.

177. Hauserman, N., Mitler, J. S., & Bond, F. T. (1976). A behavioral approach to changing self-concept in elementary school children. *Psychological Record, 26,* 111–116.

178. Lane, J., & Muller, D. (1977). The effect of altering self-descriptive behavior on self-concept and classroom behavior. *Journal of Psychology, 97,* 115–125.

179. Olszewski, P., Kulieke, M. J., & Willis, G. B. (1987). Changes in the self-perceptions of gifted students who participate in rigorous academic programs. *Journal for the Education of the Gifted, 10*(4), 287–303.

180. Scheier, M. A., & Kraut R. E. (1979). Increasing educational achievement via self-concept change. *Review of Educational Research, 49,* 131–149.

181. Schulman, J. L., Ford, R. C., & Busk, P. (1973). A classroom program to improve self-concept. *Psychology in the Schools, 10,* 481–487.

Instruments for assessing students' self-confidence are described in the following references.

182. Coopersmith, S., & Feldman, R. (1974). Fostering a positive self-concept and high self-

esteem in the classroom. In R. H. Coop & K. White (Eds.), *Psychological Concepts in the Classroom*. New York: Harper & Row.

183. Harter, S. (1982). The perceived competency scale for children. *Child Development, 53,* 87–97.

184. Katzenmer, W. G., & Stenner, A. J. (1970). *Self-Observation Scale*. Durham, NC: NTS Research Corporation.

185. Norwicki, S., & Strickland, B. (1973). A locus of control scale for children. *Journal of Consulting Psychology, 40,* 148–154.

186. Piers, E. V., & Harris, D. B. (1969). *Children's Self-Concept Scale (The Way I Feel About Myself)*. Nashville: Counselor Recordings and Tests.

Suggestions for enhancing the self-confidence of poor and non–European American students are included in the following references.

187. Draper, I. L, Kimbrough, A. H., Jones, J. W., & Pierce, B. (1992). *Using "Self-Esteem Through Culture Leads to Academic Excellence (SETCLAE)" Transmission of Culture*. Paper presented at the Council for Exceptional Children Topical Conference on Diverse Exceptional Children, Minneapolis.

188. Frasier, M. M. (1979). Rethinking the issues regarding the culturally disadvantaged gifted. *Exceptional Children, 45*(7), 538–542.

189. Hale-Benson, J. E. (1986). *Black Children: Their Roots, Culture, and Learning Styles*, (rev. ed.). Baltimore: The Johns Hopkins University Press.

190. Hankerson, H. E. (1980). Understanding the young black exceptional child: An overview. In E. Jackson (Ed.), *The Young Black Exceptional Child: Providing Programs and Services*. ERIC ED 204–919.

191. Mack, F. R-P. (1987). Understanding and enhancing self-concept in black children. *Momentum, 18*(1), 22–25.

192. Pepper, F. C. (1976). Teaching the American Indian child in mainstream settings. In R. L. Jones (Ed.), *Mainstreaming and the Minority Child*. Reston, VA: Council for Exceptional Children.

193. Wood, G. H. (1984). Schooling in a democracy: Transformation or reproduction: *Educational Theory, 34*(3), 219–239.

The following references offer guidelines and suggestions on how to make course contents more relevant and interesting to non–European American students.

194. Asante, M. K. (1991). Putting Africa at the center. *Newsweek, 118*(13), 46.

195. Kantrowitz, B. (1991). A is for ashanti, b is for black. *Newsweek, 118*(13), 45–48.

196. Cheng, L. L. (1989). Intervention strategies: A multicultural approach. *Topics in Language Disorders, 9*(3), 84–91.

197. Flores, J. M. (1989). Barrio folklore as a basis for English composition. *Equity & Excellence, 24*(2), 72.

198. Gay, G. (1988). Designing relevant curricula for diverse learners. *Education and Urban Society, 20*(4), 327–340.

199. Martinez, D. I., & Ortiz de Montellano, B. R. (1988). *Improving the Science and Mathematic Achievement of Mexican American Students Through Culturally Relevant Science*. Las Cruces: ERIC/CRESS, New Mexico State University.

200. Palmer, P. A., & Palmer, B. C. (1983). Reading interests of middle school black and white students. *Reading Improvement, 20*(2), 151–155.

201. Pugh, S. L. (1989). Literature, culture, and ESL: A natural convergence. *Journal of Reading, 34*(4), 320–329.

This reference provides examples of acceptable and unacceptable learning experiences.

202. Nazzaro, J. N. (1981). Special problems of exceptional minority children. In J. N. Nazzaro (Ed.), *Culturally Diverse Exceptional Children in School*. ERIC ED 199–993.

The following references discuss the interrelationship between socioeconomic class and ethnicity.

203. Chan, K., & Rueda, R. (1979). Poverty and culture in education: Separate but equal. *Exceptional Children, 45,* 422–427.

204. Cooper, J. G. (1977). *The Effects of Ethnicity upon School Achievement*. ERIC ED 157–675.

205. Dillard, J. M., & Perrin, D. W. (1980). Puerto Rican, Black, and Anglo adolescents' career aspirations, expectations, and maturity. *Vocational Guidance Quarterly, 28,* 313–332.

206. Havighurst, R. J. (1976). The relative importance of social class and ethnicity in human development. *Human Development, 19,* 56–64.

207. Johnson, N. J., & Sanaday, P. R. (1971). Subcultural variations in one urban poor population. *American Anthropologist, 73,* 128–143.

208. Kagan, S., & Ender, P. B. (1975). Maternal responses to success and failure of Anglo-American, Mexican American, and Mexican children. *Child Development, 46*, 452–458.

209. Laosa, L. M. (1977). Socialization, education and continuity: The importance of the socio-cultural context. *Young Children, 32*(5), 21–27.

210. Sarason, S. B. (1973). Jewishness, blackness, and the nature-nurture controversy. *American Psychologist, 28*, 962–971.

211. Wilson, W. J. (1978). *The Declining Significance of Race.* Chicago: University of Chicago Press.

These references discuss students' acculturation and how to evaluate it.

212. Ramirez, M., & Castaneda, A. (1974). *Bicultural Democracy, Bicognitive Development and Education.* New York: Academic Press.

213. Berry, J. W., Kim, U., Minde, T., & Mok, R. (1987). Comparative studies of acculturative stress. *International Migration Review, 21*(30), 491–511.

214. Cloud, N. (1990). *Measuring Level of Acculturation in Bilingual, Bicultural Children.* Paper presented at the annual meeting of the American Educational Research Association, Boston.

215. Cloud, N. (1991). Acculturation of ethnic minorities. In A. M. Ambert (Ed.), *Bilingual Education and English as a Second Language: A Research Handbook 1988–1990.* New York: Garland.

216. Cuellar, I., Harris, L. C., & Jasso, R. (1980). An acculturation scale for Mexican American normal and clinical populations. *Hispanic Journal of Behavioral Sciences, 2*(3), 199–217.

217. Franco, J. N. (1983). An acculturation scale for Mexican-American children. *Journal of General Psychology, 108*, 175–181.

218. Koh, T., & Koh, S. D. (1982). A note on the psychological evaluation of Korean school children. *P/AAMHRC Research Review, 1*(3), 1–2.

219. Lee, E. (1988). Cultural factors in working with Southeast Asian refugee adolescents. *Journal of Adolescence, 11*, 167–179.

220. Leung, E. K. (1988). Cultural and acculturational commonalities and diversities among Asian Americans: Identification and programming considerations. In A. A. Ortiz & B. A. Ramirez (Eds.), *Schools and Culturally Diverse Exceptional Students: Promising Practices and Future Directions.* Reston, VA: ERIC Clearinghouse on Handicapped and Gifted Children, Council for Exceptional Children.

221. Lin, K., & Masuda M. (1983). Impact of refugee experience: Mental health issues of Southeast Asian refugees. In R. F. Morales (Ed.), *Bridging Cultures.* Los Angeles: Asian American Health Center.

222. Mainous, A. G., III. (1989). Self concept as an indicator of acculturation in Mexican Americans. *Hispanic Journal of Behavioral Sciences, 11*(2), 178–189.

223. Martinez, R., Norman, R. D., & Delaney, H. D. (1984). A Children's Hispanic Background Scale. *Hispanic Journal of Behavioral Sciences, 6*(2), 103–112.

224. Mendoza, R. H., & Martinez, J. L. (1981). The measurement of acculturation. In A. Baron, Jr. (Ed.), *Explorations in Chicano Psychology.* New York: Holt.

225. Olmedo, E. L. (1980). Quantitative models of acculturation: An overview. In A. M. Padilla (Ed.), *Acculturation: Theory, Models, and Some New Findings.* Boulder, CO: Westview Press.

226. Olmedo, E. L., & Padilla, A. M. (1978). Empirical and construct validity of a measure of acculturation for Mexican Americans. *Journal of Social Psychology, 105*, 179–187.

227. Padilla, A. M. (1980). The role of cultural awareness and ethnic loyalty in acculturation. In A. M. Padilla (Ed.), *Acculturation: Theory, Models, and Some New Findings.* Boulder, CO: Westview Press.

228. Suinn, R. M., Rickard-Figueroa, K., Lew, S., & Vigil, P. (1987). Asian Self-Identity Acculturation Scale: An initial report. *Educational and Psychological Measurement, 47*, 401–407.

229. Szapocznik, J., & Kurtines, W. (1980). Acculturation, biculturalism and adjustment among Cuban Americans. In A. M. Padilla (Ed.), *Acculturation: Theory, Models, and Some New Findings.* Boulder, CO: Westview Press.

230. Szapocznik, J., Kurtines, W. M., & Fernandez, T. (1979). *Bicultural Involvement and Adjustment in Hispanic American Youth.* ERIC ED 193–374.

231. Wong-Rieger, D., & Quintana, D. (1987). Comparative acculturation of Southeast Asian and Hispanic immigrants and sojourners. *Journal of Cross-Cultural Psychology, 18*(3), 345–362.

232. Golden, J. G. (1990). The acculturation of three Korean American students. *Teaching and Learning, 5*(1), 9–20.

Instruments for evaluating students' learning styles are listed and discussed in the following references.

233. Dunn, R., & Dunn, K. (1978). *Teaching Students Through Their Individual Learning Styles: A Practical Approach.* Reston, VA: Reston Publishing Company.

234. Keefe, J. (1979). Learning style: An overview. In *Student Learning Styles: Diagnosing and Prescribing Programs.* Reston, VA: National Association of Secondary School Principals.

235. McCarthy, B. (1980). *The 4 Mat System: Teaching to Learning Styles with Right/Left Mode Techniques.* Oak Brook, IL: Excel.

236. Perrin, J. (1982). *Learning Style Inventory: Primary Version.* Jamaica, NY: St. John's University.

237. Renzulli, J., & Smith, L. (1978). *The Learning Style Inventory: A Measure of Student Preference for Instructional Techniques.* Mansfield Center, CT: Creative Learning Press.

Classroom/Behavior Management in a Diverse Society

This chapter provides educators with the information they require to consider their students' unique characteristics when they select classroom/behavior management techniques. It begins by noting that many educators contribute to students' behavior problems by relating to them in a discriminatory manner. Then it describes the typical ways educators can misperceive and misunderstand students' behaviors and use inappropriate responses to deal with them when they interpret students' behavior from their own perspective. The next section describes some of the student characteristics that educators should be aware of in order to understand why students are behaving in a particular way and what techniques might help them to behave differently. The final section discusses the importance of using classroom/behavior management techniques that empower rather than disempower students.

Discriminatory Classroom/Behavior Management Approaches

There is still considerable ethnic, socioeconomic, and gender bias in American schools. As was noted in Chapters 3 and 7, many educators have lower expectations for poor, African American, Hispanic American, and Native American students. They tend to evaluate them lower than objective evidence warrants, praise and call on them less often, criticize them more often, and use harsher and more punitive disciplinary techniques with them. Teachers' gender biases are demonstrated in the different expectations, attention, and feedback they typically have for male and female students, their encouragement of different behaviors in male and female students, their intolerance of male behavior patterns, and their use of more severe classroom management techniques with males. No one knows the exact degree to which behavior problems in school are caused by prejudice. However, when the evidence is considered as a whole, it is inconceivable that the discriminatory manner in which many students are treated by their teachers does not affect their attitudes and behavior. Therefore, elimination of teacher prejudice is one of the most important steps educators can take to eliminate disciplinary problems.

Chapters 3 and 4 include a number of self-quizzes and activities designed to assist you to identify and correct your biases. This chapter is also designed to provide you with some of the additional knowledge you require to provide students with nondiscriminatory classroom/behavior management.

Misperceptions

Educators do not have to be prejudiced to use biased management techniques with students. Even well-meaning teachers can misperceive and misunderstand students' behaviors when they interpret them from their own perspective. They can perceive behavior problems that do not exist, not notice problems that do exist, misunderstand the causes of students' behaviors, and use inappropriate techniques to deal with students' behavior problems.

Nonexistent Problems

Students whose ethnic or socioeconomic backgrounds differ from those of their teachers and school administrators may have values, goals, and interests that are acceptable to their families and communities, but not to the school system. As a result, educators may not be able to accept behavior that the students and their parents find completely appropriate. For example, teachers may incorrectly think that students brought up not to be assertive or to volunteer their opinions unless encouraged by adults are shy or insecure, and they may believe that students who are encouraged at home to work independently rather than with others and to judge their accomplishments for themselves rather than rely on the opinions of others do not care about others. Some specific examples of how educators may perceive nonexistent problems in the case of African American, Asian and Pacific American, and Hispanic American students follow.

African American students are particularly prone to have difficulty in school because of incompatibilities between how many of them are encouraged to behave in their communities and the expectations of their teachers (1, 4, 5, 7, 10, 13). Many African American males, and females as well, express their emotions much more intensely than most European Americans. When European American teachers observe African American males behaving aggressively and assertively, too many of them assume that the students are much angrier or more upset than they actually are. Attributing a level of anger to African American students that would be correct for European American students who behaved in a similar way, the teachers can become uncomfortable, even anxious, and concerned about what they incorrectly anticipate will happen next. As a result, they intervene when no intervention is necessary. If teachers appreciated the cultural context of African American males' seemingly aggressive behavior toward others and understood that such behavior is unlikely to cause the physical fight or whatever else they expect to occur between African American students who appear to be acting aggressively toward each other, they would be less likely to have to intervene to make themselves feel more at ease in the situation. This would lessen the likelihood that African American males would get into trouble needlessly. As two African American professionals see it:

> *Urban schooling patterns, for the most part, promote quietness and docility. Such classrooms are therefore designed to suit the learning norms of children from white families and opposed to the characteristics of Black children, making it difficult for them to comply with the demands made upon them by that system. . . . A troubled teacher-pupil relationship is the outcome. The resentful teacher and the balking student's interactions erode with daily incidents. School policy leads to a compilation of a dossier on these students so as to build up a string of minor offenses, which, when presented all at once, appear to be a massive campaign of misdeeds. (13, pp. 51–52)*

> *Most teachers are unprepared to accept the active, aggressive behavior of Black boys. The aggressive behavior of a Black child is immediately interpreted as hostile. The teacher's expectation is that the student should be compliant, docile, and responsive to authority. The student is expected to conform to a standard of behavior that the teacher is familiar with, the compliant child standard that was indicative of the teacher's up-bringing. It is as though the teacher makes an unwritten contract with the student, "If you don't behave, I won't (or can't) teach you."*

> *The next step in the process is that the teacher will make futile attempts to control the aggressive, active behavior, but abandon those efforts very quickly and conclude that the child is unmanageable. The child resists the teacher's efforts to control the behavior. More often than not, the behavior becomes more unmanageable. As the disruptive behavior increases, the amount of time and effort available to devote to attending to the instructions and acquiring academic skills decreases. In all likelihood the student prefers to avoid the academic work. Within a short period of time it becomes apparent that this unmanageable student is not functioning at grade level. This then can be interpreted, depending on the tolerance level of the teachers, as a learning problem and a justification for referral for special placement. The longer the time span involved, the greater the learning problem. (1, pp. 78–79)*

An African American educator describes how other behavior patterns that are acceptable in the African community can cause problems for students in school.

Blacks are accustomed to integrating mental, emotional, and physical activities. Schools tend to encourage compartmentalizing these areas. The Black child's involvement in cognitive classroom activities is likely to be signaled by vocal responses, exuberance, and physical movement. Teachers consider this behavior disruptive because they expect that one can be highly stimulated to intellectual activities without involving affective or psychomotor dimensions.

What teachers view as total chaos and noise may be structured activity to Blacks. What teachers consider planned activities may be perceived by Black students as prohibiting constraints. The problem of perception stems from different sets of expectations and cultural sensibilities. (4, pp. 32–33)

Elaborating on how Blacks respond to others when they are reciting, performing, and so on, Gay states:

There is more total interaction involved; all those in the social environment must play some active response role if it is only through such responses as "right on brother"....

The Black child in performing looks for verbal and kinesthetic support from his peers. The teacher hears noise and is threatened. The child's success is measured by his peers by the extent to which he stimulates the others to provide responses. When this behavior is manifested, teachers see an undisciplined and discourteous group of Blacks.

This situation arises because contrarily in white, middle-class culture the relationship between a performer and his audience demands a show of passivity on the part of the latter.... When Black children's classroom behavior is assessed using this frame of reference, the conclusions are foreordained. The culturally determined Black ways of demonstrating interest and involvement are interpreted as restlessness, inattentiveness, and sometimes hostility. (5, p. 338)

A final example of these many incompatibilities between acceptable African American students behavior at home and the expectations of the schools is the verbal dueling games such as "playing the dozens," "ribbin' and jivin'," and so on that African American students play. Although they know that these are merely part of a competitive game, European American and other non–African American teachers often perceive them as a prelude to a fight (10).

Commenting on how European American teachers may misperceive the origin and meaning of the field sensitive/dependent relationship style of Hispanic American students, Jaramillo states that

An Anglo teacher is likely to consider many of the Spanish speaking children in his class dependent in a negative sense, or perhaps he will say they are immature, or that they are retarded in their social development. In reality, these differences are purely cultural, and viewed from another perspective, these children are perfectly normal and mature for their age. (9, p. 13)

The following quotation provides insight into the kinds of cultural misperceptions educators can make with Chinese American students.

> *The child does not volunteer to answer. He just sits and waits for his teacher to call upon him. So in the eyes of the American teacher, Asian children, as compared to the American students, are dull, passive, unresponsive, and lack initiative. Most of the time, Chinese (Asian) students are ignored because of their absolute silence in class. (17, p. 11)*

Examples of the kinds of cultural misperceptions educators can make with Southeast Asian students are illustrated in the quotations that follow.

> *American straightforwardness is considered at best impolite, if not brutal. In Indochina, one does not come directly to the point. To do so is, for an American, a mark of honesty and forthrightness while a person from Indochina sees it as a lack of intelligence or courtesy. Falsehood carries no moral structure for a Cambodian, Laotian, or Vietnamese. The essential question is not whether a statement is true or false, but what the intention of the statement is. Does it facilitate interpersonal harmony? Does it indicate a wish to change the subject? Hence, one must learn the "heart" of the speaker through his/her words. In Indochina, one thinks very carefully before speaking. The American style of "speaking one's mind" is thus misunderstood.*
>
> *The Vietnamese literal equivalent of the English word "Yes" is "Da" (pronounced "Ya" in the Southern Vietnamese dialect). However, whereas the English "Yes" means unequivocally "Yes," the Vietnamese "Da" means a variety of things. In the final analysis, it can mean "Yes," but in general usage it merely means "I am politely listening to you," and it does not at all mean that "I agree with you." The listener may disagree with what he hears, but due to his politeness, cannot say no. His English "Yes" for him conveys the polite and non-committal Vietnamese "Da," but to the American it can carry only its English meaning. Thus, the Vietnamese may appear insincere, or even stupid, to the American. (14, pp. 6, 7, 19)*

It is easy to understand how educators who do not know these facts could misinterpret their students' responses. For example, they may think their students have just agreed to do what they have been asked to do and so become angry and frustrated when the students don't follow through after saying "yes."

Unnoticed Problems

Educators who are not tuned to how students from other cultures communicate can miss a request for help or assistance. They may not even realize that their students have problems. As was noted previously, Hispanic American and Asian and Pacific American students are usually brought up not to ask teachers for help.

Hispanics are expected to be sensitive to the needs, feelings, and desires of others so that it is unnecessary for others to be embarrassed by asking for help. Asian and Pacific American students believe that to do so would insult their teachers.

There is evidence that teachers are especially tolerant of Asian Pacific American students' problems (2, 8, 16, 18, 19). There appear to be two reasons for this. First, they believe that all of them are good students. As Yao puts it: "Many school teachers share a myth: that all Asian American youngsters are diligent, respectful, intelligent, good students. But teachers should not be dismayed if they find the opposite is true in their classrooms" (19, p. 82).

Dao offers the following observation.

> *There is an assumption that Asian Americans, in general, are a model minority. This notion is related to the stereotypic perception that Asian-American families place high priority on education and push their children to succeed in school. . . . Although there have been impressive occupational and educational achievements by Asian-Americans in the past, these achievements should not obscure the changes now occurring in the Asian American population. . . . The growing and changing Asian-American student population includes many children from families with life and educational experiences vastly different from children from established Asian-American families. Among the Mein and Hmong refugees, for example, the unemployment rate is 90%. Recent immigrant or refugee children from these families face the triple burden of simultaneously learning English and the new school curriculum, adjusting to a new culture, and surviving an impoverished environment. (2, p. 594)*

Second, Asian American students tend to internalize their emotional problems rather than act them out. Even though they may be experiencing serious

Teachers' Perceptions of Asian American and European American Students (18)

European Americans	Asian Americans
more extroverted	less extroverted
less cheerful	more cheerful
less emotionally stable	more emotionally stable
less kind	more kind
less obedient	more obedient
less disciplined	more disciplined
less cooperative	more cooperative
less patient	more patient
more prone to anger	less prone to anger
less academically competent	more academically competent
less able to concentrate	more able to concentrate
less organized	more organized
less persevering	more persevering
less adequate memory	more adequate memory

emotional problems, their suffering is less obvious and less disruptive than that of students who act out their problems. As a result, they are less likely to be noticed by teachers (8). Because teachers tend to welcome the quiet unobtrusive behavior of many Asian Pacific Island Americans, they often fail to recognize when it may be a sign of problems (16).

Incorrect Causes

Educators may mistakenly attribute behavior problems that are culturally determined to other causes. For example, educators who are unaware of their students' identity conflicts may attribute the students' behavior to other causes such as lack of interest and motivation to succeed in school, lack of respect for teachers, poor parenting, and other reasons. Then, instead of responding with understanding to their students' identity conflicts or helping them resolve these conflicts, they are likely to use inappropriate techniques to squash the objectionable behavior. Some of the ways non–African American teachers can misunderstand the causes of African American students' behavior are revealed in the following description of the faculty of a desegregated school.

> *The Black children displayed unfamiliar behavior that teachers found difficult to adjust to and cope with. At one time or another teachers commented:*
> *"There's so much pent-up anger in them."*
> *"They talk so loud."*
> *"When he came here he was totally nonverbal."*
> *"Did you ever see such antsyness?"*
> *Teachers called attention to kids who used "foul" language ("I'll never get used to that"), to children who spoke out in class, to antisocial behavior (fighting, spitting at other children, stealing), to short attention spans, to immaturity (e.g., thumb sucking). Each of these behaviors made the job of teaching much more difficult than it had been prior to desegregation. . . . The first and most basic teacher response to the number of problems presented by the Black children was to devise some personal explanation for the unfamiliar behavior. While these explanations varied somewhat from teacher to teacher, a common theme emerged. On several occasions unfamiliar and disturbing behavior (whether antisocial actions or difficulty mastering classroom work) was attributed to problems in a child's environment. Comments such as "I think Ben is brutalized at home" were offered as explanations for children's actions or attitudes. To a lesser extent I heard references made to children's previous schools not having demanded enough of them. Whether these explanations accurately represented fact or not, they made the problems understandable and to some extent served to legitimate the approach taken by the teachers to ameliorate the problems. (12, p. 21)*

The next two quotations describe some of the possible causes of behavior problems that teachers should consider when they interpret the behavior of Asian and Pacific American students.

> *When a Southeast Asian student misbehaves this misbehavior may be the result of one or more of the following sources of tension: frustration due to language problems and misunderstanding, imitation out of a desire for rapid adaptation, behavior learned in refugee camps where survival was paramount and included stealing and violent self defense, intragroup historical animosity among various Southeast Asian groups, adjustment difficulties because school rules here are less strict and well-defined, culture-gap in the family resulting from different rates of assimilation. (3, p. 58)*

> *One teacher was puzzled by an Asian child, because he responded with a smile when scolded. Asian children tend to "camouflage" their embarrassment by smiling. (11, p. 1)*

The final quotation reminds educators not to overlook the possibility that some of the behavior problems of limited English proficient students can be caused by their language difficulty.

> *Problem behaviors such as difficulty following directions, poor eye contact, inattention, and daydreaming could be associated with a handicapping condition, but they could also reflect a lack of English proficiency. (15, p. 52)*

Inappropriate Techniques

Even if educators recognize when students' behavior problems are culturally determined, they may still respond with techniques that are inappropriate if they do not have the knowledge needed to adapt their approaches to the cultural realities of their students.

An educator who wishes to communicate effectively with Hispanic American students benefits from understanding the differences between the cultures and how these impact the classroom.

> *Hispanic parents tend to speak more politely and indirectly when they criticize or discipline their children. In the United States educators are much more gruff and direct with students. . . . Some Hispanic students, especially males, may interpret the gruff or more direct manner of Anglos as an indication that educators do not consider them worthy or deserving of a proper relationship. When educators speak to them in a matter-of-fact or authoritarian manner, they may feel insulted, angry, or resentful and lose respect for these educators and the desire to cooperate or conform. (6, p. 102)*

At times the very techniques teachers choose to motivate individual students backfire because of different cultural values. For example, as was described in Chapter 9, rewarding Hawaiian American students for appropriate behavior can cause them to behave in less desirable ways in order to avoid being singled out for praise and recognition. On the other hand, rewarding the whole group for the improvement of one or more members of the group can cause those individuals who are not behaving appropriately to behave in a more desirable manner.

Student Characteristics

The following are some of the ways students' behavior characteristics differ. Knowledge of how ethnic, socioeconomic, and gender factors influence these characteristics may help you understand how students actually behave, why they behave as they do, and which management techniques might help them to behave differently.

Which of the four approaches described in Chapter 4 (assimilation, accommodation, biculturalism, or empowerment) you decide to use when you discover that students' behavior is the result of ethnic, socioeconomic, or gender factors is a personal matter for you to decide. However, your awareness that one or more of these factors is contributing to students' behavior problems should help you to avoid misperceiving and misunderstanding them, and it should lead you to use effective management techniques to deal with them.

Previous chapters discussed students' communication, motivational, and cognitive styles, time orientation, interests, and attitudes about acceptable and unacceptable learning activities. This chapter focuses on other student characteristics.

Perception of Authority Figures

Are students expected not to speak unless spoken to, not to ask questions, and to obey their elders just because they are the authorities? Or can they disagree with adults and ask their elders to justify why they are requiring them to do certain things or punishing them? Can teachers expect students to accept their opinions, rules, and consequences simply because they are in charge, or are they expected to justify themselves to their students?

Although many experts advise teachers to be authoritative rather than authoritarian, students from other cultures may require help in adjusting to an adult who is authoritative and not authoritarian. These students may also have difficulty participating in democratic classrooms in which the students are actively involved in establishing rules, procedures, and consequences. For example, a Filipino American teacher states:

> *Especially to a small child from grade one to grade six, the democratic atmosphere that is being provided here is an entirely new aspect. Perhaps, during the first months the Filipino student is somewhat lost. He doesn't know what to do. The Filipino child may feel insecure. In the Philippines, the teacher usually says, "do this, make this." (24, p. 21)*

Is the relationship between adolescents and adult authority figures more like that between children and adults or between adult and adult? What special rights and privileges do adolescents enjoy that are denied to children? What special instructional and classroom management techniques should teachers use with adolescents? Which techniques that are appropriate with younger students are inappropriate with adolescents?

Are the authority roles of male and female adults the same? Is one gender the authority figure and the other the nurturer? Does each gender express and enforce its authority in the same or different ways? Are students ready to accept teachers of either gender as authority figures? Are students prepared to accept the same disciplinary techniques from teachers regardless of their teachers' gender? An Hispanic American educator offers the following comment about Hispanic American males' perceptions of their female teachers. "One should be conscious of a male Chicano's lack of understanding in trying to take orders from a female teacher. He will really look up to or listen with better interest if an adult male is talking to him" (6, p. 104).

Because some Hispanic American males may have difficulty accepting the authority of female teachers, some educators suggest that females should stress nonauthoritarian methods such as requesting rather than ordering and/or request that a male administrator intervene if it becomes necessary to deal in a stern way with male students (6).

How do students express their respect for authority? As was noted in Chapter 6, in some cultures looking an adult in the eye is a sign of respect and submission. In other cultures avoiding eye contact communicates the same message. As a result, teachers may misinterpret the nonverbal messages communicated by students from other cultural backgrounds. How African American, Asian and Pacific American, Hispanic American, and other non–European American students are taught to show respect typically differs from how European American students are expected to behave.

Relationships with Others

Individual Versus Group Rights

Are the rights of individuals or the obligations of individuals to the group stressed? Are youngsters encouraged to establish their own goals and strive for individual excellence, or are they expected to be sensitive and responsive to the needs and desires of the group? Are students likely to sacrifice their desires for the benefit of their classmates?

Which group rights are respected? Some cultures expect individuals to consider the effect of their actions on other people's sensibilities. Cultures that stress people's individuality—their right to determine for themselves the way they satisfy their desires—require their members to learn to tolerate the inconvenience the rights of others may create for them. Thus, some children are taught to be considerate of others by keeping the volume on the TV or stereo low so as to avoid disturbing others; other children are taught to be considerate of others by learning how to do what they have to do even when the volume is high; and some are taught to keep the volume low and to be tolerant of others if they keep the volume high. Teachers who are unaware of this difference may mistakenly believe that some students are inconsiderate and self-centered rather than merely behaving in a culturally approved manner. The following is a description of the different approaches of many African Americans and European Americans in this respect.

> *Whites have been taught that to act on behalf of their own feelings is unjustified if someone else's sensibilities might become offended as a result. So strongly ingrained is this rule that it has the force of a moral injunction. Rather than violate it and feel guilty. . . . whites will hold back what they truly feel even if this will result in an injustice to their feelings or create for themselves an unwanted social situation.*
>
> *From a black standpoint, individuals asserting themselves in accordance with their feelings are seen not as violating the sacred rights of others but, rather, as preserving the sacred rights of self. (27, p. 121, 123)*

How should educators deal with this issue? Should they teach students to be tolerant of each others styles or to be sensitive to the needs and sensibilities of others?

Giving and Sharing

Some cultures bring up children to be better sharers than others. Some cultures train children to be generous with their possessions because it is better to give than to receive. Other cultures stress private ownership and property rights. Some students have more practice in sharing because their cultures do not provide many experiences in private ownership and personal space. Instead of having their own room, area, chair, and so on, they have to share space, belongings, and the like. Their different experiences at home can affect how they prefer to function in school.

To what extent are children and youth expected to share their things with others? How prepared are students to share their belongings with others? Will they also expect their peers to reciprocate? How will students react if their peers do not share their things with them?

> *Humanism in Hispanic children is also expressed in their unusual generosity with toys and other personal belongings, an openness of attitude which they frequently discover is not reciprocated by their Anglo-Saxon peers. (23, p. 75)*

> *When educators attempt to resolve sharing difficulties among students by explaining the rights of owners—emphasizing private property or what's mine is mine and what's yours is yours—Hispanic students may feel bewildered, confused or even rejected and insulted. (6, p. 89)*

Students' motives for doing favors for and giving presents to teachers and peers differ. In some cultures, when students do favors and give gifts to their peers and teachers they do so in order to curry favor with them; in other cultures they do so in order to place others in their debt; and in others the purpose is to express friendship. Therefore, educators should not assume they understand why students do favors for others or give them gifts if they are not knowledgeable about the students' cultural background.

Do students think helping a friend during a test is bad, cheating, and dishonest, or a way of demonstrating their helpfulness, friendliness, and brotherhood? Some Hawaiian American and Hispanic American students may feel that helping friends during a test or when they are called on to recite is necessary despite their teacher's view that it is cheating (6, 22).

How should educators react to students whose ethnic backgrounds lead them to have different attitudes about sharing their belongings and helping their peers when they are called on to recite or taking a test? Should they treat all students the same regardless of the students' beliefs or take their beliefs into consideration when they establish rules, procedures, and expectations?

Relationships with the Opposite Gender

How do children and youth relate to the opposite gender at different ages? The brother-sister and male-female relationships in the Hispanic American community have been described as follows:

> Older boys for instance, tend to assume a protective and responsible attitude toward their sisters—escorting them to and from school, dispensing lunch money to them, and defending them against intruders; as a result of their protective upbringing, girls tend to be shy and submissive toward their brothers and other boys. Neither of these typical male and female Hispanic behaviors meets the wholehearted approval of the egalitarian Anglo-American educator who tends to translate them as overaggressiveness on the one hand, and excessive dependence on the other. (23, p. 61)

At what age are students comfortable relating to peers of the opposite sex? Should they be allowed to choose to work in same-sex groups or required to participate in groups with the opposite sex? Does the students' age or the nature of the activity play a role in their ability to participate comfortably in mixed-gender groups?

In recent years an increased emphasis on nonsexist coeducational activities in the schools has been required by Title IX and supported by the courts (see Chapter 9), yet students from some cultural backgrounds may both overtly and covertly resist being required to engage in activities that are reserved for the opposite sex in their cultures. They may also balk at being made to engage in coed activities that are usually carried out in sexually segregated groups in their home culture. The problems that many Native American and East Indian American students experience in mixed gender groups are described next.

> At a school dance in which Anglo teachers were instructing Navajo students in the expected social behavior of adolescents in the dominant society, these harbingers of "culture," randomly selected young males and females and forced them to dance together. As some of these students were from the same clan, this physical

contact was akin to a sexual encounter. In their minds, incestuous relations were forced upon these students. (29, p. 23)

East Indian American students expressed great discomfort about working with someone of the opposite sex on a class assignment about how to run a household as a married couple. The Indian culture segregates males and females in all environments especially until they are married. Thus coming from a culture that believes it would be wrong to work in close contact with each other it is uncomfortable for most students to do so. All of the European American students felt totally comfortable with the project and stated that it would be a great learning experience. (33, p. 3)

How should educators deal with the requirements of Title IX? Should they respect students' ethnic preferences, encourage students to comply with them, or require them to do so?

How do males and females express interest in one another? What one group may consider an insulting form of attention or show of interest, other groups may deem acceptable. This is especially true of African American and Hispanic Americans. Thus, "piropos," compliments about how great they look or how sexy they are said to females whom one does not know, are acceptable in many Hispanic American and African American communities, but insulting to many European Americans (27, 28). How should educators deal with the problems that occur when males relate to females from different ethnic backgrounds in ways that they think are acceptable, but the females feel insulted or harassed?

Social Space

People from different cultural backgrounds prefer different amounts of personal space between them and the individuals with whom they are interacting. Thus, European American educators may find that some Hispanic students make them uncomfortable by standing to close to them, while the students feel rejected every time the teachers back away in order to feel more comfortable. These same teachers may have the exact opposite experience with some Asian and Pacific American students, who require even more personal space than they do.

The concept of social space is interpreted in widely different manners in Hispanic and American societies, with the former opting generally for a narrower interaction distance than that preferred by the latter. . . . Many an Anglo American has reacted negatively without realizing it to the "crowding" behavior of Latino children, and his instinctive withdrawal has been interpreted by them as a sign of exclusion from the inner circle of favorite students. (23, p. 65)

In the classroom situation, Oriental American students, particularly those newly arrived, have often demonstrated uneasiness when teachers sit too close to them. This is because they are not used to proximity between an adult and a youngster. In Asia, teachers are respected by both students and their parents, and the size of

> *the spatial bubble is rather extensive. Oriental teachers seldom mingle with students to help them with schoolwork. (37, pp. 68–69)*

Disciplinary Style

People from different cultures attribute disciplinary problems to different causes and use different techniques to motivate children and youth to behave in acceptable ways. Some ethnic groups rely heavily on the use of consequences to modify children's behavior; others do not. Some are quick to resort to punishments; others emphasize rewards. Some stress materialistic rewards; others train children and youth to respond to more personal ones. Therefore, it is helpful to know the kinds of disciplinary techniques that students are accustomed to in their homes and communities. How this principle applies to African American students is described next.

> *Many districts offer a single program for improving the behavior of all students based on the assumption that the student population is homogeneous. But . . . it is likely that those activities necessary to improve the behavior of African-American students will involve efforts that address those behavioral differences. Identifying alternative disciplinary actions is perhaps the most difficult of the tasks included in this approach because it involves trying to determine what actions may be more effective.*
>
> *The difficulty of the task partially reflects the reluctance of schools to develop and use strategies that specifically address the needs and problems of African-American students because they fear that they will be charged with having dual standards of discipline. (36, p. 34)*
>
> *In many instances white teachers are unable to discipline Black children because they do not "connect" culturally; the teachers do not behave as Black children expect authority figures to behave. . . . It seems that when white teachers practice the disciplinary techniques they are taught in college, Black children "run over them." (25, p. 172)*
>
> *It is much easier to dish out punishment to the child of a Black maid than to the child of a white school board president. (32, p. 16)*

Permissive Versus Strict Management

Some educators believe that a lenient, permissive approach to classroom management can backfire with students who are used to a more authoritarian approach (3, 25, 35). For example, speaking of African American students Bacon advises that

> *Those who are accustomed to a more authoritarian approach to behavior management are particularly difficult to control in an atmosphere of permissiveness, of being given freedom to choose prematurely and without training. (20, p. 7)*

In a somewhat similar vein, Tharp advises that teachers of Hawaiian Americans need to be tough.

> *To be tough, the teachers must be firm, clear, and consistent in insisting that the children comply with their directions and requests. They must dispense contingently the resources they control, such as recess, access to peers, and praise. (35, p. 354)*

However Tharp reports that the opposite is true for Navajo students

> *For Navajos, neither extreme of "tough" or "nice" is appropriate, and the reinforcing and punishing value of identical teacher behaviors is often reversed. Navajo adults are more reserved in their affectionate displays but are highly respectful of children's individuality and of children's sovereignty over their own persons. Punishment, contingent reward, or any openly manipulative effort to control the behavior of others—including children—is a violation of cultural values. (35, p. 354)*

Positive Consequences

How much praise and reward do students receive from adults? Will students expect to be rewarded and praised more often, less often, or about as often as teachers habitually praise and reward them? Providing students with less than their customary amount of praise and rewards may cause them to think that their teachers do not value them or their work. On the other hand, rewarding and praising students excessively can cause learned helplessness. Educators understand the importance of using praise to motivate students. The problem lies in the fact that what is an unnecessary or excessive amount of praise for some students may be just the amount or less than what others are accustomed to receiving. For example, as the following quote indicates, Southeast Asian children usually are not rewarded and praised as often as children from many other cultures.

> *The child should not receive rewards for the behaviors he is expected to demonstrate. Accomplishments are usually acknowledged in the form of parent encouragement to do even better and strive for higher levels of achievement. This attitude is also reflected in the family discouragement of praising oneself or family members in the presence of non-family members. When a child (or adult) is given a compliment, it is often dismissed or negated by immediate discussion of one's faults through self-deprecating remarks. (31, p. 4)*

Students' ethnic backgrounds also affects which consequences they do and do not experience as rewarding or the opposite.

> *"Time-out" from the social interaction of recess or in-class activities is a sharp punishment for Hawaiian children. In Navajo classrooms, children are quite content to be alone. (35, pp. 354–355)*

There are many other questions that educators should consider when they make decisions about whether and how to reward students. Are students brought up to strive for individual recognition or is anonymity stressed? Will students respond better to individual rewards or when the group is praised and rewarded? Should teachers recognize students' accomplishments or those of the group as a whole? When recognizing students' accomplishments should teachers do so publicly by placing their work on the walls, referring to their achievement, and using them as peer models or privately? Many non-European students, especially Asian and Pacific Americans, Hawaiian Americans, Hispanic Americans, Native Americans, and European American females, have such difficulty in classrooms that stress individual goals, and individual recognition that it is often better to recognize their achievement in a less public manner (6, 34).

Are students accustomed to receiving personal or impersonal rewards at home? Will they respond better to personal, positive reinforcements such as statements of approval, smiles, pats on the back, and so on, or impersonal ones such as treats, toys, gold stars, sweets, and the like? Is it possible that students aren't changing their behavior because they are relatively indifferent to praise and criticism from others?

Negative Consequences

Educators should also be aware of their students' characteristics when they decide to use negative consequences with them. The following are some important issues for them to consider. What kinds of negative consequences do adults use to discipline youngsters—physical punishments (spanking and slapping); loss of affection, attention, or the possibility of social interaction (statements of disappointment and anger, removal from the presence of others); loss of privileges (being grounded, loss of TV); or loss of material things (desserts, allowances)? What kinds of negative consequences will work best with the students? Which ones will be unacceptable to them or their parents? The following are a few examples of cultural differences among Hispanic Americans, Native Americans, and Southeast Asian Americans.

Hispanics tend to use corporal punishment more and deprivation of love and affection less when disciplining their children. (6, p. 161)

Native American children are seldom if ever, struck by an adult: no parents, uncles, aunts, no adults. (21, p. 45)

Such forms of punishment as locking the child outside the house, isolating the child from the family social life, shaming the child, scolding or guilt induction that results in a "loss of face" are commonplace in Southeast Asia. (30, p. 145)

What are the acceptable and unacceptable ways of criticizing or punishing children and teenagers? Are they given feedback about their behavior in public or only in private? Can students accept direct criticism or only indirect and subtle feedback? Can they tolerate being criticized in public or will they only respond positively to private criticism? Should educators write students' names on the blackboard when they misbehave and comment about their inappropriate behavior in front of others, or should they only correct students in private to make sure they do not "lose face"?

Many non–European American students may react extremely negatively to public criticism. The following quotations describe the likely response of Filipino American students to criticism.

> *Correction of students mistakes must be done tactfully. Pilipino students often have difficulty detaching themselves from their work and may view adverse comments as direct criticisms of themselves. . . . Pilipino children are particularly sensitive to criticism. When embarrassed the child may withdraw and become uncooperative. The teacher may be frustrated in all attempts to discover what is wrong. (26, p. 19)*

What tone of voice do adults use when they discipline and criticize children and teenagers? Are they gruff, emotional, and direct. Or are they gentle and indirect? European Americans tend to be more emotional and direct than many other groups. For example, among Native Americans, "Talking loud, especially while correcting children, is highly disapproved" (21, p. 45).

Group Consequences

To what extent are students motivated by the attitude of their peer group? Can teachers motivate students to change their behavior by referring to its effect on the students' peer group? As was noted earlier, in comparison to European Americans many non-European Americans are more sensitive to the effects their behavior has on their peers.

> *What motivates Hispanics to be punctual are not impersonal reasons such as it's efficient for everyone to arrive at the same time and begin at the same time. Hispanics may feel that the meeting or work could have started without them if necessary. . . . On the other hand, personal relationships do concern them. For example they may be very concerned that their lack of punctuality not be interpreted as a sign of disrespect or a lack of courtesy toward others and arrive on time to make sure they do not seem disrespectful. . . . Statements such as "if you respect your classmates you will get here when we need you" may have more effect than statements such as "we could not finish on time" or "we wasted fifteen minutes because we had to wait for you." (6, p. 95)*

Shame and Guilt

Do parents emphasize guilt (feeling bad about one's self for misbehaving), shame (feeling bad because others know one has misbehaved), or neither when they discipline children? When motivating students to behave well, should educators focus on what the students themselves should think about their behavior (guilt), how others will think of them (shame), or neither? Educators are typically advised not to make students feel guilty or to shame them even in private. In fact, many readers may feel that this discussion of the possibilities of using guilt or shame to motivate students is inappropriate. However, shame and its avoidance can be a very effective and acceptable motivator with some Hispanic American, Native American, and Southeast Asian American students (9, 21, 23, 30, 31).

> *For Native Americans, warnings about the consequences of bad behavior are couched in community terms like, "What will people say—they will laugh at you".... Shame, otherwise known as embarrassment, is a common disciplinary tool with Native Americans. (21, p. 48)*
>
> *Shame is, indeed, a powerful instrument for discipline in Hispanic culture.... Where the threat of a failing grade or detention may not succeed in producing the desired change of behavior with the student, a private and strong reminder of his family obligations may do wonders. (23, pp. 72–73)*

SELF-QUIZ: Accommodating Management Techniques to Student Characteristics

How should educators handle problems between male and female students from different ethnic or socioeconomic backgrounds that result from their different perceptions of what are and are not acceptable ways for students to relate to the opposite gender?

Do you agree that female educators should use less direct management techniques with those Hispanic males who are not accustomed to direct disciplinary approaches from females?

With which of the following ways of accommodating management techniques to students' behavioral characteristics would you feel comfortable?

- Being authoritarian with some students and authoritative with others
- Being tough with some students and the opposite with others
- Using time out as a negative consequence with some students, but not with others
- Recognizing some students' achievements, progress, and improvements publicly and those of others privately
- Using shame, guilt induction, corporal punishment, scolding, or peer pressure with students who are accustomed to such forms of discipline at home and in their communities

---

Empowering Approaches

Students who are empowered by their teachers are helped to believe they can achieve their goals, control their behavior, and meet the challenges that confront them, because they themselves have the power to shape their destinies and futures. Those that are disempowered come to believe they lack the ability or potential to do so. The following behavior management techniques can disempower students (see the section on locus of control in Chapter 10).

Deprecating students' backgrounds and treating them in a discriminatory manner has a harmful effect on their self-concepts and sense of power. Routinely and unnecessarily rewarding students may teach them to strive to please others rather than to accomplish their own internal motives and may contribute to their "learned helplessness" (38). Praising poor or non–European American students for trying even though they do not succeed or for achieving less than what is expected of others with the same ability can cause them to doubt whether they can succeed or accomplish what others can, and emphasizing teacher-management techniques over self-management techniques can lead students to believe that they are unable to manage themselves (38).

The following quotation exemplifies the view of many African American educators that using extrinsic consequences to modify the behavior of African American students does them more harm than good.

> *Perhaps one of the most overriding criticisms of externally oriented management techniques is the tendency of teachers to use these approaches as control tactics rather than teaching students to become self-directing individuals. . . . Many otherwise promising teachers resort to interpreting and utilizing traditional management approaches as control tactics, which then results in making students behaviorally stifled, docile, overcompliant, and further doubt their abilities. Additionally, the use of these approaches in this vein has the tendency to foster impulsive conformity in students and often turns them off to school and learning. (39, pp. 1–4)*

To empower students, education teachers should demonstrate their conviction that students can and will control their own behavior. And they should assist them to do so without making them dependent on excessive or unnecessary teacher praise, assistance, or supervision.

> *Our society thinks that "more discipline" will make a better world and certainly better schools. But doesn't the cry for discipline really translate to, "let's try to help people act in a responsible manner"? This society desperately needs people who accept responsibility, not simply accept discipline. (40, p. 188)*

SELF-QUIZ: Empowerment

If you have been an in-service teacher or have completed a teaching practicum, list the various classroom/behavior management techniques that you tend to use with students. Categorize them into empowering and disempowering approaches and determine which approach you employ most often.

Summary

There are many ways educators can improve their classroom/behavior management approaches. Because many educators contribute to students' behavior problems by relating to them in a discriminatory manner, they can begin by correcting their own ethnic, socioeconomic, and gender biases. Rather than interpreting students' behavior from their own perspective, educators can avoid misperceiving and misunderstanding students' behaviors by taking students' behavior styles into consideration. Finally, they can use classroom/behavior management techniques that empower rather than disempower students.

Activities

1. Ask some students from different backgrounds in the courses you are taking or some friends to describe their behavior style preferences. Do you notice any of the differences reported in this chapter?

2. Using the list of characteristics included in this chapter as a guide, prepare descriptions of the traits that you believe are characteristic of male and female students. Then ask a few of your friends or fellow students to review your list and tell you which traits they do and do not accept as being characteristic of their group.

3. Interview some individuals from an ethnic group that interests you and prepare a description of the characteristics of their group that they think educators should consider when they select management techniques.

4. Ask your friends or fellow students to answer the self-quiz on accommodating management techniques to student characteristics. Do you observe any differences between persons of different genders or ethnic backgrounds. How do your answers compare to theirs?

5. List the various classroom/behavior management techniques that your professors tend to use with students. Categorize them into empowering and disempowering approaches and determine which approach each one employs most often. Are there any differences between male and female professors?

References

Misperceptions and misunderstandings that can affect educators' choices of management approaches are discussed in the following references.

1. Dent, J. L. (1976). Assessing black children for mainstream placement. In R. L. Jones (Ed.), *Mainstreaming and the Minority Child.* Reston, VA: Council for Exceptional Children.

2. Dao, M. (1991). Designing assessment procedures for educationally at-risk Southeast Asian-American students. *Journal of Learning Disabilities, 24*(10), 594–601, 629.

3. ERIC Clearinghouse on Urban Education. (1985). The social and psychological adjustment of Southeast Asian Refugees. *Equity and Choice, 1*(3), 55–59.

4. Gay, G. (1975). Cultural differences important in the education of Black children. *Momentum*, October, 30–33.
5. Gay, G., & Abrahams, R. D. (1973). Does the pot melt, boil, or brew? Black children and white assessment procedures. *Journal of School Psychology, 11*(4), 330–340.
6. Grossman, H. (1984). *Educating Hispanic Students: Cultural Implications for Instruction, Classroom Management, Counseling, and Assessment.* Springfield, IL: Charles C Thomas.
7. Irvine, J. J. (1991). *Black Students and School Failure: Policies, Practices, and Prescriptions.* New York: Praeger.
8. Ishi-Jordan, S. (1992). *Effects of Students' Racial or Ethnic Background on Teacher Expectations and Intervention Selection for Problem Behaviors.* Paper presented at the Topical Conference on Cultural and Linguistically Diverse Exceptional Children, Minneapolis.
9. Jaramillo, M. L. (1973). *Cautions When Working with the Culturally Different Child.* ERIC ED 115–622.
10. Johnson, S. O. (1980). Minorities and discipline games. *High School Journal, 63*(5), 207–208.
11. Koh, T., & Koh, S. D. (1982). A note on the psychological evaluation of Korean school children. *P/AAMHRC Research Review, 1*(3), 1–2.
12. Kritek, W. J. (1979). Teachers' concerns in a desegregated school in Milwaukee. *Integrated Education, 17*, 19–24.
13. Morgan, H. (1980). How schools fail black children. *Social Policy, 10*(4), 49–54.
14. Nguyen, L. D. (1986). Indochinese cross-cultural adjustment and communication. In M. Dao & H. Grossman (Eds.), *Identifying, Instructing and Rehabilitating Southeast Asian Students with Special Needs and Counseling Their Parents.* ERIC ED 273–068.
15. Ortiz, A. A., & Yates, J. R. (1988). *Characteristics of Learning Disabled, Mentally Retarded, and Speech-Language Handicapped Hispanic Students at Initial Evaluation and Reevaluation.* ERIC ED 298–705.
16. Takeuchi, S. M. (1972). *Verbal Skills and the Asian American Student.* ERIC ED 097–395.
17. Wong, M. K. (1978). Traditional Chinese culture and the behavior patterns of Chinese students in American classrooms. In *Second Annual Forum on Transcultural Adaptation (Proceedings): Asian Students in American Classrooms.* Chicago: Illinois Office of Education.
18. Wong, M. K. (1980). Model students? Teachers' perceptions and expectations of their Asian and white students. *Sociology of Education, 53*, 236–246.
19. Yao, E. L. (1987). Asian-immigrants students—Unique problems that hamper learning. *NASSP Bulletin, 71*(503), 82–88.

The following references discuss student characteristics that educators should consider when selecting classroom/behavior management approaches.

20. Bacon, M. M. (n.d.). *Coping Creatively with Adolescence: Culturally Relevant Behavior Management Strategies for the Twenty-First Century.* Unpublished manuscript, Palo Alto Unified School District, Palo Alto, CA.
21. Burgess, B. J. (1978). Native American learning styles. In L. Morris, G. Sather, & S. Scull (Eds.), *Extracting Learning Styles from Social/Cultural Diversity: A Study of Five American Minorities.* Norman, OK: Southwest Teacher Corps Network.
22. Chan, K., & Rueda, R. (1979). Poverty and culture in education: Separate but equal. *Exceptional Children, 45*, 422–427.
23. Condon, E. C., Peters, J. Y., & Sueiro-Ross, C. (1979). *Special Education and the Hispanic Child: Cultural Perspectives.* Philadelphia: Temple University, Teacher Corps Mid-Atlantic Network.
24. Geschwind, N. (1974). *Cross-Cultural Contrastive Analysis: An Exploratory Study.* Unpublished masters thesis, University of Hawaii, Honolulu.
25. Hale-Benson, J. E. (1986). *Black Children: Their Roots, Culture, and Learning Styles*, (rev. ed.). Baltimore: The Johns Hopkins University Press.
26. Howells, G. N., & Sarabia, I. B. (1978). Education and the Filipino Child. *Integrated Education, 16*(2), 17–20.
27. Kochman, T. (1981). *Black and White Styles in Conflict.* Chicago: University of Chicago Press.
28. Leggio, P. (n.d.). *Contrastive Patterns in Nonverbal Communication Among Different Cultures.* Trenton: Office of Equal Opportunity, New Jersey State Department of Education.
29. Medicine, B. (1985). Child socialization among Native Americans: The Lakota (Sioux)

in cultural context. In *Indian Studies*. Cheney, WA: Eastern Washington University.

30. Morrow, R. D. (1987). Cultural differences—Be aware. *Academic Therapy, 23*(2), 143–149.

31. Morrow, R. D., & McBride H. J. (1988). *Considerations for Educators in Working with Southeast Asian Children and Their Families*. ERIC ED 299–730.

32. Robinson, S. (1989). Quoted in Wiley, E. III, Educators call for fairer, more effective means of discipline in schools: Black males most likely to be punished. *Black Issues in Higher Education, 5*(21), 3, 16.

33. Sra, D. (1992). *A Comparison of East Indian American and European American Students*. Unpublished manuscript, San Jose State University, Division of Special Education, San Jose, CA.

34. Swisher, K. (1990). Cooperative learning and the education of American Indian/Alaskan Native students: A review of the literature and suggestions for implementation. *Journal of American Indian Education, 29*(2), 36–43.

35. Tharp, G. (1989). Psychocultural variables and constants: Effects on teaching and learning in schools. *American Psychologist, 44*(2), 349–359.

36. Williams, J. (1989). Reducing the disproportionately high frequency of disciplinary actions against minority students: An assessment-based policy approach. *Equity and Excellence, 24*(2), 31–37.

37. Yao, E. L. (1979). Implications of biculturalism for the learning process of middle-class Asian children in the United States. *Journal of Education, 16*(4), 61–72.

The importance of empowering students is discussed in these references.

38. Grossman, H. (1990). *Trouble Free Teaching: Solutions to Behavior Problems in the Classroom*. Mountain View, CA: Mayfield.

39. Patton, J. M. (1981). *A Critique of Externally Oriented Behavior Management Approaches as Applied to Exceptional Black Children*. ERIC ED 204–902.

40. Sleeter C. E., & Grant, C. A. (1988). *Making Choices for Multicultural Education: Five Approaches to Race, Class, and Gender*. Columbus, OH: Merrill.

Index

Ability grouping. *See* Tracking and ability grouping
Absenteeism, 130
Abstract concepts, 26, 275
Abuse. *See* Child abuse; Child neglect; Substance abuse
Abused children
    behavioral problems of, 144
    contextual problems of, 143–148
    identifying, 145
    self-concept of, 144
    teachers and, 144–146
    See also Child abuse; Child neglect
Academic achievement
    contextual aspects of, 4
    of culturally deprived students, 34–35
    effect of nonstandard speech on, 35
    ethnic identity and, 105
    gender differences in, 189
    instructional approaches and, 5
    IQ scores as predictors of, 24–25
    lack of, factors contributing to, 53
    of LEP students, 4–5
    meritocracy theory and, 20–21
    of minority groups, 2
    motivation and, 226
    parenting and, 33–34
    self-concept and, 35–37
Academic aspirations. *See* Educational aspirations
Accents, bias against, 60–61
Accommodation, 99, 100–104, 105
    critics of, 100–104, 106, 107
    as discrimination, 103
    mutual, 110
    proponents of, 101, 103
    research, 112
Acculturation, 99

assessing the level of, 290–295
cultural conflicts and, 289
culture brokers and, 121–123
effects of, 289–290
identity conflicts and, 123–125
process of, 294–295
resistance to, 113
time frame of, 135, 290, 291
See also Assimilation
Accusations, response to, 175–176
Achievement tests
    gender differences in scores, 3, 189
    reliability and validity of, 234
    time limits on, 237
    See also IQ scores
Acquired Immune Deficiency Syndrome (AIDS), 19
Active learning, 269
Activity levels, 232
Adolescence
    concern about sexual orientation in, 215
    cultural problems of, 149–150
    parenthood in, 148
    pregnancy in, 148
    problems of, 148–150
    substance abuse in, 148
Adopted children, IQ scores of, 23
Adult relationships
    gender differences in, 266
    and learning, 263
Affection, demonstration of, 178–179
Affluent students, 142–143
African American families
    child rearing practices, 55–56
    extended, role of, 40
    father absence in, 39–40
    gender roles in, 3, 40, 63
    level of intensity in, 231
    sexism in, 40

See also African American students
African American students, 1
    academic achievement of, 30
    aspirations of, 37–38
    assessment of, 24, 224, 225, 228, 231–232, 235–236
    attitudes toward whites, 228
    behavioral problems of, 60, 63, 180, 308–310, 313
    behavior in groups, 180
    classroom behavior of, 308–310, 313
    communication styles of, 173, 175, 182, 183, 229
    contextual problems of, 138
    desegregation and, 76
    dialects spoken by, 35, 60, 162, 166, 168, 169, 170
    discipline of, 320, 321, 325
    dropout rates of, 2
    emotional expression of, 308–310, 313
    ethnic identity of, 108, 170
    evaluation of, 59–61
    experiences in groups, 180, 278–279
    females, 197, 222, 225, 265, 273
    IQ scores of, 24
    learning styles of, 263, 268, 269, 270, 272, 275
    locus of control and, 283
    males, 60, 63, 149, 199, 225, 272, 309
    perception of education, 74–75
    prejudice and bias against, 57, 59–63
    self-concept of, 285
    stereotypes of, 102, 149
    teacher expectations for, 59
    teacher interactions with, 34–35

critics of, 111
Bidialectalism, 164–169
  negative and positive effects of,
    169
  proponents of, 164–166
  techniques used for, 167
Bilingual education, 126, 160–161
  assessment in, 238
Bilingual Education Act of 1988, 126,
    159
Biological predispositions, 189–191
  hormonal differences, 189–190
  lateralization and specialization,
    190
  versus determinism, 190–191
Biomedical problems, 16–19
  AIDS-exposed infants, 19
  health care and nutrition, 16–17
  substance abuse, 16–19
Bisexual students, 215
Black dialect
  acceptance of, 169, 170
  research, 61
Black English, 60–61, 162, 166
Bloom, B.S., 26
Boudreau, F.A., 196, 198
Boykin, A.W., 231–232
Brain lateralization and specializa-
    tion, 190
Brooks, D.M., 198
Bzdykr, Olga, 183

California, 70
Cambodian American students
  prejudice against, 134
  school experience of, 127, 132
Cardenas, Gilberto, 131
Case study method, for examining
    prejudice, 97
Caste-like groups, 70
Central American students
  contextual problems of, 138
  school experience of, 127, 132
  strengths of, 134–135
Chacon, Oscar, 132
Chamberlain, K.P., 226–227
Chapter I services, 32
Cheating, 318
Chicanos, 274
Child abuse
  emotional maltreatment, 145
  physical abuse, 145
  reporting, 144
  sexual abuse, 144, 145, 146
  by substance addicted parents,
    17–19
  systematic, 143
  See also Abused children
Child care, inadequate, 143–148
Child neglect, 18, 143, 145

Child rearing practices, out of the
    mainstream, 55–56
Children of War, 96
Chinese American students
  assimilation of, 288
  classroom behavior of, 311
  identity conflicts of, 123–124
  prejudice against, 134
  reaction to language barrier, 126
Class-cultural factors. *See* Culturally
    deprived students
Class participation, 125, 137, 227,
    264
Classroom behavior management,
    307–325
  with abused children, 144
  adapting to learning styles, 127
  behavioral styles and, 314, 315–
    320, 325
  biased techniques in, 62–63, 199
  cultural differences and, 314, 315–
    320, 325
  discipline styles, 320–324
  discriminatory approaches, 307–
    308
  of discriminatory incidents, 96–97
  disruptive behavior, 309–310
  empowering approaches, 324–
    325
  giving and sharing differences,
    317–318
  with immigrant and refugee stu-
    dents, 136
  inappropriate techniques, 314,
    324
  individual versus group rights,
    316–317
  learning styles and, 269–270
  misperceptions and bias, 308–314
  misunderstanding causes of be-
    havior, 313–314
  multicultural approach to, 137
  name-calling, 96–97
  nonexistent problems, 308–311
  opposite gender relationships,
    318–319
  perceptions of authority figures
    and, 137, 315–316
  permissive versus strict, 320–321
  social space needs, 319–320
  unnecessary intervention, 309
  unnoticed problems, 311–313
  using group or peer consequenc-
    es, 323–324
  using negative consequences,
    322–323
  using praise and reward, 314,
    321–322, 324–325
  using shame and guilt, 323, 324
  See also Behavioral problems

Classrooms, open type of, 125
Coed activities, 122, 277–278, 287,
    318–319
Cognitive academic learning profi-
    ciency (CALP), 160, 161
Cognitive development
  parenting styles and, 33–34
  socioeconomic factors in, 33–34
Cognitive skills
  of culturally deprived students,
    26–27, 33–34
  See also Intelligence
Cognitive styles, 266–272
  gender differences in, 267
Communication styles, 172–179
  and assessment results, 229–230
  cultural differences in, 172–179,
    311–313
  of culturally deprived students,
    27
  direct versus indirect approaches,
    174
  emotional versus subdued, 173
  formal versus informal, 172–173
  in groups, 179–180
  honest versus dishonest, 174–175
  nonverbal, 27–28, 64, 180–184, 316
  parent-child, 27–28
  poetic and analogous, 174, 229
  resolving conflicts, 180
  responses to guilt and accusa-
    tions, 175–176
  students' versus teachers', 172
  themes discussed and not dis-
    cussed, 176–179
Communicative disparities, prob-
    lem of, 4–5
Communicatively appropriate edu-
    cation, 159–185
  communication styles and, 172–
    179
  dialectal differences, 162–172
  LEP programs, 159–162
Communist countries, students
    from, 127–128
Community college system
  critics of, 73–74
  minority representation in, 73
  tracking students and, 66, 73
Competitive games, 122
Competitive learning, 5, 276–279
Competitiveness, 224–225, 226–227
Computational skills, gender differ-
    ences in, 3, 189
Computer software, gender bias in,
    195
Condon, E.C., 281
Conflict resolution, styles of, 180
Conformity, 265
Constructivism, 192

THE ENCYCLOPEDIA OF
MYTHOLOGY

CLASSICAL

CELTIC

NORSE

ARTHUR COTTERELL

SELECT
EDITIONS

Select Editions imprint specially produced
for Selectabook Ltd

Produced by Anness Publishing Limited
Hermes House, 88-89 Blackfriars Road,
London SE1 8HA

A CIP catalogue record for this book is available
from the British Library

ISBN 1 84038 894 3

Publisher: Joanna Lorenz
Editorial Manager: Helen Sudell
Project Editor: Belinda Wilkinson
Designer: Nigel Soper, Millions Design
Illustrators: James Alexander, Nick Beale,
Glenn Steward

Printed and bound in Singapore

© Anness Publishing Limited 1996
Updated © 2000, 2001
10 9 8 7 6 5 4 3 2 1

Frontispiece: *The Forging of the Sampo* by A.
Gallen-Kallela
This page: *The Rape of Ganymede* by Peter Paul
Rubens

Author's Note

The entries in this encyclopedia are all
listed alphabetically. Where more than one
name exists for a character the entry is
listed under the name used in the original
country of origin for that particular myth.
Names in italic capital letters indicate that
that name has an individual entry. Special
feature spreads examine specific
mythological themes in more detail. If a
character is included in a special feature
spread it is noted at the end of their
individual entry.